US National Secu~ Democracy

"Professor Miller provides a timely forum for reflection on the invaluable contributions of the Church Committee to oversight of U.S. intelligence activities. Since 9/11, our country has been embroiled in a debate about the proper role of intelligence, the preservation of civil liberties, the consequences of torture, and, in many ways, the contours of American values themselves. As we engage in the current debate, we would be well-served by the historical perspectives offered by this remarkable collection of essays."

Rep. John F. Tierney (D-MA)
Chairman of the Subcommittee on National Security and Foreign Affairs, Committee on Oversight and Government Reform, and Member of the Permanent Select Committee on Intelligence in the U.S. House of Representatives

"If there is any hope of avoiding intelligence abuse in the post-9/11 era, it will only be by learning the lessons of history, and no investigation, commission, or study is more important on this subject than the Church Committee's 1975 inquiry into domestic spying. This smart and necessary collection brings together a remarkable set of scholars in the hope that we can indeed learn from our mistakes."

Professor David D. Cole
Georgetown University Law Center

"Today's warrantless surveillance springs from a different and far more calamitous set of circumstances than the warrantless surveillance at the center of the Church Committee investigations of the 1970s. Still, the parallels are stark. In its first half, this timely volume collects insightful lessons for today's version of the tensions between national security and democracy from some who played central roles inside the Church Committee's work. The contributions in the second half of the book deal thoughtfully with today's national security controversies. Overall, the collection is carefully structured and the contributors include experienced and knowledgeable scholars and practitioners from law, intelligence, and political science."

William C. Banks
Director, Institute for National Security and Counterterrorism
Syracuse University

This volume examines the investigation by the 1975 Senate Select Committee ("Church Committee") into US intelligence abuses during the Cold War, and considers its lessons for the current "War on Terror."

The Church Committee's report remains the most thorough public record of America's intelligence services, and many of the legal boundaries operating on US intelligence agencies today are the direct result of reforms proposed by the Church Committee, including the Foreign Intelligence Surveillance Act. The Church Committee also drew attention to the importance of constitutional government as a Congressional body overseeing the activities of the Executive branch. Placing the legacy of the Church Committee in the context of the contemporary debate over US national security and democratic governance, the book brings together contributions from distinguished policy leaders and scholars of law, intelligence and political science.

This book will be of much interest to students of American politics, intelligence studies, and politics and international relations in general.

Russell A. Miller teaches Constitutional Law, Comparative Law and International Law at the Washington and Lee University School of Law.

Studies in intelligence series
General Editors: Richard J. Aldrich and Christopher Andrew
ISSN: 1368-9916

US National Security, Intelligence and Democracy

From the Church Committee to the War on Terror

Edited by Russell A. Miller

Routledge
Taylor & Francis Group

LONDON AND NEW YORK

First published 2008
by Routledge
2 Park Square, Milton Park, Abingdon, Oxon OX14 4RN

Simultaneously published in the USA and Canada
by Routledge
270 Madison Ave, New York, NY 10016

Routledge is an imprint of the Taylor & Francis Group, an informa business

Transferred to Digital Printing 2009

© 2008 Selection and editorial matter, Russell A. Miller; individual
chapters, the contributors

Typeset in Times by Wearset Ltd, Boldon, Tyne and Wear

British Library Cataloguing in Publication Data
A catalogue record for this book is available from the British Library

Library of Congress Cataloging in Publication Data
A catalog record for this book has been requested

ISBN10: 0-415-44646-5 (hbk)
ISBN10: 0-415-77876-X (pbk)
ISBN10: 0-203-89496-0 (ebk)

ISBN13: 978-0-415-44646-4 (hbk)
ISBN13: 978-0-415-77876-3 (pbk)
ISBN13: 978-0-203-89496-5 (ebk)

For Idaho and three of its great sons: Senator Frank Church and my brothers Barry Miller Jr. and Todd R. Miller

Contents

Contributors

David Gray Adler is Professor of Political Science at Idaho State University, where he teaches courses on the Constitution and the presidency. Adler is coauthor (with Louis Fisher) of *American Constitutional Law* (7th edition Carolina Academic Press, 2007), and author and editor of several books on the Constitution, presidential power and foreign policy. He has published more than 100 scholarly articles and essays. Funding for this chapter was provided by a generous grant from the Idaho State University History and Social Science Committee. He is indebted to Ericka Christensen for her valuable assistance in preparation of this chapter, and to Russell Miller for his very helpful comments and suggestions.

Katherine G. Aiken is Professor of History and Dean of the College of Letters, Arts and Social Sciences at the University of Idaho. She is the author of articles on Idaho's first woman member of the United States Congress, Gracie Pfost; environmental history; twentieth-century Idaho history; and the Coeur d'Alene mining district. Her books are *Harnessing the Power of Motherhood: The National Florence Crittenton Mission, 1883–1925* (University of Tennessee Press, 1998) and *Idaho's Bunker Hill: The Rise and Fall of a Great Mining Company, 1885–1981* (University of Oklahoma Press, 2005). Aiken and Idaho State University colleagues Kevin Marsh and Laura Woodworth-Ney co-wrote a short history of Idaho under the auspices of the Idaho State Historical Society – *Idaho: The Enduring Promise*.

LeRoy Ashby is Regents Professor and Claudius O. and Mary Johnson Distinguished Professor of History at Washington State University. Professor Ashby is the author (with Rod Gramer) of a biography of Idaho Senator Frank Church entitled *Fighting the Odds* (Washington State University Press, 1994).

Elizabeth Barker Brandt is Associate Dean for Faculty Affairs and James E. Rogers Distinguished Professor of Law at the University of Idaho College of Law. Recently, Professor Brandt has published several articles on the USA PATRIOT Act and on the impact of post-September 11 policies on academic freedom. She would like to thank Aaron Johnson for his assistance on the research for this chapter, and Professor Russell A. Miller for conceiving and nurturing this project.

Stephen Dycus is a Professor at Vermont Law School. He is coauthor of *National Security Law* (4th edition Aspen Publishers, 2007) and *Counterterrorism Law* (Aspen Publishers, 2007), and author of *National Defense and the Environment* (University Press of New England, 1996). He is also founding co-Editor-in-Chief of the *Journal of National Security Law and Policy* and founding Chair of the Section on National Security Law of the Association of American Law Schools. Special thanks are due to Edward Demetriou, Matthew Einstein, Eric Goldwarg, Byron Kirkpatrick, and Emily Wetherell, all current or former Vermont Law School students, for their assistance with research for his chapter. Portions of the chapter are adapted from Stephen Dycus, "The Role of Military Intelligence in Homeland Security," 64 *Louisiana Law Review* 779 (2004), and are used here with the permission of the *Louisiana Law Review*.

Michael J. Greenlee is Head of Public Services and Associate Professor at the University of Idaho College of Law Library. Professor Greenlee extends special thanks to Suzanne Booker for her assistance in editing earlier drafts of this chapter, and to Russell A. Miller for providing the opportunity to contribute to this work.

Gary Hart represented Colorado in the U.S. Senate from 1975 to 1987 and was a member of the Church Committee. He is the author of 17 books, including *The Shield and the Cloak* (Oxford University Press, 2006) and *Restoration of the Republic* (Oxford University Press, 2004). Senator Hart has lectured at Yale, the University of California, and Oxford, where he earned a doctor of philosophy in politics. He is currently Wirth Chair Professor in the School of Public Affairs at the University of Colorado at Denver and a Distinguished Fellow at the New America Foundation. He co-chaired the U.S. Commission on National Security for the Twenty-First Century. This chapter is an adaptation of the chapter "Liberty and Security" from the book *The Courage of Our Convictions: A Manifesto for Democrats* (Times Books, 2006).

Loch K. Johnson is Regents Professor of Public and International Affairs at the University of Georgia. Professor Johnson is senior editor of the journal *Intelligence and National Security* and the author of several books and more than 100 articles on U.S. national security, including, most recently, *Seven Sins of American Foreign Policy* (Longman, 2006). Professor Johnson was special assistant to Senator Church in his capacity as Chair of the Senate Select Committee on Intelligence, in 1975–76; the first staff director of the House Subcommittee on Intelligence Oversight, in 1977–79; and special assistant to the chair of the Aspin-Brown Commission on Intelligence, in 1995–96.

Russell A. Miller is an Associate Professor at Washington and Lee University School of Law. Until 2008 he was an Associate Professor at the University of

Idaho College of Law. He teaches courses in Constitutional Law, Public International Law and Comparative Law. He has published books in those fields, including *Transboundary Harm in International Law: Lessons from the Trail Smelter Arbitration* (with Rebecca M. Bratspies) (Cambridge University Press, 2006) and *Progress in International Law* (with Rebecca M. Bratspies (Martinus Nijhoff Press, 2008). His articles have appeared in the *Washington & Lee Law Review*, the *Columbia Journal of Transnational Law* and the *American Journal of International Law*. He is the co-founder and co-Editor-in-Chief of the *German Law Journal* (www.germanlawjournal.com).

Frederick A.O. Schwarz, Jr. was Chief Counsel to the Church Committee. Together with Aziz Huq, a colleague at the Brennan Center for Justice at New York University Law School, he published *Unchecked and Unbalanced: Presidential Power in a Time of Terror* (The New Press, 2007). In addition to the Church Committee, Mr. Schwarz's government service includes serving as Corporation Counsel for New York City, as Chair of the New York City Campaign Finance Board and as Chair of the City's Charter Revision Commission. For many years, he was also a Partner at a leading New York law firm.

Richard Henry Seamon is Associate Dean for Administration and Students and Professor of Law at the University of Idaho College of Law. Professor Seamon thanks William C. Banks, Louis Fisher, Ken Gormley, Orin S. Kerr, David S. Kris, Timothy Lynch, Judge Richard A. Posner, Andrew M. Siegel and Christopher Slobogin for helpful comments on drafts of this chapter. This chapter is adapted from the article "Domestic Surveillance for International Terrorists: Presidential Power and Fourth Amendment Limits," forthcoming in the *Hastings Constitutional Law Quarterly* (Spring 2008).

Alan F. Williams is an Associate Professor of Law at the University of Idaho College of Law. Before coming to academia he served on active duty with the U.S. Marine Corps as a military judge, prosecutor, defense counsel, and Special Assistant U.S. Attorney. Prior to becoming an attorney, he served in the U.S. Intelligence Community for 12 years, including a four-year stint at the National Security Agency. Professor Williams wishes to thank Professor Russell A. Miller for his assistance in inspiring this chapter as well as Craig Stacey for his assistance in conducting research for this chapter.

Foreword

When my colleagues at the *New York Times*[1] reported in December 2005 that the National Security Agency (NSA) had bypassed the law requiring court warrants for eavesdropping in the United States, any student of America's largest and most secretive intelligence agency could sense that history was repeating itself.

General Michael V. Hayden, the agency's director from 1999 to 2005, defended the warrantless surveillance program to Congress and the press by noting that the NSA had targeted only the international communications of Americans, and only eavesdropped on those suspected of ties to terrorism. What's more, he said, the surveillance was approved by government attorneys inside and outside the agency, who concluded that the program was properly authorized under the President's constitutional powers.

General Hayden might almost have been reading from the testimony to the Church Committee in 1975 of his predecessor as NSA director, Lt. Gen. Lew Allen Jr., who had mounted the same defense of the agency's warrantless intercepts of American communications 30 years before.

"This activity was reviewed by proper authority within NSA and by competent external authority," General Allen testified at the time. And in an assertion that eerily prefigured the defense mounted by the Bush administration three decades later: "We are aware that a major terrorist act in the United States was prevented."

As a journalist who had written extensively about the NSA, I was struck by the echoes and wrote about them in a February 2006 article for the *New York Times*.[2] I called leading figures in the earlier drama, including three contributors to the current volume: former Church Committee member Senator Gary Hart; former committee counsel Frederick A.O. Schwarz, Jr.; and former Church aide Loch K. Johnson. They were riveted by the parallels between their decades-old work on the Church Committee and the new events. Walter F. Mondale, the former Vice President, who served on the Church Committee as a Democratic Senator from Minnesota, told me the eavesdropping controversy "does bring back a lot of memories."

But Mr. Mondale pointed to a major difference. Unlike the intelligence abuses being investigated by Idaho Senator Frank Church in the 1970s, the NSA's domestic eavesdropping after 2001 was ordered *despite* a reform law that was intended to prevent such actions. After becoming Vice President under Jimmy Carter, Mr. Mondale had helped usher into law a crucial Church Committee recommendation – that no eavesdropping on American soil take place without a warrant. That became the basis of the Foreign Intelligence Surveillance Act of 1978, the law that critics and at least one judge say was violated by President Bush's decision to authorize eavesdropping without court warrants on people in the United States linked to al Qaeda.

"For those of us who went through it all back then," Mr. Mondale told me, "there's disappointment and even anger that we're back where we started from."

The parallels go far beyond the NSA. Now, as then, military intelligence units in the United States monitored antiwar activists, a theme explored by Stephen Dycus in his contribution to this collection. Now, as then, the CIA, acting on the direction of the White House, took extreme action overseas: assassination plots in the earlier period; since 2001, interrogations at secret jails using methods human rights experts brand as torture.

The reactions to the media revelations, too, have followed familiar paths. The Bush administration, like the Nixon and Ford administrations, ordered leak investigations to find out how the press learned of the secret programs. Though the political fallout did not strictly follow party lines, many Republicans in both eras complained that the government's most sensitive secrets were being splashed on the front pages of newspapers. Most Democrats blasted the administration in power for violating civil liberties and American values. Even the current battle over legal immunity for the telecommunications companies that assisted the NSA closely echoes a debate that took place in 1975.

Yet there are differences between the policies and programs investigated by Church and those implemented by the Bush administration in what it calls the "War on Terror." Most significantly, the recent intelligence agency excesses, if that is what they are, followed an attack on the United States that killed 3,000 people; its perpetrators have vowed to strike again. There was no similar attack on American soil in the 1970s, even if the threat then from Soviet nuclear forces was incomparably larger than the threat from al Qaeda today.

This point was made last year by Senator Pat Roberts, the Kansas Republican who then was chairman of the intelligence committee, when he rejected comparisons of recent intelligence activities with abuses in the Watergate period. "When President Richard Nixon used warrantless wiretaps," he said, "they were not directed at enemies that had attacked the United States and killed thousands of Americans."

Nor has any domestic intrusion revealed so far since 9/11 come close to the violation of privacy, liberty and decency represented by the FBI's ruthless campaign against Martin Luther King, Jr. in the 1960s. The relatively small-scale intrusions into domestic political groups by the Defense Department, as part of a threat database called TALON, were quickly curtailed in response to complaints.

But the most extreme facets of the current policies bear the Machiavellian characteristics of the earlier abuses. Take, for example, the United States' embrace after 2001 of secret detention of terrorist suspects and harsh physical pressure during interrogations, which marked a notable break with American tradition. While such tactics had on occasion been used by Americans in Vietnam and Latin America, they had never before become overt American policies approved by the President. Even after the Bush administration backed away from the harshest interrogation tactics in 2005 and 2006, the taint of torture would prove difficult to erase from American counterterrorism programs, damaging the image of the United States and straining relations with allies.

One person who played a significant role in the Church Committee period is in the government today. As an aide to President Ford, Dick Cheney worked to curtail and counter the Church investigations. As Vice President, he has campaigned privately and publicly to expand presidential power, especially in national security matters. As Mr. Cheney has noted, his resentment of what he saw as a regrettable incursion by Congress into presidential power in the 1970s decisively shaped his approach to his vice presidency since 2001.

Asked by reporters about his views on presidential power on December 20, 2005, shortly after the disclosure of the NSA program authorized by the President, Mr. Cheney replied, "Yes, I do have the view that over the years there had been an erosion of presidential power and authority." He blamed "a lot of the things around Watergate and Vietnam, both in the '70s."

"The President of the United States needs to have his constitutional powers unimpaired, if you will, in terms of the conduct of national security policy. That's my personal view," Mr. Cheney said.

Mr. Cheney's view of presidential power, enforced by his top aide, David S. Addington, became a major factor in shaping the intelligence agencies' conduct in the years after the September 11 terrorist attacks. Without the Vice President's influence, President Bush conceivably might have asked Congress to change the Foreign Intelligence Surveillance Act rather than simply bypassing it. The President might have worked with Congress as well in designing detention and interrogation policies, leading to more moderate policies and greater oversight.

So far in the current era, then, one might say that the reaction against the Church Committee, in the person of Mr. Cheney, appears to have had greater influence than the committee itself. But since the Democrats took control of Congress following the 2006 elections, some committees have slowly grown more assertive about oversight of national security, and the Bush administration has dropped warrantless eavesdropping and scaled back harsh interrogations. No congressional inquiry has yet emulated the Church Committee, but an aggressive and comprehensive investigation of intelligence activities might yet happen, filling in the full story of the past six years and completing the historical cycle.

The various chapters of this book thoughtfully frame the historical parallels between the work of the Church Committee and the contemporary debate over security and democracy. The book's first part contains the reflections of Church Committee veterans and authorities on Senator Church himself. The authors suggest that the committee demonstrated that an insistence on constitutional governance and strong legislative oversight can improve intelligence and strengthen America.

The volume's second part gives a scholarly account of the controversial intelligence programs and security measures launched in reaction to the September 11, 2001 terrorist attacks. The contributors describe warrantless surveillance of Americans; the domestic use of military intelligence; the USA PATRIOT Act and limits on freedom of speech and association; criminal prosecutions for providing material support to targeted groups; the use of national security letters to discover Americans' library and banking habits; the theory of the unitary executive as constitutional justification for presidential action in the campaign against terrorism; and the invocation of foreign constitutional schemes in support of these measures. Each chapter considers whether the contemporary debate is touched by the legacy of the Church Committee.

If 1975 was an *annus mirabilis* of debate over the limits and oversight of intelligence, as Loch K. Johnson puts it in his chapter in this collection, then we may now have begun a similar epochal reexamination of the trade-offs between security and liberty. There are few topics of greater importance to the foundations and future of the American experiment.

Scott Shane

Notes

1 The author of this Foreword, Scott Shane, is a reporter covering national security in the Washington bureau of the *New York Times*. In 1995, at the *Baltimore Sun*, he was coauthor of a six-part explanatory series about the National Security Agency.
2 Scott Shane, For Some, Spying Controversy Recalls a Past Drama, *New York Times*, Feb. 6, 2006, at A-18.

Acknowledgments

First and foremost, I extend my warmest gratitude to Dean Donald Burnett of the University of Idaho College of Law. Dean Burnett, along with Gerald Schroeder (former Chief Justice, Idaho Supreme Court) and Jay Sturgell (former President of the Idaho State Bar), constituted the 2006 Sherman J. Bellwood Lecture Committee, which approved my plans and provided support for a reflection on the legacy of Idaho Senator Frank Church and the balance that must be struck between democratic governance and security in the confrontation with global terrorism. Most of the contributions to this book were first presented at the panels associated with that event, held on October 11–12, 2006 at the University of Idaho. The program was entitled "National Security and the Constitution" and, besides the scholarly panels that gave rise to this book, the program featured a keynote "dialogue" between former Senators Gary Hart and Alan Simpson.

I am also grateful to Dean Rodney A. Smolla of the Washington and Lee University School of Law. Dean Smolla generously supported this project during my tenure as a visitor at Washington and Lee during the 2007/08 academic year. Louise A. Halper, Professor of Law and Director of the Frances Lewis Law Center at the Washington and Lee University School of Law, provided valued resources for research support. Without that assistance, I would not have been able to work with Anna Ku and Steve McNeill (Washington and Lee Law 2008), who provided highly professional, always conscientious and sometimes clandestine copy editing. They vastly improved the quality of the book. Mark Drumbl, Class of 1975 Alumni Professor of Law and Director of the Transnational Law Institute at Washington and Lee, also provided invaluable support and encouragement during that year.

My editors at Routledge showed extraordinary support for this project. They also extended to me more than my deserved share of patience in the course of editing and producing the book. I am grateful for their professionalism and encouragement. I am also grateful for the comments of the scholars who reviewed the proposal for this book. They were insightful and constructive.

I am grateful that the following permissions were granted, allowing me to include previously published materials as substantially adapted chapters in this book:

1   Adaptation of "Security and Liberty" from THE COURAGE OF OUR CONVICTIONS by Gary Hart. Copyright 2006 by Gary Hart. Reprinted by permission of Henry Holt and Company, LLC.
2   Richard Henry Seamon, Domestic Surveillance for International Terrorists: Presidential Power and Fourth Amendment Limits, *Hastings Constitutional Law Quarterly* (forthcoming 2008).
3   Stephen Dycus, The Role of Military Intelligence in Homeland Security, 64 *Louisiana Law Review* 779 (2004).

Most importantly, I acknowledge my partner and children: Theresa, Carver and Elsa Miller. All my work is inspired and lovingly encouraged by them.

1 Introduction: U.S. national security, intelligence and democracy

From the Church Committee to the War on Terror

Russell A. Miller

The return of Senator Church

During the past half-century, two historic confrontations – one against world-wide communism and the other against international terrorism – have presented American policy makers with the inevitably, difficult challenge of balancing intelligence and security needs against fundamental commitments to constitutional government and human liberty.

America's contribution to the triumph over communism was a measure of the success with which that balance could be struck; it was as much a victory of the democratic spirit as it was of intelligence ruthlessness and military strength. U.S. Senator Frank Church (Democrat from Idaho) was among those Americans who insisted upon democracy and constitutionalism even in the face of the existential, nuclear-armed Soviet threat. As Chairman of the Senate Select Committee to Study Governmental Operations with Respect to Intelligence Activities (1975–76),[1] which came to be called the "Church Committee," Senator Church led the first independent examination of the American intelligence community's Cold War record. Senator Church's determination to expose and correct intelligence agencies' abuses of civil liberties and violations of the law resulted in the publication of 14 volumes of reports. *Newsweek* described the effort as the "most comprehensive and thoughtfully critical study yet made of the shadowy world of U.S. intelligence."[2] More than a quarter-century later, the Church Committee's work remains the most thorough public record of America's intelligence services. The Foreign Intelligence Surveillance Act,[3] which principally sought to prohibit warrantless government surveillance of U.S. citizens, is among the most prominent of the many legislative reforms that resulted from the Church Committee's reform proposals.

Of greater consequence than the resulting intelligence oversight and reform, the Church Committee's investigation stands as an historic monument to faith in constitutional governance. As a congressional body investigating the most secret realm of the Presidential empire,[4] the Church Committee represented a stubborn commitment to the Founding Fathers' vision of limited government as secured by checks and balances, even in the face of America's most vexing national trials. Repeatedly, the Church Committee's reports refer to the "fundamental principles of American constitutional government," consisting of the commands that power be checked and balanced and that the preservation of liberty requires the restraint of law.[5]

Now, following the September 11, 2001 terrorist attacks in the United States, Senator Church is back.

The U.S. intelligence community's devastating failure to discover and prevent the terrorists' plot turned attention to the effectiveness of America's intelligence apparatus.[6] Some blamed the Church Committee for hobbling America's spymasters with the millstone of congressional oversight. According to this line of thinking, the Church Committee was the cause of the intelligence breakdowns leading up to that fateful day in September 2001. Chris Mooney explained that

> [t]he Church bashing began the day of the World Trade Center massacre on ABC, when former Secretary of State James Baker said that Church's hearings had caused us to "unilaterally disarm in terms of our intelligence capabilities." The allegation was soon repeated by Republican Senator Christopher "Kit" Bond of Missouri and numerous conservative commentators. The *Wall Street Journal* editorial page called the opening of Church's public hearings "the moment that our nation moved from an intelligence to anti-intelligence footing." And the spy-mongering novelist Tom Clancy attacked Church on Fox News's *O'Reilly Factor*: "The CIA was gutted by people on the political left who don't like intelligence operations," he said. "And as a result of that, as an indirect result of that, we've lost 5,000 citizens this week."[7]

Stephen F. Knott forcefully joined this chorus, arguing that the Congressional oversight resulting from the work of the Church Committee extensively damaged the CIA. "While the old CIA may have been noted for the 'cowboy' swagger of its personnel," Knott explained, "the new [post-Church Committee] CIA" is unwilling to take risks and "act at times in a Machiavellian manner."[8] Congressional oversight, Knott complained, prevents the CIA "from acting in a shrewd and, as is sometimes necessary, ruthless manner."[9] Rather than rooting out the cancer of executive secrecy and lawlessness, Knott viewed the Church Committee as having maimed the American intelligence community, turning the CIA into "the functional equivalent of the Department of Agriculture."[10]

These contemporary accusations, especially as regards the threat of terrorism, would not have surprised Senator Church.[11] He would have been disappointed, however, by the fact that they reflect an unserious examination of the Committee's work. The Committee strongly sought to underscore the "vital" constitutional importance of intelligence activities, declaring, for example, that "intelligence agencies perform a necessary and proper function" in advancing the Constitution's preambular commitment to promoting "domestic tranquility" and "the common defense." The Committee was especially aware of the need for effective intelligence activities in combating terrorism.[12]

More troubling to Church, however, would be the notion that his twenty-first-century critics, much like those arrayed against him in the 1970s, invoke a vision of government that he passionately believed is supported neither by the text of the U.S. Constitution nor by the republican ideals to which it aspires. Whatever the U.S. Constitution stands for, Church insisted, Machiavellianism must not be one of them, not even in the hardscrabble world of intelligence and not as an expedient in responding to threats to America's national security.

The book: bridging the Church Committee and the War on Terror

This book tackles this claim by bridging the work of the Church Committee and the contemporary debate over national security, intelligence and constitutional governance in the War on Terror. It consists of two distinct parts.

Part I: the Church Committee – then and now

The book's first part contains the reflections of several key veterans of the Church Committee and authorities on Senator Church himself. These pieces point up several themes. First, they make clear that advocating constitutional governance, as Senator Church did, requires great courage. This is especially true in the face of real or perceived threats to American security. Insisting upon checks and balances, even with respect to intelligence operations, also threatens the entrenched and powerful interests of the national security state, even if the nation is not confronted with a clear and present national security threat. Second, the contributions to the book's first part establish that a commitment to constitutional governance need not come at the cost of a loss of security. To the contrary, as each of the contributors to the book's first part make clear, the respect for constitutional governance and intelligence oversight demanded by Church actually serves to strengthen America. This is true, if for no other reason, because constitutional governance and the rule of law are profoundly American. As Senator Gary Hart says in his chapter in this book (Chapter 2), "deep down, what people really respect about the United States is its Constitution and principles." The book's first part, by reminding us of the rarity of the Church Committee's integrity and vision, serves as a call to courage for our own era, one that is responsive to the adage that those who ignore history are doomed to repeat it.

Senator Gary Hart's chapter opens the first part of the book. A member of the Church Committee and now one of America's leading scholar-statesmen on issues of national security, Hart compellingly argues that the compromises made in the War on Terror have their historical precedent in the Cold War abuses documented by the Church Committee. With the anecdotal flair of an eyewitness, he recounts the most startling of the Church Committee's revelations and the resulting reform proposals. Senator Hart singles out two points for particular concern. First, he is bothered by the predictability of the extraconstitutional intelligence policies that proliferated, seemingly unchecked, in the Cold War era and which have returned in the reaction to the September 11, 2001 terrorist attacks. "What goes around comes around," he concludes. "Here we are again, 30 years later, in yet another unwise war, no wiser and once again willing to sacrifice constitutional liberties in the name of security expediency." This predictability, Hart argues, is a product of a distinct understanding of presidential authority that has never gained ascendance but that has nonetheless survived through the persistent advocacy of a handful of well-placed Americans, most prominently Vice President Richard Cheney. Second, he agonizes that compromises of American constitutional values, whatever short-term intelligence and security benefits they produce, nonetheless erode the most important national security weapon at America's disposal, "the extraordinary power of [America's] respected constitutional principles." Senator Hart's contribution poignantly engages the book's most fundamental themes, with more than just a tone of regret for lessons still unlearned.

Frederick Schwarz was the Church Committee's Chief Counsel. No one is better positioned than he to identify, as he does in his chapter, the broad elements of the Committee's findings. He notes that the intelligence community long had relied on imprecise mandates, weak or permissive oversight, and patterns of secrecy and ambiguity that undermined accountability. He supports these claims with details from the Committee's expansive reports. With Schwarz, the reader has the privilege of being led through the Committee's massive record by the man who coordinated the investigation and assembled the vast body of evidence. But Schwarz is not content with detailing the Committee as an historical artifact. He pushes forward to outline the significant reform that resulted from the Committee's investigation and the repeated assaults on that fragile oversight infrastructure, including the present challenge posed by a number of the policies in the War on Terror. Considering the precarious nature of the reform achieved by the Church Committee as demonstrated by the alleged abuses of the Bush administration, Schwarz turns his attention, in the second half of his contribution, to a consideration of the context and method that made the Committee's success possible. He emphasizes that the Committee had the benefit of working without the pressures that attend an immediate or ongoing national security crisis. What is more, the Committee's success demonstrates that "oversight should be comprehensive, non-partisan, responsible and fact based." This, it is clear, is meant to serve as a model for the approach to be taken towards the intelligence abuses being exposed today.

Professor Loch K. Johnson was special assistant to Senator Church in his capacity as Chair of the Senate Select Committee on Intelligence. Later, Johnson was the first staff director of the House Subcommittee on Intelligence Oversight. He has gone on to become one of the nation's leading scholars of the U.S. intelligence community. He was present for the creation of, and his chapter in this book carefully details, the intelligence oversight infrastructure that resulted from the work of the Church Committee. It is exactly this oversight that, as remarked earlier, came in for so much hostility following the September 11, 2001 terrorist attacks. That is a surprising accusation in light of Johnson's findings that "the level of rigor displayed by intelligence overseers in Congress has fallen below the expectations of the [Church] Committee's reformers in 1975." Johnson's chapter is a bracing introduction to American intelligence oversight, a story that begins, as it must, with the Church Committee's "chilling" revelations of constitutional indifference. After mapping the resulting oversight regime, Johnson underscores the important role of human agency in its operation. Members of Congress, he demonstrates, have pursued their oversight responsibility with varying degrees of engagement and commitment.

Chapters from Professors LeRoy Ashby and Katherine Aiken round out the book's first part. Ashby, one of Church's biographers, and Aiken, a historian of Idaho politics, provide incredibly valuable insight into the biographical significance of Church's leadership of the Committee. On the one hand, Ashby articulates Church's courage and idealism:

> [B]y questioning the huge expansion of executive powers and secrecy that were occurring in the name of national security, the committee struck a blow on behalf of the constitutional separation of powers. As Frank Church insisted time and again, no one – including the President – is supposed to act outside the law. Protecting the nation, Church said, should not come at the expense of the nation's ideals, freedoms, and Constitution.

On the other hand, Aiken underscores that courage often has a cost. Aiken's chapter confirms that Church's dedication to constitutional governance and his leadership of the Committee came at a grave political price, concluding that "[t]here is little doubt that [Church's] very public investigation of the United States' intelligence community negatively impacted Church's 1980 reelection campaign," a battle Church ultimately lost by fewer than 4,000 votes. But both Ashby and Aiken suggest that this was a risk Church was willing to take. "Church was fully cognizant at the outset that his task in investigating United States intelligence operations was fraught with controversy and represented a potential political quagmire," Aiken notes. "He genuinely believed that going forward with the investigation was the right thing to do, the only legitimate course of action."

Part II: Contemporary issues of national security, intelligence and democracy

If Part I of the book provides the mandate of history, then the book's second part makes clear that the history of the Church Committee, and its insistence on constitutional governance, is painfully relevant today. In a series of in-depth scholarly commentaries from a diverse set of researchers and advocates, the second part of the book provides a comprehensive, if not exhaustive, accounting of the questionable intelligence and security policies pursued as part of the American reaction to the September 11, 2001 terrorist attacks. The legacy of the Church Committee haunts each of these contributions like a specter.

Professor David Gray Adler, one of America's foremost experts on presidential power and the Constitution, frames the broad concern at work in each of the chapters in the book's second part by tackling the Bush administration's assertions of power under a theory of the "unitary executive." How much unaccountable and unchecked authority does the President possess? In uncompromising terms Adler asserts that any vision of executive power that vitiates the doctrines of separation of powers and checks and balances is neither constitutionally justifiable nor wise. His argument is based, in equal parts, on resort to the intention of the Constitution's framers and general political theory. Adler recognizes, in the Bush administration's assertion of sweeping powers under the theory of the "unitary executive," the same threat of executive overreaching that so troubled the Church Committee. Adler also shares the Church Committee's insistence on shared decision making in foreign and intelligence affairs. The Constitution, he concludes, demands vigilance and accountability.

Professor Richard Seamon, a prolific commentator on the USA PATRIOT Act and other national security issues, strikes a more moderate tone in his examination of the Bush administration's warrantless domestic surveillance program. The National Security Agency's warrantless domestic surveillance program, of course, is the clearest contemporary reprise of abuses uncovered by the Church Committee. Critiques like Adler's, which primarily focus on the limits imposed on the executive by the Constitution's mandated separation of powers and checks and balances, have dominated the public and legal reaction to revelations of this contemporary warrantless surveillance program. Seamon, however, turns his attention to the Fourth Amendment privacy implications of the program. He concludes that not every instance of warrantless surveillance is prohibited by the Fourth Amendment. A genuine ongoing national security emergency, for example, would justify departures from the established privacy protections of the Fourth Amendment. He cautions that this is a very narrow and limited reliance upon the theory of the "unitary executive." This is a fine distinction Adler seems unwilling to concede. Ultimately, however, Seamon finds that the emergency predicate for a departure from the Fourth Amendment is lacking in the case of the Bush administration's warrantless domestic surveillance program.

Professor Elizabeth Brandt, a scholar of national security issues and an adviser to the American Civil Liberties Union, critically examines the Bush administration's policies that are aimed at outlawing groups and prosecuting their members. Putatively meant to strike at terrorists, Brandt sees in these policies a particularly bitter repeat of the Cold War-era persecution of those living outside society's mainstream. These policies, Brandt argues, risk "sweeping innocent people into the maelstrom of terrorism prosecutions," just as innocent people were ensnared by anticommunist hysteria during the Cold War. For Brandt, the First Amendment ought to prevent this by protecting associational interests. Her careful accounting of First Amendment jurisprudence in this field is a compact and impressive survey that leads her to the conclusion that the First Amendment should advance "the notion that an individual's group associations should not be suspect unless the person knew that a group was engaged in illegal conduct and intended to carry out the group's illegal purposes." This, Brandt reminds us, is precisely the kind of liberty interest advanced by the work of the Church Committee.

Professor Stephen Dycus, one of the most widely published experts in the field of national security law, takes up the underexamined issue of the domestic activities of America's military intelligence services. This can take the relatively innocuous form of gauging threats to the U.S. military located in the homeland or providing direct intelligence support to the U.S. military's potential use of the domestic, defensive use of force. The Church Committee documented, and leveled special criticism against, more invidious domestic uses of military intelligence, including domestic surveillance of U.S. citizens. Dycus wonders if we are only one more terrorist attack from a return to such abuses; if, indeed, the rush to harmonize American intelligence capabilities since the September 11, 2001 terrorist attacks already has not eroded the traditional prohibition on domestic military activities. Dycus's chapter catalogues the legal regime in place to test whether it adequately accounts for the increasing likelihood of domestic deployment of military intelligence services. He concludes that it does not. We urgently need "to clarify our current understandings about how military intelligence activities at home should affect the balance between security and liberty." This is especially true, Dycus concludes, because the "threat to civil liberties from expanded domestic use of military intelligence is surely greater now than it was" in the Cold War.

Professor Michael Greenlee writes with a librarian's passion about national security letters. These "administrative subpoenas," used primarily for foreign intelligence and counterterrorism information gathering, have been used with increasing frequency by the Bush administration to obtain library and banking records. Greenlee is most concerned with the First Amendment implications of the nondisclosure rules that accompany the National Security Letters and broadly prohibit the recipients from publicizing (even to the person whose records have been solicited) the intelligence-gathering action. Greenlee argues that the shroud of secrecy resulting from these nondisclosure measures resembles the secret activities exposed by the Church Committee. And while he seems reassured by the courts' reinforcement of First Amendment rights in this context, Greenlee worries that current national security letter powers are more expansive than anything previously created by Congress. Like the Church Committee, he concludes that oversight and scrutiny are the only proper response.

Professor Alan Williams, a retired Marine colonel and veteran of the National Security Agency, explores a lesser-known front in the War on Terror. The government increasingly has been seeking to prosecute internet website activity (development and support) under a creative interpretation of traditional "material support" statutes. Williams makes it clear that he approves of the prosecution of internet activity that is supportive of terrorism, particularly as it helps recruit, train, organize and fund terrorists. He is convinced, however, that the traditional material support statutes are not suited to the task. As proof, he refers to the acquittal in one such prosecution that took place in Idaho, Senator Church's home state. Williams, and apparently juries, are concerned that the government's theory under the material support statutes significantly expands criminal liability and treads on constitutionally protected freedom of speech in the process. Williams uses this critique to propose a revised statute that would strike the appropriate balance between liberty, on the one hand, and the government's ability to interdict terrorist activity in the internet, on the other hand.

My chapter closes the book's second part by returning to the broader constitutional and theoretical perspective from which Professor Adler launched the second half of the book. I acknowledge that the Constitution must permit the government to promote security, and that this mandate often comes at the expense of cherished individual liberties. I argue, however, that the constitutional balance that must be struck between security and liberty is an organic matter, not readily susceptible to comparative law transplants. This claim is important because there is increasing reference to foreign constitutional systems that more explicitly anticipate threats to democracy. Germany's constitutional provisions that erect a so-called militant democracy against authoritarian and antidemocratic movements are prominent examples that frequently come in for comparative consideration. I conclude that Germany's militant democracy is ill-suited for use in the American War on Terror, but that an examination of Germany's system nonetheless provides valuable insights that might inform America's home-grown effort to combat terrorism while preserving liberty.

Conclusion

The Church Committee understood that there is an inevitable tension between a society's efforts at securing order and liberty respectively. It is an old and difficult dilemma that revisits us in the War on Terror. But this struggle, the Church Committee affirmed, is not one that lacks for clear guidance in the American tradition and law. Church and his colleagues sought to remind us of those guiding values. And, to the degree that this reminder stung when the Committee's reports were published, and continue to chafe today, it must be in part because the Committee supported its message with a massive body of evidence documenting over 40 years of intelligence abuses and lawlessness perpetrated across seven presidential administrations involving both political parties.

This book is a modest introduction to the Church Committee's impressive and vital public record. And if we can read the times as fraught with the risk of a return to unchecked government power, as many of the contributions in this book suggest, then this project must also be understood as an argument. Like the Church Committee, this book calls America to heed the fundamental principles of constitutional government: checked and balanced power and respect for human dignity and liberty. This must be equally true for the President's management of our intelligence apparatus. The Church Committee and several contributors to this book explicitly reject claims of unchecked, inherent presidential intelligence authority. The Church Committee and several chapters in this book warn that crises should not be grounds for abandoning our enduring values. The Church Committee and a number of this book's chapters are conscious that due concern for America's precious international reputation as an example of democratic government might be an added incentive for adhering to these values.

This book seeks to reaffirm, for the War on Terror, the Church Committee's understanding that

> [t]he natural tendency of Government is toward abuse of power. Men entrusted with power, even those aware of its dangers, tend, particularly when pressured, to slight liberty.
>
> Our constitutional system safeguards against this tendency. It establishes many different checks upon power. It is those wise restraints which keep men free. In the field of intelligence those restraints have too often been ignored.[13]

Notes

1 S. Res. 21, 94th Cong. (1975).
2 Inquest on Intelligence, *Newsweek*, May 10, 1976, at 40.
3 *See* Foreign Intelligence Surveillance Act of 1978, Pub. L. No. 95-511, 92 Stat. 1783 (codified as amended at 50 USC §§ 1801–1811, 1821–1829, 1841–1846, 1861–1862).
4 See, e.g., Arthur M. Schlesinger, Jr., *The Imperial Presidency* (1973).
5 See, e.g., Church Committee, Book II, Preface, p. V.
6 See generally The 9/11 Commission, *Final Report of the National Commission on Terrorist Attacks upon the United States* (2004).
7 Chris Mooney, Back to Church, *The American Prospect*, Nov. 5, 2001, available at web.archive.org/web/20061205025524/http://prospect.org/print/V12/19/mooney-c.html.
8 Stephen F. Knott, Congressional Oversight and the Crippling of the CIA, *History News Network*, Nov. 4, 2001, at http://hnn.us/articles/380.html.
9 Ibid.
10 Ibid.
11 LeRoy Ashby and Rod Gramer report that the criticism of the Church Committee's work was virulent, drawing fire from a spectrum of political and media sources, including President Ford, National Security Adviser and Secretary of State Henry Kissinger, James J. Kilpatrick, Patrick Buchanan, Paul Harvey, and *TV Guide*. See LeRoy Ashby and Rod Gramer, *Fighting the Odds* 487–88 (1994).
12 S. Rep. No. 94-755 (1976), Intelligence Activities and the Rights of Americans [Church Book II], at v, 1 and 20.
13 Ibid. at 291.

Part I

The Church Committee – then and now

2 Liberty and security

Gary Hart

Liberty and security in the "War on Terror"

For anyone with even a faint understanding of the pattern of conservative behavior in wartime, from the infamous Palmer raids after World War I through J. Edgar Hoover's excesses in the Vietnam era, it was as predictable as sunrise that the administration of George W. Bush would err on the side of extraconstitutional behavior in its conduct of the so-called War on Terror. The pattern is for Presidents to obtain legal opinions from compliant White House counsel and an equally subservient Attorney General to assure them that extraordinary circumstances justified extraordinary consolidation of power in the executive branch.

In this case, extraconstitutional behavior was further predictable because Vice President Cheney and Secretary of Defense Rumsfeld had vocally advocated more unilateral executive powers since the days of the Ford presidency in the 1970s, when excesses by the Nixon administration led Congress to take its oversight responsibilities more seriously.[1]

The persistent argument seems to be that extraordinary times require the setting aside of the intricate balance of constitutional powers fashioned in 1789, if for no other reason than that James Madison and his fellow Founders could not possibly have understood the dangers represented by fascism, communism, terrorism, or whatever the threat of the day.[2] This reasoning, of course, overlooks the profound historical fact that the Founders fashioned the Constitution with its unique checks and balances at a time when the incipient American republic was in the greatest danger of any in its long future existence.

Nevertheless, much wiser than we, the Founders clearly knew that the greatest danger came not from a long future list of "isms" but from a natural human tendency toward concentration of power. The constitutional distribution of powers, with checks and balances crafted like the finest Swiss watch, was to protect Americans from abuse of power not during times of ease but rather in times of crisis and peril.[3]

Thus came revelations in late 2005 of presidential authorization of massive electronic and other surveillance of American citizens by the National Security Agency over an almost four-year period,[4] in clear violation of federal law.[5] The U.S. government had also resorted to an unusual and undemocratic practice called "rendition," the summary kidnapping and forced transportation of suspects to torture-lenient countries where uncomfortable issues of due process and the rule of law could casually be swept aside.[6] Then, of course, there was the systematic abuse of "detainees" by U.S. military and CIA personnel[7] – "detainees" being an extralegal category, without the right of due process and other protections under the American criminal justice system, or those of prisoners of war with rights under the Geneva Conventions.[8]

Predictably also, we learned toward the end of 2005 that the FBI counterterrorism units had conducted surveillance and intelligence-gathering activities against a variety of groups having nothing to do with national security – groups concerned with the environment, animal cruelty, and poverty.[9] And we may expect further revelations of a wide variety of excesses that will not become public until those responsible are well out of power.

All of this occurred, and predictably so, in the name of the "War on Terror." We should have known that when criminal conduct by a stateless group was elevated to a "war," extraconstitutional behavior, violation of civil liberties, and abuse of power would occur in a variety of venues. Indeed, it fitted the plans of Cheney and Rumsfeld to declare war on a tactic, thereby enabling the long-sought concentration of powers in the President as commander in chief. It is doubtful in the extreme that they would have welcomed such concentration of power in a Democratic President. The Constitution, however, thank divine providence, knows no ideology or party.

Not knowing or studying their own history, many Americans seem stunned and amazed when Presidents and their administrations abuse civil liberties in the name of security. Though by no means confined to one ideology, these abuses do seem the peculiar preserve of conservative Republicans, who incline, in any case, more toward security, secrecy, and a "strong President," usually meaning one who can do whatever pleases him, than toward protection of free speech, of association, of the press, and of citizens' liberties.[10]

Democrats, however, do not approach the subjects of constitutional rights and civil liberties with totally clean hands. Franklin Roosevelt,[11] with the approbation of the U.S. Supreme Court,[12] imprisoned tens of thousands of loyal Japanese-Americans during World War II.[13] The government, rightly embarrassed by this mass violation of American principles, later – much later – paid reparations by way of expiation.[14] Harry Truman cut corners during the early years of the Cold War and during the Korean War, and John Kennedy, following the precedent of Dwight Eisenhower, gave the U.S. intelligence services enormous leeway in the form of Operation Mongoose, the effort to overthrow Fidel Castro. And Lyndon Johnson endorsed the infamous Phoenix program, which targeted thousands of village Vietnamese, who may or may not have been guilty of collaboration with the Vietcong, for summary execution.

The issue is not whose hands are dirtiest. The issue is who has learned from this history of excess. In almost every case where liberty was sacrificed to obtain a measure of security, the sacrifice turned out to be unnecessary and ineffective.

Legacy of the Church Committee

Having served on the Senate Select Committee to Study Governmental Operations with Respect to Intelligence Activities (the "Church Committee," named
after its chairman, Senator Frank Church of Idaho),[15] which investigated and
revealed similar abuses of power that occurred during the 1960s and 1970s, I
was not surprised that there would be a cyclical return to these patterns of abuse
in the name of combating terrorism. Even for those with a proclaimed heritage
of opposition to big-government power, there is an almost inevitable, reflexive
concentration of power in the President and those closest to him in the White
House whenever a threat, real or imagined, exists. It is ironic in the extreme,
however, that those so busy with concentrating and abusing government power
after the September 11, 2001 terrorist attacks in the United States were so blind
to the warnings of terrorist attacks before September 11, 2001.[16]

Three weeks after I took the oath of office in the U.S. Senate, Majority
Leader Mike Mansfield appointed me to the Church Committee.[17] The Senate
had been moved to investigate the Central Intelligence Agency, the Federal
Bureau of Investigation, the Defense Intelligence Agency, the National Security
Agency, and a host of other intelligence agencies by increasing reports of abuse
of authority both by the agencies themselves and by previous administrations
that had abused the agencies because of war fever.[18] Throughout 1975 and much
of 1976, the Committee investigated these reports and issued recommendations
to prevent future abuses. I grew up very, very fast in the course of my service on
the Church Committee. It was not the kind of education I thought I would get
when I went to the Senate.

This experience was extraordinary as much as anything else because it turned
over some rocks. It turned over rocks that a lot of American people did not want
turned over. As Americans, we should never do anything that we would be
ashamed for the world to know about, but the Church Committee was charged
with uncovering things, things that neither the Senate nor the American people
knew, or, in too many instances, wanted to know.[19] The broad issue that
emerged from the Church Committee's work was the challenge we face in
holding to principle against the pressure of expediency. What the Church Committee uncovered in its investigation was that the U.S. government had repeatedly chosen expediency over principle. In this respect, one of the most
memorable moments in the Church Committee's work was a closed session with
the then-Director of the CIA, William Colby. All members of the staff were
excluded, save the staff director and our general counsel. For two or more hours
during this meeting, Director Colby delivered to us what came to be known as
the "family jewels." The litany of abuses he reported included some things that
had been rumored or generally believed, including the overthrow of foreign governments – and in one notable case the overthrow and eventual assassination of
a duly democratically elected head of state – almost all justified by the Cold
War. He disclosed to the Committee a systematic effort to assassinate at least
half a dozen national leaders around the world, mostly in the Third World. That

effort included, with almost demented insistence, plans to assassinate Fidel Castro. And it was not a partisan effort; it had started under Eisenhower and continued under Kennedy until after the missile crisis of 1962. Senators Barry Goldwater and John Tower, as members of the Church Committee, were present for this meeting with Director Colby. Goldwater and Tower were seasoned veterans, people who knew the way the world works and were accustomed to, in many cases, believing that it was necessary to take an expedient course to protect America's interests. But as the youngest person in the room, I watched their faces very carefully during that session. Barry Goldwater was clearly shocked. The thought that America had been in the assassination business shocked him.

During our investigations, the Church Committee discovered widespread surveillance, wiretaps, and mail openings of a very large number of American citizens.[20] The excuse given by the FBI and others for this program, code-named COINTELPRO,[21] was "We are at war and we need to do everything we can to defeat our enemy."

The CIA conducted the infamous Phoenix program, which consisted of the systematic assassination of thousands of village Vietnamese accused of collaborating with the Vietcong. This was an earlier version of Abu Ghraib, with torture being replaced by "termination with extreme prejudice." During the Eisenhower and Kennedy administrations, the United States also tried to assassinate at least six foreign leaders – in the case of Fidel Castro, with almost fanatical insistence – but without success.

Many reforms were proposed and enacted in the wake of the Church Committee's findings. The Foreign Intelligence Surveillance Act of 1978 (FISA) required special intelligence courts to approve national security wiretaps.[22] In recommending this legislation, the Church Committee sought to balance national security with the Constitution. The way FISA sought to achieve this was to create special courts, staffed with specially cleared judges, to receive application for warrants for searches and seizures and wiretaps when national security is at stake. FISA has worked wonderfully up until a couple of years ago. In all but only a very small handful of cases,[23] FISA warrants have been expeditiously granted because the process recognizes that, in many cases, a grave threat requires that you find out what somebody is up to or who they are talking to very quickly. The current Bush administration has found FISA inconvenient and, predictably, has ignored it.[24]

The Church Committee also recommended presidential "findings" before extraordinary covert operations were undertaken.[25] Up to this time, Presidents had used a wink and a nod in ordering the most egregious operations. For example, the farthest we could find President Kennedy going vis-à-vis Castro was "We have got to find a way to get rid of him," or words to that effect. The phrase "get rid of" is deliberately open to interpretation. Did it indicate mere removal from office? Was it something more invidious, like assassination? This exemplifies the fact that Presidents were not in the business of clearly saying to the CIA Director, "Overthrow this government" or "Kill that man." Presidential findings require Presidents to sign a clear order. This has had some effect in causing some Presidents to think twice, at least, before ordering a major covert operation that might embarrass the United States. Importantly, the Church Committee understood this reform as a means of strengthening and protecting, not undermining, the CIA. The CIA, up to then, had been left dangling in the wind when misused by Presidents who wished to claim "plausible deniability" for operations that were discovered or did not turn out as planned. The value of this reform surfaced during another period of political abuse, the infamous Iran-Contra affair of the mid-1980s, involving Bible-shaped cakes, trading with the enemy, lying to Congress, and avoidance of accountability, when it turned out that Ronald Reagan, contrary to his own memory, had signed a "finding" authorizing the whole bizarre episode of trading arms for hostages held by Iranian-sponsored groups in Lebanon and then using the monies generated to fund the Contra rebels in Nicaragua – all in violation of federal law.[26]

Again, to support the CIA, the Church Committee laid the groundwork for the 1982 Intelligence Identities Protection Act, which prevented identification of CIA operatives.[27] This is the Act violated by the Bush White House in its ideologically motivated efforts to punish one of its critics, Ambassador Joseph Wilson, by exposing his wife, who held an undercover position at the CIA – all because Wilson had disproved administration assertions that Iraq was obtaining nuclear materials from Niger.[28] I. Lewis "Scooter" Libby, Vice President Richard Cheney's former Chief of Staff, was convicted in March 2007 of four counts of perjury and obstruction of justice in the investigation of this affair. Still, many defenders of President Bush said, "It doesn't matter. She had a desk job." They forget the history that gave rise to the Identities Protection Act: the exposure and subsequent assassination of Athens CIA Station Chief Richard Welsh on Christmas Eve 1975. I know this history well because I was asked by the Director of Central Intelligence, William Colby, to intervene with the White House chief of staff to obtain presidential approval to have Richard Welsh buried at Arlington National Cemetery – a first for a CIA agent. Ironically, that chief of staff was one Richard Cheney.

Conclusion

So, what goes around comes around. Here we are again, 30 years later, in yet another unwise war, no wiser and once again willing to sacrifice constitutional liberties in the name of security expediency. One has only to consider the behavior of the Bush administration during the Iraq war to appreciate how soon we forget, how little we learn, and how pervasive is the tendency to violate civil and constitutional liberties in the name of war. Virtually all of the reforms recommended by the Church Committee have been evaded, ignored or violated in the name of the "War on Terror." If there was one lesson all of us who served on the Church Committee learned, it was that there are no secrets, everything comes out, and the promises of improved security nearly always fail to justify the sacrifice of liberty.

I argue in my book *The Fourth Power*[29] that the United States has the extraordinary power of its respected constitutional principles. I have had the great privilege of traveling the world, and I know for a fact, whether in the former Soviet Union, Eastern Europe, the Far East, Latin America, Africa, the Middle East – wherever I have been – people envy America's economic success and the American lifestyle and standard of living. But they also admire – perhaps not always – the American political system. They envy America's military power and resent it in many cases. But deep down, what people really respect about the United States is its Constitution and principles. And when America violates those principles, it undercuts its greatest power. America cannot base its operations on expediency, whatever the threat, whatever the challenge. For if it does so, it sacrifices the power of principle. Senator Frank Church understood this. He came to the fore at a time when the country was badly divided, polarized much as today. Americans were being divided by pragmatists who urged that compromises respecting American principles were necessary. They seemed to be saying, "Well, look, we have to do this." The point was, they thought, that this is a dirty, nasty world, and we are going to have to be as dirty and nasty as our enemies. Frank Church did not believe that. Frank Church and I shared many things. One of them was a kind of irrepressible sense of idealism. What makes the United States great is that it is different. Americans are different. When America abandons that difference, it becomes like every other country.

The issue before America today is, again, liberty or security. I do not think we have to give up one to achieve the other. We can be secure if we are united, not simply if we buy the biggest weapons or invade the most countries, but if we are united, if we have a sense of purpose, and if we do not abandon our principles. If America is to prevail, it must grow up. We must learn from our mistakes, and not repeat them. It is high time we learned the lesson that the work of the Church Committee teaches: Our security cannot be ensured by the sacrifice of our own liberties.

Notes

1 For a treatment of the President's emergency powers and the theory of the unitary executive, see Seamon in this volume (Chapter 8).
2 Professor John Yoo advances this claim with respect to the post-September 11 security landscape in arguing for greater presidential authority and discretion over war powers. See generally John Yoo, War, Responsibility, and the Age of Terrorism, 57 *Stanford Law Review* 793 (2004). Yoo notes three exceptional conditions of the post-September 11 world: (1) the unique, asymmetrical nature of the threat posed by global terrorism; (2) the irrational behavior of dangerous rogue nations; and (3) the changed nature of warfare, which now more significantly implicates civilian targets and relies on far more destructive weaponry. Ibid. at 816–19. Yoo explains, "These new threats to American national security … should change the way we think about the relationship between the process and substance of the [constitutional] warmaking system." Ibid. at 819.
3 See *The Federalist No. 69*, at 446 (Alexander Hamilton) (Benjamin Wright ed., 1961). Hamilton notes:

The President is to be commander-in-chief of the army and navy of the United States. In this respect his authority would be nominally the same with that of the king of Great Britain, but in substance much inferior to it. It would amount to nothing more than the supreme command and direction of the military and naval forces ... while that of the British King extends to the *declaring* of war and to the *raising* and *regulating* of fleets and armies – all of which the Constitution under consideration, would appertain to the legislature.

(Ibid.; see also *The Federalist No. 51*, at 355–59 (James Madison) (Benjamin Wright ed., 1961))

4 James Risen and Eric Lichtblau, Bush Lets U.S. Spy on Callers without Courts, *New York Times*, Dec. 16, 2005, at A1; Seymour Hersh, Listening In, *New Yorker*, May 22, 2006, at 24.

5 *Am. Civil Liberties Union* v. Nat'l Sec. Agency/Cent. Sec. Serv., 438 F. Supp. 2d 754, 781 (E.D. Mich. 2006) (holding that the Total Surveillance Program violated the separation of powers doctrine, the APA, statutory law, the First Amendment, and the Fourth Amendment). See Washington in Brief: Lawyers Group Criticizes Surveillance Program, *Washington Post*, Feb. 14, 2006, at A6; see also Seamon in this volume.

6 See, e.g., Douglas Jehl and David Johnston, Rule Change Lets C.I.A. Freely Send Suspects Abroad to Jails, *New York Times*, Mar. 6, 2005, at 1.

7 *60 Minutes II: Army Probes POW Abuse* (CBS News television broadcast Apr. 28, 2004). *See generally The Torture Papers* (Karen J. Greenberg and Joshua L. Dratel eds., 2005); Mark Danner, *Torture and Truth: America, Abu Ghraib, and the War on Terror* (2004).

8 See generally *Hamdi* v. *Rumsfeld*, 124 S. Ct. 2633 (2004) (O'Connor, J., plurality) (concluding that the executive branch cannot indefinitely hold a U.S. citizen without basic due process protections); *Hamdan* v. *Rumsfeld*, 126 S. Ct. 2749 (2006) (finding that the military commissions to try Guantanamo Bay detainees violated the Geneva Conventions).

9 Eric Lichtblau, F.B.I. Watched Activist Groups, New Files Show, *New York Times*, Dec. 20, 2005, at A1. See Brandt (Chapter 9) and Greenlee (Chapter 11) in this volume.

10 See generally Frederick A.O. Schwarz, Jr. and Aziz Z. Huq, *Unchecked and Unbalanced: Presidential Power in a Time of Terror* (2007); *Presidential Power* (Robert Y. Shapiro *et al.* eds., 2000).

11 Exec. Order No. 9066, 3 C.F.R. 1092 (1942).

12 *Korematsu* v. *United States*, 323 U.S. 214, 223–24 (1944) (refusing to hold the Japanese internment program unconstitutional).

13 See generally *Only What We Could Carry* (Lawson Fusao Inada ed., 2000); Greg Robinson, *By Order of the President: FDR and the Internment of Japanese Americans* (2003).

14 See, e.g., Civil Liberties Act of 1988, Pub. L. No. 100-383, 102 Stat. 904.

15 S. Res. 21, 94th Cong. (1975) ("[I]n order to clear the air, in order to cleanse whatever abuses there have been in the past, so that we can recite, once and for all, the proper parameters within which [intelligence organizations] can function.").

16 See *The 9/11 Commission Report* 255–77 (2004); U.S. Commission on National Security in the 21st Century, *Road Map for National Security: Imperative for Change – Phase III Report* viii–ix, 10 (2001), available at http://govinfo.library.unt.edu/ nssg/PhaseIIIFR.pdf. See generally Gary Hart, *The Fourth Power* (2004).

17 You can tell a lot about what a congressional operation is up to by the caliber and quality of people who help in a committee's efforts, whether a standing committee or a select committee. The staff of the Church Committee was an extraordinary group of professionals, a great many of whom have gone on to distinguished careers after their

service on that Committee. We had, among others, a future District Attorney of the District of Columbia. We had a future Assistant Secretary of State on our staff. Loch Johnson has become the preeminent historian of American intelligence and a distinguished scholar on American foreign policy. And Fritz Schwarz, who served as Counsel to the Church Committee, is one of the preeminent members of the American bar.

18 See, e.g., Seymour Hersh, Underground for the C.I.A. in New York: An Ex-Agent Tells of Spying on Students, *New York Times*, Dec. 29, 1974, at 1; see also Loch K. Johnson, *A Season of Inquiry: Congress and Intelligence* 9 (1988). Johnson states:

> Reporter Seymour M. Hersh of the *New York Times* captured the attention of the public in a series of articles, beginning on December 22, 1974, which accused the CIA of "massive" spying and illegal intelligence operations directed against antiwar activists and other American dissidents. According to Hersh's sources in the CIA, files on over ten thousand American citizens had been complied by the agency, despite the language of the 1947 act that barred the CIA from any security or police function within the United States.
>
> (Ibid.)

See generally LeRoy Ashby and Rod Gramer, *Fighting the Odds: The Life of Senator Frank Church* 470–71 (1994).

19 See Aiken in this volume.

20 See S. Rep. No. 94-755 (1976) (6 Books), including *Intelligence Activities and the Rights of Americans* [hereinafter Church Book II], *Supplementary Detailed Staff Reports on Intelligence Activities and the Rights of Americans* [hereinafter Church Book III]; Johnson, *supra* note 18, at 211–37; Ashby and Gramer, *supra* note 18, at 483–84. Ashby and Gramer state:

> [I]n April 1976 [the Committee] made public its multi-volume findings. Newsweek described the report as "probably the most comprehensive and thoughtfully critical study yet made of the shadowy world of U.S. intelligence." Its existence constituted a remarkable achievement, and Church deserved a great deal of credit for it.
>
> (Ibid.)

21 Johnson, *supra* note 18, at 125–29.

22 See Foreign Intelligence Surveillance Act of 1978, Pub. L. No. 95-511, 92 Stat. 1783 (codified as amended at 50 U.S.C. §§ 1801–1811, 1821–1829, 1841–1846, 1861–1862 (2000)).

23 The Electronic Privacy Information Center (EPIC) has collected statistics from the activities of the Foreign Intelligence Surveillance Court since its creation in 1979. The EPIC website reports that only four FISA warrants were rejected by the FISC between 1979 and 2005. Over the same period, 20,814 warrants were approved. See Electronic Privacy Information Center, Foreign Intelligence Surveillance Act Orders 1979–2005 (Aug. 27, 2007), www.epic.org/privacy/wiretap/stats/fisa_stats.html.

24 See Seamon in this volume.

25 See Intelligence Authorization Act, Fiscal Year 1991, Pub. L. No. 102-88, § 503(a), 105 Stat. 441 (1991) (replacing Section 501 of the National Security Act of 1947, 50 U.S.C. § 413). Section 503(a) provides:

> The President may not authorize the conduct of a covert action by departments, agencies, or entities of the United States Government unless the President determines such action is necessary to support identifiable foreign policy objectives of the United States and is important to the national security of the United States, which determination shall be set forth in a finding that shall meet each of the following conditions....
>
> (Ibid.)

26 Report of the Congressional Committees Investigating the Iran-Contra Affair, S. Rep. No. 100-216, H.R. Rep. No. 100-433, at 3–11 (1987).
27 Intelligence Identities Protection Act of 1982, Pub. L. No. 97-200 (codified at 50 U.S.C. §§ 421–426 (1982)).
28 See David Johnston *et al.*, Cheney Told Aide of C.I.A. Officer, Lawyers Report, *New York Times*, Oct. 25, 2005, at A1; Eric Lichtblau, The Leak Inquiry: The Former-Aide; Ex-Aide Enters Not Guilty Plea in Leak Charges, *New York Times*, Nov. 4, 2005, at A1; David E. Sanger, The Leak Inquiry: White House Memo; Intrigue Has Familiar Ring for Libby and Associates, *New York Times*, Oct. 31, 2005, at A1.
29 See generally Hart, *supra* note 16.

3   The Church Committee, then and now

Frederick A.O. Schwarz, Jr.

The Church Committee

Thirty years ago, the United States Senate's Select Committee to Study Governmental Operations with Respect to Intelligence Activities – mercifully known as the Church Committee after its Chair, Idaho Senator Frank Church – completed its 17-month investigation.[1] Neither before nor since in America, or anywhere else in the world, has there been such a comprehensive investigation either of intelligence agencies – FBI, CIA and others – or of their relations with Presidents, national security advisers, Attorneys General and other high-ranking executive branch officials.[2]

The Church Committee's investigation had two significant impacts. First, it exposed in great detail decades of conduct at home that was inconsistent with American ideals, that violated the Constitution and the law, and that often was a diversion from more important objectives. Second, it revealed conduct abroad that was inconsistent with a "decent respect [for] the opinions of mankind" (to borrow a phrase from the Declaration of Independence), as well as often being harmful to America's long-term interests. Facing and fearing a powerful (and ruthless) enemy, the United States at home and abroad often adopted the tactics of the enemy. (A secret 1954 presidential task force had recommended doing so, stating that "hitherto acceptable norms of human conduct do not apply," contending that "longstanding American concepts of 'fair play' must be reconsidered," and urging that tactics "more ruthless than [those] employed by the enemy" should be adopted if necessary).[3]

A particularly chilling abuse uncovered by the Committee was the FBI's effort to destroy Dr. Martin Luther King, Jr. The effort, over many years, included an attempt to induce Dr. King to commit suicide.[4] While the King story is particularly horrible, it exemplified the pathologies that enabled the executive branch during the Cold War repeatedly to violate the law and act in ways fundamentally inconsistent with America's best traditions. Such acts were enabled by an assumption of perpetual secrecy, nonexistent oversight, and vague, fuzzy mandates. When questioned about vicious tactics used against Dr. King, the FBI official in charge of domestic intelligence echoed the rationale of the 1954 presidential task force. Intelligence is "a rough, tough business.... We have used that technique against Soviet agents. They have used it against us." Asked by Senator Fritz Mondale at a Church Committee hearing whether anybody had objected to the tactics used against Dr. King, the FBI official testified, "as far as legality is concerned, morals or ethics, was never raised by myself or anybody else."[5]

The Church Committee's multivolume reports and hearings document countless examples of abuses by the major intelligence agencies, including the FBI, the CIA, and the National Security Agency (NSA).[6] The records of Cold War abuse show how the nation dealt with an earlier generation's crisis, and how Presidents, Attorneys General, and other high-ranking executive-branch officials – as well as Congress – fell far short of their obligations to oversee and control the intelligence community.

The Committee found that, all too often, executive-branch actions – taken in the name of nebulous concepts like "national security," or "subversion," shielded by secrecy, and without the guidance of clear laws – were not "governed and controlled in accord with the fundamental principles of our constitutional system of government."[7] As a result, the Committee concluded, America's secret government did far too many "illegal, improper or unethical" deeds that did not reflect "the ideals which have given the people of this country and of the world hope for a better, fuller, fairer life."[8]

Secret intelligence action was used to harass, disrupt, and even destroy law-abiding domestic groups and citizens.[9] Too many people were spied on with excessively intrusive, and often knowingly illegal, techniques.[10] Intelligence agencies conducted secret surveillance and infiltration of entirely lawful groups.[11] Mail was illegally opened.[12] Without their knowledge, Americans were dosed with dangerous drugs to test techniques being developed to combat the Soviets.[13] Congress was provided incomplete or misleading intelligence on subjects of national concern, such as whether the Civil Rights Movement or anti-Vietnam War protests were controlled from overseas.[14] Presidents solicited intelligence agencies to spy on political opponents.[15] Among other assassination plots, the CIA attempted for years to assassinate Fidel Castro, even enlisting the Mafia in its efforts.[16] The CIA also helped foment the overthrow of Chile's democratically elected government.[17] This is just a tiny glimpse of what the Committee uncovered.

In addition to exposing illegal, improper, foolish and often counterproductive conduct by intelligence agencies, the Church Committee exposed inadequacies in oversight and control by Congress and by Presidents and other high officials within the executive branch. Underlying all the Cold War abuses and excesses at home and abroad was the assumption that the government's role would remain forever secret. Intelligence agencies did cancel a few programs out of fear of public exposure. A handful of officials resisted misuse of intelligence assets. But these were exceptions. In general, a small coterie of executive-branch decision makers acted on the assumption that improper actions would be forever shrouded in secrecy. Thus, they failed to consider the harm to the government, to America's reputation among other nations, and to Americans' own self-esteem when abuses inevitably saw the light of day.

Importantly, the Church Committee focused on the role played by Presidents, Attorneys General, and other high-level executive officials in the commission of the intelligence abuses it uncovered. The evolution of the Committee's findings on executive responsibility shows how important it is to have an in-depth inquiry into the facts.[18]

At the start, the role of senior executive-branch officials was not clear. In mid-summer of 1975, early in the assassination plots investigation, Senator Church speculated that the CIA may have acted like a "rogue elephant on a rampage," conceiving and carrying out the plots without clear authorization. Other Senators, also speculating, opined that the CIA "took orders from the top."[19] When an interim report documenting the Committee's findings on assassinations was issued in November 1975, midway through the complete investigation, the Committee declined to adopt either theory. Instead, the interim report presented the substantive evidence for both views, saying the conflicting evidence made it impossible to be certain whether or not Presidents Eisenhower and Kennedy authorized the assassination plots during their administrations.[20]

In April 1976, after the Committee's completion of its investigation into many other intelligence actions, the Committee was ready in its Final Reports to fix responsibility at the top for abuses at home and abroad. While intelligence agencies did, on occasion, fail to reveal domestic programs or acts to their superiors, when it summed up the evidence relating to "Intelligence Activities and the Rights of Americans" the Committee concluded that "the most serious breaches of duty were those of senior officials who were responsible for controlling intelligence activities and generally failed to assure compliance with the law."[21] Fault often lay with senior executive-branch officials who "demanded results" without "carefully limiting the means." These officials, moreover, gave de facto endorsement for wrongdoing by "failing to inquire further" after receiving indications that improper activities had been occurring, as well as by "delegating broad authority" through open-ended mandates and terms such as "national security" or "subversion,"[22] and then by failing to set forth adequate guidelines or procedural checks on how their wishes were carried out. Finally, senior officials "exhibit[ed] a reluctance to know about secret details of programs."[23]

In the context of a similar pattern with respect to foreign intelligence activities, the Committee explained: "On occasion, intelligence agencies concealed their programs from those in higher authority; more frequently, it was the senior officials themselves who, through pressure for results created the climate within which the abuses occurred."[24]

The Committee's conclusions on responsibility evolved due to the clarity produced by exposure to the whole record. Specific agency acts, examined in isolation, sometimes suggested that an agency acted on its own, or even misled political superiors. But the fuller record, covering many years and many agencies, made clear that ultimate responsibility was properly fixed with Presidents, Attorneys General, and other high executive-branch officials.

The Church Committee's work led to some statutory reforms. These included improving congressional oversight by creating permanent House and Senate

Committees on Intelligence, passing the Foreign Intelligence Surveillance Act of 1978 (FISA), which banned warrantless wiretapping, and passing a law that limited the tenure of the FBI Director to ten years, thus preventing a recurrence of J. Edgar Hoover's control of the FBI, which had lasted from 1924 until his death in 1972.[25]

Despite the efforts of a number of Senators, including Church Committee veteran Walter "Dee" Huddleston (aided by former Church Committee Staff Director, William G. Miller), comprehensive charters for the nation's key intelligence agencies were not enacted.[26] This happened for many reasons, including that Attorney General Edward Levi and President Gerald Ford, followed by President Jimmy Carter, had issued guidelines and executive orders in response to the Church Committee's revelations that went part of the way toward the goals of the Church Committee.[27] As the Church Committee reports pointed out, however, the problem with Attorney General guidelines and presidential executive orders (as opposed to laws) is that they can be changed much more easily.[28]

Regression from the Church Committee reforms began in the 1980s. Also in the 1980s, new theories of unilateral executive power began to be developed.[29] A leader in this effort was Dick Cheney, then Wyoming's representative in the House. In a minority report to the joint Senate/House Committee's Iran-Contra Report, Cheney (assisted by David Addington, his long-time aide and now the Vice President's Chief of Staff) defended President Reagan's practice of secretly selling missiles to Iran and then using the proceeds to evade Congressional laws barring financial aid to the Nicaraguan rebels known as the Contras. Citing the Church Committee as a prime offender, Cheney conjured up and condemned an "all but unlimited Congressional power" that he claimed "began to take hold in the 1970s in the wake of the Vietnam War." Cheney and his dissenting colleagues called for executive supremacy, akin, indeed, to English monarchs'.[30] Today, 20 years after the Iran-Contra dissent, the author of the minority report is the key member of President George W. Bush's team pressing for unilateral "monarchial" presidential power.[31]

Thirty years later: the relevance of the Church Committee to the debate on presidential power in a time of terror

The Church Committee's most fundamental lesson for today is that crisis makes it tempting to ignore the wise restraints that keep us free. In addition, the facts exposed by the Committee stand as an object lesson of how, over the course of decades, secrecy, inadequate – or nonexistent – oversight, and vague, fuzzy laws lead to abuse, excess, and foolishness. The Church Committee also documented how repeatedly – indeed, almost invariably – secret programs that started small and relatively focused expanded far beyond any conceivably defensible origin they may once have had. Out of many examples, here are just two:

- The NSA's Operation SHAMROCK, pursuant to which, for 35 years, the NSA secretly obtained from major U.S. companies every single cable sent overseas, started with the objective of examining encrypted cables sent by foreign embassies. It ended by examining the cables of anti-Vietnam War protestors and civil rights leaders.[32]

- The FBI's COINTELPRO program – an ugly, secret effort to use dirty tricks to disrupt and destroy dissenters – began with its focus on persons said to be associated with the Communist Party. But COINTELPRO moved on to war protestors and African-American organizations such as Martin Luther King, Jr.'s Southern Christian Leadership Conference – which, unbelievably, was secretly labeled within the FBI as a "Black Nationalist *Hate* Group."[33]

This common – seemingly inevitable – phenomenon of "mission creep" was colorfully captured in testimony given to the Committee by Tom Charles Huston, who coordinated from the White House in 1970 the abortive "Huston Plan," by which intelligence agencies sought presidential sanction for ongoing illegal break-ins and illegal mail opening campaigns as well as warrantless wiretaps and bugs. As Huston later testified before the Committee, unchecked intelligence activity risked a "move from the kid with the bomb to the kid with a picket sign, and from the kid with the picket sign to the kid with the bumper sticker of the opposing candidate. And you just keep moving down the line."[34]

The Church Committee's extensive exposure of the dangers of the assumption of perpetual secrecy, lack of oversight, vague and fuzzy laws, and mission creep is clearly relevant to the current national debate. The following presents a survey of the other lessons from the Church Committee that may be illuminating today.

Remember our history

Crisis has always made it tempting to ignore restraints. The Sedition Act of 1798,[35] the Palmer Raids just after World War I,[36] and the World War II internment of Japanese-Americans[37] are examples from which the Church Committee learned. In retrospect, each came to be viewed in U.S. constitutional history as unhappy overreactions to crisis – indeed, as iconic examples of what *not* to do.[38]

As the Church Committee pointed out, the public knew about all these excesses at the time they occurred, although the public may have been misled about the legitimacy of their claimed justifications. During the Cold War, secrecy was added as a new facet of executive action in a time of crisis. The very existence of whole programs was concealed for decades. A democracy cannot work where the public is kept in the dark about what is being done in its name. And the constitutional assumption of checks and balance cannot possibly work where Congress is uninformed about – or knowingly turns a blind eye to – both the conduct of the intelligence agencies it is meant to oversee, and the responsibility of Presidents, Attorneys General and other high officials it is supposed to check and balance.

Since the September 11, 2001 terrorist attacks in the United States, as during the Cold War, excessive secrecy, weak oversight and the temptation to let crisis override wise restraints all are blooming once again, spreading and choking U.S. democracy. Added today, however, is the Bush administration's theory of the President's authority to ignore or set aside laws passed by Congress.[39]

Oversight should be comprehensive, nonpartisan, responsible and fact based: how the Church Committee operated also provides lessons for today

Comprehensiveness

There has never been, before or since, in the United States or any other country, an investigation of a nation's secret intelligence or national security agencies as comprehensive as the Church Committee's. How could this have happened? Part of the reason was that the Committee was nonpartisan and responsible, as will be discussed shortly. Another part of the reason was that, after decades of Cold War secrecy, there was a pent-up interest in what the nation's secret government had been doing. Reporters, like Seymour Hersh in the *New York Times*, had begun to reveal bits of the story. Congress had perhaps become ashamed of neglecting its oversight responsibilities.[40] In addition, there were two recent events that helped make possible the Church Committee investigation.

The first was that President Gerald Ford had just taken over from Richard Nixon. Nixon, of course, was disgraced for, among other things, abusing the national security agencies and for trying desperately to conceal information, including the secret White House tapes. In the shadow of the Nixon presidency, Ford was reluctant to be accused by the Committee of withholding relevant information.

The second was that J. Edgar Hoover had died. Hoover's power arising from the FBI's enormous trove of information frightened even the most stalwart public officials.[41] Indeed, in the course of its investigation, the Church Committee learned of Hoover's ability to use information garnered from wiretaps to intimidate President Kennedy and his brother, the Attorney General.[42]

Nonpartisan and responsible nature

When the Church Committee was established in the wake of Watergate, some may have thought that it would simply expose more wrongdoing by the Nixon White House. Not so. One of the Committee's signal contributions was to show that excess and abuse had existed in every administration from that of Franklin Delano Roosevelt to that of Richard Milhous Nixon.[43] This had to help hold the Committee together, and presumably helped produce substantial majorities in the Senate and, to a somewhat lesser extent, in the House when FISA was passed in 1978.

The Committee (with six Democrats and five Republicans) never split on a partisan basis. In the early days, Vice Chair John Tower and all the Republican members helped in pushing the White House for access to documents. In later days, two Republicans, Senators Tower and Barry Goldwater, disagreed with some Committee decisions on disclosure of information, and they (along with Senator Howard Baker) disagreed on some remedies proposed by the Committee. But these never were wholly partisan disagreements.[44] And, particularly when compared to today, the atmosphere was far more collegial.

Investigating secret government programs requires access to secrets. It forces analysis of the overuse of secrecy stamps, and of the harm caused by excessive secrecy. Ultimately, it may require the describing and revealing of secrets. Nonetheless, obviously, there are legitimate secrets. Oversight, or an investigation that is heedless of that, is doomed, as well as irresponsible.

The Church Committee worked out reasonable arrangements on this subject with the White House and the intelligence agencies. The arrangements related to (1) how secret documents were provided, and (2) how the Committee's reports were produced.

The Committee was also helped enormously by its success in avoiding leaks. This record stood in stark contrast to the parallel House committee, which floundered at the outset and foundered at the end because of leaks.[45]

Fact-based approach

At its outset, the Church Committee had to decide what kind of hearings it would hold. Would it emphasize the insights of "wise men"? Or would it rely on detailed facts to make the case for reform? Chairman Church opted to emphasize the latter while not ignoring the former.

Without facts, oversight will necessarily be empty. Only with a record that is detailed and covers a wide range can one be sure one understands patterns, be confident of conclusions, or make a powerful case for change. The Committee's whole record stands as support for this approach. Without detailed facts, it is simply not possible to make a creditable case that something is wrong. Another example is the evolution (described above) of the Committee's conclusions about presidential and other high executive-branch officials' responsibility for agency wrongdoing. Another emotionally telling example occurred on the first day of the Committee's public hearings on the FBI. After counsel had provided a detailed and disturbing litany of FBI lawlessness, Chairman Church turned to questions and comments from senators, first recognizing Michigan's Senator Philip Hart. Church expressed pleasure at Hart's return after "some weeks of absence." What Church did not say – but everyone knew – was that Hart had been away being treated for the cancer that killed him the next year.

Noting that he did not "recommend that others pursue the course I took to get this advantage" (of commenting first), Hart began by telling how he had for years rejected claims of FBI impropriety:

As I'm sure others have, I have been told for years by, among others, some of my own family, that this is exactly what the Bureau was doing all of the time, and in my great wisdom and high office, I assured them that they were [*sic*] – it just wasn't true. It couldn't happen. They wouldn't do it.[46]

Then Hart described how the facts recounted by counsel had changed his mind, and set out the two broad challenges facing the Committee:

> What you have described is a series of illegal actions intended squarely to deny First Amendment rights to some Americans. That is what my children have told me was going on.
>
> The trick now, as I see it, Mr. Chairman, is for this Committee to be able to figure out how to persuade the people of this country that indeed it did go on. And how shall we insure that it will never happen again? But it will happen repeatedly unless we can bring ourselves to understand and accept that it did go on.[47]

Asking the right questions

Getting the facts is essential to telling the story – and essential (as Senator Hart put it) to "persuad[ing] the people of the United States." Why does the story matter? The Church Committee asked fundamental questions about American values and about the premises underlying the country's system of constitutional government. These questions are equally relevant today.

When faced with a powerful and unscrupulous enemy, should America adopt the tactics of the enemy? The case in favor is not trivial, as shown, for example, by the recommendations of the 1954 presidential task force mentioned earlier. But the Church Committee concluded otherwise. In words that resonate today, the Committee concluded that the acts that it had exposed "did not reflect the ideals which have given the people of the country, and of the world, hope for a better, fuller, fairer life."[48] It added:

> The United States must not adopt the tactics of the enemy. Means are as important as ends. Crisis makes it tempting to ignore the wise restraints that make [us] free. But each time we do so, each time the means we use are wrong, our inner strength, the strength which makes [us] free is lessened.[49]

As the Committee concluded in its Final Report, even in crisis, "power must be checked and balanced, and ... the preservation of liberty requires the restraint of laws, and not simply the good intentions of men."[50]

Similarly, the Committee found that those planning covert actions "rarely noted" possible harms the actions could cause, particularly to "this nation's ability to exercise moral and political leadership throughout the world."[51] Reputation matters. It matters to power[52] – as we are learning once again today.[53]

Democracy depends on an informed public. But governments – often relying on fuzzy terms like "national security" – frequently conceal basic facts from the public. Again, the Church Committee's words can resonate today:

Despite our distaste for what we have seen, we have great faith in this country. The story is sad, but this country has the strength to hear the story and to learn from it. We must remain a people who confront our mistakes and resolve not to repeat them. If we do not, we will decline; but if we do, our future will be worthy of the best of our past.[54]

The Committee was unanimous that its embarrassing findings about excess, abuse and illegality at home should be made public. In "Additional Statements" to the Final Report on "Intelligence Activities and the Rights of Americans," Democratic Senator Robert Morgan and Republican Senator Howard Baker commented in unison on the *favorable* impact of making facts, however embarrassing, public. Senator Morgan explained that "releasing this Report is a great testament to the freedom for which America stands," and expressed his "sincere hope that the Report ... will rekindle in each of us the belief that perhaps our greatest strength lies in our ability to deal frankly, openly and honestly with the problems of our government."[55] Senator Baker predicted that the abuses being "fully aired to the American people" would have a "cathartic effect" on the FBI and the CIA.[56] Baker supported this conclusion by quoting former CIA Director William Colby, who, in a 1976 *New York Times* opinion piece, said "this year's excitement" from the investigation could "strengthen American intelligence."[57]

Strengthening the intelligence services

In fact, the Church Committee's work *was* "cathartic" and *did* "strengthen" the U.S. intelligence agencies. All Committee members understood the need for strong intelligence agencies: "properly controlled and lawful intelligence is vital to the nation's interest"; it serves to "monitor potential military threats," "verify compliance with international agreements," and "combat espionage and international terrorism."[58]

Even where there were abuses, the men and women of the agencies – which play many vital roles unrelated to abuse – deserved a measure of understanding, not solely criticism. Agents received assignments that were often almost impossible to fulfill. They were expected to predict every crisis, to supply, immediately, information on any issue, and to anticipate and respond to the demands of Presidents. Under that kind of pressure, and acting in the shadow of the Soviet threat, it is no surprise that agents interpreted their ambiguous mandates as expansively as possible.

The wrongdoing that the Committee exposed needed to be stopped not only because it was illegal, improper, unwise and harmful to America's reputation but also because it got in the way of the agencies doing their vital work. Thus, for example, the Committee urged elimination of the open-ended FBI authority to investigate "subversives" – a term so vague that for over 40 years it had been used to "constitute a license to investigate about any activity of practically any group that actively opposed the policies of the administration in power."[59] Thus, the Committee concluded (in words that in many respects were ahead of its time): "The national interest would be better served if Bureau resources were directed at *terrorism*, hostile foreign intelligence activity or organized crime, all more serious and pressing threats to the nation than 'subversives'."[60]

In the foreign intelligence arena, the Committee called for intelligence reorganization to realize efficiencies sought (but not achieved) by the 1947 National Security Act. Like the 9/11 Commission decades later, the Church Committee called for limiting the Director of the CIA to running the CIA, and for a higher-level official to coordinate all the intelligence agencies, including the CIA. The Committee also expressed its concern about the dangers of overreliance on "technical collection systems" – i.e., spy satellites and complicated electronic listening devices. These should not replace human spies, because spies can provide "valuable insight concerning the motivations for activity or policies of potential adversaries, as well as their future intentions."[61] This was a lesson the nation has had to relearn after the September 11, 2001 terrorist attacks in the United States.

Conclusion

Stepping away from details of methods of spying or the importance of placing emphasis on crucial matters like terrorism and espionage rather than chasing after activities protected by the First Amendment, the Church Committee's fundamental point was to remind Americans of the premises of the U.S. Constitution. Because men are not "angels," "you must first enable the government to control the governed; and in the next place, oblige it to control itself."[62] To paraphrase Lord Acton, power corrupts and unchecked power corrupts absolutely. Foolish, wasteful, unseemly and illegal actions flowed from a lack of checks and balances. The Church Committee documented universal truths. Unfortunately, today we must be reminded of those truths once again.[63]

Notes

1 The Church Committee reports cited most extensively are: S. Rep. No. 94-755 (1976) (6 Books), including *Foreign and Military Intelligence* [hereinafter Church Book I], *Intelligence Activities and the Rights of Americans* [hereinafter Church Book II], and *Supplementary Detailed Staff Reports on Intelligence Activities and the Rights of Americans* [hereinafter Church Book III]; see also S. Rep. No. 94-465 (1975) [Addressing Assassination Plots] [hereinafter Interim Report]. For the Church Committee's public hearings, see S. Res. 21, 94th Cong. (1975) (7 vols.), including *Unauthorized Storage of Toxic Agents* [hereinafter Church Vol. 1], *Huston Plan* [Church Vol. 2], *Internal Revenue Service* [Church Vol. 3], *Mail Opening* [hereinafter Church Vol. 4], *The National Security Agency and Fourth Amendment Rights* [hereinafter Church Vol. 5], *Federal Bureau of Investigation* [hereinafter Church Vol. 6], and *Covert Action* [hereinafter Church Vol. 7]. For electronic versions, see www.aarclibrary.org/publib/church/reports/contents.htm. Books on the Church Committee include Loch Johnson, *A Season of Inquiry: The Senate Intelligence Investigation* (1985); Frank John Smist, *Congress Oversees the United States Intelligence Community, 1947–1994*, at 25–81 (1994); LeRoy Ashby and Rod Gramer, *Fighting the Odds: The Life of Senator Frank Church* 453, 468–92 (1994). See also Frederick

A.O. Schwarz, Jr., *Intelligence Activities and the Rights of Americans*, Rec. Ass'n Bar City N.Y., Jan./Feb. 1977, at 43; Frederick A.O. Schwarz, Jr., *Intelligence Oversight: The Church Committee*, in *Strategic Intelligence*, Vol. 5 (2007).

2 See Smist, *supra* note 1, for the comparative comprehensiveness of the Church Committee. The 9/11 Commission, well run (on a bipartisan basis) by former Governor Thomas Kean and former Congressman Lee Hamilton, comprehensively examined the secret records of intelligence agencies and the related record of Presidents and other high-ranking executive-branch officials. However, the 9/11 Commission had a single issue focus and also covered a shorter period of time than had the Church Committee.

   Shortly before the September 11, 2001 terrorist attacks in the United States, former Church Committee member Senator Gary Hart, who is a leader of this Idaho conference, together with former Senator Warren Rudman, chaired a commission that issued a report on *National Security/21st Century*, *available at* www.fas.org/near/docs/nwc. The Hart/Rudman Commission concluded that terrorism at home was a threat that demanded far more attention.

3 See Church Book I, *supra* note 1, at 50; Interim Report, *supra* note 1, at 259 n.1 (quoting James Doolittle *et al.*, *Report on the Covert Activities of the Central Intelligence Agency* (Sept. 30, 1954)).

4 For the Bureau's treatment of Dr. King generally, see Church Book II, *supra* note 1, at 11–12, 219–23, and Church Book III, *supra* note 1, at 79–184. For attempt to induce suicide, see Church Book II, *supra* note 1, at 11, 220–21, and Church Book III, *supra* note 1, at 158–61. See also Taylor Branch, *Pillar of Fire: America in the King Years: 1963–1965*, at 528–29, 556–57 (1998); David Garrow, *Bearing the Cross: Martin Luther King, Jr. and the Southern Christian Leadership Conference* 373–75 (1986).

5 Church Book II, *supra* note 1, at 92–93, 141 (quoting William C. Sullivan's testimony on November 1, 1975). Mondale chaired the Domestic Intelligence Subcommittee of the Church Committee. See also Walter F. Mondale, *The Accountability of Power: Toward a Responsible Presidency* (1975); Walter F. Mondale, Lecture at Minneapolis, Minnesota: Democracy's Challenge: Balancing Personal Liberty and National Security (Apr. 27, 2000) (on file with author).

6 See *supra* note 1.

7 Church Book II, *supra* note 1, at Preface, v.

8 Ibid.; S. Res. 21, § 1, 94th Cong. (1975). See also Interim Report, *supra* note 1, at 285.

9 See Church Book II, *supra* note 1, at 10–12, 65–94, 211–23; Church Book III: COINTELPRO: The FBI's Covert Action Programs against American Citizens, *supra* note 1, at 3–77.

10 See, e.g., Church Book II, *supra* note 1, at 6–7, 165–82.

11 Ibid. at 12–13, 137–63, 167–69, 172–82, 183–210; Church Book III: Warrantless FBI Electronic Surveillance, *supra* note 1, at 273–351; Ibid.: Warrantless Surreptitious Entries, at 355–71.

12 Church Book II, *supra* note 1, at 12; Church Book III: Domestic CIA and FBI Mail Opening, *supra* note 1, at 559–677.

13 Church Book I: CIA Drug Testing Programs, *supra* note 1, at 391–411.

14 Church Book II, *supra* note 1, at 167–68, 174–75, 232–33, 250–51; Church Book III, *supra* note 1, at 679–732.

15 Church Book II, *supra* note 1, at 225–52.

16 Interim Report, *supra* note 1, at 71–180.

17 Ibid. at 225–54; Staff Report, *Covert Action in Chile, 1963–1973*.

18 Contemporaneous documents and access to actual witnesses are necessary to master the intricacies of intelligence and security institutions and to learn the truth about their conduct and the conduct of their political masters. The White House and the

intelligence agencies initially resisted the Committee's demands for detailed documents. But continued pressure from the Committee eventually led to compliance. See, e.g., Johnson, *supra* note 1, at 27–44. (When CIA Director Colby first appeared to testify before the Committee, the author got him to commit to produce the key CIA documents. During the author's first visit to FBI headquarters, FBI officials attempted to divert attention from a real investigation by showing pictures of severed heads on an urban street. But the Bureau also soon cooperated by providing their secret (and highly embarrassing) documents.) With respect to witnesses, the CIA initially proposed that a "monitor" from the agency accompany any current or former intelligence official called for questioning, including preliminary questioning by staff members. In addition to observing, the monitors would give witnesses "advice." The Committee refused. Ibid. at 43. For an example of the inadequacy (indeed gross inaccuracy) of internal agency reports about the facts, see Church Book II, *supra* note 1, at 271 (describing FBI report on a COINTELPRO action that was in fact designed to provoke a killing as an effort to "drive a wedge between" two black groups in Chicago).

19 Johnson, *supra* note 1, at 57.

20 See Interim Report, *supra* note 1, at 6–7, 148–61, 260–67 (authorizing evidence and conclusions).

21 Church Book II, *supra* note 1, at 137.

22 One of the most important factual findings of the Church Committee was that "the imprecision and manipulation of labels such as 'national security,' 'domestic security,' 'subversive activities,' and 'foreign intelligence,'" led to unjustified use of highly intrusive techniques like bugs, wiretaps, break-ins and illegal mail opening. See Church Book II, *supra* note 1, at 205; see also Church Book I, *supra* note 1, at 12.

23 For "demanding results," see Church Book II, *supra* note 1, at 139. For "failing to inquire further," "delegating broad authority," failing to establish adequate guidelines and "exhibiting a reluctance to know," see ibid. at 265.

24 Church Book I, *supra* note 1, at 11.

25 See Frederick A.O. Schwarz, Jr. and Aziz Huq, *Unchecked and Unbalanced: Presidential Power in a Time of Terror* 50–56 (2007). For permanent committee, see Church Book I, *supra* note 1, at 2, 424; Johnson, *supra* note 1, 227–51; Johnson in this volume (Chapter 4). *See* Smist, *supra* note 1, at 82–83; *see also* 122 *Congressional Record* 14,673–75 (1976). For debate on S. Res. No. 400, see 122 *Congressional Record* 13,656, 13,678–95, 13,973–90, 14,149–73, 14,259–66, 14,643–79 (1976). And see Smist, quoting an interview in which Senator Church said:

> [C]ontinuing congressional oversight is built into the woodwork. We did the necessary job. Political will can't be guaranteed. The most we could do was to recommend that permanent surveillance be established. We did that knowing that the Congress being a political animal will exercise its surveillance with whatever diligence the political climate of the time makes for.

(Smist, supra note 1)

For FISA, see Foreign Intelligence Surveillance Act of 1978, Pub. L. No. 95-511, 92 Stat. 1738 (codified at 50 U.S.C. §§ 1801–1811). For the Senate Committee report, see S. Rep. No. 95-701 (1978), as reprinted in 1978 U.S.C.C.A.N. 3973. For the House Committee report, see H.R. Rep. No. 95-1720 (1978) (Conf. Rep.), as reprinted in 1978 U.S.C.C.A.N. 4048. For President Carter's signing statement, see *Statement of Signing S. 1566 into Law* (Oct. 25, 1978), available at www.cnss.org/Carter.pdf. Foreign Intelligence Surveillance Act, *Statement on Signing S. 1566 into Law* (Oct. 25, 1978), available at www.cnss.org/fisa.html. See also George Lardner Jr., Carter Signs Bill Limiting Foreign Intelligence Surveillance, *Washington Post*, Oct. 26, 1978, at A2. For further early material on FISA, see Editorial, National Security Wiretaps, *Washington Post*, Sept. 6, 1978, at A14.

For the tenure of the FBI director, see Crime Control Act of 1976, Pub. L. No. 94-503, § 203, 90 Stat. 2427 (codified at 28 U.S.C. § 532).

26 See Schwarz and Huq, *supra* note 25, at 58; Smist, *supra* note 1, at 97–99; Loch Johnson, Legislative Reform of Intelligence Policy, *Polity*, 17 (Spring) (1985), 549–73, at 567.

27 For the Levi Guidelines, which were issued in 1976, see Church Book II, *supra* note 1, at 135, 318–20; FBI Statutory Charter, Hearings before the Comm. on the Judiciary, 95th Cong., 18–26 (1978); Exec. Order No. 11,905, 41 Fed. Reg. 7703 (Feb. 18, 1976) (President Ford); Exec. Order No. 12,036, 43 Fed. Reg. 3674 (Feb. 24, 1978) (President Carter).

28 Church Book II, *supra* note 1, at 136, 318–20.

29 See Schwarz and Huq, *supra* note 25, at 158–61; see also *infra* notes 31 and 39; Seamon in this volume (Chapter 8).

30 For the Iran-Contra Minority Report, see *Report of the Congressional Comms. Investigating the Iran-Contra Affair, with Supplemental, Minority, and Additional Views*, S. Rep. No. 100-216, H. Rep. No. 100-433, at 457 (1987).

31 See Schwarz and Huq, *supra* note 25, at 1; ibid.: Chapter 7, "Kings and Presidents," at 153–86.

32 For NSA, see Church Book III, *supra* note 1, at 733–83; Church Vol. 5, *supra* note 1; James Bamford, *The Puzzle Palace: Inside America's Most Secret Intelligence Organization* (1983); James Bamford, *Body of Secrets: Anatomy of the Ultra-secret National Security Agency* (2002); L. Britt Snider, Recollections from the Church Committee's Investigation of NSA, *Studies in Intelligence*, Winter 1999–2000, 43–51.

33 For COINTELPRO generally, see Church Book II, *supra* note 1, at 10–12, 65–94, 211–23; Church Book III, *supra* note 1, at 1–79. For "ugly" program, see Frederick A.O. Schwarz, Jr., *Intelligence Activities and the Rights of Americans*, *supra* note 1, at 43, 46.

34 For Huston, see Church Book II, *supra* note 1, at 4 (quoting Tom Charles Huston's testimony on September 23, 1975); Church Vol. 2, *supra* note 1, at 45. For the Huston Plan; see Church Book II, *supra* note 1, at 111–16; Church Book III, *supra* note 1, at 921–83; Church Vol. 2, *supra* note 1; Johnson, *supra* note 1, at 78–88.

35 For the Alien and Sedition Acts of 1798, see John Chester Miller, *Crisis in Freedom: The Alien and Sedition Acts* (1951); Geoffrey R. Stone, *Perilous Times: Free Speech in Wartime: From the Sedition Act of 1798 to the War on Terrorism* 16–78 (2004).

36 *See* Stone, *supra* note 35, at 135–233; Edwin Palmer Hoyt, *The Palmer Raids* (1969); William Preston, *Aliens and Dissenters: Federal Suppression of Radicals, 1903–1933* (1963).

37 See *Korematzu* v. *United States*, 323 U.S. 214 (1944); Peter Irons, *Justice at War: The Story of the Japanese Internment Cases* (1983); Roger Daniels, *Prisoners without Trial: Japanese Americans in World War II* (1993); Stone, *supra* note 35, at 283–310.

38 See, e.g., *New York Times* v. *Sullivan*, 376 U.S. 254, 276 (1964) ("[A]lthough the Sedition Act was never tested in this Court, the attack upon its validity has carried the day in the court of history"); Schwarz and Huq, *supra* note 25, at 4, 210, n.10.

39 See Schwarz and Huq: Chapter 7, "Kings and Presidents," *supra* note 25; Charlie Savage, Bush Challenges Hundreds of Laws, *Boston Globe*, Apr. 30, 2006.

40 For comments about Congress's neglect of its oversight responsibilities pre-Church Committee, see, e.g., Smist, *supra* note 1, at 5 (quoting Clark Clifford as saying: "Congress chose not to be involved and preferred to be uninformed"); ibid. at 9 (quoting the CIA General Counsel as suggesting the lack of oversight caused *problems* for the CIA because "we became a little cocky about what we could do"); and ibid. at 50 (quoting then Senate Majority Leader Mike Mansfield in 1975 when speaking in support of the resolution establishing the Church Committee). Mansfield said:

It used to be fashionable ... for members of Congress to say that insofar as the intelligence agencies were concerned, the less they knew about such questions, the better. Well, in my judgment, it is about time that attitude went out of fashion. It is time for the Senate to take the trouble and, yes, the risks, of knowing more rather than less.

(Ibid.)

41 According to then-Congressman Hale Boggs:

Our apathy in this Congress, our silence in this house, our very fear of speaking out in other forums, has watered the roots and hastened the growth of a vine of tyranny which is ensnaring that Constitution and Bill of Rights which we are each sworn to uphold. Our society can survive many challenges and many threats. It cannot survive a planned and programmed fear of its own government bureaus and agencies.

(Church Book II, *supra* note 1, at 240 (quoting 117 Cong. Rec. 11,562 (1971)))

42 See Interim Report, *supra* note 1, at 129–30 (discussing a letter from Hoover to the White House and Attorney General Kennedy that revealed that Hoover knew that the mistress of the Mafia don hired by the CIA to kill Fidel Castro was at the same time one of the President's mistresses). (This was relevant to the Committee's analysis of the President's knowledge of the Castro assassination plots. Was she a go-between? The Committee concluded no.)

43 See, e.g., Church Book II, *supra* note 1, at viii.

44 For general comments on the Committee's nonpartisan character, see Smist, *supra* note 1, at 41 (describing the Committee's "unity and bi-partisanship" as key to its success). Among other things, Smist quoted a long-time aide of Senator Howard Baker, who contrasted the Watergate Committee ("brutally partisan") with the Church Committee ("Republicans and Democrats worked hand-in-hand on projects together").

45 For the House committee, see Smist, *supra* note 1, at 175–213.

46 Church Vol. 6, *supra* note 1, at 41.

47 Ibid.

48 Interim Report, *supra* note 1, at 285.

49 Ibid.

50 Church Book II, *supra* note 1, at v.

51 For rarely noted, see Church Book I, *supra* note 1, at 156.

52 See Joseph S. Nye, Jr., *The Paradox of American Power* (2002); Gary Hart, *The Fourth Power* (2004).

53 Pew Research Center for the People and the Press, Pew Global Attitudes Project, *America's Image Further Erodes, Europeans Want Weaker Ties* (Mar. 18, 2003), available at http://pewglobal.org/reports/display.php?ReportID=175; The Pew Research Center for the People and the Press, Pew Global Attitudes Project, *America's Image Slips, but Allies Share U.S. Concerns over Iran, Hamas* (June 13, 2006), available at http://pewglobal.org/reports/display.php?ReportID=252.

54 Interim Report, *supra* note 1, at 285.

55 Church Book II: Additional Statement of Senator Robert Morgan, *supra* note 1, at 363–65.

56 Church Book II: Additional Statement of Senator Howard H. Baker, Jr., *supra* note 1, at 373–75.

57 See William Colby, After Investigating US Intelligence, *New York Times*, Feb. 26, 1976, at A30.

58 Church Book II, *supra* note 1, at v.

59 Ibid. at 319.

60 Ibid. (emphasis added).

61 Church Book I, *supra* note 1, at 437. *See also* 121 Cong. Rec. 14,673 (1975) (discussing Senator Church's earlier speech to the Senate calling for, among other things, strengthening of the CIA's ability to provide the "best possible understanding of foreign capabilities, leaders and developing events").

62 See *The Federalist No. 51*, at 322 (Madison) (Clinton Rossiter, ed., 1961).

63 See generally Schwarz and Huq, *supra* note 25.

4   Establishment of modern intelligence accountability

Loch K. Johnson

Introduction

This chapter examines the legacy of a well-known U.S. Senate Committee investigation into the intelligence agencies in 1975, known as the Church Committee probe (after its leader, Frank Church, Democrat from Idaho). In particular, the focus here is on the consequences of this inquiry for the establishment of a reliable system of intelligence accountability on Capitol Hill. The chapter's central thesis is that the Church Committee substantially strengthened the opportunities for lawmakers to keep tabs on America's hidden government, but that the level of rigor displayed by intelligence overseers in Congress has fallen below the expectations of the Committee's reformers in 1975.

The United States has 16 major intelligence agencies. They are responsible for gathering and analyzing information about threats and opportunities around the world, and about subversive activities at home; protecting the nation's secrets through counterintelligence defenses; and attempting, on occasion, to change the course of history by means of secret interventions into the affairs of other nations (covert action).

In maintaining supervision over these secretive agencies, members of Congress have displayed a wide range of commitment. Some lawmakers have looked upon accountability of "oversight" with an attitude of benign neglect; they are referred to here as the "ostriches," who are content to bury their heads in the sand rather than examine the merits of U.S. intelligence operations. Others have become unalloyed champions of the intelligence bureaucracy, regardless of flaws in its operations (the "cheerleaders"). Still others, imbued with deep-seated misgivings about the value and morality of covert operations, have found much fault and little virtue in secret activities across the board (the "skeptics"). Finally, some in Congress have shown a capacity to step back and evaluate, in a dispassionate manner, the strengths and the weaknesses of the intelligence agencies (the "guardians").

A primary purpose of this inquiry is to examine these roles as they have been practiced in the United States since 1975, providing examples of each and probing why lawmakers have adopted one or another (or sometimes a mix) of approaches to intelligence accountability – arguably the most stringent test of

America's fabled constitutional principle of checks and balances, because so much of the reviewing must take place behind closed doors, with little public credit. Before the different roles can make sense, however, they must be understood in the context of intelligence history in the United States since the creation of the Central Intelligence Agency (CIA) in 1947. In this 60-year slice of recent history, 1975 stands out as an *annus mirabilis*, the year when the question of how to manage the nation's secret agencies emerged as a key topic of debate in Washington, D.C. During this year, the Church Committee did nothing less than revolutionize America's attitudes toward intelligence supervision.

The year of intelligence

The differences in the seriousness of intelligence accountability before and after 1975 are as stark as night and day. Because that year marked the time when Congress conducted its first major investigations into the modern intelligence bureaucracy, it became a watershed. The congressional probes arose as a result of a series of exposés on domestic spying, published by the *New York Times* in the autumn and winter of 1974.[1]

The newspaper articles shocked the nation. *Times* reporter Seymour M. Hersh alleged that, without warrants, the CIA had engaged in the widespread opening of mail sent and received by American citizens, an operation known inside "the Agency" (as insiders refer to the CIA) by the codename Operation CHAOS. Hersh also reported that the CIA had tried to manipulate the free and open democratic elections for the presidency in Chile during the 1960s and 1970s; and then, when the CIA's favored candidate lost in the 1970s, the Agency attempted to undermine the government of the successful candidate, Salvador Allende, who had been critical of the United States in the past. As newspapers across the country reprinted and commented on these stories, the CIA faced a major scandal in the making. At the beginning of 1975, lawmakers reacted to public concern about the media reports by establishing two panels of inquiry, one in the Senate and one in the House.[2] The White House, not to be left behind and accused of laxity, created its own presidential commission to investigate the allegations.[3] The so-called Year of Intelligence, triggering what intelligence professionals ruefully remember as "The Intelligence Wars," was under way.

Senator Frank Church headed the Senate investigative committee, which bore the official name "The Senate Select Committee to Study Governmental Operations with Respect to Intelligence Activities," or, more simply, the Senate Select Committee on Intelligence. As is common with panels of inquiry, it soon took on the name of its Chair: the Church Committee.[4] The counterpart inquiry in the House of Representatives stumbled at the beginning with a series of missteps, first creating and then disbanding one committee before finally settling on Representative Otis Pike (Democrat from New York) to lead its investigation. Formally labeled "The House Select Committee to Study Government Operations with Respect to Intelligence Activities," or the House Select Committee on Intelligence, it is commonly referred to as the Pike Committee. The presidential commission was formally "The Commission on CIA Activities within the United States," and informally the Rockefeller Commission – after its chair, Vice President Nelson Rockefeller (Republican).

During the first few months of 1975, these panels began to scrutinize the CIA and its operations, and as a broader picture of malfeasance began to emerge, they widened their investigations to include the CIA's companion agencies in the "intelligence community." The Rockefeller Commission remained on the investigative trail for half a year, the Pike Committee for almost a year, and the Church Committee for 16 months. Each panel produced impressively detailed and thoughtful reports, disclosing that Hersh and the *Times* were correct about CIA surveillance within the United States and covert action in Chile, but that the newspaper accounts had only scratched the surface of wrongdoing by America's secret agencies. In addition, the investigative findings demonstrated that the CIA had:

- opened the mail to and from selected American citizens, which generated 1.5 million names stored in the Agency's computer bank (CHAOS), including such "subversives" as John Steinbeck, Leonard Bernstein, Arthur Burns, and even Richard Nixon and Frank Church;
- engaged in drug experiments against unsuspecting subjects, two of whom died from side effects;
- manipulated elections around the world and even in democratic countries such as Chile, as the *Times* had reported (although without examining the global extent of such operations);
- infiltrated religious, media, and academic organizations inside the United States, in explicit violation of its founding charter (the National Security Act of 1947); and
- plotted failed assassination attempts against selected foreign leaders, including Fidel Castro of Cuba and Patrice Lumumba of Congo.[5]

Further, investigators discovered that several other intelligence agencies had joined the CIA, or acted independently, in a veiled assault on America's traditions and laws related to privacy and civil liberties. Army intelligence units, for example, had compiled dossiers on 100,000 U.S. citizens during the Vietnam War era (1965–73).[6] The vast computer facilities of the National Security Agency (NSA) had monitored every cable sent overseas or received from overseas by Americans from 1947 to 1975 (Operation SHAMROCK), and the agency had engaged as well in questionable wiretapping within the United States (Operation MINARET).[7] The Internal Revenue Service had allowed tax information to be misused by intelligence agencies for political purposes.

Among the most chilling of the Church Committee findings came from the vaults of the Federal Bureau of Investigation (FBI). The Bureau had created files on over one million Americans and carried out over 500,000 investigations of "subversives" from 1960 to 1974 without a single court conviction.[8] The FBI's schemes included a campaign to incite violence among African-Americans. As the Church Committee reported, a Bureau office in California boasted in a memorandum back to headquarters:

> Shootings, beatings, and a high degree of unrest continues to prevail in the ghetto area of southeast San Diego. Although no specific counterintelligence action can be credited with contributing to this overall situation, it is felt that a substantial amount of the unrest is directly attributable to this program.[9]

The efforts to drive African-Americans to one another's throats was just one of many operations that fell into a broad category known inside Bureau headquarters as the Counterintelligence Program (COINTELPRO). As Senator Walter Mondale (Democrat from Minnesota), one of the more active members of the Church Committee, recalled, "No meeting was too small, no group too insignificant" to escape the FBI's attention.[10] From 1956 to 1971, the Bureau carried out smear campaigns against thousands of groups and individuals simply because they had expressed opposition to the war in Vietnam or criticized the slow pace of the civil rights movement.[11] Ecumenical in its distrust of everyone who failed to fit into a Norman Rockwell portrait of a patriotic American citizen, the Bureau also went after groups on the extreme right, such as the Ku Klux Klan.[12] Target Number One for FBI Director J. Edgar Hoover, however, was the civil rights leader Martin Luther King, Jr., who became the victim of a multitude of secret smear operations, including a blackmail attempt in 1964 that sought to push him into suicide on the eve of his acceptance of a Nobel Peace Prize.[13]

The testimony of witnesses in hearings held by the Church Committee revealed an intelligence community that had drifted far away from its original mandate to protect the American people against foreign and domestic threats. Here is one exchange between Senator Mondale and the Committee's chief counsel, Fredrick A.O. Schwarz, Jr., related to the FBI's attacks against Dr. King:

MONDALE: [No one] showed up a single suggestion that Martin Luther King had committed or was about to commit at crime. Is that correct?
SCHWARZ: That is correct....
MONDALE: Was he ever charged with fomenting violence? Did he ever participate in violence? Was it ever alleged that he was about to be violent?
SCHWARZ: That was the very opposite of his philosophy, Senator.[14]

As Schwarz noted in a commentary on the Church Committee experience, suspected violation of the law is "the only legitimate ground to investigate Americans."[15] The intelligence agencies had slipped far below that standard. One of the witnesses before the Committee, Tom Charles Huston, the young architect of a master plan in 1970 to spy on American citizens (especially campus protestors against the Vietnam War), conceded in hearings that ineluctably the secret agencies would "move from the kid with a bomb to the kid with a picket sign, and from the kid with the picket sign to the kid with the bumper sticker of the opposing candidate. And you just keep going down the line."[16]

In another exchange with a witness, this time Benson Buffham, the deputy director of the NSA, Senator Mondale again probed the legal aspects of the domestic spying:

MONDALE: Were you concerned about its legality?
BUFFHAM: Legality?
MONDALE: Whether it was legal?
BUFFHAM: In what sense? Whether that would have been a legal thing to do?
MONDALE: Yes.
BUFFHAM: That particular aspect didn't enter into the discussion.
MONDALE: I was asking you if you were concerned about whether that would be legal and proper.
BUFFHAM: We didn't consider it at the time, no.[17]

Nor did the FBI give the law much thought. William Sullivan, the Bureau's Deputy Director during the COINTELPRO operations, told the Church Committee, "No holds were barred. We have used [similar] techniques against Soviet agents. [The same methods were] brought home against any organization against which we were targeted. We did not differentiate. This is a rough, tough business."[18] Sullivan testified that never had he heard a discussion about the legality or constitutionality of any aspect of COINTELPRO or any of the other FBI internal security programs. "We were just naturally pragmatic," he said. He offered this excuse for his conduct (reminiscent of Hannah Arendt's remarks on the banality of evil):[19] "I was so inured and accustomed to any damn thing I was told to do, I just carried it out and kept my resentment to myself. I was married and trying to buy a house with a big mortgage and raise a family."[20]

Historian Henry Steele Commager was correct in his observation that "perhaps the most threatening of all the evidence that [emerged] from the findings of the Church Committee" was the indifference of the intelligence agencies to constitutional restraint.[21] As a result of the *Times* reporting and the Church, Pike and Rockefeller investigations, Congress set out to change this indifference with laws, regulations and, above all, a new philosophy of meaningful and consistent legislative involvement in intelligence review, to replace the earlier era of benign neglect.

Congress develops new intelligence safeguards

The law works. That was the central conclusion reached by the Church Committee. Each of the security objectives sought by the intelligence agencies during the Cold War could have been achieved without descending into the darkness of COINTELPRO, CHAOS and the other zealous operations. The United States could fight a totalitarian state without becoming one itself. Liberty and security had to be kept in balance, if America were to stay true to its democratic values and traditions.

When Iran took U.S. diplomats hostage in Tehran during the Carter Adminis-tration, former Secretary of State Dean Rusk thought it was fortunate that the United States did not, in return, seize Iranian diplomats in Washington. "We are not that kind of country or that kind of people," he reflected.[22] A similar point of view guided a majority on the Church Committee: a conviction that the United States was different from the Soviet Union. The nation was, and remains, the world's premier democracy, and that standing has helped to win global support for America.[23] Most members of the Committee felt that when the United States ignored its bedrock democratic principles, it risked losing that support – and its identity.

The Church and Rockefeller inquiries, which focused on questions of accountability (while the Pike panel concentrated on weaknesses in intelligence collection and analysis), stressed the importance of applying traditional govern-mental safeguards to the hidden side of government – not just the more open agencies and departments. The CIA was obviously not the Department of Agri-culture, but, according to constitutional principles, both should be subject to serious and ongoing congressional review of their programs. The venerable maxim of checks and balances that undergirds the spending, subpoena and investigative powers of Congress makes America's "parliament" unique in the world in the degree of its oversight authority.[24]

Today, thanks chiefly to the work of the Church Committee, the nation's intel-ligence agencies must take into account the likely reactions to their programs of lawmakers seated on the Senate and House Intelligence Committees (created in 1976 and 1977, respectively).[25] The purpose of these new arrangements was to prevent a further erosion of American liberties at the hands of the intelligence agencies. According to one of its senior staff experts, "We can't slide back into the days of J. Edgar Hoover" was the Church Committee's core message.[26]

For the most part, intelligence officials since 1975 have agreed with the intent of the Church Committee. The major exception was William J. Casey, Director of Central Intelligence (DCI) during most of the Reagan years (1981–87), who had nothing but disdain for congressional oversight of intelligence and fre-quently referred to its overseers in scatological terms.[27] More common has been the sentiment expressed by William E. Colby, an earlier DCI (1973–76), who found himself in office and in the spotlight when the CHAOS articles broke in the *Times*. He wrote after the Year of Intelligence that the Church Committee had helpfully shed light on the boundaries "within which [the secret agencies] should, and should not, operate."[28] Robert M. Gates, another DCI, who served 1991–93, spells out why closer intelligence accountability by lawmakers has proved valuable:

> [S]ome awfully crazy schemes might well have been approved had every-one present not known and expected hard questions, debate, and criticism from [Capitol] Hill. And when, on a few occasions Congress was kept in the dark, and such schemes did proceed, it was nearly always to the lasting regret of the presidents involved.[29]

More recently, in the memoirs of embattled DCI George Tenet one will find neither the word "accountability" nor the word "oversight" in the index, a reflection perhaps of his embattled relations with the Congress during his tenure (1997–2004).[30]

The Church Committee and the other investigations of 1975 led to a sea change in attitudes within the United States about the need for supervision of the intelligence agencies. Before, supervision had been thin. Members of Congress were content to let the secret side of government go its own way for the most part during the Cold War, guided by broad directives from the White House and the National Security Council (NSC) and with only occasional spurts of interest by Congress.[31] Lawmakers were prepared to let the "honorable men" of the CIA determine what operations to conduct and when.[32] Intelligence would be an exception to the normal rules of American government and the canons of accountability; secret operations were simply too fragile, too dependent on secrecy, for the normal strictures of oversight. They simply would not fit, without endangering the country, into the Madisonian framework of legislative safeguards against executive power. Such "auxiliary precautions," as Madison phrased it in *The Federalist Paper No. 51*, were a luxury prohibited by the perils of the Cold War.[33]

Moreover, lawmakers were too busy with other activities (not the least, fundraising for reelection) to worry excessively about covert actions and other stealthy operations against the Soviet Union. Besides, the fewer Congressmen knowledgeable about CIA operations, the easier it would be for them to escape culpability if things went wrong, as they did with the Bay of Pigs fiasco in 1961. Operation CHAOS, however, brought an end to this philosophy of blind trust. Now the American public and their representatives began to understand that safeguards were required even within – especially within – the shadowy corners of government.

Yet changes in attitudes among lawmakers, though important, were not enough. Genuine accountability required explicit new rules and guidelines to serve as buoys for the intelligence agencies that would mark more clearly, as DCI Colby had hoped, the boundaries of probity. Even in the small interstice of time between the *Times* reporting in 1974 and the creation of the Church Committee in 1975, these new rules and guidelines had begun to take shape. They would continue to unfold over the next 30 years, and indeed, debate over their merits remains a lively topic today.

How well these rules have been enforced by lawmakers over the years provides an index of their commitment to intelligence oversight responsibilities. The results have been mixed, stretching from passivity, harking back to the earlier days of benign neglect, to an activism rarely seen in the era preceding the Year of Intelligence. Before these patterns can be understood, however, one must first know something about the new rules and the demands they have placed on both the intelligence agencies and their legislative supervisors.

The emergence of rules for the new intelligence oversight

From the year of the CIA's creation in 1947 until the domestic spy scandal of 1974, Congress passed no laws related to intelligence accountability. After various flaps, such as the Bay of Pigs disaster and the CIA's secret funding of the National Student Association (1952–67),[34] a few reform-minded lawmakers proposed tighter controls over the CIA.[35] These efforts were rebuffed, however, by a majority who continued to espouse the philosophy of intelligence exceptionalism, arguing that America's secret operations were just too delicate for the usual array of oversight procedures.[36] When the *Times* reporting in 1974 on Operation CHAOS made the approach of benign neglect to intelligence untenable, Congress enacted its first statutory measure to improve the supervision of the CIA: the Hughes–Ryan Act of December 1974.[37] Over the next three decades, lawmakers would periodically enact additional initiatives to enhance intelligence accountability – always mindful of the balance necessary between meaningful supervision of the secret agencies, on the one hand, and the need for sufficient flexibility, self-initiative and risk taking by the agencies, on the other hand. The key intelligence accountability laws since 1947, and their objectives, are summarized in Table 4.1.

These attempts to determine the proper balance between legislative control and executive flexibility have almost always taken shape in the crucible of a crisis, whether a scandal (the statutes passed in the 1970s and after the Iran-Contra affair in 1986) or an unacceptable intelligence failure (following the September 11, 2001 attacks and the faulty estimates about weapons of mass destruction (WMD) in Iraq in 2002). The exception was the 1982 Intelligence Identities Act, a law lobbied for by the CIA to halt left-wing organizations from "outing" its officers and agents. As significant as these statutes have been for establishing intelligence accountability, a few simple rule changes in the Congress – far short of the formality of lawmaking – have been just as important, particularly the creation of the Senate Select Committee on Intelligence (SSCI) in 1976 and the House Permanent Select Committee on Intelligence (HPSCI) in 1977.[38] "Simple" is surely the wrong word, however, because the creation of these two intelligence oversight committees was a lengthy and hard-fought proposition, with reformers finally winning the day by virtue of the *Times* reporting on CHAOS and the evidence of wrongdoing uncovered by the Church, Pike and Rockefeller inquiries.[39] At any rate, it is accurate to say that the creation of the SSCI and HPSCI did not require any formal action by the executive branch, and in that sense, their establishment was a simpler task than passage of the various laws displayed in Table 4.1.

The combination of the accountability laws and the creation of SSCI and HPSCI has placed high expectations on those lawmakers selected by the leadership in the two chambers to serve as intelligence overseers. These members of SSCI and HPSCI are expected to do what other members of committees do: hold hearings; review budgets; read reports from the executive agencies; issue their own reports, both classified and unclassified; manage sizable staffs; maintain a

Table 4.1 Accountability legislation affecting the U.S. intelligence agencies, 1947–2006

Statute	Year of enactment	Core objective
National Security Act[1]	1947	To create the Central Intelligence Agency
Hughes–Ryan Act[2]	1974	To require presidential approval of covert action and their reporting to Congress "in a timely manner" (within two days)
Foreign Intelligence Surveillance Act (FISA)[3]	1978	To prohibit improper intelligence operations through the establishment of a FISA court to review warrant requests for wiretaps and other intrusive surveillance methods
Intelligence Oversight Act[4]	1980	To require prior reporting to Congress of all intelligence activities
Intelligence Identities Act[5]	1982	To prohibit the disclosure of the names of individuals working undercover in the intelligence agencies
CIA Inspector General Act[6]	1989	To establish a CIA Inspector General answerable to Congress
Intelligence Oversight Act[7]	1991	To clarify oversight language by defining covert action more definitively and adjusting the reporting time to "prior" in most cases, but with an opportunity for presidential delay (two days) if exigencies so require
USA PATRIOT Act[8]	2001	To improve intelligence sharing and enhance collection targeted at domestic subversives
Intelligence Reform and Terrorism Prevention Act[9]	2004	To create a Director of National Intelligence to further improve the sharing of information among the intelligence agencies

Notes
1 National Security Act, Pub. L. No. 235, 61 Stat. 496 (1947) (codified as amended in scattered sections of 50 U.S.C.).
2 Hughes–Ryan Act § 662, 88 Stat. 1804 (1974) (codified as amended at 22 U.S.C. § 2422 (2000)).
3 Foreign Intelligence Surveillance Act, Pub. L. No. 95-51 (1978) (codified as amended in 50 U.S.C. §§ 1801–1811 (2000)).
4 Intelligence Oversight Act, 94 Stat. 1981 (1980) (codified as amended at 50 U.S.C. § 413 (1982)).
5 Intelligence Identities Act, Pub. L. No. 97-200, 96 Stat. 122 (1982) (codified as amended at 50 U.S.C. § 421 (2000)).
6 CIA Inspector General Act, Pub. L. No. 101-193, § 801 (1989) (codified at 50 U.S.C. § 403q (2000)).
7 Intelligence Oversight Act of 1991, Pub. L. No. 102-88, § 602, 105 Stat. 441 (1991) (codified at 50 U.S.C. § 413 (2000)).
8 USA PATRIOT Act, Pub. L. No. 107-56, 115 Stat. 272 (2001); reauthorized in Pub. L. No. 109-177, 120 Stat. 192 (2006).
9 Intelligence Reform and Terrorism Prevention Act, Pub. L. No. 108-458, 118 Stat. 3638 (2004).

dialogue with bureaucrats; respond to media reports that charge the bureaucracy with wrongdoing or failure;[40] travel at home and abroad to inspect agency organizations and activities; enact laws when appropriate; hold the President accountable for the operations of the executive branch; confirm (in the Senate) high appointments in the intelligence agencies; visit with allied foreign lawmakers who serve on counterpart committees in other lands; and maintain security on their committees.

Their duties are made more difficult in the case of the intelligence committees, however, because of the subject matter's sensitive nature. An inadvertent leak – say, accidentally mentioning the name of an agent or operation in an open hearing – could have a tragic result, leading to the death of an intelligence officer or agent, or the disruption of a vital clandestine operation abroad. No wonder the "good old days" remain attractive not just for intelligence agencies, but for lawmakers as well; prior to 1974, lawmakers did not have to worry much about all the duties outlined here, or the risk of harming a fragile operation because of something they might say. Yet in light of the abuses uncovered in 1975, for lawmakers to put their heads back in the sand would be to invite further abuses. Of course, abuses may occur anyway, given the flawed nature of human beings, but the theory of accountability, as practiced (unevenly) in the United States since the founding of the Republic, rests on the assumption that mistakes and scandals are less likely to occur – or, at least, to last as long – if members of Congress are engaged in the application of checks and balances through rigorous hearings and budget reviews.[41]

Lawmakers are torn in three directions. In the first place, they long for release from the duties of intelligence oversight, because they are time-consuming and fraught with risks – especially since intelligence has become such a controversial subject in the politically charged debates over who was responsible for the lack of preparedness with respect to the September 11, 2001 attacks and the WMD failures in Iraq. Yet conscientious lawmakers would like to see the United States become more secure, and this objective requires, in part, improvements in the conduct of intelligence, often referred to as a nation's "first line of defense." Moreover, lawmakers also understand that Americans value their privacy and civil liberties and do not wish to return to the days of CHAOS and COINTELPRO, SHAMROCK and MINARET.

Like a mule placed in the middle of three bales of hay, lawmakers find attractive, and therefore queue up for service on, the intelligence oversight committees; service on these panels sends a signal to constituents that their senator or representative is guarding their civil liberties and protecting the nation against foreign and domestic threats. In addition, there is a certain James Bond cachet that comes with membership of these secretive committees, with its closed-door briefings on CIA covert actions and the arcane technology of surveillance satellites. Yet once on the committees, lawmakers often shirk their duties because becoming expert enough on intelligence to understand the secret workings of the intelligence agencies and their budgets is time-consuming.

Another downside of service on these committees is the reality that they provide insufficient credit-claiming opportunities to impress voters back home, owing to the fact that much of the work carried out by the SSCI and HPSCI must be done in the inner sanctums of the Congress, away from the klieg lights of television. Intelligence can also trap a lawmaker in controversy – say, over whether the President has an inherent constitutional right to conduct warrantless wiretaps,[42] the issue of why the CIA does not have better agents in Iran, or how Aldrich H. Ames could have stolen top-secret documents from the CIA for over a decade without being caught. In light of these forces of attraction and repulsion, it is important to examine how well members of Congress have reacted to their new responsibilities for intelligence accountability since the days of the Church Committee and the founding of SSCI and HPSCI in the mid-1970s.

The first part of this chapter focused on the Church Committee's findings related to intelligence abuses, and its efforts to establish a more rigorous approach to intelligence accountability. The laws outlined in Table 4.1 are vital legacies of this fresh approach to intelligence supervision advocated by a majority of the Church Committee members. If these new statutes and procedures are to succeed, however, dedicated members of the two oversight committees are needed. They must be willing to ensure, through their close scrutiny of the 16 secret agencies, that intelligence is kept under the rule of law. Since the spy scandals of 1974–75, the sequence of events has been as follows: the presentation of the Church Committee's findings of abuse and its recommendations for reform (1975–76); the creation of the SSCI and HPSCI (1976–77) to carry out serious oversight; the passage of laws and rules designed to hold the secret agencies accountable (1974, 1978–80, 1989–2004); and the arrival of new generations of lawmakers, upon whom fell the burden of making sure the new system worked (1978 to the present). The next part of the chapter explores how effectively these post-Church Committee members of SSCI and HPSCI have carried forth this responsibility. How faithfully have they devoted their time and effort to supervising intelligence operations? The short answer is: inconsistently.

The role preferences of lawmakers in the supervision of intelligence activities

Intelligence accountability on Capitol Hill in the period since 1975 has been desultory for the most part, except when crises occur; then members of Congress have performed well as "firefighters," responding to alarms and putting out "fires" (that is, conducting major investigations into intelligence scandals or failures).[43] In between crises, however, lawmakers have performed day-to-day "police patrolling" duties in a manner that falls significantly short of the intense supervision espoused by reformers in 1975. Eighty-six lawmakers have served on SSCI since its creation in 1976, and 97 on HPSCI since its creation in 1977.[44] Among these individuals, the committee chairs (a total of eleven on SSCI and ten on HPSCI since 1975) have been particularly influential in determining the rigor of committee oversight.

From time to time, the ranking minority member or even a junior member –

Democrat or Republican – on one of the oversight committees will make a mark. During the early days of HPSCI (1977–79), for example, minority member J. Kenneth Robinson (Republican from Virginia) spent more time than any of his colleagues poring over intelligence budget proposals late into the afternoon; as a result, he excelled in closed hearings on funding as he pointed to sections in the authorization bill that had weak justifications and wielded a scalpel as he proceeded through the mark-ups.[45] During this same period on HPSCI, junior members Les Aspin (Democrat from Wisconsin) and Roman Mazzoli (Democrat from Kentucky), though mindful of the importance of the intelligence agencies and willing to praise intelligence witnesses and programs when warranted, became the Committee's strongest critics of questionable secret operations.[46] They played the role of guardians, achieving a commendable balance between expressions of congratulations and criticism.

This analysis does not attempt to examine the oversight activities of all 183 members of the intelligence oversight committees since they were established, but it does look into the activities of some overseers, as a means of illustrating the role typology presented here. The analysis yields four general roles that lawmakers have chosen to play while serving on the oversight panels.[47] Many members are not easily bound by a single role and instead have displayed some degree of movement between two or more roles. The four types initially presented below should be viewed more as "centers of gravity" around which most members orbit rather than sharply delineated areas of confinement for an individual lawmaker. They are "static" starting places in this analysis; the reality is that many members of Congress are inclined to move toward and away from these centers of gravity, depending on various influences. Stated another way, the model presented here is meant to be dynamic, not an artificial effort to herd complicated human beings into four high-fenced corrals. The objective is to provide a sense of the range of possible reactions to the Church Committee mandate for greater attention to intelligence accountability by future generations of lawmakers, both in theory and (only sampled here) the empirical reality.

The first type, as mentioned in the introduction, is the "ostrich" – a label selected to indicate a preference by some lawmakers to embrace the pre-1975 philosophy of benign neglect toward the intelligence agencies (see Figure 4.1). A classic illustration is Senator Barry Goldwater when he became chair of the SSCI in 1981. He had also served as a member of the Church Committee and ironically (in light of his subsequent rise to the position of chair) voted at that time against the creation of the SSCI in the first place.[48] He also opposed most of the other reforms proposed by the Church Committee.[49] Goldwater was content with the system of oversight that existed before 1975 – that is, occasional review by a few subcommittees on intelligence housed within the armed services and the Appropriations Committees in both chambers. Barrett has found that these panels were somewhat more active than the conventional wisdom would suggest, but were nonetheless relatively passive.[50] They certainly did nothing to halt CHAOS, COINTELPRO, the assassination plots, and the many other horrors uncovered in 1975. The evidence presented by the

	Responsibility for support	
	Low	High
Responsibility for evaluation Low	1 The Ostrich	2 The Cheerleader
High	3 The Skeptic	4 The Guardian

Figure 4.1 A typology of roles assumed by intelligence overseers in the U.S. Congress.

Church, Pike, and Rockefeller panels suggests that lawmakers never knew about these operations.

The second type of legislative overseer for intelligence is the "cheerleader." This is a member of Congress who has removed his or her head from the sand, but only to cheer more effectively on behalf of the intelligence agencies. The cheerleader is interested primarily in the advocacy of intelligence officers and their decisions, the support of intelligence budgets (and the quick granting of supplements when needed), and the advancement of intelligence operations at home and abroad against those who seek to harm the United States. During hearings, the cheerleader specializes in "softball" pitches – easy questions designed to be hit over the center field fence by witnesses from the secret agencies.[51] In press conferences, the cheerleader acts as a kind of defense attorney for the agencies, hinting at their behind-the-scenes, still-secret, "if you only knew" successes; lauding the heroism of intelligence officers and agents in the field, often under conditions of great danger and hardship; castigating journalists for printing leaked secrets that imperil the nation; warning of threats at home and abroad that can lead to more terrorist attacks like those in 2001 … or worse, if the intelligence agencies are shackled in any way. Such statements by cheerleaders are often true, but it is the one-sidedness that characterizes this type – the absence of a critical eye.

An illustration of the cheerleader is Representative Edward P. Boland (Democrat from Massachusetts) when he became the first chair of the HISCI in 1977. Boland had witnessed firsthand how, in 1975, the Pike Committee in the House had been excessively critical of intelligence, to the point of a shrill final report that (although it had some insights and valuable historical data) was widely discredited for its ideological anti-CIA biases.[52] Appalled by its experience with the Pike Committee, the House refused to create an intelligence oversight committee in 1976 when the Senate established SSCI.[53] It took another year of debate and cooling down before members of the House voted to establish a counterpart to the Senate Committee.[54] As a means of helping to restore the House to a more balanced perspective on the value of intelligence, Boland bent over backwards from 1977 to 1982 to display a willingness to cooperate with intelligence officials. He often swallowed his own personal skepticism about some secret operations and expressed his support for the government's secret bureaucracy, just to show that the HSPCI could be a partner in the world of intelligence and was not a reincarnation of the blunderbuss Pike Committee.[55]

A third role type is the "skeptic." This approach is similarly one-sided, only at the opposite extreme from the cheerleader. From the skeptic's point of view, nothing the intelligence agencies do is likely to be good. From this perspective, the secret agencies are inherently immoral: opening and reading other people's mail, listening in on telephone calls, stealing documents, maybe even killing people – all unsavory activities. The secret agencies are also incompetent, continues this argument, with the CIA failing to anticipate the fall of the Soviet Union, the September 11, 2001 attacks, or the absence of WMD in Iraq. For the most extreme skeptic, there is only one solution: shut down the secret agencies altogether. In 1996, for example, Senator Daniel Patrick Moynihan (Democrat from New York), a member of the SSCI dismayed by the CIA's inability to predict the collapse of the Soviet empire, called for the Agency's abolition.[56] Representative Robert Torricelli (Democrat from New Jersey) became such a zealous skeptic of the CIA in 1995 that he did what no other intelligence overseer has ever done: as a member of the HPSCI, he disclosed during a press conference classified information (regarding the CIA's employment as an agent of a notably disreputable army colonel in Guatemala) that should never have been released by a member on his own volition.[57] This behavior was a serious breach of the Committee's rules, for which Torricelli was swiftly chastised by his HPSCI colleagues and the House Committee on Standards of Official Conduct.[58]

The fourth general type is the "guardian." From the normative perspective that runs through the analysis offered here, this model conforms best with the hopes of the Church Committee and reformers in 1975, who favored a Congress that conducts a serious review of intelligence programs to prevent (or at least lessen the likelihood of) future programs like CHAOS and COINTELPRO. Representative Lee H. Hamilton, a Democrat from Indiana and the HPSCI's chair from 1985 to 1987, maintains that the ideal intelligence overseers are those members of Congress who are both "partners and critics" of the secret agencies.[59] Or, as another HPSCI member, Norm Dicks (Democrat from Washington), has put it, "Overseeing the intelligence community is like being a good parent: you have to encourage and discipline."[60]

Since not even academic specialists in international affairs focus much on the secret side of government, it is unlikely that the American people know much about the activities of the CIA and its companion agencies – beyond the superficial accounts they may see in James Bond films or read in Tom Clancy thrillers.[61] Thus, lawmakers have an obligation, within the constraints of protecting sensitive information, to inform the people about the value of these agencies and their programs. The intelligence community spends some $44 billion a year, and someone in an official capacity ought to explain this use of taxpayers' money.[62] Further, when the secret agencies legitimately need a friend when under public scrutiny, lawmakers are in a position to provide a defense, say, when skeptics argue unreasonably that the CIA should have known about some surprise calamity, when in reality no mere mortal could have known.

The job description for an effective overseer includes more than just educating the American people on the virtues of having an intelligence capability or coming to the defense of secret agencies when they are unfairly maligned. A good overseer must also search for and acknowledge program flaws, and advocate their correction. This role requires the ability, above all, to be objective; in the vernacular, to call a spade a spade, without fear or favor. Hamilton has come as close to this ideal as any member of the SSCI or HPSCI. He regularly convened HPSCI meetings; paid close attention to reports from his staff and the intelligence agencies; followed up on media reports alleging intelligence wrongdoing or mistakes; and spent a reasonable amount of time in budget reviews and conversations with intelligence professionals.[63]

Even Hamilton faltered badly, however, during the Iran-Contra scandal. He took at face value – always a mistake for overseers – the assurance of staffers on the NSC that they were not involved in those illegal operations.[64] When a Middle East periodical subsequently revealed the scandal,[65] it was clear that national security adviser Robert C. McFarlane and Lt. Col. Oliver L. North of the NSC staff had lied to the HPSCI chair and other members of the Committee, face to face at a meeting in the White House and on other occasions, about the involvement of the Council's staff in Iran-Contra.[66]

Conclusion

The government of the United States is built on a foundation of shared powers among the three branches: the executive, the legislative, and the judicial.[67] Beyond making laws, a primary duty of the legislative branch is to keep watch over the sprawling bureaucracy that lies at the feet of the President.[68] An especially difficult assignment is to keep watch over the dark side of this terrain: America's secret agencies. Before 1975, lawmakers largely overlooked the responsibility to supervise these organizations, because the job was daunting in the expertise it required, and time-consuming. It provided little opportunity to claim credit. It was fraught with risk if things went wrong (à la Bay of Pigs), especially if members of Congress might have to share culpability. Thus, for the length of the first half of the Cold War, the logic in Congress went that it was better to let the spies go their own way in the back alleys of the world, fighting the justified, if unsavory, war against global communism. The revelation in 1975 that these agencies had engaged in espionage against American citizens – the very people they had been created to protect – changed this attitude of trust and benign neglect on Capitol Hill; the domestic spy scandal forced lawmakers to take intelligence accountability more seriously.

In 1975, the Church Committee established a new attitude in the nation about the importance of maintaining intelligence accountability. Henceforth, lawmakers would be expected to devote attention to this matter, doing their best to ward off a fresh round of intelligence abuses. The era of benign neglect was a thing of the past. Yet subsequent generations of lawmakers have displayed an uneven commitment to this concept of robust accountability toward the CIA and its companion agencies.

Some members of Congress have been throwbacks ("ostriches," in the terminology used here), content to bury their heads in the sand and continue the earlier era of trust when lawmakers deferred to the decisions of the executive branch within the domains of intelligence and defense. Others have chosen to become unabashed boosters for intelligence – "cheerleaders" who view their job primarily as one of explaining the value of intelligence to the American people and supporting intelligence missions with strong funding and encouragement. Taking the opposite approach, another group of lawmakers (the "skeptics") have been so critical about intelligence that some have even called for the abolition of the CIA. While not going that far, other skeptics have consistently found fault, and little virtue, in America's attempts to spy on adversaries or overthrow regimes that fail to conform with U.S. interests. Finally, some members of Congress have been "guardians," striking a reasonable balance between serving as partners of the intelligence agencies on Capitol Hill, on the one hand, and – through a persistent examination of budgets and operations – demanding competence and law-abiding behavior from these agencies, on the other hand.

From among these roles, the frequency distribution displays a scattering of lawmakers across the range of possibilities, with a particular concentration on the role of cheerleader in recent years. Members of the congressional oversight committees in the House and Senate have sometimes migrated from one role to another, say, from adoring cheerleader to dismayed skeptic. One of the main catalysts for this mobility has been a sense of injured institutional pride, when lawmakers perceive that intelligence officials have failed to treat Congress with appropriate respect. In one instance of role transition, Senator Barry Goldwater shifted rapidly from ostrich to skeptic when DCI William Casey approached hearings with SSCI in a cavalier manner. In other cases, a deteriorating personal relationship between lawmakers and intelligence officials has led to change, as when SSCI Chair DeConcini and DCI Woolsey, or SSCI Chair Shelby and DCI Tenet, became alienated toward one another. A dramatic change in policy can also induce changes in oversight behavior, as when HSPCI chair Edward Boland could no longer countenance his role as cheerleader when DCI Casey ratcheted up the level of violent covert actions in Nicaragua during the 1980s.

This analysis only scratches the surface. Much more work remains to be done in the search for a full understanding of how lawmakers choose their oversight roles, and how these roles may change over time.[69] One would like to discern the "footprints" for each member of Congress who has served on SSCI and HPSCI. Especially important will be efforts to fathom why more members of Congress have failed to become guardians – the model widely accepted by reformers in 1975 and after as the ideal, because it balances support for intelligence with a determination to avoid (through persistent review or "police patrolling") future failures and scandals by the secret agencies. How can lawmakers be urged to spend more time on serious program evaluation? What incentives can be introduced into the culture of Capitol Hill to make accountability a more valued pursuit?

One might think that enough incentives already exist, such as warding off another domestic spy scandal (like the one pursued by the Bush Administration, which bypassed the warrant procedures for telephone wiretaps (as in the case of Operation MINARET)[70], helping to prevent another terrorist calamity, or avoiding false conclusions on WMD abroad, like the intelligence that drew the United States into war with Iraq in 2003. Most observers agree, however, that lawmakers are performing far below their potential when it comes to intelligence accountability and that generally, across the policy board, oversight remains a neglected stepchild on Capitol Hill.[71] Correcting this condition is a worthy challenge for educators, journalists, lawmakers, and indeed all public-minded citizens. As always, the vote stands ready as a powerful tool to rid the legislative branch of those who fail to understand the importance of this duty.

Notes

1 See, e.g., Seymour M. Hersh, Underground for the C.I.A. in New York: An Ex-Agent Tells of Spying on Students, *New York Times*, Dec. 29, 1974, at A1.
2 See 121 *Congressional Record* S524–29 (daily ed. Jan. 21, 1975), 121 *Congressional Record* S967–84 (daily ed. Jan. 27, 1975).
3 The White House created its own presidential commission on January 4, 1975.
4 The author served as special assistant to Senator Church throughout the inquiry. For accounts of this investigation, see generally Loch K. Johnson, *A Season of Inquiry: The Senate Intelligence Investigation* (1985); Frederick A.O. Schwarz, Jr., Intelligence Oversight: The Church Committee, *in* 5 *Strategic Intelligence* (Loch K. Johnson, ed., 2007); Frederick A.O. Schwarz, Jr. and Aziz Z. Huq, *Unchecked and Unbalanced: Presidential Power in a Time of Terror* (2007); Frank Smist, Jr., *Congress Oversees the United States Intelligence Community* (2d ed. 1994); Loch K. Johnson, Congressional Supervision of America's Secret Agencies: The Experience and Legacy of the Church Committee, *Public Administration Review* 64 (Jan.–Feb. 2004), 3–14.
5 See S. Rep. No. 94-755 (1976) (6 Books), including *Foreign and Military Intelligence* [hereinafter Church Book I], *Intelligence Activities and the Rights of Americans* [hereinafter Church Book II], *Supplementary Detailed Staff Reports on Intelligence Activities and the Rights of Americans* [hereinafter Church Book III]; see also S. Rep. No. 94-465 (1975) [hereinafter Interim Report]. The Church Committee also published seven volumes of hearings testimony. All materials are available online at www.aarclibrary.org/publib/church/reports/contents.htm.
6 See Dycus in this volume (Chapter 10).
7 See generally Seamon in this volume (Chapter 8, discussing the contemporary operations of the NSA).
8 Church Book II, *supra* note 5, at 6.
9 Ibid. at 218.
10 Interview with Walter Mondale, Minneapolis, Minn. (Feb. 17, 2000).
11 Church Book II, *supra* note 5, at 10–12, 65–94, 211–23.
12 Ibid. at 216–19.
13 Ibid. at 11, 220–21; Church Book III, *supra* note 5, at 158–61.
14 S. Res. 21, 94th Cong. (1975) (7 vols.), including *Federal Bureau of Investigation* 42

[hereinafter Church Vol. 6] (Questioning by Senator Walter F. Mondale (Democrat from Minnesota) and responding testimony by the Church Committee Chief Counsel, Frederick A.O. Schwarz, Jr.).

15 Interview with Frederick A.O. Schwarz, Jr., New York City (Apr. 27, 2000). See generally Schwarz and Huq, *supra* note 4; Schwarz in this volume (Chapter 3).

16 Church Book II, *supra* note 5, at 4.

17 S. Res. 21, 94th Cong. (1975) (7 vols.), including *The National Security Agency and Fourth Amendment Rights* 45 [hereinafter Church Vol. 5] (Testimony of NSA Deputy Director Benson Buffham).

18 Church Book II, *supra* note 5, at 141.

19 See generally Hannah Arendt, *The Origins of Totalitarianism* (1973).

20 Church Book II, *supra* note 5, at 14, 141.

21 Henry Steele Commager, Intelligence: The Constitution Betrayed, *New York Review Books*, Sept. 30, 1976, at 32, 32.

22 Dean Rusk as told to Richard Rusk, *As I Saw It* 397 (Daniel S. Papp ed., 1990).

23 As polling data from the Pew Global Attitudes Report and other reports on worldwide opinions toward the United States currently indicate, however, this high standing has been tarnished by the George W. Bush Administration's war in Iraq. See Loch K. Johnson, *Seven Sins of American Foreign Policy*, at ch. 2 (2007).

24 See generally *Who's Watching the Spies? Establishing Intelligence Service Accountability* (Hans Born, Ian Leigh and Loch K. Johnson, eds., 2005).

25 The Senate and House established these committees by way of S. Res. 400, enacted on May 19, 1976, and H. Res. 658, enacted on July 14, 1977.

26 Interview with John T. Elliff, Head of the FBI Task Force (Apr. 14, 2000).

27 See generally David M. Barrett, *Congressional Oversight of the CIA in the Early Cold War, 1947–1963, in 5 Strategic Intelligence, supra* note 4, at 1; David M. Barrett, *The CIA and Congress: The Untold Story from Truman to Kennedy* (2005); Loch K. Johnson, *America's Secret Power: The CIA in a Democratic Society* (1987).

28 William E. Colby, After Investigating U.S. Intelligence, *New York Times*, Feb. 26, 1976, at A11.

29 Robert M. Gates, *From the Shadows* 559 (1996).

30 See generally George Tenet with Bill Harlow, *At the Center of the Storm: My Years at the CIA* (2007).

31 See generally Barrett, *The CIA and Congress, supra* note 27.

32 This phrase was often used by DCIs in the 1960s and 1970s to argue that they and their fellow intelligence officers were imbued with high integrity and could be trusted to carry out espionage activities in the best interests of the United States. The phrase became the title of a DCI's memoir: William E. Colby with Peter Forbath, *Honorable Men: My Life in the CIA* (1978).

33 See *The Federalist No. 51*, at 290 (James Madison) (Clinton Rossiter ed., 1961).

34 See generally Rhodri Jeffreys-Jones, *The CIA and American Democracy* (1989); Johnson, *supra* note 27.

35 On these failed legislative efforts, see Harry Howe Ransom, *The Intelligence Establishment* 163–79 (1970). Senator Mike Mansfield, Democrat from Montana, led several of the efforts to improve intelligence accountability.

36 See, e.g., Johnson, *A Season of Inquiry, supra* note 4, at 227–37 (discussing the arguments of Church Committee Republican members John Tower (Texas) and Barry Goldwater (Arizona) during the debates on intelligence reform in 1975–76).

37 The amendment became law on December 30, 1974; 22 U.S.C. § 2422. The co-sponsors were Senator Harold Hughes (Democrat from Iowa) and Leo Ryan (Democrat from California).

38 See generally *supra* note 25 (discussing these resolutions).

39 See generally Johnson, *A Season of Inquiry, supra* note 4.

40 Responding to media reports is among the most important of these duties. As an

HPSCI member has noted, intelligence oversight is always dependent on the newspaper headlines. More Perfect Oversight: Intelligence Oversight and Reform, in Strategic Intelligence, supra note 4, at 115–40 (referencing Nolan's interview with Representative Charlie Wilson, Democrat from Texas on July 1, 2004). A savvy scholar of intelligence, Harry Howe Ransom, has referred to the media – not the Congress – as the key institution of intelligence accountability in the United States. Interview with Harry Howe Ransom (Feb. 21, 2006).

41 For insights into constitutional and political theory supporting these claims about the design of the American government, see *Myers* v. *United States*, 272 U.S. 52, 293 (1926) (Brandeis, J., dissenting); *The Federalist No. 5*, *supra* note 33; Thomas Jefferson, *Draft of the Kentucky Resolutions*, in *Jefferson* 455 (Merrill D. Peterson ed., 1984).

42 See Seamon in this volume (Chapter 8).

43 See generally Loch K. Johnson, Accountability and America's Secret Foreign Policy: Keeping a Legislative Eye on the Central Intelligence Agency, 1 *Foreign Policy Analysis* 99, 99–120 (2005). For the police patroller and firefighter metaphor, see M.D. McCubbins and T. Schwartz, Congressional Oversight Overlooked: Police Patrols and Fire Alarms, 28 *American Journal of Political Science* (1984), 165–79.

44 I am grateful to my research assistant Lawrence J. Lamanna and a graduate seminar paper written by Marie Milward at the University of Georgia for these numbers, based on searches through editions of the *Congressional Directory* since 1976.

45 Based on the author's observations as the HPSCI staff director, Subcommittee on Intelligence Oversight, 1977–79.

46 For a more detailed account, see Loch K. Johnson, *Secret Agencies: U.S. Intelligence in a Hostile World* 89–93 (1996).

47 For examples of useful political analyses using two-by-two tables, see James David Barber, *Presidential Character: Predicting Performance in the White House* (1978) (examining the typology of presidential character); Cecil V. Crabb, Jr. and Kevin V. Mulchay, *American National Security: A Presidential Perspective* (1991) 175–92 (examining the role playing by national security advisers). The observations offered in this chapter are qualitative and impressionistic, based on the author's experiences as a participant observer (as the staff director of the HPSCI Oversight Subcommittee, 1977–79), supplemented by the author's interviews with SSCI and HPSCI members and staff over the years since 1976. Future research will need to develop more empirical indices of member involvement in intelligence oversight, such as hearings attendance records and the frequency (and seriousness) of witness questioning in hearings. For an example of the latter, see Loch K. Johnson, Playing Ball with the CIA: Congress Supervises Strategic Intelligence, in *The President, the Congress, and the Making of Foreign Policy* 49, 49–73 (Paul E. Peterson ed., 1994).

48 For this vote, see 121 *Congressional Record.* S7567 (daily edition May 19, 1975); Johnson, *A Season of Inquiry*, supra note 4, at 247–48 (1986).

49 For an account of Senator Goldwater's opposition throughout the Church Committee proceedings, see generally Johnson, *A Season of Inquiry*, supra note 4; Schwarz, *supra* note 4; Schwarz and Huq, *supra* note 4; as well as the formal dissents printed at the end of the Church Book I, *supra* note 5, and Church Book II, *supra* note 5. Votes taken informally by the Church Committee during the course of the investigation were never released to the public; therefore, until they are released, one must rely on these memoirs and scholarly studies of the panel to learn about what happened behind its closed doors in 1975–76.

50 See generally Barrett, *The CIA and Congress, supra* note 27.

51 On softball and hardball pitches to CIA witnesses by lawmakers, see Johnson, *supra* note 47.

52 Some unknown person leaked the Pike Committee Report to a New York newspaper; it was published as The CIA Report the President Doesn't Want You to Read: The

Pike Papers, *Village Voice*, Feb. 16 and 23, 1976. For criticism of the report's biases, see Johnson, *A Season of Inquiry*, *supra* note 4; and Smist, *supra* note 4.

53 Interviews with Edward P. Boland and other members of the HPSCI, in Washington, D.C. (Jan.–Feb. 1978).

54 On these debates and votes, see *supra* note 25.

55 Based on the author's observations as a staff member on the Boland Committee (HPSCI in its early years) from 1977 to 1979, plus the author's periodic interviews with staff and members on HPSCI during Boland's remaining tenure as HPSCI chair (until 1985).

56 Daniel Patrick Moynihan, Do We Still Need the C.I.A.? The State Department Can Do the Job, *New York Times*, May 19, 1991, at E17.

57 See generally Mark M. Lowenthal, *Intelligence: From Secrets to Policy* (3d edition 2006).

58 See ibid. at 271.

59 See F. Davies, GOP-Controlled Senate Expected to Give Less Scrutiny to War on Terror, *Miami Herald*, Nov. 7, 2002, at A1 (quoting Representative Hamilton).

60 *More Perfect Oversight*, *supra* note 40, at 115 (discussing the interview by Cynthia Nolan in Washington, D.C., on Oct. 15, 2003).

61 On the inattention of international relations scholars to intelligence studies, see Amy B. Zegart, *Cloaks, Daggers, and Ivory Towers: Why Academics Don't Study U.S. Intelligence*, *in* 1 *Strategic Intelligence*, *supra* note 4, at 21, 21–34.

62 This figure has been cited frequently in the media. For instance, see Mark Mazzetti, Spymaster Tells Secret Size of Spy Force, *New York Times*, Apr. 21, 2006, at A18.

63 Interviews with HPSCI staff, in Washington, D.C. (1985–87).

64 Ibid.; see also Report of the Congressional Committees Investigating the Iran-Contra Affair, S. Rep. No. 100-216, H.R. Rep. No. 100-433 (1987).

65 See Lawrence E. Walsh, *Firewall: The Iran-Contra Conspiracy and Cover-Up* 7–8 (1997). The periodical was the Lebanese publication *Al Shiraa*; Walsh was the independent counsel in the Iran-Contra investigation.

66 Ibid. at 5, 141. Public hearings by this joint investigative committee brought the mendacity of both men to light. Both faced criminal prosecution, but President George H.W. Bush (who had been Vice President during the scandal) pardoned all of the Iran-Contra conspirators. See generally William S. Cohen and George J. Mitchell, *Men of Zeal: A Candid Inside Story of the Iran-Contra Hearings* (1988), written by two senators on the panel of inquiry.

67 See generally Richard E. Neustadt, *Presidential Power* (1960); James M. Lindsay, Deference and Defiance: The Shifting Rhythms of Executive–Legislative Relations in Foreign Policy, 33 *Presidential Studies Quarterly* 530 (2003).

68 See generally Joel Aberbach, *Keeping a Watchful Eye: The Politics of Congressional Oversight* (1990); Louis Fisher, *Constitutional Conflicts between Congress and the President* (1985).

69 For some suggestive research directions, see generally Aberbach, *supra* note 68.

70 James Risen and Eric Lichtblau, Bush Lets U.S. Spy on Callers without Courts, *New York Times*, Dec. 16, 2005, at A1. The two journalists won a Pulitzer Prize for their reporting about how the second Bush Administration seemed to have violated the 1978 Foreign Intelligence Surveillance Act, which requires judicial warrants for national security wiretaps (see Table 4.1). See Seamon in this volume.

71 See generally Aberbach, *supra* note 68; Lee H. Hamilton with Jordan Tama, *A Creative Tension: The Foreign Policy Roles of the President and Congress* (2002).

5   The Church Committee's history and relevance

Reflecting on Senator Church

LeRoy Ashby

The Church Committee's record

On January 27, 1975, the U.S. Senate created the Select Committee to Study Governmental Operations with Respect to Intelligence Activities.[1] Frank Church, an Idaho Democrat, chaired it. Some 25 years later, following the September 11, 2001 terrorist attacks on the World Trade Center towers and the Pentagon, a number of critics asserted that Church and his committee had left the United States naked before its enemies. "The CIA was gutted by people on the historical left," the popular novelist Tom Clancy charged. "As an indirect result of that, we have lost 5000 citizens."[2] The noted historian John Lewis Gaddis apparently agreed, contending that congressional efforts in the 1970s to harness U.S. intelligence capacities had made the nation virtually "its own worst enemy."[3]

The Committee indeed deserves remembering – but *not* for the reasons that such critics claim. It in fact provided one of the more luminous chapters in American history, harkening back to some of the nation's most important constitutional principles and most honored ideals. By publicizing the astonishing abuses in America's intelligence-gathering activities that had occurred over a period of some 20 years, it revealed the extent to which Cold War policies contradicted the uplifting rhetoric about freedom and democracy, sullying in the process America's reputation abroad, and undercutting its moral authority. And by questioning the huge expansion of executive powers and secrecy that were occurring in the name of national security, the Committee struck a blow on behalf of the constitutional separation of powers. As Frank Church insisted time and again, no one – including the President – is supposed to act outside the law. Protecting the nation, Church said, should not come at the expense of the nation's ideals, freedoms and Constitution.[4]

In retrospect, however, the Church Committee appears to have been an historical accident. It is amazing that it existed, let alone that it accomplished what it did. In the mid-1970s, it marked a surprising and extremely significant challenge to America's "national security state," one of the Cold War's most notable and enduring creations. In the 1940s, following World War II, as fear of the Soviet Union and communism gripped the United States, the emerging Cold

War facilitated the growth of government secrecy, presidential power and cloak-and-dagger excesses abroad – all ostensibly to keep Americans safe.[5] Although, on paper, congressional supervision of new intelligence-gathering offices such as the Central Intelligence Agency (CIA) existed,[6] Senate watchdog committees had ignored CIA actions.[7] As Senator Leverett Saltonstall, the dignified Massachusetts Republican, once told Church, "It's better for gentlemen not to know what's going on."[8]

The Cold War setting provided a powerful cultural consensus that encouraged public acceptance of an enlarged and more intrusive government, along with an unquestioning toleration of America's expansive role abroad. A triumphalist, idealized view of that role had strengthened during World War II – the "good war" – when the United States had defeated aggressive totalitarian governments, setting the stage for what publisher Henry Luce optimistically hailed as "the American Century."[9] But, like a skeleton at the feast, anxieties festered over the threat of nuclear war as well as the spreading communist influence of the Soviet Union (and, after 1949, China). The Cold War's hold on American politics was evident in the Red-baiting of McCarthyism and in the 1960 presidential campaign, when John Kennedy and Richard Nixon each tried to show that he was the tougher Cold Warrior.[10]

By the 1970s, however, the Vietnam War was ripping and tearing the Cold War consensus. A 1969 poll revealed that a solid majority of Americans had decided that the war was a mistake, even though most of those people detested the antiwar protestors.[11] Richard Nixon took office that year, after narrowly winning the 1968 presidential election, partly because of his claims that he had a "secret plan" to end the war. The war would not end until early 1973, however. The additional 30,000 American deaths, along with countless numbers of Vietnamese, under Nixon's watch further battered Cold War assumptions that masked a foreign policy increasingly based on secrecy, lies and deception. By the time the war was winding down, revelations about the crimes and conspiracies of the Watergate scandals were surfacing, shattering Nixon's administration and demonstrating the dangers of what critics were now calling "the imperial presidency."[12]

On December 22, 1974, *New York Times* journalist Seymour Hersh jarred the public with sensational revelations: the CIA had conducted a "massive" domestic surveillance campaign, targeting thousands of Americans, especially antiwar activists.[13] Hersh's story prompted the U.S. Senate, by an 82–4 vote in early 1975, to establish the Select Committee on Intelligence Activities, which was supposed to operate for about nine months.[14] Meanwhile, the House of Representatives launched its own investigation, with New York Democrat Otis Pike as Chair.[15] President Gerald Ford, who in August had succeeded the disgraced Nixon, worried about a legislative "circus" and thus set up a commission under Vice President Nelson Rockefeller to investigate Hersh's charges.[16]

In sum, events had created a kind of historical crease as they bent and twisted the Cold War consensus. The Church Committee took shape in that crease. Vietnam, Nixon's scandals and Hersh's stunning depiction of American citizens as themselves victims of Cold War policies created a rare opportunity to question central tenets and consequences of both American foreign policy and swelling presidential powers.

Frank Church was especially qualified to head the Senate Select Committee. A few weeks earlier, he had won election to a fourth term. Since joining the Senate in 1957 at the age of 32, he had compiled a notable liberal record on many domestic issues, including civil rights, the environment and the needs of elderly citizens. As a member of the Foreign Relations Committee, he had been one of the first senators to question America's growing involvement in Vietnam. "How Many Dominican Republics and Vietnams Can We Take On?" he asked in an article in the *New York Times*.[17] Since late 1964, he had been an increasingly vocal critic of Lyndon Johnson's interventionism, not just in Vietnam but also in places such as the Dominican Republic. In mid-1967, he noted sadly that the United States had become "the principal arms dispenser of the world," and was apparently more devoted to "furnishing swords that plowshares."[18] By 1968, he had become one of the best-known Senate "doves," and during Nixon's administration he had co-sponsored a number of bills aimed at extricating the United States from Vietnam.[19]

He also took aim at enhanced presidential powers. In mid-1970, he listened incredulously when Secretary of Defense Melvin Laird claimed that President Nixon had the legal authority to keep U.S. troops in Cambodia even if Congress cut off funding. According to Laird, such authority rested in the form of the Feed and Forage Act of 1861, an obscure Civil War statute that permitted the cavalry to buy feed for its horses even if it ran out of funds and Congress was no longer in session. Laird argued that Nixon could use that act to override Congress and continue paying the U.S. troops in Cambodia.[20] Shocked at the testimony, Church wondered "what other laws were in the books which might be construed as permitting the President to govern without leave of Congress."[21] For two years, starting in mid-1972, Church co-chaired the Special Committee on National Emergencies, a major effort to rein in the national security state with its expansive presidential authority.[22] Existing emergency powers, in Church's words, "were like a loaded gun lying around the house, ready to be fired by any trigger-happy [p]resident who might come along."[23]

But it was as Chair of the Senate Foreign Relations Subcommittee on Multinational Corporations in the 1970s that Church was instrumental in documenting a genuine political shocker – one that subsequently helped to inspire the Select Committee to study intelligence: the CIA had conspired with a huge corporation, ITT, to block the election of Chilean President Salvador Allende and then to destabilize and topple that legally elected government.[24] In March 1972, the muckraking journalist Jack Anderson had first made such charges public.[25] Church had quickly obtained Senate approval for "an in-depth study of the role of multinational corporations and their relationship to foreign policy" and also to examine the CIA's role in Chile.[26] The CIA tried unsuccessfully to shift testimony regarding Chile to the Senate Armed Services Subcommittee on CIA Oversight, a body that met infrequently, seldom asked questions, and followed the "shut-your-eyes" advice of its chair, Mississippi's John Stennis.[27]

The multinational hearings exposed the ITT–CIA intervention in Chile for what it was: immoral, because it violated the American ideal of self-determination; impractical, because it was ultimately counterproductive and bad for business; and subversive, because it contravened democratic and constitutional processes. "So the tangled web we weave entraps us," Church said sadly. "The imagination is set free to assume the United States is involved in every shady deal on God's earth."[28] Even worse, he conceded, those suspicions might be correct. "Who can blame others for thinking the worst of us?" he asked, in light of America's recent record. On September 10, 1973, a few months after the ITT–CIA hearings, Church stared dejectedly at a note that an aide had handed him. A military coup had just toppled Allende's government in Chile. Church gloomily scrawled on the back of the note, "The military will inherit the world."[29]

When Church learned that several people, including former CIA director Richard Helms, had lied to the multinationals subcommittee about the destabilization of Chile, he pushed for a larger inquiry. He blamed "the Vietnam syndrome" for the growing willingness to lie to Congress and stated firmly, "it's a habit the Congress is going to have to break."[30]

After President Ford defended the CIA's covert activities in Chile on grounds that communist countries spent "vastly more money than we do for the same kind of purpose," Church was aghast. "He equates us with the Russians," the Senator fumed. "I thought there was a difference, and the difference is what it's all about."[31] But even then, only a few of Church's colleagues favored investigating America's intelligence activities. The Senate was supposed to oversee the CIA but, as Church complained, "the watchdog committee never really watched the dog."[32] Indeed, from 1947 to 1974 only two of some 150 proposals to improve congressional oversight of the CIA even reached the floor of Congress.[33] By December 1974, it still seemed that Congress would not open an inquiry into the CIA.[34]

Then came Seymour Hersh's detonation, charging that the CIA had illegally conducted intelligence operations against thousands of Americans, particularly antiwar activists. Congress now acted quickly and Ford responded by setting up his own commission to offset any legislative "circus." During several days of heated debate on Capitol Hill, Church pressed hard for an investigation, noting that the CIA had "deceived" the multinationals subcommittee about Chile. A few senators summoned up familiar Cold War arguments. "What's wrong with overthrowing the government of Chile?" demanded Mississippi's James Eastland. "It was a commie government, wasn't it?"[35] The Senate nevertheless voted overwhelmingly on January 27 to establish a Senate Select Committee on Intelligence Activities. As senators walked down the halls, there was considerable discussion about "the end of an era."[36]

Church's leadership of the committee

While the decisions to investigate U.S. intelligence activities suggested "the end of an era," and were the products of a particular confluence of events, the Senate

Select Committee's successes were just as unexpected and owed much to Church, who "almost knocked down [Majority Leader Mike] Mansfield's door" in order to gain the Chair's position. Ironically, despite the notable credentials he brought to that job, a number of individuals fretted about his leadership qualities. Going into the multinational national inquiry a few years earlier, for example, such influential senators as J. William Fulbright (Democrat from Arkansas) and Clifford Case (Republican from New Jersey) expressed concerns that Church's actions typically did not match his strong rhetoric.[37] From his first days in the Senate, Church had labored under a boy-orator reputation whose rather florid oratorical style bothered individuals who thought he was a bit pompous, deserving his "Frank Sunday School" nickname. Part of the problem reflected a sense that he compromised too much too soon – a tendency that could prove disastrous in the face of the enormous political pressures that the intelligence investigations faced. At first glance, Church's sensitivity and accommodating disposition raised questions about whether he was tough enough for the job. "The normal rule of thumb in the Senate," joked Jack Blum, a key staffer on the multinationals subcommittee, "is that the more you are concerned with humanity at large the worse you treat the people within thirty feet of you."[38] But Church's kind demeanor and personality seemed antithetical to a tough-guy role. Church was, in Blum's words, "so acutely aware of the feelings of others that he fell over himself to accommodate those feelings. That's the worst guy on earth for negotiation."[39]

In fact, Church's diplomatic skills proved crucial in making the Senate Select Committee on Intelligence work. Whereas the parallel investigation in the House of Representatives virtually fell apart as the bickering factions squared off, Church maneuvered his Committee through exceedingly stormy political waters with amazing success. His achievement in that regard was especially striking in light of the Committee's wide ideological spectrum, ranging from Democratic liberals such as Michigan's Philip Hart, Minnesota's Walter Mondale, and Colorado's newly elected Gary Hart (who had been instrumental in George McGovern's 1972 presidential campaign) to the staunchly right-wing Republicans who seemed determined to protect the CIA: Arizona's Barry Goldwater and Texas's John Tower.[40]

Partisanship indeed plagued the Committee. At one point, Goldwater leaked information concerning its proposed agenda to the White House.[41] Tower, who conceded that the Republican minority leader Hugh Scott wanted him to be the Grand Old Party's "damage control officer" on the Committee, blocked Church's move to go public with hearings on the National Security Agency (NSA).[42] And the large staff of 150 was anything but free of party politics. Goldwater's staff designee admitted to the Committee's chief counsel, F.A.O. ("Fritz") Schwarz, "Fritz, I'm not here to work for you. I'm here to spy on you."[43] Meanwhile, the administration worried that the Committee's "massive efforts" put it on the defensive, giving the public the impression "that leadership rests in Congress rather than with the White House."[44] The administration thus looked for ways to circumscribe and even discredit the Committee's activities.

As a way "to bolster" efforts to restrain the Church Committee, President Ford's advisers considered cracking down on journalist Seymour Hersh and the *New York Times* – if necessary by seeking a warrant to search Hersh's apartment and grand jury indictments of both Hersh and the *Times*.[45]

Church's own staff sometimes expressed frustration at their boss's continuing efforts to build a consensus. But the Senator, who invariably viewed politics as the art of the practical, emphasized the need for harmony on the Committee and in his negotiations with the executive branch. "You don't win by losing," he told one staffer.[46]

The Senator's willingness to compromise in no sense meant that he was unwilling to battle for principles. On the one hand, he very much recognized the need to gather intelligence to protect the nation. During World War II, he had served in the Asian theater as an army intelligence officer. Indeed, his "daily presentations to the Combined Staff sections," according to a citation he received, "were so unanimously acclaimed that the Commanding General personally commended him."[47] And during his early Senate years, he had seldom questioned either America's Cold War foreign policy or the CIA. But, during the 1960s, the nation's military intervention in a number of countries, ranging from Vietnam to the Dominican Republic, increasingly troubled him. More and more, he questioned U.S. foreign policy. In the mid-1960s, he supported Senator Eugene McCarthy's unsuccessful call to investigate the CIA's role in shaping that policy.[48] By 1973, when he learned about the CIA's unseemly activities in Chile, he was emerging as a leading critic of expanding presidential powers and America's role abroad. It was impossible, he declared, "to insulate our constitutional and democratic processes at home from the kind of foreign policy we have conducted."[49]

On this level, the intelligence investigations of the 1970s tapped Church's moralistic, crusading side. "America," he liked to say, "does best when it follows its best instincts."[50] According to William Miller, the staff director for the Committee, who knew the Senator well, Church liked the prospects of "cleaning the Augean stables. That was a part of him that made him feel good: To right something. If it was wrong, get rid of it, clean it out."[51] Indeed, his desire to set things right sometimes made him resemble a minister. Morality was in him "as big as a horse," recalled one old friend.[52] Church's moralizing tendency annoyed some people. The Senator "took his name too seriously," scoffed the longtime congressional doorkeeper, William "Fishbait" Miller. "Church. Christ, he's more like a cathedral."[53]

Unquestionably, for Church, vital principles were at stake in the intelligence investigation. He became more and more outspoken about U.S. interventionism and the growth of the national security state. In that regard, his chairing of the Intelligence Committee was "the culmination of what he has been talking about for years," as an associate observed: "America doped on *hubris*, playing God in the world. It ties together his foreign policy and civil libertarian views."[54] Philosophically, Church recognized the tensions within American history between nationalism and the constitutional guarantees regarding justice, personal freedom, and government under law. "Nationalism," he once said, "has always been the enemy of the republic."[55] By feeding a rally-round-the-flag mentality, it jeopardized individual liberty and enhanced the powers of the state. To salvage America's basic freedoms, Church believed the investigation of the intelligence community could be nothing less than "redemptive."[56]

Church was convinced that the Committee's most important findings were those that documented "CIA murder plots and murder attempts abroad" – with targets ranging from Cuba's Fidel Castro to the Belgian Congo's Patrice Lumumba and South Vietnam's Ngo Dinh Diem. When the Rockefeller Commission largely ducked the assassination topic, relegating specifics to a secret 80-page report for the President, Church angrily told the press, "It is simply intolerable that any agency of the government of the United States may engage in murder." According to Church, the Rockefeller Commission had revealed only "the tip of the iceberg," and done little more than murmur, "naughty, naughty, tich, tich." A number of Committee staffers soon concluded that the assassination issue was leading Church into a swamp, consuming precious time and diverting attention from other forms of covert action and domestic spying. Church disagreed: "I knew we had to face it."[57] Throughout the summer and into the fall of 1975, the Committee pursued the grim assassinations subject. To his credit, Church did not back off from the fact that some of the worst CIA abuses had occurred under the watch of John Kennedy and Lyndon Johnson, Presidents from his own political party. Moreover, when it appeared that the Committee might honor President Ford's plea to keep the assassination findings secret, Church threatened to resign. His stunned colleagues sat quietly for several minutes. Then, overwhelmingly, in one of the few votes the Committee took, they recommended that the Committee's findings be made public.[58] In retrospect, staffer Rick Inderfurth marveled at how Church had not caved in to the opposition but instead "hung in there again and again."[59]

Racing the clock, the Committee ultimately conducted over 800 interviews, met as a group 126 times, held 21 public and 250 executive hearings, and gathered over 110,000 pages of documentation. It probed the FBI's domestic counterintelligence programs (COINTELPRO), which had virtually declared war against civil rights groups and Native American organizations such as the American Indian Movement. The FBI had, for example, implemented a number of strategies, including illegal wiretaps and vicious slander, to destroy Martin Luther King, Jr. – to knock him "off his pedestal," in the words of one agency document. The Church Committee revealed also that a special unit with the Internal Revenue Service had "politically harassed" thousands of political activists, and that, for over 30 years, major communications companies such as ITT and RCA had routinely provided the CIA with access to telegrams that Americans sent abroad. The Committee probed as well the Nixon White House's efforts to cajole the FBI, CIA, National Security Agency, and the Defense Intelligence Agency to mount a massive, and grossly illegal, domestic surveillance program. A major target was the antiwar movement. One of the most chilling documents that the Committee found, in that regard, involved the so-called Huston Plan. White House aide Tom Charles Huston had drafted it, gaining the approval of CIA director Richard Helms and FBI head J. Edgar Hoover. The plan rested on the premise that intelligence agencies needed to ignore the Bill of Rights and other laws because student radicals were supposedly aiding America's enemies.[60]

Another set of revelations concerned biological weapons. The Committee determined, for example, that the CIA had stored enough deadly shellfish toxin to kill thousands of people, despite a presidential order in 1970 to destroy it.[61] According to the director of the Project on National Security and Civil Liberties, Morton Halperin, the Committee's investigation of biological weapons constituted nothing less than "the beginning of a public education in how the CIA functions."[62]

Newsweek magazine summed up the Committee's work as "probably the most comprehensive and thoughtfully critical study yet made of the shadowy world of U.S. intelligence."[63] Columnist Mary McGrory wrote that "the Committee turned up some maggoty horrors" – what the *New York Times* viewed as "inexcusable products of an amoral secret bureaucracy that endangered democratic ideals, freedom, and a government of laws." Church was convinced that the Committee marked a "tidal shift in attitude" regarding governmental secrecy and accountability in a free society.[64]

Later, when Richard Nixon defended the warrantless wiretapping of Americans in the antiwar movement, he said: "When the President does it, that means it is not illegal."[65] Such a view of presidential powers frightened Church. "Like Caesar peering into the colonies," Church said, Nixon had watched the Chilean elections; and after deciding that the Chileans had elected the wrong leader, he had instructed the CIA to bring down their democratically chosen government.[66] The sad truth, in Church's opinion, was that definitions of America's "national security" often disguised the most sordid acts. U.S. policies, the Senator argued, typically hinged far less on real issues of national security than on inflated views of America's role abroad, exaggerated fears, and the desire to shield powerful interest groups. An ironic result was that, in the name of protecting the United States, authorities were creating a security system that more and more resembled "a mirror image of the evil it is designed to combat."[67]

Church paid a heavy price for his criticism of U.S. foreign policy as well as of the abuses of intelligence gathering and presidential powers. "We seem to face increasing resistance on every front," he wrote during the Committee's work.[68] Continually he encountered warnings that he and his panel were destroying America's defense community and endangering national security. President Ford and Vice President Rockefeller both accused him and the Committee of aiding America's enemies by exposing U.S. intelligence operations.[69] Years later, Henry Kissinger continued to say that Church had "practically wrecked" the CIA.[70] Kissinger, former CIA director Richard Helms, and others believed that Church was naive and held a "boy-scoutish" view of the world. From that perspective, Church and his ilk expected the United States, in the words of columnist James Kilpatrick, to "go abroad in a dangerous world, accoutered like

Little Lord Fauntleroy, to play patticake with gangs who fight with switchblade knives."[71] "Sen. Church aids Reds," a Missouri newspaper charged.[72] Mail from across the country descended on Church's office attacking him as unpatriotic. A CIA person declared bitterly, "You don't have a country, you have a church – no pun intended."[73] Newscaster Paul Harvey rebuked the Committee for "sticking pins in the FBI" and ignoring the bureau's "mission to protect our established order against the wreckers."[74] An editorial in *TV Guide* claimed that "a hundred KGB agents working overtime for the Kremlin" could not have damaged national security as much as had Church's Committee.[75] A vigilante group, "Veterans Against Communist Sympathizers," threatened to kill the Senator.[76]

In 1980, a furiously vicious right-wing assault on Church resulted in his narrowly losing his bid for a fifth Senate term. The National Conservative Political Action Committee flooded Idaho with literature, including a flyer, "Frank Church's Record of Shame," saying that "the anti-CIA witch hunt" had gutted America's national defense. One constituent razored out Church's throat from a campaign photo and accused him of selling out "to the commies." "*Go to Hell! You God Damn Communist*," wrote another person.[77]

The Church Committee's relevance today

Three decades after the Church Committee submitted its report, the newly declared "War on Terror" has nevertheless made the work of the Committee disturbingly relevant. Indeed, Church's words and the Committee's findings could hardly be more compelling or timely, given "the New Paradigm" that has emerged during the administration of President George W. Bush. This paradigm, as the journalist Jane Mayer has described it, "rests on a reading of the Constitution that few legal scholars share – namely, that the President, as commander in chief, has the authority to disregard virtually all previously known legal boundaries if national security demands it."[78] Vice President Richard Cheney, arguably the most powerful Vice President in U.S. history,[79] and his chief of staff, David Addington, have been the leading voices in shaping the paradigm. Both view as reprehensible the Church Committee and the intelligence reforms it spawned (such as the Foreign Intelligence Surveillance Act of 1978, which requires, for example, judicial review to legitimatize wiretaps of foreign suspects in the United States[80]). As one observer noted, "They've focused on restoring the Nixon Presidency. They've persuaded themselves that, following Nixon, things went all wrong."[81] Cheney served as Gerald Ford's chief advisor during the Church Committee investigations and was subsequently the ranking Republican on a House select committee that examined the Iran-Contra scandal during the Reagan administration. In December 2005, the Vice President praised the 1987 House select committee's minority report, which accused *Congress* – not the Executive branch – of abusing its powers.[82] Reagan, according to the report, had acted out of "a legitimate frustration" with Congress's efforts to diminish the President's authority over foreign policy. Cheney candidly says that he has been determined to rebuild presidential power.[83]

The "War on Terror" has been immensely useful in that regard. According to the head of the New York Bar Association's International Law Committee, strongly influential individuals in the administration want to "overturn two centuries of jurisprudence defining the limits of the executive branch."[84] As former Senator and Church Committee member Gary Hart wrote recently with the historian Joyce Appleby:

> George W. Bush and his most trusted advisers, Richard B. Cheney and Donald H. Rumsfeld, entered office determined to restore the authority of the presidency. Five years and many decisions later, they've pushed the expansion of presidential power so far that we now confront a constitutional crisis.[85]

That crisis is evident in such policies as warrantless wiretapping of American citizens[86] and in claims that the President can imprison indefinitely, without hearing, any person whom he labels an "enemy combatant." It also reflects assertions that the executive can waive such cherished legal rights as allowing accused individuals to know what evidence is being used against them. Bush has asserted that, as a wartime President, he must act as he sees fit to protect the nation.[87]

But a crucial aspect of Bush's approach has taken the shape of a deliberate effort to circumvent Congress and has occurred largely behind the scenes. "Through secrecy and contemptuous treatment of Congress, the Bush White House has made the executive branch less accountable than at any time in modern American history," the long-time Washington observer Elizabeth Drew has written.[88] Although the Constitution says that Congress shall "make all laws" and the President shall faithfully execute them, "Bush claims the power to execute the laws as he interprets them, ignoring congressional intent."[89] He has done so via the unparalleled usage of over 800 "signing statements" – statements which the President has attached to legislation that he intends to ignore or interpret without regard to Congress's intent. The proposition that Attorney General Alberto Gonzalez and others in the executive branch have pushed is a throwback to the ancient Roman dictum "In time of war, the laws are silent." In that regard, the War on Terror has spawned a way of thinking – and a long list of policies and actions – that resemble Cold War America's most draconian features. According to Elizabeth Drew, "For the first time in more than thirty years, and to a greater extent than even then, our constitutional form of government is in jeopardy."[90]

What of the lessons of the Church Committee? Insofar as people have remembered the intelligence investigations of the mid-1970s, they have mainly chastised them for endangering the United States and providing a model of what not to do. Following the September 11, 2001 terrorist attacks in the United States, a number of influential leaders and commentators have been emphatic: criticism of, and inquiries into, intelligence gathering and presidential powers make America vulnerable and jeopardize national security. In the nearly six years since the horrors of the September 11, 2001 attacks, a rally-round-the-flag mentality has generally prevailed. There is no equivalent of the Church Committee. Indeed, the Bush administration warned that one of the most important threats in the November 2006 elections could come from a reshaped Congress that might launch a series of investigations into government policies, including a centerpiece of Bush's battle against terrorism: the Iraq war. These warnings have proven true. Following the ascension of the Democrats to majorities in the House and Senate there has been a flurry of congressional oversight and investigative undertakings. Still, until well after his 2004 reelection, even as disturbing questions about the administration's decision to attack Iraq surfaced, the public and mainstream press overwhelmingly endorsed Bush as a take-charge President who was leading a charge against terrorism.

In December 2005, a frustrated John Conyers, Jr. (Democrat from Michigan) asked the House to form "a select committee to investigate the Administration's intent to go to war before congressional authorization, manipulation of pre-war intelligence, encouraging and countenancing torture, retaliating against critics, and to make recommendations regarding grounds for possible impeachment."[91] After his proposal received virtually no attention in the House or in the press, Conyers had his own staff gather evidence from a growing flood of reports in newspapers, books, and congressional testimony about the abuse of presidential powers. The result, in early 2006, was a 182-page report, with over 1,000 footnotes: *The Constitution in Crisis: The Downing Street Minutes and Deception, Manipulation, Torture, Retribution, and Coverups in the Iraq War.*[92] The Conyers report provides a host of examples of presidential misconduct – most serious of which is Bush's alleged "conspiracy to commit fraud" by deliberately manipulating and falsifying evidence to take the United States into war against Iraq.[93] When news broke that the President had ordered the NSA to monitor telephone and e-mail traffic in the United States, without first obtaining a court order, Bush maintained that the executive's wartime powers justified his directive.[94] The Justice Department went so far as to argue that Congress cannot restrict the President's strategies of how to "engage the enemy."[95] Even when Bush signed legislation barring "cruel, inhuman and degrading treatment" of possible terrorists,[96] he implied that no such congressional act would bind him. He would act "in a manner consistent with the constitutional authority of the President to supervise the unitary executive branch and as Commander in Chief."[97]

Challenges to such a sweeping view of presidential powers have nevertheless grown, placing the Church Committee in a more favorable light. In April 2006, Senator Russ Feingold (Democrat from Wisconsin) recalled the issuance of the Committee's final report as "a watershed moment" in which Congress seemed ready "to assume its critical role in overseeing the U.S. intelligence community."[98] Such a perspective suggested that events and trends reminiscent of those that set the historical stage for the Committee's work might again be in motion. History does not repeat itself, certainly, but it often has a way of making past experiences powerfully relevant.

Through the midpoint of President Bush's second term, the Iraq war – like the Vietnam War earlier – had lost public favor. And Bush's initially very favorable ratings had dropped significantly. Criticism of the President grew in the mainstream press and even from some of his conservative allies. "Congress and the courts must rein in this presidential power grab," editorialized the conservative *Salt Lake Tribune* on July 29, 2006. "To do otherwise would be to court tyranny."[99] Bruce Fein, a Republican who served as Ronald Reagan's associate deputy attorney general and voted for Bush in 2000 and 2004, has recently expressed strong reservations about the President. According to Fein, Bush "presents a clear and present danger to the rule of law." Indeed, Fein is convinced that Bush

> has made claims that are really quite alarming. He's said there are no restraints on his ability, as he sees it, to collect intelligence, to open mail, to commit torture, and to use electronic surveillance.... All the world's a battlefield – according to this view. He could kill someone in Lafayette Park if he wants! It's got the sense of Louis XIV: "*I* am the State."

Fein worries that if Bush "maintains this disregard or contempt for the coordinate branches of government, it's that conception of an omnipotent presidency that makes the occupant a dangerous person."[100] Even Grover Norquist, a leading conservative, and someone who has been close to the Bush White House, expressed worry: "They're not trying to change the law; they're saying that they're above the law and in the case of the NSA wiretaps, they break it." If such a view prevails, Norquist has said, "you don't have a constitution: you have a king."[101]

Although *Rolling Stone Magazine* is not a major public influence, it is a profitable biweekly magazine with a sizable readership among young people. And it has published a growing number of hard-hitting critiques of the administration. Essays in mid-2006, for example, focused on the use of torture at Guantanamo and on Iraq as "a fake 'War on Terror' to scare voters into supporting" Bush's initiatives.[102]

Perhaps more tellingly, *Harper's Magazine*, for decades one of the most prestigious of popular journals of commentary on American public life, has also published a host of sharply critical essays – including editor Lewis Lapham's *The Case for Impeachment: Why We Can No Longer Afford George W. Bush*. Lapham quoted Bush as saying on December 19, 2005, "We're at war ... we must protect America's secrets." Scoffing at the President's argument, Lapham retorted, "No, it's not America's secrets that the President seeks to protect ... the secrets are those of the Bush administration."[103]

In August 2006, the highly influential *Wall Street Journal* published financier George Soros's opinion piece, asserting that the War on Terror "has led to a dangerous extension of executive powers; it has tarnished our adherence to universal human rights; it has inhibited the critical process that is at the heart of an open society."[104] And the equally prestigious *New Yorker* magazine has published a series of devastating evaluations of Bush and the Iraq war. One of the contributors has been none other than Seymour Hersh, whose articles on the CIA's domestic surveillance campaigns prodded Congress in the mid-1970s to launch investigations of America's intelligence agencies.[105]

Perhaps no essay has had the political effect of Hersh's writings some 30 years ago, but, together, the outpouring of journalistic pieces may well reflect another reorientation of American politics. In sum, an increasingly unpopular war, an administration that has time and again displayed a willingness to ignore constitutional restrictions and existing laws, and a growing restiveness on the part of a host of sources – many of them mainstream and well established, on the right as well as the left – may be setting the stage for investigations such as those of the Church Committee.

By the fall of 2006, at least two ingredients were still missing, however. One involved the political makeup and will of Congress. Unlike the situation in 1975, when a Democratic Congress wrestled with a Republican White House, Congress had been in the control of the President's party since he was first elected in 2000. As Senator Chuck Hagel, a Nebraska Republican, has said, "Congress has essentially been complicit" during the Bush years. "If it was a Clinton presidency we'd be holding hearings."[106] But with both the Senate and House in the President's camp, Congress has served as "simply an echo chamber of presidential politics," in the words of columnist David Broder.[107] Two scholars with different political orientations concluded recently that Congress is now "The Broken Branch" of government, a weakened institution that refuses to deal with major issues such as runaway budgets and conscientious oversight of executive agencies.[108]

Another missing ingredient may be the absence of a Frank Church. At the least, however, Church's example and words from 30 years earlier still resonate. Senator Feingold recently quoted Church: "Our experience as a nation has taught us that we must place our trust in laws, and not solely in men. The founding fathers foresaw excess as the inevitable consequence of granting any part of government unchecked power."[109] Church, considering his era, also said, "Our tragedy in recent years springs from a leadership principally motivated by fear."[110] In his opinion, "Our Founding Fathers were a different breed. They acted on their faith, not their fear. They did not believe in fighting fire with fire; crime with crime; evil with evil; or delinquency by becoming delinquents." They instead constructed "a government that would obey the law."[111]

Church's belief in 1976 that a "tidal shift in attitude" had occurred concerning government secrecy and accountability was at best premature. Still relevant, however, were his warnings that the executive branch's "imperial view" of its powers jeopardized the right of people in a democracy to know what their government is doing. Totalitarian governments, he argued, hide their evils behind veils of secrecy; democracies depend upon well-informed electorates. "Our society," he said proudly, "has drawn its inspiration from the Biblical injunction, 'Ye shall know the truth and the truth shall make you free.' "[112]

The fate of Church's comments hinged ultimately on his faith in democracy and what the public wants to know. Ominously, in that regard, Richard Nixon once instructed John Kennedy that voters care little about the law and statesman-like actions; they prefer bold leadership instead. Or, as a social activist observed sadly, "The facts just bounce off people." Against that backdrop, the challenges facing constitutional government are always formidable. As George Orwell observed years ago, "In a time of universal deceit, telling the truth is a revolutionary act."[113]

The Church Committee engaged in some truth telling. That was its triumph. And its legacy.

Notes

1 S. Res. 21, 95th Cong. (1975) (enacted).
2 Chris Mooney, Back to Church, *American Prospect*, Nov. 5, 2001, at 6–7.
3 Tony Judt, *New York Review of Books*, Mar. 23, 2006, at 15.
4 For scholarly treatments of the Committee, see Loch Johnson, *A Season of Inquiry: The Senate Intelligence Investigation* (1985); Loch Johnson, Congressional Supervision of America's Secret Agencies: The Experience and Legacy of the Church Committee, 64 *Public Administration Review* 3–14 (January 2004); Frank J. Smist, *Congress Oversees the United States Intelligence Community, 1947–1989* (1990); Kathryn S. Olmsted, *Challenging the Secret Government: The Post-Watergate Investigations of the CIA and FBI* (1996); and LeRoy Ashby and Rod Gramer, *Fighting the Odds: The Life of Senator Frank Church* 411–92 (1994).
5 The "intelligence community," as it developed during the early Cold War, included 13 major agencies. Literature on the Cold War is voluminous, but for an overview, see Harry Howe Ransom, *The Intelligence Establishment* (1970); Thomas G. Paterson, *On Every Front: The Making and Unmaking of the Cold War* (1992); Thomas G. Paterson, *Meeting the Communist Threat: Truman to Reagan* (1988); Walter LaFeber, *America, Russia, and the Cold War, 1945–1996* (1997); and Johnson, Congressional Supervision, *supra* note 4. For a different emphasis, see the works of John Lewis Gaddis, particularly *The Cold War: A New History* (2006), which Judt critiques insightfully in A Story Still to Be Told, supra note 3, at 11–15. For a particular emphasis on the CIA, see John Ranelegh, *The Agency: Rise and Decline of the CIA* (1986–87); Thomas Powers, *The Man Who Kept the Secrets: Richard Helms and the CIA* (1979); John Prados, *Presidents' Secret Wars: CIA and Pentagon Covert Operations from World War II through Iranscam* (1986); and Rhodri Jeffrey-Jones, *The CIA and American Democracy* (1989). Popular culture helped to build the anti-communist consensus, reflecting mixed emotions of fear and triumph, and romanticizing a system that works along with government efforts to protect Americans. See Olmsted, *Challenging the Sacred Government, supra* note 4, at 14, and LeRoy Ashby, *With Amusement for All: A History of American Popular Culture since 1830* 282–300 (2006).
6 Following the CIA's creation in 1947, two Senate committees – Armed Services and Appropriations – had oversight responsibilities for U.S. Intelligence. Smist, *supra* note 4, at 5. See also Loch Johnson, The U.S. Congress and the CIA: Monitoring the Dark Side of the Government, *Legislative Studies Quarterly* 477–99 (Nov. 1980).
7 As Clark Clifford, adviser to Presidents Truman and Lyndon Johnson, recalled in 1983, "Congress chose not to be involved and preferred to be uninformed." Smist, *supra* note 4, at 4–9.
8 Interview by Rod Gramer with Frank Church, Senator from Idaho (June 24, 1979) (regarding Saltonstall).

9 Henry R. Luce, The American Century, *Life*, Feb. 17, 1941.

10 For a good, albeit brief overview, see Richard Fried, *Nightmare in Red: The McCarthy Era in Perspective* (1990).

11 See *Opposition to the Vietnam* War (n.d.), http://en.wikipedia.org/wiki/Opposition_ to_the_Vietnam_War; *Public Opinion and the Vietnam War* (n.d.), www.digital history.uh.edu/learning_history/vietnam/vietnam_publicopinion.cfm.

12 See, e.g., Arthur Schlesinger, Jr., *The Imperial Presidency* (1973).

13 Seymour Hersh, Huge CIA Operation Reported in U.S. against Anti-War Forces, Other Dissidents in Nixon Years, *New York Times*, Dec. 22, 1974.

14 S. Res. 21, 95th Cong. (1975) (enacted).

15 H. Res. 138, 95th Cong. (1975) (enacted). The House voted 286–120 to approve the resolution. See Smist, *supra* note 4, at 135.

16 See, e.g., Year of Intelligence, *New York Times*, Feb. 8, 1975, at 24; Olmsted, *supra* note 4, at 49–50. For the administration's concerns about heading off congressional investigations, see Richard Cheney, Handwritten Notes (Dec. 27, 1974) (on file with the Gerald R. Ford Presidential Library, Ann Arbor, Mich., in the White House Operations, Richard Cheney Files, 1974–77, Box 5).

17 Frank Church, How Many Dominican Republics and Vietnams Can We Take On?, *New York Times Magazine*, Nov. 28, 1965, at 44–45, 177–78.

18 Frank Church, To All the World with Love, *Esquire*, July 1967, at 68, 83–85, 123–24.

19 Referencing the Church–Hatfield Sense of the Senate Resolution in 1969 urging a more rapid withdrawal of U.S. troops from Vietnam, see Ashby and Gramer, *supra* note 4, at 295–96. In 1970 and 1971, Church joined John Sherman Cooper (Demo-crat from Kentucky) in sponsoring, with mixed success, a series of amendments to appropriations bills aimed at keeping the war from spreading into Laos, Thailand, and Cambodia, or at disengaging U.S. troops from all of Southeast Asia. Ibid. at 299–305, 312–31, 335–40. Church also voted for the McGovern-Hatfield end-the-war motion, which the Senate rejected on Sept. 1, 1970. Ibid. at 331–32.

20 Church discussed Laird's testimony in his article Ending Emergency Government, *ABA Journal* 197 (Feb. 1977).

21 Ibid.

22 See U.S. Cong., Senate, *The National Emergencies Act (Public Law 94–112), Source Book: Legislative History, Texts, and Other Documents* (1976). See also Harold C. Relyea, Reconsidering the National Emergencies Act: Its Evolution, Implementation, and Deficiencies, in *The Presidency and National Security Policy*, at 274–323 (R. Gordon Hoxie, ed., 1984); Ashby and Gramer, *supra* note 4, at 412–16.

23 See, e.g., Church, *supra* note 20, at 197; Frank Church, speech in Fresno, Calif., (Sept. 20, 1976) (regarding the "loaded gun") (on file with the Frank Church Collec-tion, MSS 56, Boise State University, Series 10.6, Box 1, Folder 17) [hereinafter referred to as Church Collection, Series *X*, Box *Y*, Folder *Z*].

24 Ashby and Gramer, *supra* note 4, at 427–31. See also 94th Cong., *Hearings Before the Subcomm. on Multinational Corporations* (1976).

25 Jack Anderson with George Clifford, *The Anderson Papers* 13–62, 112 (1973); Ashby and Gramer, *supra* note 4, at 416.

26 See Staff Memorandum, Origins of the Subcommittee on Multinational Corpora-tions (Mar. 21, 1975) (on file with the Church Collection, Series 10.6, Box 4).

27 See Memoranda from Theodore G. Shackley for the Director of Central Intelligence (Feb. 21 and 24, 1973) (on file with the Henry Jackson Papers, Univ. of Washington, 3560–6, 51/52) (regarding the CIA's efforts to head off Church); Johnson, *Season of Inquiry*, *supra* note 4, at 7 (quoting Stennis).

28 Church news release, In the Aftermath of the Chilean Affair (Dec. 13, 1974) (on file with the Church Collection, Series 2.2, Box 46, Folder 3); (regarding self-determination);

Letter from Frank Church, Senator from Idaho to Milton J. Berrey (Aug. 27, 1975) (on file with the Church Collection, Series 2.2, Box 4, Folder 17).

29 Notes from Kissinger confirmation hearings (Sept. 10, 1973) (on file with the Church Collection, Series 10.6, Box 3, Folder 21).

30 *New York Times*, Sept. 12, 1974 (quotations).

31 *New York Times*, Sept. 17, 1974; *Chicago Tribune*, Sept. 18, 1974 (regarding Ford); *Commonweal*, Oct. 18, 1974 (quoting Church).

32 *Chicago Tribune*, Sept. 22, 1974.

33 Thomas G. Paterson, Oversight or Afterview? Congress, the CIA, and Covert Actions since 1947, in *Congress and United States Foreign Policy: Controlling the Use of Force in the Nuclear Age*, at 160 (Michael Barnhart, ed. 1987).

34 Judith Miller, Criminal Negligence: Congress, Chile, and the CIA, *Progressive*, Nov. 1974, at 19 concluded, for example, that Congress was apparently going to "do what it has done in the past – nothing."

35 A Peek in the CIA's Closet, *Newsweek*, Jan. 27, 1975, at 30 (quoting Eastland).

36 *New York Times*, Jan. 15 and 21, 1975; Johnson, *Season of Inquiry*, *supra* note 4, at 9–11.

37 Transcript of Senate Historical Office Oral History Interview by Don Ritchie with George Tames (Jan. 13 to May 18, 1988) ("knocked down"); Johnson, *Season of Inquiry*, *supra* note 4, at 22 (regarding Church's credentials); Rod Gramer interview with Jack Blum (Aug. 10, 1984) [hereinafter Gramer interview with Blum]; Rod Gramer interview with Jerome Levinson (Aug. 2, 1984); interview with Jerome Levinson (May 11, 1987) (regarding skepticism of Fulbright and Chase). Levinson was chief counsel of the multinationals subcommittee; Blum was associate counsel.

38 Gramer interview with Blum, *supra* note 37. See Ashby and Gramer, *supra* note 4, at 102–03 (describing "Frank Sunday School" and Church's reputation); see also Johnson, *Season of Inquiry*, *supra* note 4, at 22.

39 Gramer interview with Blum, *supra* note 37.

40 Others who constituted the Committee were Democrats Walter Huddleston of Kentucky and Robert Morgan of North Carolina, along with Republicans Charles Mathias, Jr., of Maryland, Howard Baker of Tennessee, and Richard Schweiker of Pennsylvania.

41 Memorandum from Patrick O'Donnell, to Roderick Hills (July 31, 1975) (on file with the Gerald R. Ford Presidential Library, Ann Arbor, Mich., in the William T. Kendall Files, Box 3) (regarding Goldwater).

42 Bob Wolthuis notes of GOP Leadership Meeting (Sept. 24, 1975) (on file with the Gerald R. Ford Presidential Library, Ann Arbor, Mich., in the Robert K. Wolthuis Files, Box 2); John Tower, *Consequences: A Personal and Political Memoir* 132 (1991).

43 Smist, *supra* note 4, at 48.

44 Memorandum from Roderick Hills, to Phil Buchen *et al.*, Counselors to the President (July 19, 1975) (on file with the Gerald R. Ford Presidential Library, Ann Arbor, Mich., in the John Marsh Files, Box 81).

45 Cheney's handwritten notes (May 28, 1975) (on file with the Gerald R. Ford Presidential Library, Ann Arbor, Mich., in the White House Operations, Richard Cheney Files, 1974–77, Box 6).

46 Johnson, *Season of Inquiry*, *supra* note 4, at 121.

47 Forrest Church, *Father and Son: A Personal Biography of Senator Frank Church of Idaho* 28 (1985).

48 Memorandum from Eugene McCarthy, Senator from Minn., to Richard Russell (Feb. 27, 1967) (on file with the National Archives, Washington, D.C., in the Carl Marcy Papers, Senate Foreign Relation Committee Papers, Box 1967).

49 Miller, *supra* note 34, at 15 ("insulate").

50 Senator Frank Church, *Multinational Corporations and East Asia: The Foreign Policy Implications of the Lockheed Affair*, Address before the Harvard East Asia

Conference (Oct. 15, 1976) (transcript available in the Church Collection, Series 10.6, Box 4, Folder 11).

51 Interview by Rod Gramer with William Miller (July 27, 1984).

52 Interview with Patrick Shea (Oct. 15, 1988) (regarding minister analogy); interview by Rod Gramer with Stan Burns (Apr. 24, 1984).

53 William "Fishbait" Miller, *Fishbait: The Memoirs of the Congressional Doorkeeper* 323 (1977).

54 James Barron and Marjorie Arons, The Flexible Liberalism of Frank Church, *Boston Phoenix*, Nov. 18, 1975.

55 Ashby and Gramer, *supra* note 4, 472.

56 Frank Church, Senator from Idaho, Speech, *Neither a Vendetta nor a Whitewash* (Feb. 27, 1975) (on file with the Church Collection, Series 7.7, Box 2, Folder 5) ("redemptive"); interview by Rod Gramer with Frank Church, Senator from Idaho (June 24, 1979); *Washington Star News*, Jan. 29, 1975.

57 Ashby and Gramer, *supra* note 4, at 474 (quoting Church), Mary McGrory, Column, *Washington Star*, June 15, 1975; interview with Frank Church, Senator from Idaho, in *Charleston Gazette* (W.Va.), Nov. 13, 1975; see also The Cloak Comes Off, *Newsweek*, June 23, 1975, at 16–18.

58 Johnson, *Season of Inquiry*, *supra* note 4, at 61–62 (regarding the Committee's handling of JFK); ibid. at 109 (regarding the threatened resignation).

59 Interview with Rick Inderfurth (Sept. 14, 1993).

60 Johnson, Congressional Supervision, *supra* note 4, at 3–14, includes an excellent summary of these matters. See also S. Res. 21, 94th Cong. (1975) (7 vols.), including *Unauthorized Storage of Toxic Agents* [hereinafter Church Vol. 1], *Huston Plan* [hereinafter Church Vol. 2], *Internal Revenue Service* [hereinafter Church Vol. 3], *Mail Opening* [hereinafter Church Vol. 4], *The National Security Agency and Fourth Amendment Rights* [hereinafter Church Vol. 5], *Federal Bureau of Investigation* [hereinafter Church Vol. 6], and *Covert Action* [hereinafter Church Vol. 7].

61 See Church Vol. 1, *supra* note 60.

62 Morton Halperin, CIA: Denying What's Not in Writing, *New Republic*, Oct. 4, 1975, at 11–12 (quotation).

63 Inquest on Intelligence, *Newsweek*, May 10, 1976, at 40.

64 McGrory, *supra* note 57; *N.Y. Times*, Nov. 22, 1975; Olmsted, *supra* note 4, at 2 (noting the tidal shift).

65 David Cole, NSA Spying Myths, *The Nation*, Feb. 20, 2006, at 5.

66 *Tomorrow Show* (NBC television broadcast Jan. 21, 1976) (transcript on file with the Church Collection, Series 12, Box 3, Folder 16).

67 Senator Frank Church, Speech, *The Last Quarter of the Twentieth Century: A Senator's Perspective* (Oct. 26, 1976) (on file with the Church Collection, Series 12, Box 3, Folder 16; Frank Church, Covert Action: Swampland of American Foreign Policy, *Bulletin of the Atomic Scientists*, Feb. 1976, at 7–11.

68 Church interview in *Charleston Gazette*, *supra* note 57.

69 Johnson, *Season of Inquiry*, *supra* note 4, at 168; Rockefeller in *New York Times*, May 5, 1976; see also Gerald R. Ford, *A Time to Heal: The Autobiography of Gerald R. Ford* 265 (1979) (regarding "the Church probe as sensational and irresponsible"); Henry Kissinger, *Years of Upheaval* 495 (1982) (describing Church as "our scourge on Vietnam and constant critic of 'deceitful' methods").

70 *Lewiston Tribune* (Idaho), 22 Oct. 1988.

71 Clipping of Kilpatrick column (1976) (on file with the Church Collection, Series 2.6, Box 1, Folder 4); interview by Rod Gramer with Richard Helms (Aug. 2, 1984).

72 *Post-Tribune* (Jefferson City, Mo.), Aug. 20, 1975.

73 Transcript of Jack Anderson story (Nov. 9, 1975) (quoting the CIA) (on file with the Church Collection, Series 12, Box 2, Folder 16).

74 Clipping of Harvey column (1976) (on file with the Church Collection, Series 2.6, Box 1, Folder 4).

75 Johnson, *Season of Inquiry, supra* note 4, at 168.

76 *Washington Star,* Dec. 30, 1975.

77 Flyer, *Frank Church's Record of Shame* (on file with the Church Collection, Series 2.2, Box 5, Folder 19). See other examples in the Church Collection, Series 12, Box 3, Folder 19.

78 Jane Mayer, The Hidden Power, *New Yorker,* July 3, 2006, at 44.

79 See, e.g., Jo Becker and Barton Gellman, Angler: The Cheney Vice Presidency (pts. 1 and 2), *Washington Post* Weekly Edition, July 9–15, 2007, at 6–12, July 16–22, 2007, at 8–10; James MacGregor Burns and Susan Dunn, The "Kitchen Cabinet" of one … Dick Cheney, *Los Angeles Times,* Jul. 12, 2007, available at http://hnn.us/roundup/entries/40890.html.

80 See Seamon in this volume (Chapter 8).

81 Mayer, *supra* note 78, at 48–49.

82 Ibid. at 49.

83 Ibid. at 44, 46; see also Joan Didion, Cheney: The Fatal Touch, *New York Review of Books,* Oct. 5, 2006, at 51–55.

84 Mayer, *supra* note 78, at 44, 46.

85 Joyce Appleby and Gary Hart, The Founders Never Imagined a Bush Administration, *History News Network, available at* www.hnn.us/articles/23297 (last visited March 27, 2006).

86 See Seamon (Chapter 8) and Greenlee (Chapter 11) in this volume.

87 See, e.g., David Cole, Why the Court Said No, *New York Review of Books,* Aug 10, 2006, at 41.

88 Elizabeth Drew, Power Grab, *New York Review of Books,* June 22, 2006, at 10 (accountable).

89 Ibid.

90 Ibid. at 15; Rhonda Chriss Lokeman, Bush v. The Constitution, *Spokesman-Review,* Aug. 2, 2006, at B4. See also Didion, *supra* note 83, at 52 (regarding the statements). "The first forty-two presidents combined," according to Didion, resorted to signing statements "fewer than six hundred times. George W. Bush, by contrast, issued more than eight hundred … during the first six years of his administration." Ibid.

91 Lewis H. Lapham, The Case for Impeachment, *Harper's Magazine,* March 2006, at 27.

92 *The Constitution in Crisis: The Downing Street Minutes and Deception, Manipulation, Torture, Retributions, and Coverups in the Iraq War,* available at www.afterdowningstreet.org/constitutionincrisis (updated 273-page report); Lapham, *supra* note 91, at 27–32 (regarding the Conyers Report); see also ibid. at 28 (describing the key arguments).

93 The words "conspiracy to commit fraud" are Lapham's from *supra* note 91, at 28. Among the best examinations of the administration's manipulation of the facts are James Bamford, *A Pretext for War: 9/11, Iraq, and the Abuse of America's Intelligence Agencies* (2005); and Mark Danner, *The Secret Way to War: The Downing Street Memo and the Iraq War's Buried History* (2006).

94 See Seamon in this volume.

95 Department of Justice, *Legal Authority Supporting the Activities of the National Security Agency Described by the President* (Jan. 19, 2006); Cole, *supra* note 65, at 7.

96 See Press Release, Presidential Press Secretary (Dec. 30, 2005), available at http://usinfo.state.gov/gi/Archive/2006/Jan/03–762801.html.

97 Cole, *supra* note 65, at 7.

98 John Nichols, *Frank Church and the Abyss of Warrantless Wiretapping* (April 26,

2006), available at www.commondreams.org/cgi-bin/print.cig?file=/views06/0426–30.html.

99 Editorial, Power Play: Congress Should Rein in President's Signing Statement, *Salt Lake Tribune*, July 29, 2006, at Opinion.

100 Lapham, *supra* note 91, at 33–34; *see also* Mayer, *supra* note 78, at 46.

101 Drew, *supra* note 88, at 10.

102 Jeff Tietz, The Unending Torture of Omar Khadr, *Rolling Stone*, Aug. 24, 2006, at 60–68, 102–04; Robert Dreyfuss, The Phony War, *Rolling Stone*, Sept. 21, 2006, at 42–49.

103 Lapham, *supra* note 91, at 27–35 (quotation on 34).

104 George Soros, A Self-Defeating War, *Wall Street Journal*, Aug. 15, 2006.

105 Seymour Hersh, The General's Report, *New Yorker*, Jun. 25, 2007, at 58–69.

106 Drew, *supra* note 88, at 10 (Hagel).

107 David S. Broder, Congress Is Failing America, *Spokesman-Review* (Spokane, Wash.), Sept. 3, 2006.

108 Thomas E. Mann and Norman J. Ornstein, *The Broken Branch: How Congress Is Failing America and How to Get It Back on Track* (2006); *see also* Robert Kuttner, A Slight Oversight, *American Prospect*, Oct. 2006, at 36–40.

109 Nichols, *supra* note 98.

110 Forrest Church, Church of America, *Inlander* (Spokane, Wash.), June 29, 2006, at 19, available at www.thenation.com.

111 Ibid.

112 Frank Church, typescript (statement in response to Gerald Ford's Oct. 31, 1975 letter urging the suppression of the Committee's assassination report) (on file with the Church Collection, Series 10.6, Box 1, Folder 21); see also Letter from Frank Church, Senator from Idaho, to Bing Crosby (Jan. 9, 1975) (on file with the Church Collection, Series 2.6, Box 1, Folder 2).

113 Richard M. Abrams, *America Transformed: Sixty Years of Revolutionary Change, 1941–2001* 333 (2006) (regarding Nixon); Bob Moser, White Heat, *The Nation*, Aug. 28–Sept. 4, 2006, at 14 (giving facts).

6 Senator Church and his constituents

Katherine G. Aiken

Introduction

While something of a cliché, it is nonetheless true that Idaho is a long way from Washington, D.C. – a long way indeed. In fact, most observers would suspect that Idahoans usually allow their elected officials a free hand in terms of foreign policy, preferring to concentrate on domestic issues. Nothing could be further from the truth. A look at how Idahoans viewed Senator Frank Church's chairmanship of the Senate Select Committee to Study Governmental Operations with Respect to Intelligence Activities (1975–76) provides an excellent opportunity to show otherwise.

In the wake of Watergate and earlier Senate and House investigations, questions regarding the conduct of United States intelligence had been bandied about for several years. Senator Frank Church had often expressed concerns regarding this issue, especially after his chairmanship of the Subcommittee on Multinational Corporations. In that capacity, Church had learned about illegal operations in Chile in particular.[1] In December 1974, investigative reporter Seymour Hersh's front-page article in the *New York Times* revealed that the Central Intelligence Agency (CIA) had conducted intelligence operations against American citizens.[2] This infuriated Frank Church and eventually prompted the United States Senate to vote 82–4 to establish a Select Committee on Intelligence Activities. Majority Leader Mike Mansfield named Democrats Frank Church, Walter Mondale, Philip Hart, Walter Huddleston, Roger Morgan, and Gary Hart to the Committee. The five Republicans were Charles Mathias, Jr., Howard Baker, John Tower, Richard Schweiker and Barry Goldwater.[3] Frank Church lobbied hard for his appointment as Chair of the Committee, which became his when Mansfield's first choice, Senator Phil Hart, declined owing to illness.[4] His chairmanship of what came to be called the Church Committee handicapped his run for the White House in 1976, and probably contributed to Frank Church's close reelection loss in 1980. It also illustrates the complexity of representative government and the balance of power in the United States system. Frank Church believed it was a constitutional responsibility of Congress to oversee intelligence operations. A February 10, 1975 news release quoted the Senator as saying, "The task of reviewing the activities of the executive agencies falls properly upon the legislative branch. The constitution assigned Congress that role."[5] However, members of Congress have to be elected and reelected. Regardless of the validity of Frank Church's constitutional claim, he still was accountable to his constituency.[6] He recognized the considerable political risks involved, but was convinced of the necessity, in fact of his responsibility, to investigate United States intelligence operations.

Frank Church viewed the situation from a moral perspective. According to Church biographers LeRoy Ashby and Rod Gramer, "Frank Church was at his best as a kind of 'moral lightning rod.' By the 1970s, his moralistic tendencies were increasingly apparent, challenging his innate caution."[7] Ashby and Gramer's words certainly describe Frank Church's conviction that Congress should investigate U.S. intelligence operation and his determination to follow that investigation wherever it might lead and regardless of any negative repercussions for his own political reputation.

Frank Church said in an interview on *Face the Nation*, February 2, 1975:

> A free society depends upon maintaining a delicate balance between preserving individual freedom, on the one hand, and maintaining a good order on the other, and if that equilibrium ever tips too far in one direction, it results in tyranny. If it tips too far in the other, it results in anarchy.[8]

In response to a question from Seymour Hersh, the *New York Times* reporter who broke the domestic surveillance story and fueled the calls for congressional oversight, Church agreed that finding that balance was a "kamikaze mission." Frank Church was fully cognizant at the outset that his task in investigating U.S. intelligence operations was fraught with controversy and represented a potential political quagmire. He genuinely believed that going forward with the investigation was the right thing to do, the only legitimate course of action. At the same time, Senator Church recognized that the process would require him to use every bit of his considerable political acumen – both in terms of making the inquiry a success and in navigating the treacherous political waters of Idaho. He wrote to a constituent:

> [Y]ou can be sure our investigation of the CIA will look into all aspects of illegal or unwise activities regardless of the political consequences. I made this pledge at the beginning of this investigation, as you can see from the enclosed statement, and intend to keep that commitment. I will be only too happy to stand on that record at anytime, with my own political party and the people of Idaho.[9]

Examining Idahoans' opinions and ideas on this issue – coupled with an analysis of Senator Frank Church's responses – sheds light on Idaho politics, on Church's own political philosophy, and on questions of national security that continue to be asked today.

Idahoans respond

In the first place, Idahoans recognized that their Senator had received a singular honor and that he would occupy a national stage when Frank Church was chosen to chair the Senate Select Committee to Study Governmental Operations with Respect to Intelligence Activities. A constituent from Pocatello wrote, "I am impressed that someone from Idaho would be selected. I wish you luck in your assignment."[10] One from Buhl simply noted, "Thanks very much – and again we're proud of you."[11] At the same time, Idahoans acknowledged the constitutional significance of Church's assignment. A graduate of the University of Idaho noted, "I feel your chairmanship of the committee investigating the CIA and FBI is probably the greatest responsibility you will ever have."[12] A Hayden Lake man emphasized the potential significance of the investigation, "[T]his is the big one. This will make Watergate look like a frolic in the park." However, the same writer claimed, "The basis for the Jefferson Democracy demands it.... We must know the truth no matter the consequences."[13] These statements clearly outline both the significance of the issues involved and of Church's chairmanship.

Some Idahoans thought that at least there were questions surrounding American intelligence operations that needed to be answered. They believed that Frank Church's integrity made him the right person for the job. "I am sure that a lot of people would sure like to find out what has been going on for at least 20 years and maybe more!" wrote a Coeur d'Alene resident.[14] The principal of Deary [Idaho] High School noted, "I want to congratulate you on the manner in which you are pursuing the present investigations of the CIA etc. It is about time we had someone who is not inclined to cover up or sweep something under the rug."[15] The YMCA Youth Legislature's 1975 session passed a resolution supporting Church and the work of his Committee, claiming that Idahoans "commend you for your fine work for Idaho and America."[16]

There were certainly Idahoans who supported Senator Frank Church's investigations into the activities of American intelligence agencies. These constituents echoed Church's concerns that these agencies had run amok and had, in fact, overstepped their constitutional bounds. A woman from Idaho Falls proclaimed, "We in Idaho are right behind you in your honest endeavors to try and block the CIA. God Bless you."[17]

One female Mountain Home resident's October 23, 1975 words more clearly delineate the issues at hand:

> I wish to thank you on behalf of all my family, and we are numerous, for the *very fine* job you are doing in your CIA investigations and the horror we feel that our Constitutional rights have been so flagrantly violated.[18]

A Boise woman shared Senator Church's anger of the entire situation. She wrote, "I support your committee's objective investigation into the allegation that the CIA has spied on Americans in this country. Then, if you find this allegation is true, please give them hell!"[19]

Other Idahoans believed just as strongly that Church had simply exceeded his authority and that the entire investigation was unnecessary. One woman succinctly noted, "I just wonder who you think you are.... So who do you think you are to question every aspect of our government?"[20] An Idaho Falls man wrote, "I don't believe that the CIA or FBI are [sic] out of bounds in keeping files on private citizens in our country."[21] However, most objections to Church's actions were not so simplistic. They involved what continue to be difficult questions for Americans in terms of the balance between individual rights and the general security and well-being of society as a whole.

A significant number of voters in Idaho expressed concern that the Church Committee investigations and disclosures would jeopardize the United States' standing and image with other nations. One Harrison man worried about this damage: "I sincerely hope and trust ... you will consider what steps can be taken to repair the damage to our position as leaders of the free world."[22] A Twin Falls resident seconded this idea: "Also, I would appreciate it if you would stop trying to be 'Mr. Clean' and stop investigating the CIA for any criminal actions abroad. Our national secrets should not be revealed for the whole world to see."[23] A Macks Inn man made a similar point in no uncertain terms:

> I do not appreciate your actions against the CIA. We love this Country and feel that you are tearing it down – especially to our foreign friends – when what we need is to create the very best image we can. I know that the wrong doings of the CIA should be exposed, but I do not approve of the lengths to which you are going.[24]

These sentiments reflected ideas that national observers put forward as well. The *Idaho Statesman* carried a number of columns by James Kilpatrick that criticized Senator Church and his actions:

> It will be a long time before the damage done by this report can be undone – before friendly nations will again cooperate with our intelligence service, before truly competent and dedicated servants can be attracted anew to the CIA.[25]

Not only did Idaho citizens read the column, but many of them clipped it from the paper and forwarded it to Senator Church in an effort to make certain that he was aware of its contents.

Many Idahoans believed that more than just the United States' image abroad was at stake. They were worried that the Church Committee revelations might adversely affect the ability of the CIA and FBI to fight communists and other subversives. A Boise man anxiously wrote, "Your policy seems to be to do away with the FBI and CIA and all foreign defense against Russia and let them take us over."[26] Another added, "I think it is a *damned* outrage to persecute FBI agents for using surreptitious means to investigate terrorist organizations. I'm sure the Communist conspirators in this country are pleased."[27] A Rupert family warned, "[A]s far as we are concerned, it's nice to know that the CIA and the FBI are 'checking' here at home!"[28] Many of these sentiments actually called Church's own patriotism into question, or at the very least maintained that the Senator was unknowingly playing into the hands of enemies of the United States. As one constituent claimed, "You are going to frizt [sic] around until we have no security at all and the Russians ... can just walk in and take over."[29] Or as one Idaho couple noted, "It looks to many people as though *you* and others would destroy our way of keeping track of what our enemy the Soviet Union is doing."[30]

Idahoans were convinced that their senator and the rest of the investigators were indicting the activities of intelligence agencies that were precisely those necessary in order to maintain national security. A handwritten constituent note proclaimed, "To refresh memories, these agencies [sic] objectives are to protect our citizens from unlawful persons and from people involved in *Un-American activities*!"[31] Or even more clearly, as another Idahoan put it, "And the final blow is you heading a committee investigating the CIA and FBI because they have files on extremists, subversives and the Congress."[32] One Idaho resident wondered, "Just what are the CIA and FBI supposed to do if it isn't to check on aliens, communists, and etc. and subversive activities."[33] This fear that Church's inquiries actually aided and abetted the actions of subversives was a noteworthy one. An Idaho Falls man who was opposed to the Committee opined, "We have degenerated in this nation to the unbelievable state of the criminal, the traitor, the ner-do-well [sic] of every type and description consistently having the upper hand in every way."[34]

Some Idahoans believed that the very tactics that Church questioned were those that should be lauded:

> [B]ut if we don't have tough cloak and dagger men we might just as well not have any. Due to the nature of their business they have to operate under a set of rules, or more honestly, lack of rules, that would be very offensive and deplorable in the eyes of most Americans, but you have to fight fire with fire. The CIA would be completely ineffective if it was an open book operation.[35]

Closely related to this position was the conviction that United States intelligence operatives had to utilize every method of inquiry available to America's enemies if they were to have any hope of competing with them. According to a Pocatello woman:

> If wiretapping and opening the mail of prime suspects is what brought results to stamp out the invidious terrorist schism, which it did, then this is just fine with me! These agents should be given an award and not punishment. They have my respect and admiration.[36]

An organized mailing campaign resulted in postcards from all across Idaho that told Church, "I strongly urge you to demand the United States Justice Department halt the witch hunt against our FBI, and turn its attention to those who seek to undermine our free nation."[37]

Some of his constituents thought that Church was remarkably naïve in his investigation and in his demand for certain standards of constitutionality from the intelligence agencies. One letter to the editor said:

> You would think he had just discovered that there wasn't a Santa Claus.... All the big boys play with real guns and real money and mean real business. And if we don't play the same way we better fold our tents and go home.[38]

A Coeur d'Alene woman seconded this view: "The communists play every dirty game in the book, so why shouldn't we?"[39]

As was true for many Americans, some Idahoans worried that the Church Committee investigation might jeopardize United States security by publicizing secrets that should remain undisclosed. A Boise man wrote, "As far as I'm concerned one of the surest ways to make sure that a secret becomes public knowledge is to tell it to a Senator!"[40] A resident of St. Anthony noted, "[W]e need an agency through which we can combat the ever growing threat presented by the spread of communism, and the CIA is that agency. I feel it is wrong to put them in the spotlight."[41] Idahoans were not alone in this sentiment. An *Enquirer* reader poll found that the "vast majority ... believe that the publicity being given to secret CIA activities is harming America – and should be stopped."[42]

Not surprisingly, some Idaho objections to Senator Frank Church's chairmanship of the Senate Select Committee to Study Governmental Operations with Respect to Intelligence Activities were more parochial. A Boise resident questioned, "Why don't you exert some effort to solve the problems of your voters in Idaho?" (To which Church bristled, "My record of accomplishments for Idaho speaks for itself."[43])

Equally unsurprising were the complaints that the entire investigatory process was too expensive. One Idahoan complained, "I resent such use of valuable resources when we should be attempting to curtail unnecessary government spending and waste," and added, "As a concerned constituent, I feel that you should know that many of my contemporaries here in Boise feel as I do."[44] Another Idaho voter was more virulent:

> Realize we are sick of being played for stupid taxpayers-consumers-voters-citizens – by a vote-greedy [C]ongress. We want security from excessive taxation and overloading-with-taxes-consumer goods-and-services. And we want our counterintelligence agencies PROTECTED – *Not* Destroyed!!![45]

Senator Church maintained that the Committee had been frugal. He wrote a Boise man, "The entire investigation, which lasted a year and a half, and employed over 100 people was accomplished for under 3 million dollars. I believe that is a small price to pay for protecting the individual liberties of U.S. citizens."[46]

Several Idahoans expressed a stereotypical distrust of the government in Washington, D.C., and indicated that the CIA and other intelligence agencies were probably perfectly correct in investigating members of Congress – of course, without noting the irony that it was the government conducting the covert intelligence gathering? A Coeur d'Alene woman explained:

> They should have files on every Senator and Congressman in the U.S. I don't believe that the people in this great state of Idaho or the U.S. give a tinker's damn as to the Senators and Congressman's sex life but do believe they are interested in knowing who the Communists are and where they are and how soon they plan to take over this great country.[47]

People in Idaho were not certain that there were not subversives in the United States government itself and they were clearly not willing to concede that the United States Senate itself was beyond reproach.

Frank Church's reaction

Senator Frank Church knew what was at stake when he sought the chairmanship of the Senate Select Committee to Study Governmental Operations with Respect to Intelligence Activities. As soon as his appointment became public, Idahoans expressed concern. Church's early response (repeated in most correspondence) explained:

> I regret that we are in disagreement about the necessity of an investigation of the intelligence activities by the Senate. I intend to do the best job I can, fairly and objectively, and would ask that you judge at the end whether the effort has been worthwhile.[48]

Senator Church thought that criticism that preceded the Committee's report was especially troublesome and unwarranted. He did not believe that anyone could or should make a judgment about the Committee's efficacy until the results were published.

Within a couple of months, Church had refined his argument and his position, and he delivered it in numerous letters to his Idaho constituents:

> I will certainly try to conduct the investigation of the FBI and CIA with fairness and objectivity. We do not intend to diminish in any way their ability to protect our national security or to carry out those duties outlined in their respective charters. We do, however, intend to correct any abuses which may exist and to write new legislation where necessary to prevent recurrence of these abuses.[49]

In Church's view, his position was clear-cut and unequivocal. He had absolutely no desire to curtail American intelligence activities completely or to hinder intelligence efforts to protect American security interests. At the same time, he was convinced that the intelligence agencies had become accustomed to acting without oversight, that they resorted to illegal tactics for convenience not for necessity, and that Congress had a responsibility to rectify matters. He told a Paul, Idaho, couple, "I have no intention of dropping our guard against subversion by the Soviet Union or reducing the legitimate needs for intelligence through the work of the committee I head."[50] Church was, however, determined to see the investigation through to its conclusion.

As the investigation began to reveal what Church and others viewed as, at the very least, inappropriate behavior on the part of members of the American intelligence community – behavior that might even be illegal – Frank Church became even more convinced that constitutional governance demanded that all the United States' institutions abide by the country's laws and precepts. He explored this idea in a speech to the San Francisco Commonwealth Club on October 5, 1975 when he declared, "[I]f we are to restore respect for the law to a position of primacy in our society, we will have to begin at the top." He reminded his audience, "Within the federal government, the place to start is with the keepers of the law – those agencies charged with law enforcement and secret intelligence activities. If they won't respect the law, who will?"[51]

Even Church was not beyond being impressed with celebrity. When Bing Crosby (claiming some standing due to his birth in nearby Washington and to the time he spent at his summer home near Hayden Lake) wrote to the Senator regarding this issue, Church urged his staff to make certain he had a "good" letter in response. With staff help, Church crafted an answer that first emphasized the need for the public to know what was happening in government. "I and the other members of the Committee believe in the right of the public to know what the instrumentalities of their Government have done. Our democracy depends upon a well-informed electorate." He continued:

> We on the Committee have considered and rejected the contention that the facts disclosed in the investigation should be kept secret because they are embarrassing to the United States. Despite the temporary injury to our national reputation, the Committee believes that foreign peoples will, upon sober reflection, respect the United States more for keeping faith with its democratic ideal than they will condemn us for the misconduct revealed. I doubt that any other country would have the courage to make such disclosures.[52]

As the Committee completed its work, Senator Frank Church became even more thoughtful. He wrote a long letter to a Boise resident in December 1976:

> It is also my firm belief that we must maintain a strong and viable intelligence service which can counter the activities of the Soviet Union and the other communist nations. But I believe that the best method of countering them abroad is not to imitate their tactics of subversion and deceit but to provide an example of decency and honesty for other countries to emulate.[53]

Church was particularly sensitive to charges that his work with the Senate Select Committee to Study Governmental Operations with Respect to Intelligence Activities was part of a strategy designed to garner him the Democratic Party's presidential nomination. This was a distraction to the entire Committee effort, one that, according to Church Committee staffer Loch Johnson, the Senator recognized from the very outset.[54] An Albion man wrote, "[C]learly for example, as a legislator whose candidacy for higher office is being seriously discussed, you should not have accepted the chairmanship of the special committee to investigate the CIA."[55]

In Church's own words, "I recognize that it's a tightrope. Whatever I do as chairman will be subject to criticism from some quarters." One newspaper explained, "[I]n the end, the committee's work (and his presidential chances) can be judged only on the basis of the reports we issue and the public hearings we conduct."[56] Church wrote one Idahoan, "First, I have publicly stated – repeatedly, for that matter, that I will in no way engage in Presidential politics while serving as Chairman of the Select Committee on Intelligence Activities."[57] On another occasion, he noted:

> As I cannot jeopardize this important assignment by mixing my role as Chairman of such an investigation with any involvement in Presidential politics, I asked those people who have expressed an interest in such a candidacy to call off their efforts on my behalf. This will – and must – remain my position for as long as the investigation lasts.[58]

According to Ashby and Gramer, "Church put his word ahead of his political ambition" when he decided to complete the Committee's work, even though it delayed his announcement and campaign for the presidency.[59]

Most observers lauded the fact that Senator Frank Church and the ranking Republican on the Committee, Texas Senator John Tower, refrained from constant partisanship during the Committee's operation. Some political pundits thought that this united front was only more evidence that Church was using the Committee chairmanship as a springboard to the White House. However, even political columnist David Broder thought this bipartisanship rose above campaign posturing.[60]

Even following the formal announcement of his candidacy for the presidency on March 18, in Idaho City, Church found himself called upon to account for his Committee activities often during the campaign. Johnson later wrote, "Despite the public backlash against the investigation in some quarters, Church revealed with every campaign stop a passionate belief in the importance of intelligence reform."[61] In the final analysis, Church's intelligence investigations clearly harmed whatever chance he had to become a presidential or vice-presidential nominee.

The Church Committee's findings

While the entire investigation attracted broad public attention, there were two particular incidents that warrant mention and particular areas of analysis that Idahoans and people across the country especially discussed. During a post-hearing press briefing, Church wondered if "[t]he agency [Central Intelligence Agency] may have been behaving like a rogue elephant on the rampage." According to one observer, "Government spent years trying to live down 'that damning epithet.'"[62] It is the phrase most often associated with the Church Committee and one that illustrates Church's attitudes toward the CIA. On another occasion, Senator Church brandished a gun that allegedly could be used to deliver poisoned darts. *Time* labeled a photo of Church with the weapon one of the most memorable images of 1975, and that entire line of testimony detracted from many other, more substantive aspects of the investigation.[63]

The Senate Select Committee to Study Government Operations with Respect to Intelligence Activities quickly found the topic of U.S. government efforts to assassinate political opponents to be one of its main areas of focus. Other congressional committees had looked at this issue, including the so-called Rockefeller Commission, but Church described the report of that Committee as being no more than "the tip of the iceberg."[64] In June 1975, he pressed toward public hearings with the assassination question "agenda item A."[65] In what the *Christian Science Monitor* deemed a "temperately written, unanimous 347-page senate report," the six Democrats and five Republicans found a 20-year pattern of United States intelligence involvement in various assassination plots. The paper gushed, "The Senate report may be a best seller. It is believed no other government has published anything like it."[66]

Beyond the assassination report, Idahoans and other Americans were shocked when the Church Committee found that the CIA had widespread access to the domestic mail. According to one study, between 1953 and the time of the Church investigation, the CIA had looked at more than 28 million pieces of mail and had, in fact, opened 215,820 letters. Frank Church said, "I cannot think of a clearer case that illustrates the attitude that the CIA lives outside the law, beyond the law, and that, although others must adhere to it the CIA sits above it and you cannot run a free society that way."[67] For many Americans, the U.S. mail is sacrosanct, and this long-term abuse on the part of the CIA shocked Church and his constituents alike.

Another Church Committee disclosure was that the FBI had attempted to damage Dr. Martin Luther King, Jr.'s reputation. FBI surveillance of King offended Senator Frank Church and concerned his Idaho constituents. As a result of the Select Committee's work, the FBI admitted to a "nationwide, secret, extralegal campaign to disrupt left-of-center and other organizations, of which the six year drive to harass and discredit civil-rights leader Martin Luther King Jr. was the most spectacular." Senator Church described the FBI interactions with King as "the dirty covert attempt to destroy Martin Luther King, Jr.," something Church found to be "particularly abhorrent."[68] The disclosures (now well known) were so troubling to Committee members that the Committee voted not to publish the surveillance tape transcripts because the members did not want to make King's personal life a topic for public scrutiny.[69]

As has been the case since it occurred, the John F. Kennedy assassination seemed to fascinate Idahoans and other Americans. Consequently, it too became a Church Committee topic. Many people in Idaho thought this should not be brought to the fore again. A Nampa man wrote, "I can see no benefits to be gained from reopening the Kennedy Assassination."[70] Even though it was primarily a House of Representatives committee focus, people in the state asked Senator Church to use whatever influence he might have to oppose further investigation. An Athol woman wrote, "Today, I listened to the world news and found that the tax payers were paying over $6 million for an investigation into assignation [*sic*] of King and Kennedy. My question is why is this important, *now*?"[71] However, a Parma constituent urged Senator Church to find out whether or not the CIA had been involved in President Kennedy's death.[72] Church wrote a Moscow, Idaho, woman, "Our Senate Committee did study the Kennedy assassination and could not find evidence that anyone other than Oswald assassinated President Kennedy, but we did find additional information concerning the intelligence agencies' activities during the period which were not reported."[73]

Vaughn Shelton of the *Idaho State Journal* sent a copy of his political cartoon depicting President Kennedy's gravestone with the phrase "Church was here!" scrawled across it in graffiti. Shelton reminded Senator Church that he had sent him evidence concerning the assassination on November 5, 1975, and that Church should have paid attention. He claimed to have evidence that two "star witnesses" had perjured themselves before the Warren Commission. Shelton offered to send the report to Church, if Church would tell him "how to address it to your attention *only*."[74] A number of other Idahoans claimed to have evidence regarding the assassination as well.

Church sought to keep his focus despite the attempts of Idahoans and others to suggest the investigation should go elsewhere. The National Council of Irish Americans was slighted when the Committee did not look into CIA and FBI surveillance of Irish-Americans. Church wrote to Alvin Josephy, Jr., that the Pine Ridge and Rosebud reservation incidents were outside the purview of the Committee. He sent a similar message to People's Temple pastor Jim Jones, who claimed that his church was targeted as a result of its being "an interracial, socially active church."[75]

The Committee conducted over 800 interviews, held 21 public and 350 executive hearings and gathered over 110,000 pages of information.[76] The final report was released in April 1976. The Church Committee's report found that U.S. intelligence agencies had, indeed, acted inappropriately and illegally. "Our findings reflect not isolated occurrences but a pattern in which the Constitution, the statues of the land, and the orders of the President have been ignored all too frequently by the intelligence professionals." Senator Frank Church distributed copies of the reports to people in Idaho who expressed an interest. An Athol woman's response was not atypical:

Thank you for the Intelligence Committee Report you had sent to me. You are to be commended for a very thorough job in exposing the illegal activities of the CIA in foreign governments. Now Senator Church, in the interest of Fair Play and Loyalty to our country, would it not be possible to expose the illegal activities of foreign agents in our domestic affairs? (KGB-GRU).[77]

Another constituent chided Church, "As hard as you tried to beef yourself up at the expense of us tax payers you should see you can't make it nationally without trying to look after the people of Idaho."[78]

Senator Church continued to object to critics who claimed that the Senate Select Committee to Study Governmental Operation with Respect to Intelligence Activities had placed American agents and/or security efforts in jeopardy. He reminded people that "our committee never published the name of any active agent of the intelligence services, here or abroad." He added:

Over the long run this investigation will have strengthened them [intelligence agencies]. A body with a cancerous growth is made healthier by its removal: so, too, will the elimination of the misguided practices of our intelligence agencies make them healthier and stronger.[79]

It is clear that his role in the Committee had mixed results. One Idahoan wrote:

I do not know whether you are aspiring to the Presidential Candidacy or not, but let me tell you that I have talked to many people here at home and they are all dissatisfied with the grandiose way in which you have handled the CIA matter.[80]

Another was more forthright: "Hoping this will help you remember that some of us in Idaho are watching your actions because there will be another election coming up soon."[81]

The *Idaho Statesman* carried columnist James J. Kilpatrick's indictment of the Committee's final report. Kilpatrick deemed it a "Massive Folly" and noted, "What is the first accomplishment of the committee's long investigation and report? It is to belittle the CIA, to stigmatize the honorable men who have served it, and to make the agency's successful performance vastly more difficult." Very critical of Frank Church's approach, Kilpatrick went on to chide:

It is childish, or so it seems to me, to strike the virtuous pose that we must never emulate the Communist techniques. It is not wise, it is stupid, to suggest that the United States should go abroad in a dangerous world, accoutered like Little Lord Fauntleroy, to play patticake [*sic*] with gangs who fight with switch-blade knives.[82]

When a Boise man sent the clipping to Church and asked for comment, Church wrote a two-page letter defending his position. Included was his statement "I do disagree with James J. Kilpatrick when he suggests that we should imitate the Communists' techniques; for if we do that then, as a country, we cannot help but become like them."[83] This was the crux of Church's argument in favor of his Committee's investigations and report, but he nevertheless wrote to a California couple, "Our duty has not been pleasant, but our mandate was clear in Senate Resolution 21."[84]

All of this took on even greater importance when the CIA station chief in Athens, Richard S. Welch, was assassinated on December 23, 1975.[85] Some observers claimed that Welch's murder was just the kind of result one could expect when American intelligence agencies were subjected to public scrutiny and investigation. Johnson was adamant in his opinion that this criticism was totally unfair.[86] Johnson noted that Church took pride in the Committee's ability to keep intelligence agencies' secrets.

Even months after the Church Committee's work had been completed, Idahoans continued to contact Senator Church regarding intelligence issues. Idahoans were especially concerned about the FBI and its investigations of the New Left Weathermen. This was particularly true when FBI employee John J. Kearney was singled out for possible punishment. A Pocatello woman told Church, "If wiretapping and opening the mail of prime suspects is what brought results to stamp out the invidious terrorist schemes, which it did, then this is just fine with me! These agents should be given an award and not punishment."[87] Church responded to a similar letter:

> I agree with you that we need a strong intelligence and law enforcement capability that will protect the average citizen and deter crime. I also believe that the individual rights of those same citizens must be protected. It is important to recognize that all Americans are equally protected under the law.[88]

Over a year after the Committee issued its report, Church worked on a statement regarding Senate efforts to pass legislation designed to reform the intelligence agencies. He reflected:

> Through our new emphasis upon human rights we are returning to those ideals which made our country a beacon of hope for all mankind. I believe that our investigation of the abuse of secret power that had grown up even in this country was a step in the same direction.

He went on to highlight what he viewed as the most extreme examples of misconduct:

> Are we in the Congress going to act to prevent things like: anonymous letters designed to break up marriages of civil rights workers, boasts that the

FBI had secretly caused violence among black gangs, informers placed in the Women's Liberation Movement, break-ins to steal documents, opening the letters of thousands of law-abiding Americans, the use of taps and bugs against many American citizens who our Committee found "posed no criminal or national security threat to the country," the dirty covert attempt to destroy Martin Luther King, Jr., and yes, the misuse of the FBI for political purposes by all administrations of both parties from Franklin Roosevelt's to Richard Nixon's.[89]

In 1979, Church became chairman of the Senate Foreign Relations Committee – a position of considerable power. He took with him his concerns regarding the practices of United States intelligence agencies. He wrote to Pocatello attorney Richard Black:

We need a strong reliable intelligence service that can provide timely analyses of international situations as well as protect us here at home. I am hopeful that the new legislation will assist in curbing the abuses of which you speak and strengthen the intelligence community.[90]

There is little doubt that his very public investigation of the United States' intelligence community negatively impacted Church's 1980 reelection campaign.[91] This, in part, reflected the growing power of the New Right in American politics in general and a definite move to the right for Idaho politics specifically. Conservative groups brought former intelligence agents to Idaho to campaign against Church.[92] As early as 1979, the National Conservative Political Action Committee targeted Church. A NCPAC flyer, "Frank Church's Record of Shame," accused Church of doing irreparable damage to the country through his instigation of "the anti-CIA witch hunt."[93] Church was defeated by some 4,000 votes (less than 1 percent of the total). In such a close election, his well-publicized indictments of American intelligence efforts impacted his ability to garner sufficient Idaho votes to retain his senate seat.

Conclusion

Despite the passage of more than a quarter of a century since the appearance of the Senate Select Committee to Study Governmental Operations with Respect to Intelligence Activities' report, assessing its place in United States history continues to be complicated.

Even at the time the report was released, *Newsweek* reported, "Yet even as the report was making headlines last week, there were strong indications that a public atmosphere conducive to any far-reaching reform of the nation's intelligence community had all but vanished."[94] While Americans might have expressed temporary shock or dismay regarding intelligence agencies' activities, it was difficult to maintain the public interest.

There were a number of key individuals who were critical of the Church

Committee at the time and continued to voice that opinion. President Gerald R. Ford maintained, "The Church probe was sensational and irresponsible." Senator John Tower, the ranking Republican member, maintained in his political memoir, "We did succeed in controlling some of the damage, however, the repercussions of the Church Committee's misguided zeal are still being felt today."[95]

Many scholars applaud Church's work with the Select Committee to Study Governmental Operations with Respect to Intelligence Activities. They especially laud the fact that the Committee brought difficult issues to the public's attention. Rhodri Jeffreys-Jones called it "[t]he most extensive debate ever undertaken on the role of intelligence in a democracy, and on the relationship between the two." He went on to claim:

> The result was a wider comprehension of the CIA and its work – a valuable, if incomplete educative process that more than compensated for the discomfiture and demoralization of the CIA personnel at the time. Many people now agreed on the need for covert-operational guidelines, for the legitimization of objective intelligence, and for enhanced status for the CIA director. Democracy had triumphed over the impediments of secrecy, partisanship, and opportunism.[96]

James Patterson described the Church Committee Report as "impressive."[97] Ashby and Gramer maintained that Church's investigation of the intelligence community represented some of his "finest hours."[98] And John Prados has recognized that "The fundamental issue was to balance the requirements for secrecy with those of American democracy."[99]

In the short term, Church lost several battles. When President Gerald R. Ford named George H.W. Bush to head the CIA, he was confirmed despite Church's questions and objections.[100] In this sense, Church had not persuaded the Senate of the gravity of the Committee's revelations. More poignantly, Church's leadership of the Committee negatively impacted his political future. In the long term, the historical significance of the Committee cannot be denied. The Church Committee's work led to a number of fundamental pieces of legislation that reshaped the intelligence landscape in America and provided a greater measure of oversight.

The similarity between Idahoans' responses to the Church Committee over 30 years ago and Americans' responses to security issues confronting the United States today might be the Committee's most important legacy.[101] It would be a simple task to substitute current members of the United States Senate for Church and to apply the arguments Idahoans made – both pro and con – to current discussions of American intelligence. The questions Church and the Committee explored continue to be asked today. Who controls American democracy? How should national security by defined? How can the United States' need for security be balanced with the requirement that the U.S. Constitution and all it represents be followed? Idahoans identified the key issues in 1975, and continue to debate them today. The Church Committee provides an exemplary model for how that debate might be conducted while balancing an earnest commitment to constitutional governance and recognition of the need to provide security.

Notes

1 John Prados, *Presidents' Secret Wars: CIA and Pentagon Covert Operations since World War II* 321, 326 (1986).
2 Seymour Hersh, Huge C.I.A. Operation Reported in U.S. against Antiwar Forces, Other Dissidents During Nixon Years, *New York Times*, Dec. 22, 1974, at 1. See Frank J. Smist, Jr., *Congress Oversees the United States Intelligence Community, 1947–1994*, at 261 (1994).
3 *Senate Approves Investigation of CIA, FBI*, 33 *Congressional Quarterly Weekly Report* 240, 242 (1975) (profiling the Church Committee members).
4 LeRoy Ashby and Rod Gramer, *Fighting the Odds: The Life of Senator Frank Church* 472 (1994).
5 Senator Frank Church News Release (Feb. 27, 1975) (on file with the Frank Church Collection, MSS 56, Boise State University, Series 2.6, Box 1, Folder 1) [hereinafter referred to as Church Collection, Series *X*, Box *Y*, Folder *Z*].
6 See Seamon in this volume (Chapter 8).
7 Ashby and Gramer, *supra* note 4, at 44.
8 *Face the Nation* (CBS television broadcast, Feb. 2, 1975). The typescript of this interview is also available on file in the Church Collection at Boise State University, Series 2.6, Box 2, Folder 1.
9 Letter from Frank Church, Senator from Idaho, to W.E. Hansen, Boise, Idaho resident (Aug. 8, 1975) (on file with the Church Collection, Series 2.6, Box 2, Folder 2).
10 Letter from Scott Blackburn, Pacatello, Idaho, resident, to Frank Church, Senator from Idaho (Feb. 17, 1975) (on file with the Church Collection, Series 2.6, Box 1, Folder 1).
11 Letter from Grady Spradling, Buhl, Idaho, resident, to Frank Church, Senator from Idaho (Feb. 10, 1975) (on file with the Church Collection, Series 2.6, Box 1, Folder 1).
12 Letter from Kenneth H. Parks, Fairfield, Wash, resident, to Frank Church, Senator from Idaho (Feb. 20, 1975) (on file with the Church Collection, Series 2.6, Box 1, Folder 1).
13 Letter from Mic Watson, Hayden Lake, Idaho, resident, to Frank Church, Senator from Idaho (Apr. 26, 1975) (on file with the Church Collection, Series 2.6, Box 1, Folder 2).
14 Letter from M.E. Orr, Coeur d'Alene, Idaho, resident, to Frank Church, Senator from Idaho (Feb. 20, 1975) (on file with the Church Collection, Series 2.6, Box 1, Folder 1).
15 Letter from Dennis Raciot, Deary, Idaho, resident, to Frank Church, Senator from Idaho (on file with the Church Collection, Series 2.6, Box 1, Folder 2).
16 YMCA Youth Legislature 1975 Resolution (on file with the Church Collection, Series 2.6, Box 1, Folder 2).
17 Letter from Eleanor Swatsenbarg, Idaho Falls, Idaho, resident, to Frank Church, Senator from Idaho (Feb. 11, 1975) (on file with the Church Collection, Series 2.6, Box 1, Folder 1).
18 Letter from Mrs. Everett R. Simpson, Mountain Home, Idaho, resident, to Frank Church, Senator from Idaho (Oct. 23, 1975) (on file with the Church Collection, Series 2.6, Box 1, Folder 4).
19 Letter from Janet Rogers, Boise, Idaho, resident, to Frank Church, Senator from

Idaho (Jan. 21, 1975) (on file with the Church Collection, Series 2.6, Box 1, Folder 1).

20 Letter from Mrs. Lorene Brainard, Idaho Falls, Idaho, resident, to Frank Church, Senator from Idaho (Feb. 3, 1975) (on file with the Church Collection, Series 2.6, Box 1, Folder 1).

21 Letter from E.G. McCallum, Idaho Falls, Idaho, resident, to Frank Church, Senator from Idaho (Feb. 1975) (on file with the Church Collection, Series 2.6, Box 1, Folder 1).

22 Letter from Hugh O. Smith, Harrison, Idaho, resident, to Frank Church, Senator from Idaho (Mar. 1, 1976) (on file with the Church Collection, Series 2.6, Box 1, Folder 4).

23 Letter from David Marron, Twin Falls, Idaho, resident, to Frank Church, Senator from Idaho, (July 28, 1976) (on file with the Church Collection, Series 2.6, Box 2, Folder 3).

24 Letter from Melvin Harris, Macks Inn, Idaho, resident, to Frank Church, Senator from Idaho (Jan. 10, 1976) (on file with the Church Collection, Series 2.6, Box 1, Folder 4).

25 James Kilpatrick, CIA Report Called "Massive Folly," *Idaho Statesman* (on file with the Church Collection, Series 2.6, Box 1, Folder 7).

26 Letter from W.R. Smith, Boise, Idaho, resident, to Frank Church, Senator from Idaho (Aug. 23, 1976) (on file with the Church Collection, Series 2.6, Box 1, Folder 5).

27 Letter from Clifton Dixon, Gooding, Idaho, resident, to Frank Church, Senator from Idaho (May 9, 1977) (on file with the Church Collection, Series 2.6, Box 1, Folder 9).

28 Letter from Helen Bryngelson and John Bryngelson, Rupert, Idaho, residents, to Frank Church, Senator from Idaho (Jan. 30, 1975) (on file with the Church Collection, Series 2.6, Box 1, Folder 1).

29 Letter from Lorene Brainard, Idaho Falls, Idaho, resident, to Frank Church, Senator from Idaho (Feb. 3, 1975) (on file with the Church Collection, Series 2.6, Box 1, Folder 1).

30 Letter from Mr. and Mrs. Melvin Rosa, Paul, Idaho, residents, to Frank Church, Senator from Idaho (Aug. 19, 1975) (on file with the Church Collection, Series 2.6, Box 1, Folder 2).

31 Letter from Katie Lintelman, Hagerman, Idaho, resident, to Frank Church, Senator from Idaho (Feb. 3, 1975).

32 Letter from Claude Andrews, Fruitland, Idaho, resident, to Frank Church, Senator from Idaho (Jan. 31, 1975) (on file with the Church Collection, Series 2.6, Box 1, Folder 1).

33 Letter from Mrs. Frank Neilsen, Coeur d'Alene, Idaho, resident, to Frank Church, Senator from Idaho (on file with the Church Collection, Series 2.6, Box 1, Folder 1).

34 Letter from R.B. Van Sice, Idaho Falls, Idaho, resident, to Frank Church, Senator from Idaho; James McClure, Senator from Idaho; George Hansen, Representative from Idaho; and Steve Symms, Representative from Idaho (Apr. 17, 1977) (on file with the Church Collection, Series 2.6, Box 1, Folder 4).

35 Letter from Jack Streeter, Mountain Home, Idaho, resident, to Frank Church, Senator from Idaho (July 14, 1978) (on file with the Church Collection, Series 2.6, Box 1, Folder 2).

36 Letter from Edda B. McDaniel, Pocatello, Idaho, resident, to Frank Church, Senator from Idaho (Apr. 12, 1977) (on file with the Church Collection, Series 2.6, Box 1, Folder 9).

37 See generally Boise State University Church Collection, Series 2.6, Box 1, Folder 9.

38 *Idaho Statesman* letter to the editor from Jack Streeter (on file with the Church Collection, Series 2.6, Box 1, Folder 2).

39 Letter from Mrs. Frank Nielsen, Coeur d'Alene, Idaho, resident, to Frank Church, Senator from Idaho (Feb.18, 1975) (on file with the Church Collection, Series 2.6, Box 1, Folder 1).

40 Letter from R.R. Phillips, Boise, Idaho, resident, to Frank Church, Senator from Idaho (May 16, 1975) (on file with the Church Collection, Series 2.6, Box 1, Folder 2).

41 Letter from Paul Birch, St. Anthony, Idaho, resident, to Frank Church, Senator from Idaho (Dec. 24, 1975) (on file with the Church Collection, Series 2.6, Box 1, Folder 4).

42 Letter from Mr. and Mrs. W.T. McKinney, San Diego, Calif., resident to Frank Church, Senator from Idaho (May 19, 1976) (enclosing newspaper article entitled *Latest Results of* Enquirer *Poll: 90% Believe Publicizing of Secret CIA Activities Should Be Stopped*) (on file with the Church Collection, Series 2.6, Box 1, Folder 4).

43 Letter from Verl Kersey, Boise, Idaho, resident, to Frank Church, Senator from Idaho (Jan. 18, 1975) (on file with the Church Collection, Series 2.6, Box 1, Folder 1); letter from Frank Church, Senator from Idaho, to Verl Kersey, Boise, Idaho, resident (Feb. 6, 1975) (on file with the Church Collection, Series 2.6, Box 1, Folder 1).

44 Letter from James Maloney, Boise, Idaho, resident, to Frank Church, Senator from Idaho (Jan. 29, 1975) (on file with the Church Collection, Series 2.6, Box 1, Folder 1).

45 Letter from Lewis Bonner, Boise, Idaho, resident, to Frank Church, Senator from Idaho (Nov. 25, 1975) (on file with the Church Collection, Series 2.6, Box 1, Folder 3).

46 Letter from Frank Church, Senator from Idaho, to James Malone, Boise, Idaho, resident (Dec. 14, 1976) (on file with the Church Collection, Series 2.6, Box 1, Folder 7).

47 Letter from Mrs. Frank Nielsen, *supra* note 39.

48 Letter from Frank Church, Senator from Idaho, to Lucille Johnson, Burley, Idaho, resident (Mar. 5, 1975) (on file with the Church Collection, Series 2.6, Box 1, Folder 1).

49 See, e.g., letter from Frank Church, Senator from Idaho, to Mrs. Frank Nielsen, Coeur d'Alene, Idaho, resident (Mar. 5, 1975) (on file with the Church Collection, Series 2.6, Box 1, Folder 1).

50 Letter from Frank Church, Senator from Idaho, to Mr. and Mrs. Melvin Rosa, Paul, Idaho, residents (Sept. 12, 1975) (on file with the Church Collection, Series 2.6, Box 1, Folder 2).

51 A Clean US: Start at Top, *San Francisco Sunday Examiner & Chronicle*, Oct. 5, 1975, at A17.

52 Interoffice memorandum from Frank Church to his staff ("Please prepare *good* reply, FC") (on file with the Church Collection, Series 2.6, Box 1, Folder 2); letter from Frank Church, Senator from Idaho, to Bing Crosby (Jan. 9, 1976) (on file with the Church Collection, Series 2.6, Box 1, Folder 2).

53 Letter from Frank Church, Senator from Idaho, to James E. Maloney, Jr., Boise, Idaho, resident (Dec. 14, 1976) (on file with the Church Collection, Series 2.6, Box 1, Folder 7).

54 Loch K. Johnson, *A Season of Inquiry: The Senate Intelligence Investigation* 16–17 (1985).

55 Letter from Ralph Orlett, Albion, Idaho, resident, to Frank Church, Senator from Idaho (Mar. 17, 1975) (on file with the Church Collection, Series 2.6, Box 1, Folder 1).

56 No Presidential Politics – Now, *San Francisco Sunday Examiner & Chronicle*, Oct. 5, 1975, at A17.

57 Letter from Frank Church, Senator from Idaho, to Verl Kersey, Boise, Idaho, resident (Feb. 6, 1975) (on file with the Church Collection, Series 2.6, Box 1, Folder 1).

58 Letter from Frank Church, Senator from Idaho, to Ralph Orlett, Albion, Idaho, resident (Mar. 17, 1975) (on file with the Church Collection, Series 2.6, Box 1, Folder 1).

59 Ashby and Gramer, *supra* note 4, at 486.

60 David Broder, When No News Is Good News, *Washington Post*, Feb. 23, 1975.

61 Johnson, *supra* note 54, at 61.

62 Prados, *supra* note 1, at 337.

63 Smist, *supra* note 2, at 66. See *Time*, Jan. 5, 1976, at 107.

64 *Newsweek*, June 23, 1975, at 16.

65 The Cloak Comes Off, *Newsweek*, June 1, 1975.

66 Richard L. Strait, FBI-CIA Disclosures Evoke New Public Doubts, *Christian Science Monitor*, Nov. 4, 1975, at 4.

67 *Intelligence Activities: Mail Openings* (Vol. 4), S. Res. 21, 94th Cong. 24 (1975).

68 *Christian Science Monitor*, Nov. 24, 1975 (on file with the Church Collection, Series 2.6, Box 1, Folder 9); Letter from Frank Church, Senator from Idaho, to Joseph Galligan, San Bruno, Calif., resident (Jan. 23, 1976) (on file with the Church Collection, Series 2.6, Box 1, Folder 3).

69 John G. Tower, *Consequences: A Personal and Political Memoir* 137 (1991).

70 Letter from R.G. Larson, Nampa, Idaho, resident, to Frank Church, Senator from Idaho (May 13, 1976) (on file with the Church Collection, Series 2.6, Box 1, Folder 4).

71 Letter from Janey Swain, Athol, Idaho, resident, to Frank Church, Senator from Idaho (Jan. 1, 1977) (on file with the Church Collection, Series 2.6, Box 1, Folder 8).

72 Letter from Gertrude Obendorf, Parma, Idaho, resident, to Frank Church, Senator from Idaho (Jan. 31, 1975) (on file with the Church Collection, Series 2.6, Box 1, Folder 1).

73 Letter from Frank Church, Senator from Idaho, to Mrs. W.R. Parish, Moscow, Idaho, resident (Dec. 21, 1976) (on file with the Church Collection, Series 2.6, Box 1, Folder 7).

74 Letter from Vaughn Shelton, *Idaho State Journal* cartoonist, to Frank Church, Senator from Idaho (Feb. 20, 1977) (on file with the Church Collection, Series 2.6, Box 1, Folder 8).

75 Letter from William Driscoll, Press Officer, National Council of Irish Americans, to Frank Church, Senator from Idaho (May 11, 1976) (on file with the Church Collection, Series 2.6, Box 1, Folder 4); letter from Frank Church, Senator from Idaho, to Alvin Josephy, Jr. (Jan. 5, 1976) (on file with the Church Collection, Series 2.6, Box 1, Folder 6); letter from Frank Church, Senator from Idaho, to Richard D. Trapp, Executive Assistant to the Pastor, People's Temple of the Disciples of Christ (Nov. 18, 1976) (on file with the Church Collection, Series 2.6, Box 1, Folder 7).

76 Rhodri Jeffreys-Jones, *The CIA and American Democracy* 214 (1989); Prados, *supra* note 1, at 336.

77 Letter from Florence Fuller, Athol, Idaho, resident, to Frank Church, Senator from Idaho (Feb. 10, 1976) (on file with the Church Collection, Series 2.6, Box 1, Folder 4).

78 Letter from W.R. Smith, *supra* note 26.

79 Letter from Frank Church, Senator from Idaho, to Stewart R. Horn, Burbank, Calif., resident (May 20, 1976) (on file with the Church Collection, Series 2.6, Box 1, Folder 4).

80 Letter from Melvin L. Harris, *supra* note 24.

81 Letter from W.E. Hanson, Boise, Idaho, resident, to Frank Church, Senator from Idaho (July 24, 1975) (on file with the Church Collection, Series 2.6, Box 1, Folder 2).

82 Kilpatrick, *supra* note 25.

83 Letter from Frank Church, Senator from Idaho, to James Maloney, Jr., Boise, Idaho, resident (Dec. 14, 1976) (on file with the Church Collection, Series 2.6, Box 1, Folder 7).

84 Letter from Frank Church, Senator from Idaho, to Mr. and Mrs. W.T. McKinney, San Diego, Calif., residents (May 31, 1976) (on file with the Church Collection, Series 2.6, Box 1, Folder 4).

85 See Hart in this volume (Chapter 2).

86 Johnson, *supra* note 54, at 161; Ashby and Gramer, *supra* note 4, at 485; Smist, *supra* note 2, at 64–65; *The CIA & the Security Debate: 1975–1976*, at 142–47 (Judith F. Buncher *et al.*, eds., 1977).

87 Letter from Edda McDaniel, *supra* note 36.

88 Letter from Frank Church, Senator from Idaho, to Gerald Hawkes, Pocatello, Idaho, resident (May 2, 1977) (on file with the Church Collection, Series 2.6, Box 1, Folder 9).

89 Draft of Church speech (July 12, 1977) (on file with the Church Collection, Series 2.6, Box 1, Folder 9).

90 Letter from Frank Church, Senator from Idaho, to Richard Black (Dec. 7, 1978) (on file with the Church Collection, Series 2.6, Box 1, Folder 10).

91 Smist, *supra* note 2, at 33.

92 Johnson, *supra* note 54, at 277.

93 Ashby and Gramer, *supra* note 4, at 580.

94 Inquest on Intelligence, *Newsweek*, May 10, 1976, at 40.

95 Gerald R. Ford, *A Time to Heal: The Autobiography of Gerald R. Ford* 265 (1979); Tower, *supra* note 69, at 133.

96 Jeffreys-Jones, *supra* note 76, at 215.

97 Thomas G. Patterson, *Meeting the Communist Threat: Truman to Reagan* 248 (1988).

98 Ashby and Gramer, *supra* note 4, at 490.

99 Prados, *supra* note 1, at 337.

100 Jeffreys-Jones, *supra* note 76, at 210.

101 Scott Shane, For Some, Spying Controversy Recalls a Past Drama, *New York Times*, Feb. 6, 2006, at A18.

Part II

Contemporary issues of national security, intelligence and democracy

7   George Bush, the unitary executive and the Constitution

David Gray Adler

[Y]our President may easily become king.

Patrick Henry[1]

Introduction

Neither Julius Caesar nor his fellow Romans could have grasped the full implications for the Republic of his decision to cross the Rubicon. "A Roman," it has been observed, could not have "conceive[d] of the Republic's collapse," and all that was associated with it – the ancient liberties of free speech and private property, a thousand years of self-government, and the rule of law itself.[2] If the restoration of the Republic proved equally elusive, the explanations for its demise have found a measure of agreement. Gibbon has famously written, "The principles of a free constitution are irrevocably lost, when the legislative power is dominated by the executive."[3]

Has America, under the leadership of George W. Bush, approached the banks of the Rubicon? It may be fairly remarked that the extraordinary concentration of power in the hands of President Bush is pregnant with menace. The Bush administration has advanced a theory of executive supremacy, particularly in matters of war and foreign relations, that has reduced Congress and the courts to the role of spectator and has launched the executive on a trajectory toward the realm of unchecked, unfettered power.[4]

In his capacity as a wartime executive who advocates the theory of a "unitary presidency," President George W. Bush has adduced, in the name of national security, broad authority under the banner of inherent presidential power, the commander in chief clause, and the sole organ doctrine in terms that vitiate the doctrines of separation of powers and checks and balances.[5] The President, according to the Bush administration, may initiate preventive war without authorization from Congress. As commander in chief, he has the sole and exclusive authority to conduct war. Congressional directions and instructions are invidious, constitute micromanagement, and represent an encroachment on presidential power. The President may institute domestic surveillance of Americans' telephone calls and e-mails as part and parcel of his authority to wage war on terrorism. Statutes in conflict with the President's policies represent a violation of executive authority. It is contended that the President may designate, seize and detain any American citizen as an "enemy combatant" and imprison him or her in solitary confinement, indefinitely, without access to legal counsel and a judicial hearing. The Constitution, it has been asserted, provides no right of habeas corpus to American citizens. It is maintained, moreover, that the President possesses the authority to suspend the Geneva Convention and the federal laws that prohibit torture. Among other powers asserted, the President, as commander in chief, may establish military tribunals, terminate treaties, order acts of extraordinary rendition, and take actions that he perceives as necessary to the maintenance of national security and the common defense. Under this theory, any law that restricts the commander in chief's authority is presumptively unconstitutional. At all events, the President may exercise an "override" authority in the unlikely event that Congress would, by statute, seek to restrain the President. Courts have no role to play in matters of war and peace, but if they do entertain lawsuits, they should defer to the President and refrain from second-guessing his foreign policy.[6]

In the wake of the 2006 midterm elections, which saw the Democrats capture control of both houses of Congress, it might have been reasonable to assume that the Bush White House would be suffused with humility and that the President might temper his claims to power. With a little more than a year left in the Bush presidency, however, there was no evidence of a retreat from the high-flying conceptions of power that had been trumpeted with confidence. The Bush administration has continued to brandish the concept of the "Unitary Presidency" and its soaring assertions of executive power. It has asserted as "absolute" the presidential power to remove U.S. attorneys, which unleashed a firestorm of controversy.[7] As a means of defending that "absolute" power, the President adduced an "outlandish" version of executive privilege to prevent White House aides, former aides, and Justice Department officials from answering questions posed by members of the House Judiciary Committee and the Senate Judiciary Committee investigating firings.[8] When committee chairs threatened to hold these reluctant witnesses in contempt of Congress, the Bush administration announced that it would prohibit the Justice Department from enforcing the contempt charges. With this maneuver, President Bush erected a firewall around the White House that placed administration officials beyond the reach of Congress and diminished executive-branch accountability.[9] And the administration, it bears reminder, has not brooked criticism; indeed, various officials have sought to intimidate critics and characterize dissidents as "unpatriotic." Criticism, it has been said, has served the cause of terrorism. In July 2007, Senator Hillary Clinton was upbraided by Undersecretary of Defense Eric Edelman for publicly recommending a partial withdrawal of troops from Iraq. In a letter to Senator Clinton, Edelman warned that such discussion "reinforces enemy propaganda."[10]

With the possible exception of Richard Nixon, no American president has asserted such a thoroughly Cromwellian view of executive power.[11] And that may be unfair to Nixon. Former Nixon White House Counsel John Dean, an outspoken critic of the Bush administration, has aptly characterized the Bush White House as "Worse than Watergate."[12] Bruce Fein, a former Reagan Justice Department attorney and an ardent critic of the Bush administration, has perceived, in the Bush theory of presidential power, a distressing agenda: "It's part of an attempt to create the idea that during conflicts, the three branches of government collapse into one, and it is the president."[13] The sheer breadth of the aggregate powers asserted and the Machiavellian tendencies of the Bush Administration, with its apparent, though unarticulated, embrace of the philosophy that "the ends justify the means," threatens to render the Constitution superfluous – an obstructive and cursed scrap of paper. Its disdain for constitutional government may be glimpsed in the remarks of then-White House Counsel and one-time U.S. Attorney General Alberto Gonzales, who declared, in the midst of the revelations in the "Torture Memos" of cruel and inhumane treatment of prisoners in Abu Ghraib, that concerns about constitutional principles in the context of the "War on Terrorism" are "quaint."[14]

The Bush administration's theory of executive supremacy, one that derives power from necessity and justification from the climate of crisis – real or imagined – represents a grave threat to the republic and the rule of law. And, extreme though the present case may be, one of the great lessons of the Church Committee is that the threat to constitutional government from an overreaching executive has long been with us and transcends political parties.[15] The other great lesson of the Church Committee, of course, is that we must demand vigilance and accountability from those institutions charged with providing it, not only in the context of a protracted or chronic war – which is how the "War on Terror" is perceived – but at all times.

The place to start, then, is with an analysis of the planks and pillars of President Bush's platform of power. Bush's assertion of sweeping executive authority, anchored in the theory of inherent or prerogative powers, has greatly diminished executive accountability – an issue that absorbed the Church Committee. I will then turn to the centrality of the rule of law in the American democracy and the means by which it may be restored to a position of prominence. The historic work of the Church Committee provides a model for what must be done.

Inherent executive powers

The Bush administration has maintained that the Constitution vests in the President sweeping powers to conduct the nation's foreign affairs, including inherent power as chief executive and commander in chief to order the use of military force to advance and defend America's security interests. Two weeks after the September 11, 2001 terrorist attacks in the United States, John Yoo, an attorney in the Office of Legal Counsel, wrote a memorandum in which he concluded:

[T]he Constitution vests the President with the plenary authority, as Commander in Chief and sole organ of the Nation in its foreign relations, to use military force abroad – especially in response to grave National emergencies created by sudden, unforeseen attacks on the people and territory of the United States.[16]

Using English history as a basis, Yoo had earlier written:

[T]he Framers created a framework designed to encourage presidential initiative in war. Congress was given a role in war-making decisions not by the Declare War Clause, but by its power over funding and impeachment. In addition, federal courts were to have no role at all.[17]

There is in the Yoo Memorandum the voice of the Stuart monarchy.

In the early stages of the "War on Terror," attorneys in the Bush administration more specifically adduced sweeping inherent presidential powers to create military commissions,[18] to designate American citizens as "enemy combatants,"[19] to engage in "extraordinary rendition,"[20] to order domestic surveillance,[21] to justify torture as a lawful means of interrogation,[22] and to terminate and suspend treaties.[23] The administration's exorbitant claims of executive authority in the realm of foreign relations are betrayed by the text of the Constitution and its design for foreign affairs, and by the intentions of the Framers, who rejected executive unilateralism.

The Framers might have adopted the English model for reasons of familiarity, tradition and simplicity as a means of promoting and securing its vaunted values of unity, secrecy and dispatch – but they did not. Like other nations, Britain concentrated virtually unfettered authority over foreign policy in the hands of the executive. The Framers, of course, were thoroughly familiar with both the vast foreign affairs powers that inhered in the English Crown by virtue of the royal prerogative, and the values, sentiments and policy concerns that justified this arrangement. In his *Second Treatise of Government*, John Locke described three powers of government: the legislative, the executive and the federative. Federative power was the power over foreign affairs – "the power of war and peace, leagues and alliances, and all the transactions with all person and communities without the Commonwealth." The federative power was "almost always united" with the executive. Locke warned that the separation of executive and federative powers would invite "disorder and ruin."[24]

In light of Locke's admonitions, the Constitutional Convention's rejection of the English model, and the inherent unbridled and discretionary authority wielded by the King, could not have been more emphatic. Its penchant for enumeration of powers, as a method of avoiding doubts on the repository of key powers and protection against executive claims of inherent power, was ably explained by Madison in *The Federalist No. 45*: "The powers *delegated* by the proposed constitution are *few and defined* ... [they] will be exercised principally on *external* objects, as war, peace, negotiations, and foreign commerce."[25] The Framers' blueprint for foreign affairs reflects their determination to establish a republic that is grounded on collective decision making, a principle that reflects confidence in the crossfire of discussion and debate as a method for producing superior laws, policies and programs. The preference for collective, rather than unilateral, decision making runs throughout the constitutional provisions that govern American foreign policy. The Constitution assigns to Congress senior status in a partnership with the President for the purpose of conducting foreign policy. Article I vests in Congress: broad, explicit, and exclusive powers to regulate foreign commerce; raise and maintain military forces; grant letters of marque and reprisal; provide for the common defense; and initiate hostilities on behalf of the United States, including full-blown war. As Article II indicates, the President shares with the Senate the treaty-making power and the authority to appoint ambassadors. The Constitution exclusively assigns two foreign affairs powers to the President. He is designated commander in chief of the nation's armed forces, although, as we shall see, he acts in this capacity by and under the authority of Congress. The President also has the power to receive ambassadors, but the Framers viewed this as a routine administrative function, devoid of discretionary authority.[26] This list exhausts the textual grant of foreign affairs authority to Congress and the President. The President's constitutional powers are few and modest, and they pale in comparison to those vested in Congress. The American arrangement for the conduct of the nation's foreign affairs bears no resemblance to the English model. In fact, the convention discarded the British model as obsolete and inapplicable to the republican manners of the United States. Hamilton captured this sentiment in *The Federalist No. 75*:

> The history of human conduct does not warrant that exalted opinion of human virtue which would make it wise in a nation to commit interests of so delicate and momentous a kind, as those which concern its intercourse with the rest of the world, to the sole disposal of a magistrate created and circumstanced as would be a president of the United States.[27]

The Founders' deep-seated fear of the abuse of power, which resonated from the colonial period and reflected their reading of history, made the quest for an effective foreign affairs system an arduous task. The pervasive fear of a powerful executive, particularly a President who might wield unilateral authority in an area as sensitive and critical as that of foreign relations, was reinforced by the republican ideology that permeated the Convention. The Framers' attachment to collective judgment – joint participation, consultation and concurrence – and their decision to create a structure of shared powers in foreign affairs provided, in the words of James Wilson, "a security to the people."[28] The emphasis on collective decision making came at the expense of unilateral presidential authority, of course, but that consequence was of little moment, given the Founders' overriding aversion to unrestrained executive power. But that was the point, precisely. The Framers contrived a new constitutional arrangement for foreign affairs – a distinctively American contribution to politics and political science – and it was epitomized in their judgment that, in the newly minted Republican Era, the executive unilateralism exalted by prevailing models was a shopworn, outdated method that belonged to an age and a means of governance that they had rejected and discarded. The assertion of a constitutional design for foreign affairs that exalts presidential power is constitutionally untenable and wilts in the face of historical evidence.

The Bush administration's assertions of inherent executive power in the realm of war and foreign affairs, including the authority to "override" statutes, essentially the Stuart Monarchs' claim of a suspending power, are deeply troubling and without constitutional warrant. Manifestly, they are not confined to the Hamiltonian indulgence of presidential authority to act in the *absence* of legislation, as seen in the claim of Pacificus that President George Washington possessed the constitutional power to declare neutrality and thus keep the nation out of war *until Congress chooses war or peace.* Rather, legal advisers to President Bush have embraced a bolder, more virulent species of inherent power than that ever advanced by Hamilton. If we shake out the weasel words of the Administration's position, the President's inherent executive power is broad enough, on the premise of a "commander in chief override authority," to *defy* the law if he perceives it necessary to meet the nation's security needs.[29]

Does the Constitution confer upon the President authority to violate the law? Is there, indeed, room in the Constitution for governmental actors to defy the instrument from which they derive their authority? Assertions of an executive authority to trample constitutional restraints invites Chief Justice John Marshall's rejoinder in *Marbury* v. *Madison*: "To what purpose are powers limited, and to what purpose is that limitation committed to writing, if these limits may, at any time, be passed by those intended to be restrained?"[30] Alexander Hamilton, the darling of executive enthusiasts, *never* in his career urged a presidential power to violate the law. Indeed, he rejected such an assertion: "[A] delegated authority cannot alter the constituting act, unless so expressly authorized by the constituting power. An agent cannot new model his commission."[31] Is it possible for governmental officials to swear an oath to uphold the Constitution and at the same time to ignore its provisions or assert the authority to violate the Constitution and the laws of the land? May a President who perceives a grave emergency invoke inherent authority to stay in office for six years rather than four? If so, where is the constitutional repository for such authority? There is, in this line of inquiry, a question of fundamental importance for constitutional government: Is there authority, drawn from some nook or cranny, for the proposition that in times of emergency or crisis a new set of legal norms may be invoked to replace constitutional principles enshrined as the rule of law? That is the threshold question, certainly, given that the Bush administration's assertion of an inherent power represents, essentially, the claim of an executive power to improvise legislation. Does the President possess a revisory power?

Advocates of an inherent presidential power have sought, primarily, to ground presidential prerogative in the Vesting Clause. Their assertions, however, find no support in the text of Constitution, the debates in Philadelphia, the discussions of various state ratifying conventions, or contemporaneous writings. The Vesting Clause provides that "[t]he executive Power shall be vested in a President of the United States of America." The question of whether this provision will bear the weight assigned it may be illuminated by what the delegates to the Constitutional Convention actually said. It is instructive as well to recall the understanding of the term "executive power" on the eve of the Convention. The renowned legal historian Julius Goebel observed:

> "[E]xecutive," as a noun ... was not then a word of art in English law – above all it was not so in reference to the Crown. It had become a word of art in American law through its employment in various state constitutions adopted from 1776 onward.... It reflected ... the revolutionary response to the situation precipitated by the repudiation of the royal prerogative.[32]

The use of the word "prerogative," as Robert Scigliano has demonstrated, was, among the Founders, a term of derision – a political shaft intended to taint an opponent with the stench of monarchism.[33] The rejection of the use of the word "prerogative" in favor of the new and more republic-friendly noun "executive" necessitated discussion and explanation of its scope and content.

The provisions of the state constitutions conveniently frame and illustrate the meager scope of authority granted to state executives. In his 1783 work *Draft of a Fundamental Constitution for Virginia*, Thomas Jefferson stated:

> By Executive powers, we mean no reference to the powers exercised under our former government by the Crown as of its prerogative.... We give them these powers only, which are necessary to execute the laws (and administer the government).[34]

This understanding of "executive power" and its implementation were reflected in the Virginia Plan, which Edmund Randolph introduced to the Constitutional Convention, and which provided for a "national executive ... with power to carry into execution the national laws ... [and] to appoint to offices in cases not otherwise provided for."[35] For the Framers, the phrase "executive power" was limited, as James Wilson said, to "executing the laws, and appointing officers."[36] Roger Sherman "considered the Executive magistracy as nothing more than an institution for carrying the will of the Legislature into effect."[37] Madison agreed with Wilson's definition of executive power. He thought it necessary "to fix the extent of Executive authority ... as certain powers were in their nature Executive, and must be given to that departmt [*sic*]," and added that "a definition of their extent would assist the judgment in determining how far they might be safely entrusted to a single officer."[38] The definition of the executive's authority should be precise, thought Madison; the executive power "[should] be confined and defined."[39] And so it was.

To the extent that there was a debate on "executive power," it centered almost entirely on the question of whether there should be a single or a plural presidency. There was no challenge to the definition of executive power held by Wilson, Sherman and Madison, nor was an alternative understanding advanced.

Moreover, there was no argument about the scope of executive power; indeed, any latent fears were quickly allayed by James Wilson, who assured his colleagues that "the Prerogatives" of the Crown were not "a proper guideline in defining the Executive powers."[40]

It was in this context that the Constitutional Convention designed the office of the presidency. Far from establishing an executive resembling a monarch, the Framers in fact severed all roots to the royal prerogative. The Framers' rejection of the British model, grounded in their fear of executive power and reflected in their derision of monarchical claims and prerogatives, was repeatedly stressed by defenders of the Constitution. William Davie, a delegate in Philadelphia, explained to the North Carolina Convention that "jealousy of executive power which has shown itself so strongly in all the American governments would not admit" of vesting the treaty powers in the President alone, a principle reaffirmed by Hamilton in *The Federalist No. 75*: "[T]he history of human conduct does not warrant that exalted opinion of human virtue which would make it wise" to commit "its intercourse with the rest of the world to the sole disposal" of the President.[41] Hamilton, in fact, was at the center of Federalist writings that attempted to allay concerns about the creation of an embryonic monarch. In *The Federalist No. 69*, he conducted a detailed analysis of the enumerated powers granted to the President as commander in chief.[42]

The confined nature of the presidency, a conception rooted, for example, in Wilson's observation that the President is expected to execute the laws and make appointments to office, or in Sherman's remark that "he considered the Executive magistracy as nothing more than an institution for carrying the will of the Legislature into effect," represented a characterization that was *never* challenged throughout the Convention.[43] No delegate to the Constitutional Convention advanced a theory of inherent power. Madison justly remarked, "The natural province of the executive magistrate is to execute laws, as that of the legislature is to make laws. All his acts, therefore, properly executive, must presuppose the existence of the laws to be executed."[44] Manifestly, the concept of an inherent executive power, a Lockean Prerogative to "improvise" law to act in the absence of legislation or in violation of it, does not "presuppose the existence of the laws to be executed."

At the time of the American Revolution, it was widely understood that the principle of the rule of law implied executive subordination to the law. In fact, it was clear that republican government differed from the monarchies of Europe in precisely this respect. The Framers, it may be said, did not even squint in the direction of presidential prerogative. Certainly there is nothing in Philadelphia that would provide footing for such a claim – nothing at all in the arguments, discussion or train of thought of the Convention. There is, finally, no evidence to suggest that the Founders, who in 1776 had introduced the term "executive power" to avoid the stench of prerogative, had by 1787 found the odor any less repugnant. Proponents of inherent power will need to look beyond the Framers' conceptions of executive power to justify presidential prerogative powers.

President Bush's advocacy of inherent executive power faces a virtually

insurmountable problem, moreover, in his effort to reconcile presidential prerogative with the Take Care Clause, which provides that the President "shall take
care that the laws be faithfully executed." The proposition that the duty to
execute the laws carries with it the power to defy, violate or create them would
have surprised the Framers. Among other things, the concept of an undefined
reservoir of discretionary power in the form of a Lockean Prerogative would
have unraveled the carefully crafted design of Article II and repudiated the
Framers' stated aim of corralling executive power. The Convention avoided that
problem, however, by imposing on the President a solemn duty to "faithfully
execute the laws" and, as a necessary consequence, stripped him of all pretenses
to the Stuart Kings' dispensing and suspending prerogative – powers that were
utterly discordant with the President's duties under the Take Care Clause. In
fact, according to Lord Mansfield, by 1766 the King's prerogative no longer
entailed a suspending or dispensing power:

> I have a very simple notion of it, and it is this, that prerogative is that share
> of the government which, by the constitution, is vested in the King alone....
> I can never conceive the prerogative to include a power of any sort to
> suspend or dispense with laws, for a reason so plain that it cannot be over-
> looked, unless because it is plain; and that is, that the great branch of the
> prerogative is the executive power of government, the duty of which is to
> see the execution of the laws, which can never be done by dispensing with
> or suspending them.[45]

If, therefore, the Framers had decided to vest in the President legal authority to
suspend or dispense with the enforcement of laws, it would have involved the
resurrection of an old prerogative that the English themselves had discarded, a
prerogative that ran against the tides of history, which were surging toward
republicanism. Given the notorious and odious reputation of the dispensing
power, and the Framers' derisive references to monarchical prerogatives, it is
beyond belief that the Framers would have incorporated an executive prerogative within their constitutional scheme.

Finally, there remains the need to consider the impact of the prerogative to
suspend laws and to dispense with their enforcement on the congressional power
of impeachment. The Framers, it will be recalled, considered that the President
would be rendered vulnerable to impeachment for failure to perform his duty
under the Take Care Clause, a criterion invoked against Andrew Johnson, and
one that resonates across a vista of two centuries of American history.[46] Manifestly, the violation of the Take Care Clause could not constitute an impeachable
offense if the executive possessed a dispensing or suspending power, or a
general legal authority to violate the law in the event of an emergency. It is
particularly noteworthy that no early legal treatise, or commentary, from the
pens of Wilson or Kent, Story or Rawle spoke of an executive authority to
violate laws in the context of an emergency.

Viewed from another angle, the Founders' conception of an executive power to execute the laws hinged on the presence of a statute to be executed. Charles Francis Adams observed, "The legislative power is the precise measure of the executive power."[47] Justice Oliver Wendell Holmes embraced this understanding in a dissenting opinion in *Myers* v. *United States*: "[T]he duty of the President to see that the laws be executed is a duty that does not go beyond the laws."[48] Justice Louis Brandeis echoed Holmes's opinion in his own dissent in *Myers*: "The President performs his full constitutional duty, if, with the means and instruments provided by Congress and within the limitations prescribed by it, he uses his best endeavors to secure faithful execution of the laws enacted."[49] The attribution to the President of authority to improvise legislation and improvise the means to implement it would represent a fusion of the legislative and executive powers – the very antithesis of the aims of the separation of powers, to wit, the prevention of oppression, and even tyranny.[50]

The claim that the Framers attributed to the President an undefined inherent power to act in the absence of legislation or in violation of it to meet emergencies encounters stiff resistance at every turn. The delegates' effort, in Madison's words, to "confine and define" presidential power included enumeration of the relatively trivial – and seemingly obvious – powers to the chief executive. Thus, the assertion of a deep, unconfined and discretionary reservoir of presidential power seems quite anomalous in the face of an express grant to the President of the constitutional authority "to require the Opinion in writing" of each department head, which, Justice Robert Jackson rightly observed, "would seem to be inherent in the Executive if anything is."[51] Hamilton agreed in *The Federalist No. 74*, and regarded that power as a "mere redundancy" on the assumption that "the right for which it provides would result of itself from the office."[52] If Hamilton and Jackson were correct in their assumption that the authority of the chief executive to require in writing opinions of department heads is "inherent" if anything is, then the very enumeration of this presidential power supplies refutation of the premise itself.

The claim of inherent executive power, denied sustenance by anything said or done in Philadelphia, emerges for the first time in 1793 in the context of Hamilton's defense of President George Washington's Proclamation of Neutrality. In the course of his essays, written as "Pacificus," Hamilton applied the initial gloss on "executive power" in his claim of an "inherent" presidential power. Hamilton emphasized the differences between the Constitution's assignment to Congress in Article I of "all legislative Powers herein granted" and the more general grant in Article II of the executive power to the President. Pacificus claimed that the Constitution embodies an independent, substantive grant of executive power. The subsequent enumeration of specific executive powers was, he argued, only "intended by way of greater caution, to specify and regulate the principal articles implied in the definition of Executive Power." He added, "The general doctrine then of our constitution is, that the EXECUTIVE POWER of the Nation is vested in the President; subject only to the *exceptions* and *qualifications* which are expressed in the instrument."[53]

Hamilton's assertions are vulnerable on several counts. For example, the

Convention debates provide no basis for ascribing any significance to the difference in phraseology between the legislative powers "herein granted" and "[t]he executive Power." In brief, the reference to Congress likely represented an effort to reaffirm the limits of federalism and the regulatory authority of Congress and to allay concerns of states, which feared for their legislative authority, rather than an effort to recognize a substantive conception of executive power. Certainly, Congress is not limited to the powers expressly stated, as evidenced by the Necessary and Proper Clause. Congress enjoys express powers as well as others. Hamilton's explanation that the Framers intended merely to specify and *regulate* what he termed the "principal" articles implied in the definition of executive power raises additional questions. His use of the word "regulate" implies limitations – a concept at the core of the Framers' effort, in Madison's words, to "confine and define" executive power, but one at odds with a broad grant of undefined residual authority. Moreover, why would the Convention, from Hamilton's perspective, proceed to enumerate a presidential power to require opinions in writing if the President possessed a broad residuum of executive authority? Pacificus's argument that the Convention enumerated only those executive articles that were "principal" articles seems at odds with the concept of inherent power, given the understanding that nothing is seemingly more inherent in executive power than the authority to require a subordinate to submit an opinion in writing.

Additional problems plague Hamilton's theory of inherent power. The argument he adduced as Pacificus, as Madison noted, contradicted his explanation of presidential power in *The Federalist No. 69*. Hamilton's apparent reevaluation of executive power in 1793 did not alter the Convention's understanding, which Hamilton reported in *The Federalist No. 69* in his analysis of each of the enumerated powers of the President, an analysis on which delegates to the state conventions relied in their adoption of the Constitution. His analysis in *The Federalist No. 69* served to allay fears that the President would exercise the powers of an overweening executive. In *The Federalist No. 75*, he explained that fears of unilateral presidential power precluded executive control of foreign affairs. But suddenly, as Pacificus, Hamilton asserted a broad "comprehensive grant" of executive power to the President.

As a consequence, one is left to wonder at the capacious scope and theoretical limits of an inherent power and how it might be reconciled with Madison's reminder in *The Federalist No. 51* that "in republican government, the legislative authority necessarily predominates."[54] Obviously, the Convention did not endow the President with more power than it vested in Congress, but with less. However, the allocation of power between the executive and legislative branches, presumably clarified by an enumerative scheme, may be blurred and corrupted by an inherent executive power capable of overwhelming powers that are constitutionally enumerated and assigned to Congress. Unless we are willing, therefore, to abandon the concept of a *constitutionally limited* inherent presidential power, however broadly it may be construed, and to view it as a consuming, cannibalistic power, there remains the need to address some conceptual limits.

Hamilton's approach to the parameters of inherent power permits an understanding, at a minimum, that, under the banner of executive power, the President may not lay claim to any of the powers, express or implied, that are allocated to either Congress or the judiciary. Thus, it seems indisputable, for example, that the President derives from the Constitution no lawmaking authority, the quintessential congressional power. In *The Federalist No. 78*, Hamilton sharply repudiated the claim that the President may revise the Constitution:

> Until the people have, by some solemn and authoritative act, annulled or changed the established form, it is binding upon themselves collectively, as well as individually; and no presumption, or even knowledge, of their sentiments, can warrant their representatives in a departure from it, prior to such an act.[55]

The Hamiltonian–Madisonian line of reasoning, it should be said, prohibits circumvention of the Constitution and preserves the rule of law – the very marrow of which consists of executive subordination to the Constitution.

Restoring the rule of law

President Bush's theory of unfettered executive power, manifested in a series of usurpations and unconstitutional acts, is freighted with historical baggage that plumbs the depths of America's vision of itself, the rule of law, republicanism, constitutionalism, and its essential vulnerabilities. The fear of tyranny in the United States has long gripped the imaginations of Americans. Senator Church, who labored over documents rife with incidents of governmental lawlessness and immorality, was better positioned than most to sketch the shadow of tyranny that might descend on America. In an August 17, 1975 session of the popular television talk show *Meet the Press*, Church discussed the dangers of tyranny in America. "If this government ever became tyrannical there would be no place to hide," he said, "and no way to fight back, because the most careful effort to combine together in resistance to the government – no matter how privately it was done – is within the reach of the government." Church observed that he now grasped the capacity of government to impose tyranny. "We must see to it that all agencies which possess this technology operate within the law and under proper supervision so that we never cross over that abyss. That's the abyss from which there is no return."[56]

The loss of the republic – in an abyss or in the Rubicon – like the decline of the Roman Republic has haunted the American political consciousness since the colonists began to discuss, debate, and analyze power. "What gripped their minds," Bernard Bailyn has observed, "what they knew in detail, and what formed their view of the whole of the ancient world was the political history of Rome."[57] For a generation that felt itself threatened by executive power, corruption and oppression, the image of Rome lay in the colonists' characterization of their plight, for it was clear to them, as expressed by John Adams, that Britain was to America "what Caesar was to Rome."[58] As a consequence, "[a]nalogies to the decline and fall of Rome sprang to the lips of almost every commentator as the crisis in Anglo-American affairs deepened."[59]

The Framers, it is familiar, feared the menace of arbitrary power. In fact, "their distrust of official power," Willard Hurst observed, constituted "a very basic principle of our constitutionalism,"[60] and inspired their commitment to written limits on governmental power. Thomas Jefferson explained:

> It is jealousy and not confidence which prescribes limited constitutions to bind down those whom we are obliged to trust with power.... In questions of power, then, let no more be heard of confidence in man, but bind down from mischief by the chains of the Constitution.[61]

Jefferson's colorful yet exacting metaphor captured the essence of the Framers' bid to implement the rule of law: the subordination of the government to the law. What John Hart Ely said of the Supreme Court applies equally to the President. The court "is under obligation to trace its premises to the charter from which it derives its authority."[62] Certainly the President enjoys no dispensation from adherence to the Constitution, which he has sworn an oath to defend. The Constitution reflects the fundamental choices made by the people, and the government has the solemn duty to enforce them, to effectuate "the consent of the governed." "The people," explained James Iredell, one of the most acute constitutional theorists in the founding period, "have chosen to be governed under such and such principles. They have not chosen to be governed or promised to submit upon any other."[63] Accordingly, as Chief Justice Marshall stated in *Marbury*, once limits are established, they may not "be passed at pleasure." It was owing to the perception of constitutions as bulwarks against oppression, he explained, that "written constitutions have been regarded with so much reverence."[64]

The requirement of governmental adherence to the Constitution was, for the Founders, an article of faith. In 1785, Madison had declared that rulers "who overleap the great barrier which defends the rights of the people ... are tyrants."[65] No agent, Hamilton explained, "can new-model his commission."[66] The denial to government of authority to replace the choices of the people with their own values, to ignore in effect the norms and principles enshrined in the Constitution, constituted subversion of the Constitution through rank usurpation of power – one of the most serious of impeachable offenses. Thus, Justice Joseph Story, the most scholarly of Justices, wrote, "We are not at liberty to add one jot of power to the national government beyond what the people were granted by the constitution."[67] Usurpation was no idle word for a generation that imposed on its agents the duty to swear an oath to uphold the Constitution, violation of which was impeachable.[68] But the Framers knew, as Madison noted in *The Federalist No. 48*, that all "power is of an encroaching nature, and that it ought to be effectually restrained from passing the limits assigned to it."[69] Government officials were not immune from the temptation of power and thus the question of restraining them from constitutional violations was the great challenge confronting the nation in 1787. It was the great challenge that Senator Frank Church took up with such enthusiasm and integrity in 1975. It is the challenge confronting the nation today. In *The Federalist No. 51*, Madison set forth the question in words made famous: "In framing a government which is to be administered by men over men, the great difficulty lies in this: [Y]ou must first enable the government to control the governed; and in the next place oblige it to control itself."[70] The Framers, of course, relied on the structural mechanisms of separation of powers and checks and balances as means by which the government might "control itself." Then, too, there was the proposition that "the people would constitute an 'auxiliary precaution' and maintain vigilant watch over their government."

Remedies for President Bush's violations of the Constitution and his mockery of the rule of law are available, and they are familiar from Senator Church's era: judicial checks; congressional checks, including impeachment; vigorous and sustained oversight, and public repudiation. But the checks must be triggered, of course, and the fact that the Bush Administration has succeeded, for example, in reducing Congress to the role of spectator indicates that institutional mechanisms have not been implemented and that Senator Church's leadership, courage, and constitutional vision are lacking.[71] In varying degrees, partisanship and a paucity of institutional pride are to blame.

At all events, the Bush Administration's assertion of executive supremacy – what Bruce Fein dubbed "one branch rule" – has effectively served Vice President Dick Cheney's publicly stated goal of expanding presidential power to its pre-Watergate status.[72] Given the many failures of the Bush presidency, particularly the tragedy of Iraq, the one goal that the administration has achieved, ironically enough, is the mischief that the Framers of the Constitution greatly feared: a largely unfettered executive that exhibits contempt for the Constitution and the rule of law and that has reduced Congress to the role of cipher. The President's successes on this front virtually guarantee that he will not reverse course in his final years of his term and become a "uniter" – a champion of checks and balances, collective decision making in foreign affairs, republicanism, and the rule of law. For the Bush administration, the only currency is power, and it has asserted power with a rubber hose. There is, then, no reason to expect the administration to relax, let alone renounce, its grasp of power to restore the rule of law.

If America is going to witness the restoration of the rule of law, it will occur during the remainder of the Bush presidency only if Congress rebounds from its state of lethargy and regains its institutional integrity and pride. Who will sound the trumpet call for a revival of the spirit, fortitude and integrity of the Church Committee? Who will rise to the defense of republicanism in the name of Church, Mondale, Hart, and the other senators and staffers whose work and commitment reminded a nation of its link to the Framers of the Constitution? It is possible, of course, that the next President will forswear President Bush's extravagant claims to power and genuinely seek to navigate the ship of state back to its constitutional moorings. That is an intriguing question but one that cannot be addressed at this juncture.

Is it feasible to believe that Congress will regain its institutional pride and prevent the further deterioration of the American Republic? Will it avoid the historical allusions to the passive, lethargic, and impotent legislature in Rome that ceded the Republic to Caesar? Its record since the September 11, 2001 terrorist attacks in the United States is a far cry from the integrity and fortitude displayed by Church's Committee. It has unconstitutionally delegated the war power to President Bush through the passage of the Authorization to Use Military Force (AUMF) in the fall of 2001 and again in the fall of 2002 in the Iraqi Resolution. It has ceded control over the appropriations power in the form of a $10 billion blank check to the President in the days following the outrage over the terrorist attacks. And it has stood idly in the fog created by the event while the President usurped the congressional legislative power to create offices as well as the Senate's share of power in cabinet-level appointments when President Bush created the Department of Homeland Security and picked Pennsylvania Governor Tom Ridge for the post.[73] When President Bush unilaterally terminated the ABM Treaty with Russia in December 2002, few members of the Republican-controlled Congress seemed to notice, and fewer still raised any constitutional objections, as leading conservative Senator Barry Goldwater had a generation earlier when he rightly brought suit against President Jimmy Carter for unilaterally terminating the 1954 Mutual Defense Treaty with Taiwan.[74] In the reign of George W. Bush, Congress has been quiescent and it has granted the President's wishes: AUMF, the USA PATRIOT Act, legislation stripping federal courts of habeas corpus jurisdiction, and revisions in the Foreign Intelligence Surveillance Act (FISA), among others.

As a body, Congress has been gripped by both partisanship and a paucity of institutional pride – damnable traits Church was able to avoid in the work of his Committee. Of course, this is by no means a new story.[75] But if America hopes to find its legislative branch asserting its oversight function with the admirable vigor of the Church Committee[76] and its vast foreign affairs powers in a robust manner befitting its central role in the constitutional system, for the purpose of renewing a moribund doctrine of checks and balances, Congress must recover its institutional character and curb its partisan loyalties to the occupant of the White House. It may be difficult, of course, but it can be done, as seen in the work of the Church Committee.

This congressional reversal will require leadership, and quite possibly the leadership that arises from an aroused citizenry. In what was one of his greatest and most impassioned speeches – a speech that lasted two days in the Virginia Ratification Convention and one that shook the earth when he reached his peroration: "Must I give my soul, my lungs to Congress?" Patrick Henry brought a razor to our problem: "If you depend on your President's and Senator's patriotism, you are gone."[77] In a republic, there is no substitute for a vigilant citizenry. "The only real security of liberty," James Iredell declared, "is the jealousy and circumspection of the people themselves. Let them be watchful over their rulers."[78] In his state's ratifying convention, Edmund Randolph told his fellow Virginians: "I hope that my countrymen will keep guard against every arrogation of power."[79] Heightened public awareness about presidential usurpation of power and the subversion of the Constitution, as seen in the public repudiation of Richard Nixon's "Saturday Night Massacre," can trigger profound political change, as it played a key role in driving Nixon from the White House.[80] It may well be that the acid test of a republic is whether a President could survive in the face of a resolute public repudiation of his illegitimacy.

Conclusion

In the presidency of George W. Bush, the trumpet sound of the rule of law has been reduced to tinkling crystal. Monarchial prerogatives and pretensions, the Framers recognized, were irreconcilable with republican values. As a consequence, the President's powers were constitutionally "confined and defined," as Madison observed, a design the Framers believed would protect the nation from an overweening executive and maintain the rule of law. The Framers were entitled to believe that they had succeeded in their quest. However, they could not have anticipated the breakdown – indeed, the utter collapse – of the doctrine of checks and balances, and the acquiescence of Congress in presidential usurpation of power, particularly in the areas of war making and foreign policy. The abdication by Congress of its foreign affairs powers and responsibilities has shredded the constitutional design for the conduct of American foreign policy. As a result, the Bush presidency has grown autocratic, and it may be said that it poses a permanent threat to the Republic.

Scholars and concerned citizens have proffered remedies; presidential humility, congressional resurgence and judicial responsibility, in one form or another, have been recommended as antidotes. Yet the institutional prescriptions are, so far, yet unavailing. Is it too late to recover republican principles? There is little doubt that the challenge becomes more daunting by the day, particularly in the Age of Terrorism, in which governmental officials are likely to exploit the public's fears to facilitate their circumvention of constitutional provisions. But there remains hope, hope modeled so brilliantly by the Church Committee, which, if it achieved anything, ought to have persuaded American citizens to appreciate the virtues and values of constitutionalism. If summoning Frank Church will not suffice, it may help if Americans summon the ghosts of 1776 – those harpies of power that compelled a generation to answer the trumpet call: an imperious executive, oppression, assaults on liberties, absolutist pretensions, disregard for constitutional principles and limitations, and the assertion of arbitrary power. The rule of law is fleeting. Church boldly reached out and seized it. It remains within our grasp, however tenuous. As Charles McIlwain wrote, "The two fundamental correlative elements of constitutionalism for which all lovers of liberty must yet fight are the legal limits to arbitrary power and a complete responsibility of government to the governed."[81] Frank Church could not have said it better himself.

Notes

1 3 Jonathan Elliot, *The Debates in the Several State Conventions, on the Adoption of the Federal Constitution, as Recommended by the General Convention at Philadelphia in 1787*, at 58 (1836), available at http://memory.loc.gov/ammem/amlaw/lawhome.html.
2 Tom Holland, *Rubicon: The Last Years of the Roman Republic* 286 (2005).
3 1 Edward Gibbon, *The History of the Decline and Fall of the Roman Empire* 54 (1897).
4 Professor Levinson has justly observed that the Bush Administration is "contemptuous of the claims of any other institution or of the citizenry to engage in independent constitutional judgment." Stanford Levinson, Constitutional Norms in a State of Permanent Emergency, 40 *Georgia Law Review* 1, 48 (2006). Levinson is surely correct in his view that the administration is "stunningly ambitious with regard to its view of executive power." Ibid. For a recent penetrating critique of President Bush's vast claims to war and foreign relation powers, see Fredrick A.O. Schwarz, Jr. and Aziz Huq, *Unchecked and Unbalanced: Presidential Powers in a Time of Terror* (2007). See also Arthur Schlesinger, Jr., *War and the American Presidency* (2005), the last of his many distinguished works.

   The literature discussing presidential abuse of power in war and foreign affairs is extensive. See, e.g., *The Constitution and the Conduct of American Foreign Policy* (David Gray Adler and Larry N. George eds., 1996); Louis Fisher, *Presidential War Power* (2nd rev. edition 2004); Michael J. Glennon, *Constitutional Diplomacy* (1990); Harold H. Koh, *The National Security Constitution* (1990); Richard Pious, *The War on Terrorism and the Rule of Law* (2006); Schwarz and Huq, *supra*; Schlesinger, *supra*; David Gray Adler, George Bush as Commander in Chief: Toward the Nether World of Constitutionalism, 36 *Presidential Studies Quarterly* 525 (2006).
5 The unitary presidency would gather all executive power directly under the control of the President, thus precluding independent commissions, independent counsels, congressional involvement in administrative details, and statutory limitations on the President's power to remove executive officials. Needless to say, it would concentrate power in the executive. As such, it would ignore the aims and values of the Framers that shaped the creation of the presidency. For discussion, see Steven G. Calabresi and Saikrishna B. Prakash, The President's Power to Execute the Laws, 104 *Yale Law Journal* 541 (1994); Steven G. Calabresi, Some Normative Arguments for the Unitary Executive, 48 *Arkansas Law Review* 23 (1995). See also Seamon in this volume (Chapter 8).
6 See *The Presidency and the Challenge of Democracy* (Michael A. Genovese and Lori Cox Han, 2006), *including* Louis Fisher, From the Presidential Wars to American Hegemony: The Constitution after 9/11, at 23; Nancy Kassop, The Constitutional Checks and Balances That Neither Check nor Balance, at 73; Robert J. Spitzer, The Commander in Chief Power and Constitutional Invention in the Bush Administration, at 93, and David Gray Adler, The President as King: The Usurpation of War and Foreign Affairs Powers in the Modern Age, at 159. See generally Adler, *supra* note 4; Schwarz and Huq, *supra* note 4; Levinson, *supra* note 4.
7 Bruce Fein, a conservative commentator and former official in the Justice Department during the Reagan Administration, derided Bush's claim of an "absolute" power to remove the attorneys: "The president is wrong." Bruce Fein, Executive Nonsense, *Slate*, July 11, 2007, available at http://slate.com/id/2170247/. Fein, of course, is right.
8 Ibid.
9 Of course, the House and Senate could order the Sergeant at Arms to take the witnesses into custody and "jail" them in the capital. For an examination of the contempt power of Congress, see Congressional Research Service, *Congressional Investigations: Subpoenas and Contempt Power* (Apr. 2, 2003).

10 Kate Phillips, The Pentagon Issues Warnings to Clinton, *Washington Post*, July 19, 2007, at A1.
11 While it is true, in important respects, that some of Bush's predecessors have claimed similar authority, as in unilateral executive war making and treaty termination, no one, I think, has claimed the aggregate of powers adduced by Bush. His aggrandizement of power represents not merely a difference of degree, but a difference in kind. For discussion of the aggrandizement of executive power, see generally David Gray Adler, The Condition of the Presidency: Clinton in Context, in *The Presidency and the Law: The Clinton Legacy* 175 (David Gray Adler and Michael A. Genovese eds., 2002).
12 John W. Dean, *Worse than Watergate: The Secret Presidency of George W. Bush* (2004).
13 Bob Egelko, Gonzales Says the Constitution Doesn't Guarantee Habeas Corpus, *San Francisco Chronicle*, Jan. 24, 2007, at A1.
14 Derek Jinks and David Sloss, Is the President Bound by the Geneva Conventions?, 90 *Cornell Law Review* 97, 97 (2004). In *Wickard* v. *Filburn*, 317 U.S. 111 (1942), Justice Jackson held that the "cumulative effects" of statutory violations constituted the mischief that required remedy. The aggregate of President Bush's unconstitutional acts should be viewed in this light. For discussion, see David Cole, *Enemy Aliens* (2003); Schwarz and Huq, *supra* note 4, at 122–48.
15 See Hart (Chapter 2), Schwarz (Chapter 3) and Ashby (Chapter 5) in this volume.
16 Memorandum from John C. Yoo, Deputy Assistant Attorney Gen., to Timothy Flanigan, Deputy Counsel to the President 1 (Sept. 25, 2001), available at www.usdoj.gov/olc/warpowers925.htm. The assertion that the President possesses broad, inherent power as sole organ of American foreign policy, and in his capacity as commander in chief, provides the foundation for the Bush Administration's claims of sweeping executive power. For example, on January 19, 2006, the Justice Department invoked "the President's well-recognized inherent constitutional authority as Commander in Chief and sole organ of the nation in foreign affairs," to defend the authority of the National Security Agency (NSA) to intercept international communications between people in the United States and others allegedly associated with al Qaeda or the terrorist organizations. U.S. Department of Justice, *Legal Authorities Supporting the Activities of the National Security Agency Described by the President* (Jan. 19, 2006), available at www.usdoj.gov/opa/whitepaperonnsalegalauthorities.pdf.
    One of the infamous "Torture Memos," the work of Office of Legal Counsel (OLC) head Jay S. Bybee, referred to the "President's complete authority over the conduct of war," to "detain and interrogate every combatant." Memorandum from Jay S. Bybee, Assistant Attorney General, Office of Legal Counsel, to James B. Comey, Deputy Attorney General 34–35 (Dec. 30, 2002) (regarding the legal standards applicable under 18 U.S.C. §§ 2340–2340A (2000)). Scholars have savaged the legal analysis in the Bybee Memorandum. Professor Cass Sunstein, for example, has justly observed that the analysis was "very low level … very weak, embarrassingly weak, just short of reckless." Adam Liptak, Legal Scholars Criticize Memos on Torture, *New York Times*, June 25, 2004, at A14 (quoting Sunstein). In the *Confirmation Hearings on the Nomination of Alberto R. Gonzales to Be Attorney General of the United States before the Senate Committee on the Judiciary*, 109th Cong. 158 (2005), Dean Harold Hongju Koh of the Yale Law School stated, "In my professional opinion … the [Bybee] Memorandum is perhaps the most clearly erroneous opinion I have ever read."
17 John C. Yoo, The Continuation of Politics by Other Means: The Original Understanding of War Powers, 84 *California Law Review* 170 (1996).
18 In litigation defending President Bush's order of November 13, 2001 to provide for the trial through military commissions of noncitizens attached to al-Qaeda, the President cited

[t]he authority vested in me as President and Commander in Chief of the Armed forces of the United States by the Constitution and laws of the United States of America, including the Authorization for use of Military Force [AUMF] Joint Resolution (Public Law 107–40, 11 Stat. 224) and sections 821 and 836 of title 10, United States Code.

> (Press Release, White House, President Issues Military Order (Nov. 13, 2001), available at www.whitehouse.gov/news/releases/2001/11/20011113–27.html)

AUMF authorized war against Afghanistan. The Title 10 sections refer to Military Commissions. If congressional support "were not so clear," the Justice Department argued, "the President has inherent authority to convene military commissions to try and punish captured enemy combatants in wartime – even in the absence of any statutory authorization." Brief for Respondent, *Hamdan* v. *Rumsfeld*, 126 S. Ct. 2749 (2006) (No. 05-184).

19 The 1971 Detention Act, 18 U.S.C. § 4001 (2000), provides that "no citizen shall be imprisoned or otherwise detained by the United States except pursuant to an Act of Congress." But the administration contended that it was not controlled by the statute since "Article II alone gives the President the power to detain enemies during wartime, regardless of congressional action." Press Release, Department of Defense, DOD Responds to ABA Enemy Combatant Report (Oct. 2, 2002), available at www.defenselink.mil/releases/release.aspx?releaseid=3492.

20 As recently as 1979, the OLC echoed the department's historic position that "the president cannot order any person extradited unless a treaty or statute authorized him to do so." 4A OLC Ops. 149 (1979). But officials in the Bush Administration asserted the need to detain and interrogate suspected terrorists outside the country. Dana Priest, Ex-CIA Official Defends Detention Policies, *Washington Post*, Oct. 27, 2004. This is a clear claim of inherent authority to defy the law.

21 On December 19, 2005, Attorney General Gonzales held a press briefing on the National Security Agency (NSA) program of domestic surveillance and declared that "the President has the inherent authority under the Constitution, as Commander-in-Chief, to engage in this kind of activity." Press Secretary Briefing, Alberto Gonzales, U.S. Attorney Gen. (Dec. 19, 2005), available at www.whitehouse.gov/news/releases/2005/12/20051219-1.html. On January 19, 2006, the OLC affirmed the President's "inherent power" to conduct warrantless surveillance. Department of Justice Office of Legal Counsel, *Legal Authorities Supporting the Activities of the National Security Agency Described by the President* (Jan. 19, 2006), available at www.usdoj.gov/opa/whitepaperonnsalegalauthroities.pdf. This is a clear example of presidential defiance of FISA.

22 In the initial "Torture Memo," Yoo and Delahunty claimed that al-Qaeda members are not protected by the Geneva Convention. It was asserted that Congress, by statute or treaty, may not interfere with the President's authority as commander in chief over detainees. Memorandum from Robert J. Delahunty and John Yoo, Department of Justice Office of Legal Counsel, to William J. Haynes II, Gen'l Counsel, Department of Defense (Jan. 9, 2002), available at www.texscience.org/reform/torture/yoo-delahunty-9jan02.pdf.

23 Ibid. at 16. For a valuable discussion of the Bush administration's assertion of inherent power, see Special Issue: Invoking Inherent Powers, 37 *Presidential Studies Quarterly* 1–152 (2007). See also David Gray Adler, Steel Seizure Case and Inherent Presidential Power, 19 *Constitutional Commentary* 155–213 (2002).

24 John Locke, *The Second Treatise of Government*, sec. 146–48 (Thomas P. Peardon, ed., 1952).

25 *The Federalist No. 45*, at 260 (James Madison) (Clinton Rossiter, ed., 1961) (emphasis added).

26 See David Gray Adler, The President's Recognition Power, *in The Constitution and*

the Conduct of American Foreign Policy, supra note 4, at 133–58. For a discussion of the Framers' prescriptions, see David Gray Adler, Court, Constitution and Foreign Affairs, in *The Constitution and the Conduct of American Foreign Policy, supra* note 4, at 19–57.

27 *The Federalist No. 75* (Alexander Hamilton), *supra* note 25, at 419.

28 2 Elliot, *supra* note 1, at 507.

29 For Hamilton's arguments as "Pacificus," see 15 *Papers of Alexander Hamilton*, 33–39 (H.C. Syrett and J. Cooke, eds., 1969).

30 *Marbury* v. *Madison*, 5 U.S. (1 Cranch) 137, 176 (1803).

31 6 Alexander Hamilton, *Works of Hamilton* 166 (H.C. Lodge ed., 1904).

32 Julius Goebel, *Ex Parte Clio*, 54 *Columbus Law Review* 450, 474 (1954).

33 Robert Scigliano, The President's Prerogative Power, *in Inventing the Presidency* 236, 248 (Thomas F. Cronin, ed., 1989).

34 Charles Warren, *The Makings of the Constitution* 177 (1947) (quoting Jefferson).

35 1 Max Farrand, *The Records of the Federal Convention of 1789*, at 62–63 (1911), available at http://memory.loc.gov/ammem/amlaw/lawhome.html.

36 Ibid. at 66.

37 Ibid. at 65

38 Ibid. at 66–67.

39 Ibid. at 70.

40 Ibid. at 65.

41 4 Elliot, *supra* note 1, at 134; *The Federalist No. 75* (Alexander Hamilton), *supra* note 25, at 419.

42 See Adler, *supra* note 4, at 525–41; David Gray Adler, The Constitution and Presidential Warmaking: The Enduring Debate, 103 *Political Science Quarterly* 1–36 (1988).

43 1 Farrand, *supra* note 35, at 65.

44 6 James Madison, *Writings of James Madison* 145 (G. Hunt, ed., 1906).

45 Lucius Wilmerding, Jr., The President and the Law, 67 *Political Science Quarterly* 122 (1952) (quoting Mansfield). Early in the nineteenth century, the judicial branch, emphatically rejected the proposition that the President possessed a dispensing or suspending power. See, e.g., *Little* v. *Barreme*, 6 U.S. (2 Cranch) 170 (1804).

46 Raoul Berger, *Impeachment: The Constitutional Problems* 263–310 (1973).

47 Wilmerding, *supra* note 45, at 126 (quoting Adams).

48 *Myers* v. *United States*, 272 U.S. 52, 177 (1926).

49 Ibid. at 292.

50 See generally Francis D. Wormuth, *The Origins of Modern Constitutionalism* (1949). Charles Pinckney observed in the Convention that the President "cannot be clothed with those executive authorities, the Chief Magistrate of a Government often possesses; because they are vested in the Legislature and cannot be used or delegated by them in any, but the specified mode." 3 Farrand, *supra* note 35, at 111. Madison regarded the separation of powers as "a fundamental principle of free government." 2 Farrand, *supra* note 35, at 56.

51 *Youngstown Sheet & Tube Co.* v. *Sawyer*, 343 U.S. 579, 640–41 (1952).

52 *The Federalist No. 74* (Alexander Hamilton), *supra* note 25, at 415.

53 Alexander Hamilton, *Writings* 33, 39 (2001).

54 *The Federalist No. 51* (James Madison), *supra* note 25, at 290.

55 *The Federalist No. 78* (Alexander Hamilton), *supra* note 25, at 437.

56 Loch Johnson, *A Season of Inquiry: The Senate Intelligence Investigation* 71–72 (1985) (quoting Church).

57 Bernard Bailyn, *The Ideological Origins of the American Revolution* 346 (enlarged version, 1992).

58 Ibid. at 26.

59 Ibid. at 137.

60 *Discussion in Supreme Court and Supreme Law* 75 (E. Cahn, ed., 1954).

61 4 Elliot, *supra* note 1, at 543. In the Virginia Ratification Convention, Francis Corbin state, "Liberty is secured, sir, by the limitation of its [the government's] powers, which are clearly and unequivocally defined." 3 Elliot, *supra* note 1, at 110.

62 John Hart Ely, The Wages of Crying Wolf: A Comment on *Roe* v. *Wade*, 82 *Yale Law Journal* 920, 949 (1973). Madison stated in the Constitutional Convention that "it would be a novel and dangerous doctrine that a legislature could change the Constitution under which it held its existence." 2 Farrand, *supra* note 35, at 92.

63 2 Griffith J. McRee, *Life and Correspondence of James Iredell* 145 (1857–58).

64 *Marbury* v. *Madison*, 5 U.S. (1 Cranch) 137, 178 (1803).

65 2 James Madison, *Writings of James Madison* 185 (G. Hunt ed., 1900–10). Oliver Ellsworth, speaking in the Connecticut Ratification Convention, echoed the principle when he stated that Congress may not "overleap their limits." 2 Elliot, *supra* note 1, at 196.

66 Letters of Camillus, in *Works of Hamilton*, *supra* note 31, at 166.

67 *Houston* v. *Moore*, 18 U.S. (5 Wheat.) 1, 48 (1820) (Story, J., dissenting).

68 For impeachable offenses, see Berger, *supra* note 46, at 56–108.

69 *The Federalist No. 48* (James Madison), *supra* note 25, at 276.

70 *The Federalist No. 51* (James Madison), *supra* note 25, at 290.

71 The Church Committee braved charges of disloyalty, cries of treason, accusations of betraying the nation's security and dismissal of it, in the words of Henry Kissinger and others, as naïve and "boy-scoutish." Senator Barry Goldwater, a member of the Senate Select Committee on Intelligence, who refused to support the Committee report, was an apologist for the illegal behavior of the CIA and the intelligence agencies. Goldwater asserted that the issue was not what the agencies had done; rather, it was a question of what strategies and tactics were necessary. He stated, "If the intent is to keep us from national harm," then "dirty tricks" were a function of necessity and loyalty. *See* LeRoy Ashby and Rod Gramer, *Fighting the Odds: The Life of Senator Frank Church* 488 (1994) (quoting Goldwater). James Angleton, the renowned chief of counterintelligence, bemoaned the revelations of the agencies' illegal acts. He complained to the staffer (and now eminent scholar) Loch Johnson that the United States had been toppled: "We have been occupied by Congress." Ibid. Kissinger continued to maintain that Church had "practically wrecked" the CIA. Ibid.

72 See Barton Gellman and Jo Becker, Pushing the Envelope on Presidential Power, *Washington Post*, June 25, 2007, at A1.

73 See generally Adler, *supra* note 11, at 175, 186.

74 See generally David Gray Adler, The Law: Termination of the ABM Treaty and the Political Question Doctrine: Judicial Succor for Presidential Power, 34 *Presidential Studies Quarterly* 156 (2004); David Gray Adler, *The Constitution and the Termination of Treaties* (1986).

75 See the recent excellent discussion of these issues in Norman J. Ornstein and Thomas E. Mann, When Congress Checks Out, 85 *Foreign Affairs*, Nov./Dec. 2006, at 67–82; William Howell and Jon Pevehouse, Congress and the War, 86 *Foreign Affairs*, Sept./Oct. 2007, at 95–108.

76 For insightful analysis and discussion, see Johnson, *supra* note 56; Schwarz and Huq, *supra* note 4, at 1–64.

77 3 Elliot, *supra* note 1, at 148, 149, 164; Bailyn, *supra* note 57, at 346.

78 4 Elliot, *supra* note 1, at 130.

79 3 Elliot, *supra* note 1, at 207.

80 There is in this task a rich opportunity for those who labor in the groves of academe. What Justice Frankfurter said of the judiciary surely applies to the executive: "Scholarly exposure of the Court's abuse of its powers" would "bring about a shift in the Court's viewpoint." Quoted in Joseph P. Lash, *From the Diaries of Felix Frankfurter* 59 (1975).

81 Charles McIlwain, *Constitutionalism: Ancient and Modern* 146 (rev. edition 1947).

8   NSA domestic surveillance

Presidential power and the Fourth Amendment

Richard Henry Seamon

Introduction

In 2001, the President began spying on Americans again, under circumstances that recalled abuses disclosed almost 30 years earlier by the Church Committee.[1] The domestic spying program began soon after the September 11, 2001 terrorist attacks in the United States and was conducted by the National Security Agency (NSA) for the purpose of detecting and thwarting threats posed by international terrorists.[2] The NSA program, which came to be known as the "Terrorist Surveillance Program" (sometimes hereinafter referred to as TSP or the NSA Program) raised two legal issues of continuing importance. One issue is whether the TSP violated the Foreign Intelligence Surveillance Act of 1978 (FISA), or whether, instead, FISA itself is unconstitutional to the extent it purported to bar the TSP.[3] This first issue arose because the TSP involved electronic surveillance (e.g., wiretapping) that was subject to FISA but occurred without FISA compliance. The issue of whether the TSP trumped FISA, or vice versa, is a separation of powers issue that continues to haunt the President's conduct of national security surveillance, which lacks statutory authorization. The second issue is whether the TSP violated the Fourth Amendment.[4] The Fourth Amendment issue arose because surveillance under the TSP occurred without prior judicial authorization or traditional probable cause.[5] It is proper that public debate on the surveillance program distinguished the separation of powers issue from the Fourth Amendment issue; they require different analyses. Public debate did not, however, pay enough attention to the connection between the FISA issue and the Fourth Amendment issue. This chapter attempts to fill the gap.

I reach a twofold conclusion. First, the President may defy FISA in certain circumstances by authorizing electronic surveillance that is subject to FISA but that occurs without compliance with FISA or any other statutory authorization. Such defiance of FISA does not violate separation of powers doctrine. Furthermore, the very same circumstances that justify such surveillance "outside FISA" can often cause the surveillance to satisfy the Fourth Amendment even though conducted without a warrant or traditional probable cause. By the same token, when circumstances do not justify surveillance outside FISA, the government's violation of FISA presumptively violates the Fourth Amendment. A genuine national security emergency excuses the President from compliance with both FISA and traditional Fourth Amendment requirements.

Although I believe the President has inherent power to defy FISA in a genuine national security emergency, this power does not justify the NSA surveillance program in the years following the September 11, 2001 terrorist attacks in the United States. Because the surveillance was pursued as an ongoing broad "program," it cannot properly be regarded as an exercise of the President's "genuine emergency" power. The genuine emergency power is limited in scope and duration when it is exercised against the backdrop of legislation that is a generally valid regulation of the President's power to conduct domestic surveillance for national security purposes. FISA is an example of such legislation. Thus, the President may well have had broad power to conduct surveillance outside FISA in the days and weeks immediately after the September 11, 2001 terrorist attacks in the United States. That power subsided, however, as time and a still-functioning civil government permitted the President to consult Congress on the appropriate scope of surveillance powers. As the years following 2001 unfolded without another terrorist attack in the United States, the President still might have had the power to authorize surveillance outside FISA, but that power existed only when FISA's shortcomings rendered surveillance outside FISA reasonably necessary for national security purposes. In sum, as time passed following the terrorist attacks, and relative peace and security prevailed, the President's "genuine emergency" power no longer supported a broad surveillance program that constituted a violation of a generally valid act of Congress.

My further contention, developed over the next two parts of this chapter, is that the NSA program violated the Fourth Amendment precisely because it violated FISA. The statutory violation presumptively established the constitutional violation. In other words, the NSA program violated the Fourth Amendment – because FISA is on the books – even though the program may very well *not* have violated the Fourth Amendment before FISA was enacted and might very well not have constituted a violation of the Fourth Amendment if FISA were repealed. Congress's enactment of a statute that is within Congress's power and that is designed to implement the Fourth Amendment alters the Fourth Amendment analysis of whether a government search or seizure is "reasonable." In this sense, Congress can affect the substance of the Fourth Amendment. Recognizing Congress's power to enact statutes that alter Fourth Amendment analysis illuminates the linkage between the Fourth Amendment and separation of powers doctrine. In addition, an understanding of the connection informs the broader debate on the roles of legislatures and courts in enforcing the Fourth Amendment.[6]

Presidential power to conduct domestic electronic surveillance for national security purposes within Fourth Amendment constraints

The analysis of whether the NSA's Terrorist Surveillance Program violated FISA differs from, but overlaps with, the analysis of whether the program violated the Fourth Amendment. The issue of whether the program violated FISA requires a separation of powers analysis that draws a line between the President's power and Congress's power. The issue of whether the program violated the Fourth Amendment entails a reasonableness analysis that strikes a balance between governmental and individual interests. Despite this difference in analyses, the FISA issue and the Fourth Amendment issue overlap when it comes to identifying what the President can and cannot do.

Specifically, FISA is unconstitutional – and the President can therefore disregard it when doing so is required by exigent circumstances of national security. Furthermore, electronic surveillance conducted under exigent national security circumstances will satisfy the Fourth Amendment – even if it does not meet the traditional Fourth Amendment requirements of prior judicial approval and probable cause – if, as will often be true, the surveillance falls within the exigent circumstances doctrine of Fourth Amendment law. However, when national security exigencies do not exist, the President's failure to comply with FISA exceeds his authority and presumptively violates the Fourth Amendment.

The connection between the separation of powers issue and the Fourth Amendment issue reflects that both separation of powers doctrine and Fourth Amendment doctrine recognize plenary executive power when necessary to protect national security. Outside of such exigent circumstances, both separation of powers and Fourth Amendment doctrine support legislative and judicial checks on the executive to prevent executive abuse of individual rights.

Presidential powers in a "genuine emergency"

The President seemingly admitted that after the September 11, 2001 terrorist attacks in the United States, he authorized "electronic surveillance" within the meaning of FISA without following FISA's requirements. Because this Terrorist Surveillance Program was not authorized by another statute, only the President's "inherent powers" can support the program, and they can do so only to the extent that those inherent powers cannot validly be restricted by FISA. To say that FISA invalidly restricts the President's inherent powers reflects a conclusion that FISA violates the separation of powers doctrine.[7] Hence, the statutory issue whether the President violated FISA poses a separation of powers question.

Though not providing clear guidance, history and precedent suggest that the President has congressionally irreducible power to "repel sudden attacks" on the country.[8] In *The Prize Cases*, for example, the court upheld President Lincoln's power to blockade southern ports in the days after the Confederacy's attack on Union forces at Fort Sumter.[9] The court made clear that his power did not depend on legislative authorization, stating:

> If a war be made by invasion of a foreign nation, the President is not only authorized but bound to resist force by force. He does not initiate the war, but is bound to accept the challenge without waiting for any special legis-

lative authority.... He must determine what degree of force the crisis demands.[10]

More recently, two Justices in *Hamdi* v. *Rumsfeld* recognized a similar emergency power to respond to threats to national security.[11] In *Hamdi*, Justice Souter (joined by Justice Ginsburg) dissented from a decision upholding the detention of an asserted enemy combatant who is also a U.S. citizen.[12] Justice Souter concluded that an act of Congress barred the detention.[13] He suggested, however, that the executive branch might be able to detain a citizen, even in violation of the statute, "in a moment of genuine emergency, when the Government must act with no time for deliberation."[14] This suggestion in the *Hamdi* dissent implies that the President's power to take action "incompatible with the expressed or implied will of Congress" may include the power to take immediate action to respond to a "genuine emergency" threatening national security.[15] Furthermore, the *Hamdi* dissent did not limit its implication of presidential power to situations involving an actual attack. Indeed, even before *Hamdi*, many commentators believed that the President's power encompasses the taking of defensive measures necessary to thwart imminent attacks.[16]

The court's decision in *Hamdan* v. *Rumsfeld*, issued two years after the *Hamdi* decision, might be read to reject plenary power in the President to defy an act of Congress when he believes it necessary to respond to a national security threat.[17] In *Hamdan*, the court held that the President violated an act of Congress – namely, the Uniform Code of Military Justice (UCMJ) – when he established military tribunals to try aliens detained in the war on terrorism.[18] Thus, the court in *Hamdan* enforced a congressional restriction on the President's exercise of authority in the war on terrorism.

Some believe that *Hamdan* casts serious doubt on the legality of the TSP because the TSP, like the President's rules for tribunals, violates an act of Congress: namely, FISA.[19] The provisions of the UCMJ at issue in *Hamdan*, however – unlike the FISA provisions with which the TSP conflicts – were not challenged by the government as unconstitutionally infringing on the President's inherent powers. As Justice Thomas noted in his *Hamdan* dissent, the court did not need to decide whether the President has inherent authority to use military tribunals to try suspected terrorists.[20] The issue before the court was whether the President's action fell within "certain statutes, duly enacted by Congress ... in the *proper* exercise of its powers as an independent branch of government."[21] Perhaps the government in *Hamdan* did not challenge the UCMJ provisions as unconstitutionally infringing on the President's power because those provisions, in fact, leave room for the President to act as necessary in genuine national security emergencies.[22] This is a feature that FISA lacks. Because of this difference, *Hamdan* does not control the validity of the TSP, nor does it undermine the existence of presidential power to defy an act of Congress in a genuine national security emergency.

Moreover, the pre-*Hamdan* precedent, recognizing a congressionally irreducible "genuine emergency" power in the President, is supported by the

Constitution's creation of a "unitary executive."[23] The Constitution provided for only one President so, in appropriate occasions, someone can act for the nation without consulting others.[24] The Framers thought a unitary executive was particularly important for conducting foreign affairs. A unitary executive enables the country to speak to other countries with one voice.[25] It ensures quick action when necessary to protect national security.[26] It also helps ensure the secrecy of sensitive foreign intelligence.[27] Thus, the court has often referred to the President as the "sole organ" of foreign affairs.[28] The "sole organ" concept cannot, however, be stretched so far that it puts the President indefinitely above the law. Rather, it makes sense to let the President act as the "sole organ" if – but only so long as – it is necessary in a genuine national security emergency for him or her to so function.[29]

This reliance on the unitary executive concept to support presidential authority in genuine national security emergencies is deliberately narrow. It does not embrace broader claims that have been asserted under the unitary executive theory. Those broader claims assert presidential power to ignore congressional restrictions on removal of executive-branch officials and congressional enactments vesting exclusive power to administer statutory programs in officials other than the President.[30] In particular, recognition of congressionally irreducible presidential power in national security emergencies does not imply that the President has a greater role than Congress in the prosecution of war.[31] The position staked out here does, however, reject the view that "there is no constitutional impediment to Congress restricting the President's ability to conduct electronic surveillance within the United States and targeted at U.S. persons."[32] That view would apparently preclude the President's violation of statutory surveillance restrictions even if the President reasonably concluded that violation of those restrictions was necessary to respond to a national security emergency.

By any standard, the September 11, 2001 terrorist attacks in the United States constituted a genuine national security emergency.[33] They accordingly empowered the President to take some immediate actions that he reasonably thought necessary, even if those actions violated federal statutes.

Of course, the President's "genuine emergency" power has limits. The Japanese attack on Pearl Harbor created a "genuine emergency," but that emergency did not last for the entire war.[34] Nor did the attack on Pearl Harbor necessarily justify every measure that the President deemed reasonable, including the mass internment of Japanese-Americans.[35] The existence of genuine emergency powers in the President – and the relaxation of Bill of Rights limits on those powers – must be limited in time and scope.[36] Otherwise, the separation of powers system cannot work effectively, and Bill of Rights freedoms become fair-weather friends.

I propose two limits on the President's "genuine emergency" powers. First, the President's power depends on the legislative framework within which it is exercised. The President can defy an act of Congress in a national security emergency only if defiance of the legislation is necessary to respond to the emergency. If the President can respond effectively to the emergency while obeying the statute, the President lacks power to defy it.[37] Second, the President's emergency powers are residual when Congress has enacted generally valid legislation in the same area. Congress and the President share power in many areas, including the waging of war.[38] In matters of shared governance, the separation of powers doctrine gives Congress the power to make rules and the President power not to *unmake* Congress's rules, but to *break* them when reasonably necessary in a genuine emergency.

Fourth Amendment constraints on presidential powers in a "genuine emergency"

Ordinarily, the Fourth Amendment requires the government to get a warrant before electronically intercepting people's phone calls or reading their mail (presumably including their e-mail).[39] In addition, the Fourth Amendment ordinarily requires a particularized showing that the monitoring of each phone user or e-mailer is likely to reveal evidence of crime.[40] The traditional Fourth Amendment requirements of a warrant and an individualized showing of probable cause for a search do not, however, apply in the context of a genuine national security emergency. The exigent circumstances doctrine of Fourth Amendment law justifies immediate, warrantless surveillance of phones and e-mails. Moreover, although the exigent circumstances doctrine normally requires a particularized showing of probable cause of criminal activity,[41] that showing is unnecessary when "special needs, beyond the normal need for law enforcement," make the probable cause requirement impracticable.[42] In a "genuine emergency," the President can take immediate action reasonably necessary to protect national security, even if the action violates statutory restrictions, and if the President's action entails a search or seizure (as does presidentially authorized electronic surveillance), exigent circumstances in the "special needs" context of national security will often excuse ordinary Fourth Amendment requirements.

The overlap between separation of powers limits and Fourth Amendment limits on the President's power in emergency situations is not happenstance. Rather, it reflects an overlap between the separation of powers doctrine and Fourth Amendment doctrine.[43] The system of separated powers provides a unitary executive to encourage prompt and focused exercises of executive power, especially in foreign affairs. Yet to prevent abuses of executive power, separation of powers requires the President to obey limits imposed in statutes enacted by Congress (while acting within its powers) and in judgments entered by the federal courts (while acting within their powers). The Fourth Amendment, like the separation of powers doctrine, is designed to prevent abuses of power by any of the three branches. Thus, both the separation of powers and the Fourth Amendment are power-limiting provisions, neither of which speaks in absolutes. In a genuine national security emergency, the President needs some room to act unilaterally, even in defiance of congressional restrictions, and without the usual Fourth Amendment constraints. Recognition of this unilateral emergency power reflects that neither the separation of powers doctrine nor the Fourth Amendment operates as a "suicide pact."[44]

As is true of presidential power to ignore generally valid statutes, presidential power to act free of ordinary Fourth Amendment constraints has limits. Specifically, a search that is justified at its inception by exigent circumstances violates the Fourth Amendment if conducted in a way that is not reasonably related to the circumstances that justified it in the first place.[45] Thus, police officers who enter a house without a warrant to help a shooting victim cannot stay in the house to search for evidence of crime after they have rendered the help.[46] Likewise, a wide-scale surveillance program that violates an existing statute but that is justified by a national emergency such as the September 11, 2001 terrorist attacks in the United States becomes unreasonable under the Fourth Amendment as days and weeks pass without further attacks and give the executive branch an opportunity to have Congress consider whether to amend the statute to allow the program.[47]

Analysis of the NSA program as an exercise of the President's genuine national security emergency powers

Whether the NSA program falls within the President's power even though the program violates FISA

As discussed above, precedent suggests that the President has congressionally irreducible power to take immediate action reasonably necessary to respond to a genuine national security emergency; that power is limited, however, by the legislative framework within which it is exercised and by the nature of the exigency to which the government is responding. The Terrorist Surveillance Program authorized by President Bush and undertaken by the NSA beginning in 2001 exceeded those limits.

Let us assume that in the days and weeks after the terrorist attacks that the President could have established a "program" of domestic, electronic surveillance outside FISA. The President's power to maintain such a program, which violated a facially valid statute, subsided as weeks passed without further attacks and provided "time for deliberation"[48] within a system of civilian government that continued to function.[49] Indeed, deliberations on appropriate responses to the terrorist attacks *did* occur within and among the executive branch and Congress. The result was enactment of the USA PATRIOT Act, which expanded surveillance power by, among other changes, amending FISA.[50] It is hard for the President to argue that it was reasonably necessary to establish a far-ranging surveillance "program" in defiance of FISA when the President did not first attempt to change FISA to avoid the need to violate it.[51]

In judging the significance of the President's departure from FISA, it is important to recall that FISA prescribes "the *exclusive* means by which electronic surveillance [for foreign intelligence purposes] ... may be conducted" in the United States.[52] FISA's legislative history confirms that Congress intended

FISA to govern all domestic electronic surveillance for foreign intelligence purposes.[53] Congress made FISA exclusive because it wanted to stop executive abuses exposed in the 1970s through efforts such as the Church Committee investigations.[54] The Church Committee revealed that Presidents since Franklin D. Roosevelt had authorized warrantless surveillance of Americans.[55] Although Presidents claimed "inherent" power to authorize this surveillance for "national security" purposes, the surveillance often targeted people because of their political views.[56] By enacting FISA in 1978, Congress intended to "prohibit the President, notwithstanding any inherent powers," from conducting domestic electronic surveillance for foreign intelligence purposes without complying with FISA.[57] This background is important because it shows that FISA reflected Congress's intent to cabin the President's power within Fourth Amendment limits, as Congress understood them.

True, FISA has shortcomings. The shortcomings reflect changes in surveillance technology and in international terrorism. Those shortcomings could very well justify surveillance outside FISA – even today – if the President reasonably determines that, in a particular instance, it is reasonably necessary to depart from FISA. Specifically, FISA may have three shortcomings that could create "genuine emergencies" justifying event-specific departures from FISA.

First, it can take too long to get a FISA surveillance order. The Attorney General can authorize "emergency orders" approving FISA surveillance without prior court approval,[58] but this statutory emergency authority has drawbacks. The Attorney General must personally determine the existence of both an emergency and the factual basis for the issuance of an order.[59] Until he or she does so, emergency surveillance cannot occur.[60] NSA, however, may need to start surveillance the instant that it determines the surveillance is justified, without waiting for Attorney General authorization.[61] Furthermore, the Attorney General is only one person, and he or she may be called upon personally and very quickly to make dozens or hundreds of "emergency" determinations. The Attorney General could become a bottleneck. Finally, the government must advise the FISA court of each emergency order and apply within 72 hours for a surveillance order from the court to ratify the Attorney General's emergency order.[62] This supposedly expedited application process, required for every emergency order, could keep dozens of government lawyers employed on a continual fire drill without coming close to achieving the instantaneous authorization that is sometimes required for national security surveillance.

Second, the standards for getting FISA surveillance orders can be too high. NSA monitors phone calls and e-mails into and out of the United States involving people whom NSA has a "reasonable basis" for believing are associated with al Qaeda.[63] The government may not have probable cause to believe that these people are "agents of a foreign power" who can be targeted under FISA.[64] Indeed, the person in the United States whose phone calls or e-mails are monitored may be entirely innocent, if it is the person *outside* the United States who is associated with al Qaeda and who triggers NSA surveillance.[65] To cite another example, perhaps the person in the United States who is being monitored *is* associated with al Qaeda but the association does not make that person a foreign agent.[66] Even so, the government may have good reason to monitor the communication.[67]

Third, FISA orders could be too narrow. FISA authorizes surveillance of one target at a time.[68] The government, however, sometimes needs to conduct whole-sale surveillance – for example, by monitoring phone calls to all persons in the United States from particular individuals outside the United States[69] Wholesale surveillance may very well violate FISA but be reasonably necessary in a genuine national security emergency, such as when the government has strong evidence that someone outside the United States is planning terrorist attacks on a U.S. target with accomplices inside the United States.[70]

In sum, the President may have power to authorize surveillance "outside FISA" in situations presenting a "genuine emergency." That power, however, exists only when national security exigencies make it reasonably necessary to ignore FISA. Even so, the power justifies surveillance outside FISA even today, to the extent FISA's shortcomings create exigent circumstances precluding resort to the FISA process. This residual power does not support the continuation of President Bush's NSA surveillance "program" in the peaceable months that followed the 2001 terrorist attacks, especially when the program authorized wholesale departures from FISA.[71]

Whether the NSA program violates the Fourth Amendment because surveillance under the program occurs without a warrant or traditional probable cause

Before Congress enacted FISA in 1978, several lower federal courts upheld warrantless electronic surveillance conducted for national security purposes.[72] Those courts interpreted the Fourth Amendment to create an exception to the warrant requirement for searches conducted for foreign intelligence purposes.[73] After September 11, the government relied on these cases to argue that President Bush's NSA program of domestic surveillance did not violate the Fourth Amendment even though it occurs without a warrant or probable cause to believe the surveillance will reveal evidence of crime.[74] Opponents of the NSA program countered that these cases are inapposite because they concern surveillance conducted *before* FISA was enacted.[75] Thus, the opponents believe that FISA's enactment affects Fourth Amendment analysis. Neither opponents nor supporters of the NSA program, however, elaborated on how FISA affects Fourth Amendment analysis. I believe for several reasons that FISA influences any Fourth Amendment analysis of the NSA program and should carry particular weight in a court's analysis of the program.

First, FISA changes the legal landscape within which the Fourth Amendment reasonableness of the NSA program will be judged.[76] Prior to FISA, the alternative to conducting warrantless electronic surveillance for national security purposes was to seek a warrant for a physical search using the warrant application process used by prosecutors to search for evidence of crime.[77] That traditional warrant application process caused problems because it was designed for physical searches, not electronic surveillance, and for criminal investigations, not for national security surveillance.[78] With the ordinary criminal warrant process as an alternative, warrantless national security surveillance might have been reasonable. Warrantless surveillance is not necessarily reasonable when the alternative to it is the FISA process that Congress engineered with electronic surveillance and national security in mind. Thus, experience under FISA could establish that the NSA program was unreasonable, and therefore violated the Fourth Amendment, even though the same program might have been reasonable prior to FISA. In short, determining whether warrantless NSA surveillance is reasonable requires a consideration of the alternatives. FISA has created an alternative that, experience shows, facilitates the process of getting judicial approval for national security surveillance. Thus, the existence of FISA and experience under FISA bear on the reasonableness of proceeding without resort to that process in somewhat the same way as rules authorizing telephonic warrants bear on the reasonableness of police proceeding without a warrant.[79]

So, too, the existence of FISA bears on Fourth Amendment analysis in essentially the same way as it bears on separation of powers analysis. To the extent that FISA provides a process adequate for conducting surveillance in a genuine national security emergency, the government's failure to use that process is unreasonable. To the same extent, the failure to use that process cannot be justified by the President's congressionally irreducible power to violate a statute when reasonably necessary to respond to a genuine national security emergency.

Thus, the creation of the FISA process for obtaining judicial authorization of electronic surveillance would be relevant to any Fourth Amendment analysis of the NSA program.

Legislative rules enforcing the Fourth Amendment can facilitate judicial enforcement not only by requiring prior judicial authorization for executive surveillance but also by prescribing substantive standards for the surveillance and remedies for violations of those standards. Indeed, FISA prescribes an exhaustively considered standard for surveillance.[80] Legislatively prescribed standards for surveillance can benefit from the legislature's ability to gather information relevant to balancing government interests in surveillance against individual privacy interests.[81] Furthermore, legislatures may be able to make clearer standards than those made by courts. Clear rules, in turn, help officials obey the law and give the public notice of what privacy intrusions are authorized.[82] In addition, the public may better accept surveillance rules made by their elected representatives than rules made by unelected federal judges.[83] Legislative rules can be revised if they become unacceptable to the public.[84] Legislation can restrict the use of information derived from surveillance,[85] and impose sanctions for violations of those restrictions, including criminal sanctions.[86] In short, courts have good reasons to give significant weight to legislation that enforces Fourth Amendment limits on surveillance by prescribing substantive standards, enforceable by prescribed remedies, for such surveillance.[87]

Allowing the President to ignore statutorily prescribed procedures and standards for surveillance encourages executive lawlessness. Courts should discourage that behavior by preferring Fourth Amendment interpretations that encourage the executive branch to collaborate with the legislature to frame such rules, rather than defying them. After all, how are the public to feel when an act of Congress supposedly provides the "exclusive" authority for a specified type of surveillance yet they learn that a program exists "outside" that authority and has been going on for years?[88] Such a situation is likely to undermine public confidence that the nation's leaders obey the rule of law. It undermines faith in the legislative branch's willingness and ability to check executive abuse and in the President's willingness to abide by legislative restrictions.

To promote respect for legislation, such as FISA, that is carefully designed to enforce the Fourth Amendment, courts should presumptively treat surveillance "outside FISA" as a violation of the Fourth Amendment. After all, FISA reflects Congress's judgment, formed with extensive input from the executive branch, of what the Fourth Amendment requires. Treating FISA violations as presumptive Fourth Amendment violations simply reflects that when surveillance violates a statute that Congress and the executive branch designed to enforce the Fourth Amendment, the surveillance is likely to violate the Fourth Amendment. Thus, this presumption of unconstitutionality works like the presumption that the warrantless search of a home violates the Fourth Amendment.[89] The latter presumption reflects the fact that warrantless searches of homes are likely to violate the Fourth Amendment.[90] In addition to this probabilistic basis for the presumption against warrantless searches of homes, that presumption encourages police to obtain warrants, just as the presumptive unconstitutionality of surveillance outside FISA encourages compliance with FISA.[91] In short, both presumptions are rooted in common sense and further the Fourth Amendment's function of preventing abuses of power by encouraging advance judicial authorization.

Of course, the presumptive unconstitutionality of surveillance outside FISA may be overcome. First and foremost, as this chapter has argued, the presumption is overcome by proof that the surveillance was justified by a genuine national security emergency.[92] Furthermore, FISA has some requirements that are not related to enforcing the Fourth Amendment.[93] The government should be able to show that surveillance that violates FISA nonetheless satisfies the Fourth Amendment because the violation is only technical or insubstantial. If the government cannot make this showing, however, the courts should find surveillance outside FISA to be also outside the Fourth Amendment. By presuming the unconstitutionality of surveillance outside FISA, courts can moderate the current NSA surveillance program by limiting surveillance largely to instances in which it is reasonably necessary to respond to genuine national security emergencies.[94]

Conclusion

Surveillance outside FISA presumptively violates the Fourth Amendment except when the surveillance is justified by genuine national security emergency. Surveillance outside FISA that is justified by a genuine emergency not only satisfies the Fourth Amendment but also falls within the President's power even though the surveillance violates FISA. That is because FISA violates the separation of powers doctrine to the extent that FISA tries to forbid the President from taking measures that he or she reasonably believes necessary to respond to genuine national security emergencies. However, President Bush's NSA surveillance program violated the Constitution because it exceeds the President's congressionally irreducible power to respond to genuine national security emergencies.

As this summary shows, the post-September 11, 2001 situation involved unconstitutional conduct by the President (in authorizing NSA surveillance that is not justified by a genuine national security emergency) and by Congress (in enacting a statute, FISA, that in some instances infringes on the President's plenary powers under the Constitution). Beyond violating the Constitution, the President and Congress created great legal uncertainty: Congress says one thing in FISA, the President is doing another in the NSA program. Thus, the surveillance law on the books differs from the surveillance law "on the streets." This is no way to fight a war on terrorism.

Most supporters and opponents of the NSA program appear to agree on the need to make the surveillance law on the books congruent with the surveillance law on the streets. A similar consensus produced FISA.[95] As with FISA, new legislation will be contentious and take time. Although Congress enacted temporary legislation to authorize the TSP in part, that legislation sunset in six months and did little but delay the difficult work of striking a workable legislative framework for surveillance.[96] As with FISA, the contentiousness surrounding future legislation stems from the need to strike two difficult balances: (1) the balance between national security and "the right of the people to be secure in their persons, houses, papers, and effects, against unreasonable searches, and seizures";[97] and (2) the balance between the President's power and Congress's power to strike that first balance. Even rancorous and protracted debate on those issues is better than the current situation, in which the President and Congress appear to be acting outside the law.

This chapter seeks to contribute to the debate in two ways. First, it sheds light on a connection that has not received enough attention: the connection between the President's power to defy an act of Congress and Fourth Amendment limits on that power. Second, in exploring that connection, the chapter offers an analysis that is more nuanced and stakes out a more moderate position than those offered by most opponents and supporters of President Bush's NSA program. The separation of powers analysis offered here neither denies the existence of congressionally irreducible power in the President nor supports the President's disregard of generally valid legislation. Similarly, the Fourth Amendment analysis offered here recognizes Congress's authority to enforce the Fourth Amendment without treating that authority as absolutely binding on the executive branch or the courts. It is hoped that principled legal analysis will facilitate principled and politically feasible proposals for legislative reform.

Notes

1 Elizabeth B. Bazan and Jennifer K. Elsea, Congressional Research Service, *Presidential Authority to Conduct Warrantless Electronic Surveillance to Gather Foreign Intelligence Information* 1–2 (Jan. 5, 2006) [hereinafter CRS Report on Warrantless Surveillance], available at www.fas.org/sgp/crs/intel/m010506.pdf; James Risen and Eric Lichtblau, Bush Lets U.S. Spy on Callers without Courts, *New York Times*, Dec. 16, 2005, at A1. The Church Committee's revelations in the 1970s of abusive executive surveillance led to enactment of the Foreign Intelligence Surveillance Act, which was at the center of the controversy over the surveillance undertaken starting in 2001. *See* Scott Shane, For Some, Spying Controversy Recalls a Past Drama, *New York Times*, Feb. 6, 2006, at A18.
2 *See ACLU* v. *NSA*, 438 F. Supp. 2d 754, 758 (E.D. Mich. 2006), *vacated*, 493 F.3d 644 (6th Cir. July 6, 2007), *pet'n for cert. filed* (No. 07-468 Oct. 3, 2007); Letter from Alberto R. Gonzales, Attorney Gen. of United States, to Arlen Specter, Senator from Pennsylvania 1 (Feb. 28, 2006) [hereinafter Attorney General Letter of Feb. 28, 2006], available at www.fas.org/irp/congress/2006_hr/022806gonzales.pdf (stating that the President authorized the "Terrorist Surveillance Program" in October 2001, before signing the USA PATRIOT Act).
3 50 U.S.C. §§ 1801–1862 (2000). For a description of FISA, see Richard Henry Seamon and William Dylan Gardner, The Patriot Act and the Wall between Foreign Intelligence and Law Enforcement, 28 *Harvard Journal of Law and Public Policy* 319, 337–58 (2005).
4 U.S. Const. amend. IV.
5 See *Wartime Executive Power and the NSA's Surveillance Authority: Hearing before the S. Comm. on the Judiciary*, 109th Cong. 436 (2006) [hereinafter Senate Hearing, *Wartime Executive Power*] (testimony of Ken Gormley, Professor of Constitutional Law, Duquesne University) (arguing that "the program directly collides with … the Fourth Amendment").
6 See generally Orin S. Kerr, The Fourth Amendment and New Technologies: Constitutional Myths and the Case for Caution, 102 *Michigan Law Review* 801, 804 (2004) (critiquing the "popular view" that courts should take a primary role in enforcing privacy threatened by technology; urging an important role for legislature); *cf.* Daniel J. Solove, Fourth Amendment Codification and Professor Kerr's Misguided Call for Judicial Deference, 74 *Fordham Law Review* 747 (2005) (criticizing Professor Kerr's critique).
7 See, e.g., Attorney General Letter of Feb. 28, 2006, *supra* note 2, at 5; Andrew C. McCarthy, David B. Rivkin, and Lee A. Casey, NSA's Warrantless Surveillance Program: Legal, Constitutional, and Necessary, 33–34 in The Federalist Society, *Terrorist Surveillance and the Constitution* (n.d.), www.fed-soc.org/pdf/terroristsurveillance.pdf; see also *Buckley* v. *Valeo*, 424 U.S. 1, 126, 138–39 (1976); *Myers* v. *United States*, 272 U.S. 52, 176 (1926).
8 See, e.g., Committee on International Security Affairs of the Association of the Bar of the City of New York, The Legality and Constitutionality of the President's Authority to Initiate an Invasion of Iraq, 41 *Columbia Journal of Transnational Law* 15, 19 n.13 (2002); see also War Powers Resolution, Pub. L. No. 93-148, § 2(c), 87 Stat. 555 (1973) (codified at 50 U.S.C. § 1541(c) (2000)); Jane E. Stromseth, Understanding Constitutional War Powers Today: Why Methodology Matters, 106 *Yale Law Journal* 845, 852–63 (1996) (reviewing Louis Fisher, *Presidential War Power* (1995)). See Louis Fisher, *Constitutional Conflicts between Congress and the President* 259–60 (rev. 4th edition 1997). Until recently, Presidents exercised the power but later sought authorization from Congress. Ibid. at 260–62.
9 *The Brig Amy Warwick* (The Prize Cases), 67 U.S. (2 Black) 635 (1863).
10 Ibid. at 670.

11 *Hamdi* v. *Rumsfeld*, 542 U.S. 507 (2004); see also Joseph R. Biden, Jr., and John B. Ritch III, The War Power at a Constitutional Impasse: A "Joint Decision" Solution, 77 *Georgetown Law Journal* 367, 372 (1988) (proposing a "joint decision" model under which presidential power to use force in absence of statutory authorization "derives from the concept of emergency: the need to repel an attack on the United States or its forces, to forestall an imminent attack, or to rescue United States citizens whose lives are imperiled").

12 *Hamdi*, 542 U.S. at 539–54 (Souter, J., concurring in part, dissenting in part, and concurring in the judgment) (joined by Ginsburg, J.).

13 Ibid. at 541.

14 Ibid. at 552.

15 *Youngstown Sheet and Tube Co.* v. *Sawyer*, 343 U.S. 579, 635–38 (1952) (Jackson, J., concurring).

16 See Biden and Ritch, *supra* note 11, at 398–99 (proposing legislation that authorizes the President, without additional statutory authority, "to forestall an imminent act of international terrorism known to be directed at citizens or nationals of the United States"); Stromseth, *supra* note 8, at 862–63; Jane E. Stromseth, Collective Force and Constitutional Responsibility: War Powers in the Post-Cold War Era, 50 *University of Miami Law Review* 145, 159 (1995); William Van Alstyne, Congress, the President, and the Power to Declare War: A Requiem for Vietnam, 121 *University of Pennsylvania Law Review* 1, 9 (1972).

17 *Hamdan* v. *Rumsfeld*, 126 S. Ct. 2749 (2006).

18 Ibid. at 2790–98.

19 See David Cole, Reviving the Nixon Doctrine: NSA Spying, the Commander-In-Chief, and Executive Power in the War on Terror, 13 *Washington & Lee Journal of Civil Rights & Social Justice* 17, 29–30 (2006); Harold Hongju Koh, Setting the World Right, 115 *Yale Law Journal* 2350, 2366 (2006).

20 *Hamdan*, 126 S. Ct. at 2825 n.2 (Thomas, J., dissenting).

21 Ibid. at 2799 (Kennedy, J., concurring in part) (emphasis added).

22 See ibid. at 2791, 2794 (holding that President's action violated UCMJ Articles 21 and 36, 10 U.S.C. §§ 821, 836); see also ibid. at 2774 (observing that UCMJ Article 21, 10 U.S.C. § 821, obligates the President to follow the "laws of war" in the use of military tribunals, but the laws of war, in turn, authorize the use of military tribunals "in cases of 'controlling necessity'"); UCMJ Art. 36, 10 U.S.C. § 836 (2000) (authorizing the President, when establishing military tribunals, to depart from the rules for court martial if it is "impracticable" to use identical rules).

23 See, e.g., *Clinton* v. *Jones*, 520 U.S. 681, 712–13 (1997) (Breyer, J., concurring in the judgment); *The Federalist No. 70*, at 452 (Alexander Hamilton) (Benjamin Fletcher Wright ed., 1961); Christopher S. Yoo, Steven G. Calabresi and Anthony J. Colangelo, The Unitary Executive in the Modern Era, 1945–2004, 90 *Iowa Law Review* 601 (2005).

24 See 10 *Annals of Congress* 613 (1800) (argument of John Marshall that "the President is the sole organ of the nation in its external relations, and its sole representative with foreign nations").

25 *United States* v. *Curtiss-Wright Exp. Corp.*, 299 U.S. 304, 319 (1936) ("The President is the constitutional representative of the United States with regard to foreign nations") (quoting 8 US Senate Reports Committee on Foreign Relations 24 (Feb. 15, 1816)).

26 See *The Federalist No. 70*, *supra* note 23, at 451–52 ("Energy in the executive … is essential to the protection of the community against foreign attacks," and an ingredient of energy is "unity"); see also Louis Fisher, *Presidential War Power* 6 (1995).

27 See *Chi. and S. Air Lines, Inc.* v. *Waterman S.S. Corp.*, 333 U.S. 103, 111 (1948); *Curtiss-Wright*, 299 U.S. at 320; Edward S. Corwin, *The President: Office and Powers* 5–7, 200–01 (Randall W. Bland *et al.* eds., 5th edition 1984) (citing among

President's advantages over Congress in the conduct of foreign policy the unitary nature of the Presidency, its ability to collect and maintain secrecy of relevant information, and to act quickly); see also *The Federalist No. 64*, at 422 (John Jay) (Benjamin Fletcher Wright ed., 1961).

28 *Pasquantino* v. *United States*, 544 U.S. 349, 369 (2005); see also *Am. Ins. Ass'n* v. *Garamendi*, 539 U.S. 396, 414 (2003); *Sale* v. *Haitian Ctrs. Council, Inc.*, 509 U.S. 155, 188, (1993); *First Nat'l City Bank* v. *Banco Nacional de Cuba*, 406 U.S. 759, 769 (1972) (Rehnquist, J., plurality).

29 *Cf.* Michael Stokes Paulsen, The Constitution of Necessity, 79 *Notre Dame Law Review* 1257, 1257–58 (2004).

30 See Saikrishna Prakash, The Essential Meaning of Executive Power, 2003 *University of Illinois Law Review* 701, 713 (2003); Christopher Yoo, Steven G. Calabresi, and Anthony J. Colangelo, The Unitary Executive in the Modern Era, 1945–2004, at 90 *Iowa Law Review* 601, 607 (2005); cf. Michael Froomkin, The Imperial Presidency's New Vestments, 88 *Northwestern University Law Review* 1346, 1347 (1994).

31 See John C. Yoo, The Continuation of Politics by Other Means: The Original Understanding of War Powers, 84 *California Law Review* 167, 174 (1996) (arguing that Congress can check President's waging of war only by use of spending power or by impeachment); but cf. Louis Fisher, Lost Constitutional Moorings: Recovering the War Power, 81 *Indiana Law Journal* 1199, 1200 (2006) (arguing that Constitution "vest[ed] in congress the authority to take the country from a state of peace to a state of war against another country"); Martin S. Flaherty, The Most Dangerous Branch, 105 *Yale Law Journal* 1725, 1729 (1996) ("[T]he unitarian executive attributed to the Founding is 'just myth'" (quoting Lawrence Lessig and Cass R. Sunstein, The President and the Administration, 94 *Columbia Law Review* 1, 4 (1994)).

32 Cole, *supra* note 19, at 29–30.

33 See Declaration of National Emergency by Reason of Certain Terrorist Attacks, 66 Fed Reg. 48,199 (Sept. 14, 2001).

34 See *Ex parte Milligan*, 71 U.S. 2, 80 (1866); ibid. at 127; see also *Hirabayashi* v. *United States*, 320 U.S. 81, 113 (1943) (Murphy, J., concurring).

35 See *Hirabayashi*, 320 U.S. at 102; see also *Korematsu* v. *United States*, 323 U.S. 214, 217–18 (1944).

36 Cf. *Korematsu*, 323 U.S. at 234 (Murphy, J., dissenting). Justice Murphy writes:

> The judicial test of whether the Government, on a plea of military necessity, can validly deprive an individual of any of his constitutional rights is whether the deprivation is reasonably related to a public danger that is so "immediate, imminent, and impending" as not to admit of delay and not to permit the intervention of ordinary constitutional processes to alleviate the danger.
>
> (Ibid.)

37 The President has claimed that the NSA surveillance program is "crucial to our national security." Letter from William E. Moschella, Assistant Attorney General, Office of Legislative Affairs, US Department of Justice, to Senator Pat Roberts *et al.* 1 (Dec. 22, 2005), available at www.fas.org/irp/agency/doj/fisa/doj122205.pdf. The President has not (publicly, at least) shown why it is necessary to ignore FISA in conducting that program.

38 *Hamdan* v. *Rumsfeld*, 126 S. Ct. 2749, 2773 (2006); *Hirabayashi* v. *United States*, 320 U.S. 81, 93 (1943); see also, *e.g.*, *Rumsfeld* v. *Forum for Academic and Inst'l Rights*, 126 S. Ct. 1297, 1306 (2006).

39 See *Berger* v. *New York*, 388 U.S. 41, 45–54 (1967); *Ex parte Jackson*, 96 U.S. 727, 733 (1877); *United States* v. *Forrester*, 495 F.3d 1041, 1048–50 (9th Cir. 2007); see also Orin S. Kerr, Internet Surveillance Law After the USA PATRIOT Act: The Big Brother That Isn't, 97 *Northwestern University Law Review* 607, 628–29 (2003).

40 See ibid.

41 See, e.g., *Warden of Md. Penitentiary* v. *Hayden*, 387 U.S. 294, 307 (1967).

42 See *Griffin* v. *Wisconsin*, 483 U.S. 868, 873 (1987).

43 See *United States* v. *Keith*, 407 U.S. 297, 317 (1972); see also *Katz* v. *United States*, 389 U.S. 347 (1967) (Douglas, J., concurring); Raymond Shih Ray Ku, The Founders' Privacy: The Fourth Amendment and the Power of Technological Surveillance, 86 *Minnesota Law Review* 1325, 1342 (2002); *cf.* Timothy Lynch, In Defense of the Exclusionary Rule, 23 *Harvard Journal of Law and Public Policy* 711, 737 (2000).

44 *Kennedy* v. *Mendoza-Martinez*, 372 U.S. 144, 160 (1963).

45 See, e.g., *New Jersey* v. *T.L.O.*, 469 U.S. 325, 341–42 (1985); Mincey v. Arizona, 437 U.S. 385, 393 (1978).

46 See *Mincey*, 437 U.S. at 392.

47 In commenting on a draft of this chapter, Louis Fisher asked the fair question: How long after the September 11, 2001 terrorist attacks in the United States will the President's power to defy FISA last? E-mail from Louis Fisher, Senior Specialist in Separation of Powers, Congressional Research Service, Library of Congress, to Richard Henry Seamon, Professor of Law, University of Idaho College of Law (July 12, 2006) (on file with author). He notes that President Lincoln waited several months after Congress returned from recess to seek legislation authorizing Lincoln's emergency actions (including suspension of the writ of habeas corpus) in April 1861. Ibid.; see also Fisher, *supra* note 8, at 260–61. I agree with the standard that Fisher proposes: When Congress is in session, the President must go to Congress as soon as possible. In the case of the September 11, 2001 terrorist attacks in the United States, that date came less than one week after September 11, for that is how quickly the Administration was able to draft and present to Congress the bill later enacted as the Patriot Act. See *Administration's Draft Anti-Terrorism Act of 2001: Hearing before the Judiciary Committee of the House of Representatives*, 107th Cong. 67–90 (2001) (reproducing the Bush Administration's proposed bill).

48 *Hamdi* v. *Rumsfeld*, 542 U.S. 507, 552 (2004).

49 *Ex parte Milligan*, 71 U.S. 2, 80 (1866); *cf. Hamdan* v. *Rumsfeld*, 126 S. Ct. 2749, 2799 (2006) (opinion of Breyer, J., concurring).

50 United and Strengthening America by Providing Appropriate Tools Required to Intercept and Obstruct Terrorism Act of 2001, Pub. L. No. 107-56, §§ 206–208, 214, 215, 218, 225, 115 Stat. 272, 282–83, 287–88, 291, 295–96 (2001) (codified in scattered sections of 50 U.S.C.).

51 See *supra* note 47 and accompanying text (arguing that the President had power to act only while there was no time for deliberation). One argument that the President has made is that the terrorists might have been alerted if the President had consulted with Congress about the NSA surveillance program. This argument is difficult to analyze because so little relevant information is publicly available.

52 18 U.S.C. § 2511(2)(f) (2000) (emphasis added). Section 2511(2)(f) also authorizes "electronic surveillance ... and the interception of domestic wire, oral, and electronic communications" to occur under Title III of the Omnibus Crime Control and Safe Streets Act of 1968 (Title III) and under Chapter 121 of Part I of Title 18, 18 U.S.C. §§ 2701–2712. Title III authorizes wiretaps for criminal investigations, *see* 18 U.S.C. §§ 2516, 2518(3)(a), and Chapter 121 concerns access to stored electronic communications, such as e-mail messages for the investigation of criminal offenses. See 18 U.S.C. § 2701(a); ibid. § 1803(a), (d). See generally Orin S. Kerr, A User's Guide to the Stored Communications Act, and a Legislator's Guide to Amending It, 72 *George Washington Law Review* 1208 (2004). The government has not claimed that either Title III or Chapter 121 supports the current NSA surveillance program, leaving FISA as the "exclusive" means of surveillance, under § 2511(2)(f). In addition to the exclusivity provision in § 2511(2)(f), FISA provides: "A person is guilty of an offense if he intentionally engages in electronic surveillance under color of law except as authorized by statute." 50 U.S.C. § 1809(a)(1).

53 The exclusivity provision in § 2511(2)(f) of FISA (*see supra* note 52 and accompanying text) replaced a provision in Title III stating that Title III did not limit the President's power to "take such measures as he deems necessary" to protect national security. Omnibus Crime Control and Safe Streets Act of 1968, Pub. L. No. 90-351, tit. III, § 802, 82 Stat. 214, repealed by Foreign Intelligence Surveillance Act of 1978, Pub. L. No. 95-511, § 201(c), 92 Stat. 1797. Congress enacted § 2511(2)(f) instead of proposed provisions that continued to recognize possible inherent presidential power to conduct national security surveillance without statutory authorization. See S. 3197, 94th Cong. § 2528 (1976) (bill provision stating that legislation proposed in the bill would not "limit the constitutional power of the President to order electronic surveillance" for national security purposes); H. Rep. No. 95-1270, at 35 (1978) (Conf. Rep.) (observing that the House version provided that FISA and Title III would be "the exclusive statutory means" by which President could conduct surveillance, but Conference selected the Senate version, "which omits the word 'statutory'"); Ira S. Shapiro, The Foreign Intelligence Surveillance Act: Legislative Balancing of National Security and the Fourth Amendment, 15 *Harvard Journal of Legislation* 119, 123 n.11 (1977). Other legislative history expresses Congress's intent in FISA to eliminate the President's inherent power to conduct national security surveillance. See S. Rep. No. 95-604, pt. I, at 6, 64 (1978); ibid.; H.R. Rep. No. 95-1283, pt. 1, at 24 (1976).

    See also Senate Hearing, *Wartime Executive Power, supra* note 5, at 126 (testimony of Attorney General Gonzales) ("There is no question..., that Congress intended to try to limit whatever president's inherent authority existed").

54 See, e.g., S. Rep. No. 95-604, at 8 (1977) (the bill that became FISA "is designed ... to curb the practice by which the Executive Branch may conduct warrantless electronic surveillance on its own unilateral determination that national security justifies it"); see also Richard Henry Seamon and William Dylan Gardner, The Patriot Act and the Wall between Foreign Intelligence and Law Enforcement, 28 *Harvard Journal of Law and Public Policy* 319, 336–37 and nn. 66–71 (2005).

55 See, e.g., S. Rep. No. 95-604, at 7–8 (1977).

56 See, e.g., ibid. at 8.

57 See *supra* note 53; see also H.R. Rep. No. 95-1283, pt. I, at (1978). The report states:

> [D]espite any inherent power of the President to authorize warrantless electronic surveillances in the absence of legislation, by this bill [and Title III]..., Congress will have legislated with regard to electronic surveillance in the United States, that legislation with its procedures and safeguard prohibit the President, notwithstanding any inherent powers, from violating the terms of that legislation.
>
> (Ibid.)

    Section 111 of FISA makes clear that Congress intended FISA to apply – to the exclusion of the President's inherent powers – even during wartime. Section 111 says, "[T]he President, through the Attorney General, may authorize electronic surveillance without a court order ... to acquire foreign intelligence information for a period not to exceed fifteen calendar days following a declaration of war by the Congress." 50 U.S.C. § 1811 (2000). I thank Louis Fisher for pointing out to me the significance of this provision. E-mail from Louis Fisher, *supra* note 47.

58 50 U.S.C. § 1805(f) ("Emergency orders").

59 50 U.S.C. § 1805(f)(1) and (2); letter from William E. Moschella, Assistant Attorney General, U.S. Dep't of Justice, to Hon. F. James Sensenbrenner, Jr., Chairman, U.S. House of Rep. Judiciary Comm., encl. at 12 (Mar. 24, 2006) [hereinafter Moschella Letter of Mar. 24, 2006] (stating that Attorney General must "personally" determine that factual basis for emergency FISA surveillance exists).

60 See Moschella Letter of Mar. 24, 2006, *supra* note 59, encl. at 39.

61 See Alberto R. Gonzales, Prepared Remarks at the Georgetown University Law

Center (Jan. 24, 2006), available at www.usdoj.gov/ag/speeches/2006/ag_speech_0601241.html.

62 50 U.S.C. § 1805(f).

63 See United States Department of Justice, *Legal Authorities Supporting the Activities of the National Security Agency Described by the President* 5 (Jan. 19, 2006) [hereinafter cited as "DOJ White Paper"].

64 50 U.S.C. § 1801(b) (defining "agent of a foreign power"); see also ibid. § 1805(a)(3) (requiring a judge to find "probable cause" that the target of proposed FISA surveillance "is a foreign power or an agent of a foreign power").

65 Senate Hearing, *Wartime Executive Power, supra* note 5, at 459 (testimony of former CIA Director James Woolsey); Douglas Waller, A Better Way to Eavesdrop?, *Time*, Feb. 2, 2006; Richard A. Posner, Wire Trap, *New Republic*, Feb. 6, 2006, at 15.

66 See Seamon and Gardner, *supra* note 3, at 345 (footnotes omitted). See *also* McCarthy *et al.*, *supra* note 7, at 90; Posner, *supra* note 65, at 16.

67 See John Cary Sims, What NSA Is Doing ... and Why It's Illegal, 33 *Hastings Constitutional Law Quarterly* 105, 129 (2006) (concluding that "the warrantless surveillance program violates the applicable statutes" because it targets United States persons in the United States for interceptions without having probable cause that they are agents of a foreign power).

68 See Senate Hearing, *Wartime Executive Power, supra* note 5, at 425 (testimony of former CIA Director James Woolsey).

69 See Posner, *supra* note 65, at 16; K.A. Taipale, Whispering Wires and Warrantless Wiretaps: Data Mining and Foreign Intelligence Surveillance, *New York University Review of Law and Security*, No. VII Supplement, *Bulletin on Law and Security*. The NSA and the War on Terror, at 4–6 (Spring 2006), available at http://whispering-wires.info/.

70 The government can also avoid FISA by conducting electronic surveillance that falls outside FISA's definition of "electronic surveillance." The definition does not, for example, cover surveillance of a "United States person" if the surveillance is conducted outside the United States or if it does not "intentionally [target] that United States person." 50 U.S.C. § 1801(f) (2000). Thus, the government would not be subject to FISA if it targeted persons who are located abroad – even U.S. persons – if the surveillance occurred abroad. If conducted inside the United States, however, the surveillance would be subject to FISA. See 50 U.S.C. § 1801(f)(2); see also NSA Debate: Federalist Society: *Rivkin* v. *Levy* (posted on Jan. 23, 2006) (remark by David Rivkin), available at www.freerepublic.com/focus/f-news/1563282/posts.

71 I am arguing for a considerably narrower scope of plenary power than Professor Sims attributes to the present (George W. Bush) Administration. Sims, *supra* note 67, at 136 (understanding the present administration to be advancing an "unformed constitutional theory" that would give the President a "blank check"). Another commentator, however, appears to find no room for "exclusive" presidential power when its exercise "directly contradicts" FISA. Brian R. Decker, "The War of Information": The Foreign Intelligence Surveillance Act, *Hamdan* v. *Rumsfeld*, and the President's Warrantless Wiretapping Program, 9 *University of Pennsylvania Journal of Constitutional Law* 291, 345 (2006).

72 In *re Sealed Case*, 310 F.3d 717, 742 (FISA Ct. Rev. 2002); see *United States* v. *Truong Dinh Hung*, 629 F.2d 908, 913 (4th Cir. 1980); *United States* v. *Butenko*, 494 F.2d 593, 606 (3d Cir. 1974) (*en banc*); *United States* v. *Brown*, 484 F.2d 418, 426 (5th Cir. 1973). But cf. *Zweibon* v. *Mitchell*, 516 F.2d 594, 613–14 (D.C. Cir. 1975) (Wright, J., plurality); see also ibid. at 651.

73 See, e.g., *Truong*, 629 F.2d at 913.

74 See, e.g., DOJ White Paper, supra note 63, at 8.

75 See, e.g., Am. Bar Association, *Task Force on Domestic Surveillance in the Fight against Terrorism, Report 13* (Feb. 2006).

76 See, e.g., *Samson* v. *California*, 126 S. Ct. 2193 (2006).
77 See generally Fed. R. Crim. P. 41.
78 See *United States* v. *Truong Dinh Hung*, 629 F.2d 908, 913–15 (4th Cir. 1980); see also Memorandum of the Constitution Project and the Center for National Security Studies in Response to the U.S. Department of Justice's Defense of Warrantless Electronic Surveillance at 42, In *re* Warrantless Electronic Surveillance (FISA Ct. Feb. 28, 2006), available at www.cnss.org/FISC%20Memorandum%20(signed).PDF.
79 See *Steagald* v. *United States*, 451 U.S. 204, 222 (1981); cf. *Minnesota* v. *Dickerson*, 508 U.S. 366, 382 (1993) (Scalia, J., concurring).
80 See *Dickerson*, 508 U.S. at 427–35 (discussing the legislative history of FISA's surveillance standard).
81 Ku, *supra* note 43, at 1375.
82 Cf. *New York* v. *Burger*, 482 U.S. 691, 703 (1987); Anthony G. Amsterdam, Perspectives on the Fourth Amendment, 58 *Minnesota Law Review* 349, 418 (1974); but cf. *United States* v. *Grubbs*, 126 S. Ct. 1494, 1501 (2006).
83 Senate Hearing, *Wartime Executive Power*, *supra* note 5, at 815 (prepared statement of Morton Halperin, Senior Fellow, Center for American Progress).
84 See ibid. (prepared statement of Morton Halperin, Senior Fellow, Center for American Progress, and Executive Director, Open Society Policy Center).
85 See 50 U.S.C. § 1806 (2000) (regulating the use of information obtained in FISA surveillance); see also *Ferguson* v. *City of Charleston*, 532 U.S. 67, 78 (2001).
86 See, e.g., 50 U.S.C. § 1809 (FISA provision prescribing criminal penalties); cf. Amsterdam, *supra* note 82, at 428–29 (arguing that police-made rules could include administrative sanctions).
87 Cf. *Hamdi* v. *Rumsfeld*, 542 U.S. 507, 536 (2004); Richard A. Posner, *Not a Suicide Pact: The Constitution in a Time of National Emergency* 94–103 (2006).
88 See *supra* notes 52–54 and accompanying text. At least before FISA, Title III notified the public that the President might have the power to conduct surveillance outside statutory constraints. See *supra* note 53.
89 See *Groh* v. *Ramirez*, 540 U.S. 551, 564 (2004).
90 *Kyllo* v. *United States*, 533 U.S. 27, 31 (2001).
91 See *Illinois* v. *Gates*, 462 U.S. 213, 236 (1983).
92 See *supra* notes 41–47 and accompanying text. The government might also rely on exigencies not directly related to a national security emergency or on Fourth Amendment doctrines, besides the exigent circumstances doctrine, that allow warrantless searches. As a practical matter, however, these alternatives are not likely to arise often.
93 For example, FISA prescribes the contents of court orders authorizing surveillance. 50 U.S.C. § 1805(c) (2000). The prescribed contents include a judicial direction that officials "compensate, at the prevailing rate," anyone who helps officials accomplish the surveillance – including the landlord who uses her passkey to open the apartment in which a telephone tap is to be placed. Ibid. § 1805(c)(2)(D). A surveillance order that omits this direction technically violates FISA, as does a surveillance operation in which a landlord assists without receiving compensation. Yet neither of these technical violations should lead to a conclusion that the surveillance violates the Fourth Amendment.
94 Courts can presumably review surveillance under the NSA program when the government seeks to use evidence derived from such surveillance in criminal prosecutions. Cf. *United State* v. *Dumeisi*, 424 F.3d 566, 578–79 (7th Cir. 2005) (reviewing the district court's ruling on the defendant's motion to suppress evidence derived from FISA surveillance). Judicial review may also be available in civil litigation challenging the program, though this remains to be determined. *Am. Civil Liberties Union* v. *Nat'l Sec. Agency*, 493 F.3d 644 (6th Cir. 2007), *petition for cert. filed* (U.S. Oct. 3, 2007) (No. 07-468).
95 See Seamon and Gardner, *supra* note 3, at 336–37 and nn. 66–71 (2005).
96 Protect America Act of 2007, Pub. L. No. 110-55, 121 Stat. 552.
97 U.S. Const. amend. IV.

9   Free association rights in a time of terror

Elizabeth Barker Brandt

Introduction

Throughout the history of the United States, controversial groups have been persecuted in the name of national security. In 1959, lamenting the failure of a majority of the U.S. Supreme Court to overturn a contempt of Congress conviction arising from the defendant's refusal to testify before a subcommittee of the House Committee on Un-American Activities, Justice Black observed that

> [h]istory should teach us then, that in times of high emotional excitement minority parties and groups which advocate extremely unpopular social or governmental innovations will always be typed as criminal gangs and attempts will always be made to drive them out.[1]

Erwin Chemerinsky, a leading contemporary constitutional scholar, citing the government's persecution of suspected communists during the Red Scare, among other incidents, concluded:

> In the four years since September 11, 2001, one of the worst aspects of American history has been repeating itself. For over 200 years, repression has been the response to threats to security. In hindsight, every such instance was clearly a grave error that restricted our most precious freedoms for no apparent gain.[2]

Since the September 11, 2001 terrorist attacks in the United States, the U.S. government has pursued policies outlawing groups and prosecuting their supporters that mirror the failed policies of the Red Scare[3] and those directed at antiwar and civil rights activists during the 1960s and 1970s.[4] The government's failed anticommunism policies were the fertile ground upon which much of the Supreme Court's jurisprudence developed regarding the right of free association. The government's domestic surveillance of civil rights and anti-Vietnam War groups and activists triggered the Church Committee's investigation of secret domestic spying activities. The aftermath of that investigation was the adoption of legislation and policies aimed, in part, at limiting the ability of government to pursue individuals based on guilt by association.[5]

In the preface to its final conclusions and recommendations, the Church Committee mirrored Justice Black's cautionary conclusions, observing that

> [t]he crescendo of improper intelligence activity in the latter part of the 1960s and the early 1970s shows what we must watch out for: In times of crisis, the Government will exercise its power to conduct domestic intelligence activities to the fullest extent. The distinction between legal dissent and criminal conduct is easily forgotten.[6]

One of the key findings of the Committee was that the FBI should be prohibited from "interfering with lawful ... assembly, organizational activity, or association of Americans"[7] and that the FBI should be prohibited from "maintaining information on the political beliefs [or] political associations of Americans."[8]

The focus of this chapter is on the right of free association. To fully protect that right, courts must implement a judicial standard that guards against imposing individual liability based solely on guilt by association and that curtails the government's ability to blacklist groups on the basis of their rhetoric. Prior to the mid-1940s, the court's approach to free association incorporated such standards, requiring that the government prove that a person knew of a group's illegal activities and intended to carry them out as a condition of imposing civil or criminal sanctions on the person – the "knowledge and intent" test. When regulating groups directly, this approach required that government show that a group is engaged in illegal activities and that the government bear a heavy burden of justification based on facts to support its policies. The knowledge and intent test informed the court's early decision making on the right of free association. While it dropped from the court's analytical framework in the mid-1950s, it was revived in the waning days of McCarthyism as the court belatedly moved to strike down the policy framework of anticommunism. The notion that an individual's group associations should not be suspect unless the person knew that a group was engaged in illegal conduct and intended to carry out the group's illegal purposes also informed the Church Committee's recommendations.[9]

Despite its historical importance, the knowledge and intent test has disappeared from modern approaches to the right of free association. The test must be reinvigorated because it is essential to limiting governmental investigations and prosecutions of individuals based solely on their group association and to limiting the government's ability to blacklist controversial groups. The knowledge and intent test ensures that government actions against individuals focus on an individual's knowledge and activities and not on political rhetoric or association. It fills a gap in the court's current approach to free association, by limiting the imposition of "guilt by association" and ensuring that the investigative and surveillance activities of government are focused on evidence and not assumptions.

The right of free association in the Supreme Court

Most analysts divide the Supreme Court's current free association jurisprudence into three lines of authority. First, *associational privacy* turns on the individual right of members of an organization not to have their association with the organization disclosed.[10] Second, the *intimate association* cases focus on the privacy rights of individuals to form and maintain intimate relationships free of governmental intervention.[11] Third, the *expressive association* cases deal with the ability of groups to define themselves and to control their message.[12]

Yet these three categories of cases neglect a traditional line of free association cases that limited the government's ability to impute guilt based on an individual's associations. These now-neglected cases demonstrate that the government could not presume bad intent or attach negative consequences to an individual merely from the fact of association. They required strong fact-based justifications that a group was engaged in illegal activity to support official governmental policies condemning the group.

When the cases that comprise the guilt by association doctrine are considered, the gaps in the law of free association left by the associational privacy and expressive association doctrines become clear. Neither doctrine offers any protection to individuals who are investigated and targeted precisely because of their associations. Neither doctrine provides a strong basis for striking down a conviction for providing material support to a terrorist organization, for example, because a person who is prosecuted for material support is not required necessarily to violate the privacy of other group members. Likewise, material support prosecutions do not directly interfere with a group's expressive purpose in the sense that the government, in such prosecutions, is not requiring the group to admit nonadherents or to sponsor the speech of nonadherents. Reinvigorating the guilt-by-association standard and limiting the blacklisting of groups fills this gap in current free association jurisprudence and ensures that an individual could not be the subject of surveillance, investigation or punishment based exclusively on his or her associations.

The importance of reinvigorating the knowledge and intent test is underscored by historical analysis. As Justice Black, the Church Committee, and Chemerinsky make clear, courts have not, in the past, withstood the crush of fear in times of national insecurity. Any judicial approach to guilt by association must acknowledge the historical failure to protect individuals and groups from the rush to judgment of the fearful majority.

Modern association jurisprudence: associational privacy and expressive association

The doctrines of associational privacy and expressive association reflect a narrow understanding of the free association that views associational rights as derivative rights that are not protected unless they are necessary to the exercise of speech, religion or other fundamental rights.[13] Thus, while the associational privacy and expressive association cases go some way toward protecting rights of free association, neither doctrine addresses the problem of guilt by association.

Guilt by association

The guilt by association cases fall into two categories. The first group of cases deals with the circumstances under which the government may attach negative consequences to an individual strictly because of his or her associations. In its early cases, the Supreme Court reasoned that civil and criminal penalties could not attach to individuals on the basis of group associations without its having been shown that the person knew of the group's illegal activities and intended to participate in or advance them. This standard, the "knowledge and intent" test, is the key aspect of free association jurisprudence that protects individuals against guilt by association. The second group of cases deals with the circumstances under which the government may blacklist or outlaw groups and by doing so attach negative consequences to group members. Here the court's approach is less clear. Nonetheless, it has held that the government may not blacklist a group without providing notice that the group is to be listed, notice of the evidence against the group, and a hearing at which the group may present evidence in its defense. Moreover, the court has made clear that a heavy burden is on the government to justify its decision and that the government's decision must be supported by the facts.

Knowledge and intent

A line of cases in the middle of the twentieth century recognized limits on government's ability to impose penalties on individuals based solely on their association with a particular group. The first of these cases was *De Jonge* v. *Oregon*.[14] There, the court adopted a knowledge and intent test[15] holding that an individual could not be charged with criminal conduct solely on the basis on his or her association with a group alleged to engage in illegal conduct; some evidence that the defendant engaged in illegal conduct or that illegal conduct took place at a meeting organized by the defendant was required.[16] The *De Jonge* court rooted its requirement squarely on the First Amendment protection of peaceful assembly:

> If the persons assembling have committed crimes elsewhere, if they have formed or are engaged in a conspiracy against the public peace and order, they may be prosecuted for their conspiracy or other violation of valid Laws. But it is a different matter when the State, instead of prosecuting for such offenses, seizes upon mere participation in a peaceable assembly and a lawful public discussion as the basis for a criminal charge.... The defendant was none the less entitled to discuss the public issues of the day and thus in a lawful manner, without incitement to violence or crime, to seek redress of

alleged grievances. That was of the essence of his guaranteed personal liberty.[17]

De Jonge was applied in a number of early cases in which labor leaders and political dissenters were convicted of offenses arising from the coordination of, or participation in, lawful but controversial public meetings.[18]

During the late 1940s and 1950s, however, *De Jonge* fell out of favor. Although it was never overruled, the court, mirroring the anticommunist fervor of the time,[19] often overlooked *De Jonge*, and upheld the imposition of civil and criminal penalties based solely on a person's association with alleged subversive or disfavored groups.[20] Yet the knowledge and intent requirement persisted. For example, in *Wieman* v. *Updegraff*,[21] the court, without citing *De Jonge* but incorporating its rationale, struck down an Oklahoma statute requiring all employees to swear that they were not affiliated with outlawed organizations. The *Wieman* court reasoned that "[i]ndiscriminate classification of innocent with knowing activity must fall as an assertion of arbitrary power."[22]

The *De Jonge* test was revived as the court began to incrementally chip away at the framework of anticommunism.[23] For example, citing *De Jonge*, in *Shelton* v. *Tucker*,[24] the court struck down an "unlimited and indiscriminate" Arkansas statute requiring teachers to list all their associations as a condition of employment. In *United States* v. *Robel*,[25] the Supreme Court overturned a conviction based on the employment of the defendant, who had at one time been a member of the Communist Party, at a defense facility after it was designated as off-limits to such individuals.[26] The court concluded that "the statute quite literally establishes guilt by association alone, without any need to establish that an individual's association poses the threat feared by the government in proscribing it."[27]

The full extent of the revived knowledge and intent requirement was clarified in *NAACP* v. *Claiborne Hardware Co.*[28] There, the court reversed a state damage judgment against members of the NAACP arising from an NAACP boycott of white-owned businesses because the liability judgment violated the First Amendment rights of the boycotters. While a few participants in the boycott had engaged in illegal conduct, the state court liability judgment was levied against all the identified boycott participants. Rejecting this all-encompassing approach, the court concluded:

> Civil liability may not be imposed merely because an individual belonged to a group, some members of which committed acts of violence. For liability to be imposed by reason of association alone, it is necessary to establish that the group itself possessed unlawful goals and that the individual held a specific intent to further those illegal aims.[29]

Outlawing groups

The U.S. Supreme Court has not often addressed governmental policies that outlaw groups directly. Of course, most of the anticommunist cases arose because the government wanted to drive the Communist Party out of the United States. The anticommunist policies were based on various findings that the party was engaged in illegal activity, including espionage against the United States, and that it advocated the overthrow of the U.S. government. Because these findings were not seriously questioned by the court, it never truly engaged the underlying goal of the policies.[30]

One of the few cases to directly raise the propriety of outlawing groups is *Joint Anti-Fascist Refugee Committee* v. *McGrath*.[31] The plaintiffs were three activist organizations that had been designated as communist organizations by the Attorney General and had been referred to the Loyalty Review Board.[32] They challenged both the procedure used to make the designations and the substantive accuracy of the designations. The Supreme Court reversed the dismissal of the complaint, finding that, on the basis of the pleadings, a case had been stated that the Attorney General's designation was arbitrary and violated the procedures established by the President's executive order. While the court did not question the constitutionality of the executive order itself,[33] it did require notice to the organization that it was to be designated, notice of the evidence on which the designations were based, and administrative hearings at which the organizations could present evidence on their behalf.[34]

In one of the last opinions issued by the court in which it deferred to Congressional findings about the evils of communism, *Communist Party of the United States* v. *Subversive Activities Control Board*,[35] the court again addressed the question of official condemnation of groups. It upheld the designation of the Communist Party of the United States as a "communist-action organization" by the Subversive Activities Control Board. This designation had comprehensively negative impacts.[36] In his dissenting opinion, Justice Douglas concluded that "the plan of the Act is to make it impossible for an organization to continue to function."[37]

Justice Frankfurter, under the guise of avoiding premature constitutional questions, declined to address any of the constitutional issues. Instead, he addressed only the question of registration itself.[38] With this narrow approach to the issues, Frankfurter upheld the registration requirement deferring to the findings of Congress in support of the legislation.

Although *Communist Party* would seem to be strong authority that the government may constitutionally blacklist groups, it also stands out as a decision motivated more by its time than by the law.[39]

The *Communist Party* case captures the dilemma of context – when fear about safety and security drive policy making, limits on the scope of governmental power intended to protect dissidents fall by the wayside. Ideally, courts are the check that ensures such tyranny of fear does not target dissidents unjustifiably.[40] Yet the waxing and waning of the knowledge and intent test itself illustrates that courts have fallen victim to the prevailing mood of fear.

More recently, and in a different context, the court addressed government policies aimed at stigmatizing groups in *Healy* v. *James*.[41] There, the court rejected the decision of Central Connecticut State College to withhold official recognition from a student chapter of Students for a Democratic Society (SDS) based on assumptions and innuendo regarding the connection of the student group to the national SDS. Summarizing its earlier approaches to free association, the court concluded that it had "consistently disapproved governmental action ... denying rights and privileges solely because of a citizen's association with an unpopular organization."[42] Emphasizing the knowledge and intent test, the court went on, "In these cases it has been established that 'guilt by association alone without [establishing] that an individual's association poses the threat feared by the government' is an impermissible basis upon which to deny First Amendment Rights."[43] The college had a "heavy burden" to justify its decision to deny official recognition by showing a "legitimate interest in preventing disruption on campus."[44]

This trio of cases is difficult to reconcile. But if *Communist Party* is acknowledged as a product of its context, it can stand as a reminder of the dangers of outlawing groups. *McGrath* and *Healy* then provide the outlines of a principled approach to free association and controversial groups, even in times of fear and insecurity. First, while the Supreme Court has not announced a doctrine that would bar the blacklisting of groups, per se, certain procedures must accompany the decision to blacklist a group. *McGrath* requires notice of the blacklisting action, notice of the evidence upon which the government's action is based, and a hearing at which the group may present evidence in its defense. *Healy* makes clear that the government justification for the blacklisting must be based in facts and that the government has a heavy burden to justify the blacklisting decision. These requirements are the corollary of the knowledge and intent test, the effect of which is to ensure that if the government is going to pursue the individual because of his or her associations, it must have evidence of wrongdoing by the individual. The *McGrath/Healy* test ensures that if the government is first going to blacklist the group, it must have evidence that the group is engaged in illegality or wrongdoing. In either case, the government may not base its action on the speech of the group or its members, or on assumptions about such speech that are not borne out by the facts.

A reinvigorated three-pronged approach to free association

Reinvigorating the guilt-by-association standard of *De Jonge* and pursuing the *Healy/McGrath* approach to blacklisting groups provides a coherent basis for avoiding guilt by association. The knowledge and intent test combined with limitations on blacklisting groups together ensure that an individual could not be the subject of surveillance, investigation or punishment based exclusively on his or her associations. Recognition of the knowledge and intent standard must also entail a clear recognition of its central role in association jurisprudence and self-consciously acknowledge the court's failure to apply the test during past times of insecurity, if it is to stand against the current or future waves of fear and insecurity.

Targeting groups and their members and contacts in response to the "War on Terror"

The protection provided by the *De Jonge* standard is more important now than has been the case in many years. The U.S. government has radically increased its infringement of associational freedoms as part of the "War on Terror," building on the more invasive infrastructure established during the 1990s.

Designation of groups as terrorist organizations

One of the central features of the U.S. Government's response to the September 11, 2001 terrorist attacks in the United States has been to inaugurate a so-called "War on Terror."[45] A tactic of this war has been to target individuals for investigation on the basis of their associations either with controversial groups or with other controversial individuals. This process began before 2001 pursuant to the Antiterrorism and Effective Death Penalty Act (AEDPA),[46] which permits the Secretary of State to designate groups as "foreign terrorist organizations."[47] In order to make a designation, the Secretary of State must find that: (1) the group is foreign; (2) the group engages in terrorist activity[48] or terrorism,[49] or has the capability and intent to engage in terrorist activity or terrorism; and (3) the group's terrorist activity or terrorism threatens the national security of the United States or its nationals.[50] In addition to directly sanctioning the group,[51] the designation triggers criminal sanctions and immigration consequences for those associated with designated groups.[52]

The AEDPA power to designate foreign terrorist organizations is not the only blacklisting power used by the federal government in the War on Terror. In addition, since the mid-1970s the President has had the power under the International Emergency Economic Power Act (IEEPA)[53] to designate terrorist groups for the purpose of freezing assets and blocking transactions with the terrorist entities.[54] Prior to the Clinton Administration, this law had primarily served as a basis for freezing assets of other governments; it had not been used against private groups or individuals.[55]

The official condemnation of groups is the result of a process that began at the time of the first World Trade Center bombings in 1993[56] and the Oklahoma City bombings in 1995.[57] Government officials sought to strengthen U.S. policy criminalizing support for terrorism.[58] Policy makers were dissatisfied because the law did not criminalize the provision of financial support for nonterrorist purposes to organizations that also engaged in terrorism. The AEDPA provision criminalizing the provision of material support to terrorist organizations emerged in response to this perceived need.[59] As originally adopted, the statute did not require proof that an individual intended to support terrorism or knew of their support for terrorist activity.[60] Alan Williams's chapter in this volume (Chapter 12) engages more specifically with the First Amendment implications of the criminalization of "material support" and proposes a legislative reform that addresses some of the concerns I raise here.[61]

The crime of providing material support to terrorist organizations is part of a larger web of government policies aimed at outlawing groups labeled as terrorist. The USA PATRIOT Act also extended to the Secretary of State the power to exclude individuals from the country because of their association with "group[s] whose public endorsement of acts of terrorist activity" undermines the United States.[62] Also, since 2001 a number of governmental entities have begun maintaining less formal lists of domestic terrorist groups, including the National Counterterrorism Center[63] and the Department of Homeland Security.[64] The Department of Justice now has a division called the Terrorist Screening Center, which has responsibility, in part, for consolidating terrorist watch lists maintained by a number of different agencies.[65]

The inflammatory context of fear of terrorism has led to attenuated and unsubstantiated allegations that groups are terrorist organizations accompanied by investigation and prosecution of group members. The comparison to the context of fear that fueled U.S. anticommunist policies is unavoidable. The same ingredient is missing from both the historic discourse on communism and the modern discourse on terrorism: a self-conscious awareness by policy makers and courts of the danger of fear and possibility of guilt by association.

In several prominent instances, the government has made public allegations that an organization is a terrorist organization, but has not pursued designation and has not made the case for designation in related proceedings. For example, in 2003 the government alleged that an organization called Help the Needy was a terrorist organization. Although the sponsor of the organization was convicted of money laundering, the government was unable to prove that he had provided material support to terrorism and did not pursue a designation of the organization.[66] In another incident, Sami Omar Al-Hussayen was charged with, and later acquitted of, providing material support for terrorism because he developed websites for the Islamic Assembly of North America (IANA). The government intimated that IANA was a terrorist organization but neither sought designation of the group nor charged Al-Hussayen with providing material support to a terrorist organization in relation to IANA or any other terrorist organization.[67] In this type of fear-filled, high-profile setting, attention to the government's heavy burden of justification is crucial to ensure accuracy and to protect against unfounded designations and allegations of terrorism or terrorist connections.

Terrorist designations and free association

These developments raise significant concern regarding free association rights and demonstrate the importance of reviving the court's neglected guilt by association jurisprudence. The case law that has developed in the lower federal courts around the designation of foreign terrorist organizations does not consider the possibility. On the one hand, many of the cases involve factual records that appear, as reported, to support both the designation of certain groups as terrorist organizations[68] and the prosecution of individuals for providing support to those organizations.[69] On the other hand, the serious nature of the facts seems to be driving a lack of attention to the possible constitutional issues and historical standards prohibiting guilt by association.

Designation of terrorist organizations

Several aspects of the group designation process raise constitutional issues in light of the *McGrath/Healy* framework. Though their views are anathema to most Americans, these terrorist groups may be expressive associations.[70] They certainly meet any definition of expressive association advanced in the case law. They seek to inculcate values. The groups advocate political positions that are controversial. The groups engage in many activities, some of which are purely conduct, some of which are purely speech, and some of which are conduct that has an expressive function. In the same way that membership in the NAACP would have been deterred if membership lists were made public, so, too, support of and membership in these groups will be deterred if the associational privacy interests of members is not protected. These impacts should only be justified within the U.S. constitutional system if a group is engaged in illegal activities and the government meets its heavy burden justifying coercive regulation of the group.

McGrath makes clear that in the course of determining whether a group is so engaged, a certain process is required. *Healy* makes clear that in establishing that groups engage in illegal activities, the burden on the government is heavy and that the decision must be based on substantial evidence. The procedures for designating terrorist organizations do not meet these standards. This failure is important not only because of the risk that regulation of groups will chill legitimate associational activity but also because such coercive regulation represents a slippery slope – sliding toward more casual infringement of less obviously dangerous groups.

Terrorist organization designations are made initially without prior notice to the terrorist organization. The Secretary of State makes a designation of a group as a foreign terrorist organization by first informing Congress of the designation in a classified communication. After a period of time during which members of Congress may object, the classification is published in the *Federal Register*. No provision is made for notice to the group prior to publication of the designation.[71] The Secretary of State is required to make an administrative record to support the designation.[72] But that record does not necessarily consist of evidence that is available to the organization or that is offered in defense of the organization.[73] The record may consist of classified information and may also be based on hearsay, newspaper reports, information on the internet and other third-hand information.[74] The designation statute provides for judicial review by the Court of Appeals for the D.C. Circuit, and such review is limited solely to the administrative record.[75] In *United States* v. *Rahmani*, the court explained, "At no point in the proceedings establishing the administrative record is the alleged terrorist organization afforded notice of the materials used against it or a right to comment on such materials or the development of the administrative record."[76]

This process is not consistent with *McGrath*. In *National Council of Resistance of Iran* v. *Secretary of State*, recognizing that designation impaired the exercise of fundamental rights, the D.C. Circuit held that the Secretary of State must permit a pre-designation hearing and must permit the group "the opportunity to present, at least in written form, such evidence as those entities may be able to produce to rebut the administrative record or otherwise negate the proposition that they are foreign terrorist organizations."[77] This holding is enigmatic, however, because despite its conclusion that the designation process violated due process, the court declined to set aside the designation at issue because of unexplained "foreign policy and national security" concerns and because the designation expired after two years.[78]

The D.C. Circuit's requirement of pre-designation protects core free association interests. The notice and hearing requirements of *McGrath* were aimed at providing the opportunity to a blacklisted group to avoid the negative effect on association that would result from designation. The impact of erroneous or unjustified designations is substantial. Membership in the United States will be deterred by the threat of prosecution for material support of the organization. Non-U.S. citizens associated with the group will be excluded or deported from the United States. Group assets in the United States will be frozen. The group would be effectively shut down.

The *National Council* court did not go far enough, however, to ensure the protection of free association rights. In addition to procedural defects in designating groups, the burden of proof employed in the designation proceedings does not meet the government's heavy burden of justification required by *Healy* as a condition for blacklisting organizations. First, the statute does not establish a standard by which the Secretary of State is to make her or his initial decision regarding designation. The designation statute provides and the D.C. Circuit has held that the Secretary of State's decision is reviewed solely on the basis of the administrative record.[79] The designation statute further provides that the scope of judicial review is limited; designations may be set aside only if they are:

a   arbitrary, capricious, an abuse of discretion, or otherwise not in accordance with law;
b   contrary to constitutional right, power, privilege, or immunity;
c   in excess of statutory jurisdiction, authority, or limitation, or short of statutory right;
d   lacking substantial support in the administrative record taken as a whole or in classified information submitted to the court under paragraph (2), or
e   not in accord with the procedures required by law.[80]

Applying this standard, the D.C. Circuit has reasoned that "the record need provide only a sufficient basis for a reasonable person to conclude that [the organization] was likely behind such a [terrorist] threat."[81] This approach permits designation on a bare minimum of evidence and does not ensure that even the minimal evidence is reliable.

Moreover, the use of secret evidence in these group designation hearings is not consistent with the standard of *McGrath* and *Healy*. *McGrath* specifically requires that a blacklisted group must be permitted to respond to the evidence against it. This requirement is consistent with the due process requirements that have developed to govern governmental decisions depriving an individual of a liberty interest.[82] The constitutionally protected interest – the First Amendment rights of group members to associate for political purposes – is substantial. If that were not a grave enough interest, however, the interests of individual defendants in material support cases is also at stake; designation is a predicate to many of the material support cases and cannot be challenged in those cases.[83] The government's interest in maintaining the confidentiality of classified national security information is also strong in these cases. Nonetheless, the burden of justification is on the government. It is difficult to see how the government can on the one hand proceed with a policy that substantially impairs the First Amendment rights of group members, and on the other hand argue that it should be relieved of its burden of justification because of its need to keep evidence classified. At least one commentator has suggested that, at a minimum, the government must be required to produce unclassified summaries of the classified information upon which it relies in designation proceedings.[84] Even this minimum standard is troubling when the secret evidence used in a designation proceeding becomes the basis for a criminal prosecution.[85]

Finally, the designation statute purports to limit the ability of an individual to question the designation of an organization as a defense to a charge of providing material support to a terrorist organization.[86] The designation statute also provides that where a designation is revoked or otherwise set aside, that action is not retroactive.[87] While one court originally held this restriction to be unconstitutional, its decision was reversed on appeal.[88] Every other court has upheld the restriction on raising designation as a defense to material support.[89] This limitation increases the possibility of assessing guilt by association since the only intent required to support a conviction for providing material support to a terrorist organization is knowledge that the organization was designated.[90] If the process by which the designation occurs is not structured to ensure that the government meets its heavy burden of justification before designating a group as a terrorist organization, and if knowledge of the designation can itself support a conviction for providing material support to a terrorist organization, and if a defendant cannot raise the defects in the designation process, the guilt by association circle is truly complete.

The possibility of this harm is illustrated in the *Afshari/Rahmani/National Council* line of cases. There, at least one of the defendants was subject to possible conviction for contributing money to an organization that had been designated in a process that had been declared defective by the D.C. Circuit (although the court did not set aside the designation) and she was precluded from raising the constitutional defect as a defense in her criminal trial. Summarizing her untenable situation, Judge Kozinski wrote:

Rahmani is being criminally prosecuted, and almost certainly will be convicted, for contributing to an organization that has been designated as terrorist with none of the protections that are constitutionally required for such a designation. Worse, Rahmani will in all likelihood spend many years in prison for contributing to an organization whose designation the D.C. Circuit has held does not even meet the requirements of due process.[91]

Given these consequences of designation, the process employed must comply with that established in *McGrath*, and the government must be held to its heavy burden of justification as articulated in *Healy*, or the American constitutional principle barring guilt by association has been abrogated.

Material support for terrorist organizations

The material support cases raise a different version of the guilt by association problem. Because most terrorist organizations pursue both legal and illegal activities, the question is whether an individual may be convicted solely on the basis of knowledge of the organization's illegal activities even though the person did not intend to directly support those activities. To date, the cases have abandoned the knowledge and intent test.[92]

The material support cases have limited the knowledge and intent[93] test to situations in which the law prohibits mere membership in a terrorist organization. Since the material support provision does not, by its express language, prohibit mere membership or affiliation with a terrorist entity, the courts have concluded that it is not unconstitutional.[94] Yet the definition of "material support" is so broad[95] that it is hard to conceive of how individuals could become members or affiliate in any way with a designated terrorist organization without violating the material support statute. The express language of the statute criminalizes such things as the payment of membership dues or providing transportation (even for oneself) to and from meetings. If the person has any specialized knowledge, advocacy that incorporates such knowledge could be considered expert assistance. A lawyer, for example, who advocated for the free association rights of the organization could be providing expert assistance (assistance based on specialized knowledge) in violation of the statute.[96]

In addition to limiting the free association cases to mere membership, the courts have also characterized the activities involved in the cases as unprotected conduct, as opposed to protected speech and association. Avoiding the free association argument by focusing on conduct is uncomfortably close to the analytical method employed to justify the communist witch-hunts of the Red Scare in cases such as *Adler*, *Dennis* and *Douds*. *Adler* made the association–conduct distinction when the court reasoned that the defendant's First Amendment rights were not abridged because he was not barred from membership in a communist organization; rather, the statute in question regulated his employment with a state employer.[97] Likewise, in *Douds*, the court relied on the speech–conduct distinction, reasoning that

[g]overnment's interest here is not in preventing the dissemination of Communist doctrine or the holding of particular beliefs because it is feared that unlawful action will result therefrom if free speech is practiced. Its interest is in protecting the free flow of commerce from what Congress considers to be substantial evils of conduct that are not the products of speech at all.[98]

Dennis also turned on the speech–conduct distinction:

Congress [in criminalizing activities to organize the Communist Party in the Smith Act] did not intend to eradicate the free discussion of political theories, to destroy the traditional rights of Americans to discuss and evaluate ideas without fear of governmental sanction. Rather Congress was concerned with the very kind of activity in which the evidence showed these petitioners engaged.[99]

When the court reinvigorated the knowledge and intent test, it implicitly rejected the speech–conduct distinction of these cases because it recognized that the act of association with a group was itself protected absent knowledge and intent. The speech–conduct distinction now serves the same purpose it did then: to deflect the First Amendment argument. It is as vacuous now as it was eventually acknowledged to be then.

Conclusion

The U.S. constitutional commitment to the importance of political associations grows, in part, out of a shared history of the problem of guilt by association. The Red Scare prosecutions of alleged communists were based on the assumption that a contact with the Communist Party was the equivalent of endorsement of alleged illegal activities of the party. When they look back on that time period, many Americans are chagrined at their government's anticommunist policies. It should be recognized that the surveillance and undermining of political groups deterred people from speaking out, and led to a state of repression and fear. Today, in the face of a new and dangerous threat, America is embarked on a policy that has abandoned the lessons that should have been learned. The policy has been justified because it is believed that the present threat is more real and substantial than was the threat posed by communism. Yet there is a risk of sweeping innocent people into the maelstrom of terrorism prosecutions because Americans have not been vigilant and exacting in applying the rules that protect against assessing guilt by association, which require that government decisions to blacklist groups are justified by substantial evidence and that individuals are not prosecuted or otherwise penalized in the absence of proof that they intend to further that illegal activity.

Notes

1 *Barenblatt* v. *United States*, 360 U.S. 109, 150–51 (1959) (Black, J., dissenting).
2 Erwin Chemerinsky, Civil Liberties and the War on Terrorism, 45 *Washburn Law Journal* 1 (2005).
3 The United States experienced two waves of anticommunism popularly labeled "Red Scares" beginning in 1919 and extending though the mid-1960s. *See* Regin Schmidt, *Red Scare: FBI and the Origins of Anti-communism in the United States* (2000); Ellen Schrecker, *The Age of McCarthyism: A Brief History with Documents* (1994); Christina E. Wells, Fear and Loathing in Constitutional Decision-Making, 2005 *Wisconsin Law Review* 115, 121–22 (2005); William M. Wiecek, The Legal Foundations of Domestic Anticommunism: The Background of *Dennis* v. *United States*, 2001 *Supreme Court Review* 375 (2001). Both Red Scares are also discussed in Linda E. Fisher, Guilt by Expressive Association: Political Profiling, Surveillance and the Privacy of Groups, 46 *Arizona Law Review* 621, 629–31 (2004). The release of previously classified documents by both the United States and Russia in the mid-1990s indicates that there were strong ties between the Communist Party in the Soviet Union and American communists, and that the Soviets used the Communist Party in the United States to enlist spies to assist with the conduct of espionage. While most American communists were well-meaning and did not engage in activities that threatened American interests, the U.S. anticommunist policy framework never focused effectively on the actual espionage threat and swept many innocent and harmless activists into its net. See Martin Redish, *The Logic of Persecution: Free Expression and the McCarthy Era* (2006).
4 See S. Rep. No. 94-755 (1976) (6 Books), including *Intelligence Activities and The Rights of Americans* [hereinafter Church Book II], *Supplementary Detailed Staff Reports on Intelligence Activities and the Rights of Americans* [hereinafter Church Book III], and *Supplementary Reports on Intelligence Activities* [hereinafter Church Book VI], available at www.aarclibrary.org/publib/church/reports/book3/contents. htm (documenting incidents of surveillance directed at antiwar and civil rights activists).
5 See ibid. (Church Books II and III, in particular, focus on the government's domestic surveillance activities). See also Loch K. Johnson, *A Season of Inquiry: The Senate Intelligence Investigation* (1985) (documenting and explaining the work of the Church Committee); LeRoy Ashby and Rod Gramer, *Fighting the Odds: The Life of Senator Frank Church* 412–92 (1994) (describing Senator Church's involvement in intelligence issues). Largely as a result of the Church Committee Report, Congress adopted the Foreign Intelligence Surveillance Act, 50 U.S.C. §§ 1801–1811, 1821–1829, 1841–1846, 1861–1862 (2000), limiting domestic surveillance activities. There is dispute among scholars as to the origins and rationale for the so-called wall of separation that arose in the last half of the twentieth century between criminal investigations and intelligence gathering. Turf wars between agencies and the complexity of the government's response to and use of new technologies for surveillance certainly played a role in the development of such policies. In addition, however, it seems clear that the Church Committee Report emboldened and lent support to the view that criminal investigation and intelligence gathering should be separated. See William Funk, Electronic Surveillance of Terrorism: The Intelligence/Law Enforcement Dilemma – A History, 11 *Lewis and Clark Law Review* (forthcoming 2007) (manuscript on file with the author) (detailing the development of the so-called wall between intelligence gathering and criminal wiretapping in the contest of the development of electronic surveillance); Diane Carraway Piette and Jessica Radack, Piercing the "Historical Mists": The People and Events behind the Passage of FISA and the Creation of the "Wall," 17 *Stanford Law and Policy Review* 437, 444–48 (2006) (describing the development of Department of Justice policy separating intelligence gathering and criminal investigations).

6 Church Book II, *supra* note 4, at 289.

7 Ibid. at 317 (Recommendation 40(b)).

8 Ibid. at 318 (Recommendation 41).

9 In the preface to its final recommendations, the Church Committee observed that "no citizen should have to weigh his or her desire to ... join a group, against the risk of having lawful association ... used against him." Church Book II, *supra* note 4 at 291. In answering the question "When should an American be the subject of an investigation at all?" the Committee cautioned,: "We attempt to change the focus of investigations from constitutionally protected association and advocacy to dangerous conduct." Ibid. at 294. To accomplish this, the Committee recommended that investigations not be permitted unless the government had a reasonable suspicion that an individual was engaged in terrorism, hostile foreign intelligence activities, or criminal conduct. Ibid. at 317–24.

10 In connection with associational privacy, the court has recognized that advocacy of ideas is "undeniably enhanced by group association" and that "[i]nviolability of privacy in group association may in many circumstances be indispensable to preservation of freedom of association, particularly where a group espouses dissident beliefs." *NAACP* v. *Alabama ex rel. Patterson*, 357 U.S. 449 (1957) (holding that maintaining the privacy of group members was essential to the furtherance of the NAACP's purposes). "Effective advocacy of both public and private points of view, particularly controversial ones," the court reasoned, "is undeniably enhanced by group association." Ibid. at 462.

11 This chapter will not focus on this line of authority. It grows out of the Court's recognition that government should have a diminished role in regulating the characteristics of intimate personal relationships. See, e.g., *Bd. of Dir. of Rotary Int'l.* v. *Rotary Club of Duarte*, 481 U.S. 537, 545 (1987). For general discussion, see Kenneth Karst, The Freedom of Intimate Association, 89 *Yale Law Journal* 624 (1980).

12 *Boy Scouts of Am.* v. *Dale*, 530 U.S. 640 (2000). See also Nan D. Hunter, Expressive Identity: Recuperating Dissent for Equality, 35 *Harvard Civil Rights–Civil Liberties Review* 1 (2000) (discussing the developing expressive association doctrine and arguing that both expression and group membership are inextricably linked in the context of identity). In *Dale*, the court recognized that when individuals come together for expressive purposes, they form "expressive associations" that are protected from government interference in their internal operations or with their message. Because the groups have a core expressive purpose, the court has held that the government cannot regulate them in a way that undermines the ability of such groups to convey their message.

13 The derivative view of free association ignores the express language of the First Amendment regarding peaceable assembly. U.S. Const. amend. I ("Congress shall make no law ... abridging ... the right of the people peaceably to assemble"). Early free association cases were more expansive. See *De Jonge* v. *Oregon*, 299 U.S. 353 (1937) (striking down a conviction for organizing a public meeting affiliated with the Communist Party, and concluding that "peaceable assembly for lawful discussion cannot be made a crime"); *Thomas* v. *Collins*, 323 U.S. 516 (1945) (rejecting the state's argument that the right of peaceful assembly was not implicated because the meeting in question was private). See David Cole, Hanging with the Wrong Crowd: Of Gangs, Terrorists, and the Right of Association, 1999 *Supreme Court Review* 203, 226–27 (1999) (arguing that that the notions of association and assembly were synonymous to the founders); Jason Mazzone, Freedom's Associations, 77 *Washington Law Review* 639 (2002) (arguing that freedom of assembly incorporated free association in the notions of popular sovereignty in the early Republic). For more general discussion about the important value of group association in a democratic polity, see Ronald Garet, Constitutionality and Existence: The Rights of Groups, 56 *Southern California Law Review* 1001, 1018–23 (1983) (arguing that the associational privacy

cases err by treating the right of association as derivative of free speech rights and fail to recognize the intrinsic value of groups); Stanley Ingber, Rediscovering the Communal Worth of Individual Rights: The First Amendment in Institutional Contexts, 69 *Texas Law Review* 1, 5–9 (1990) (arguing that the court has failed to recognize the roll of community in further expressive activities).

14   299 U.S. 353 (1937). De Jonge was charged with violating Oregon's criminal syndicalism statute after he coordinated a peaceful meeting sponsored by the Oregon Communist Party to protest alleged illegal raids on the homes of workers at which a number of individuals associated with the Communist Party spoke. Ibid. at 257.

15   See Cole, *supra* note 13, at 215–19 (referring to a later version of the *De Jonge* test as a specific intent test). See also Fisher, *supra* note 3, at 661–72 (arguing that government should have a reasonable suspicion of criminal activity before surveillance of political groups is warranted).

16   See Cole, *supra* note 13, at 260.

17   *De Jonge*, 299 U.S. at 365.

18   See, e.g., *Thomas* v. *Collins*, 323 U.S. 516 (1945) (reversing the conviction of a union organizer for failing to register prior to speaking at an otherwise lawful gathering); *Herndon* v. *Lowry*, 301 U.S. 242, 258–57 (1937) (reversing conviction for attempting to incite insurrection by organizing meetings of the Communist Party); *Bridges* v. *Wixom*, 326 U.S. 135, 165 (1945) (reversing deportation and detention based on an immigrant's membership in the Communist Party); *Taylor* v. *Mississippi*, 319 U.S. 583, 590 (1943) (reversing conviction for communicating views disloyal to the government).

19   See Wells, *supra* note 3, at 117–18 (arguing that courts were unable to withstand public fears and pressure around national security issues and that the Cold War decade of the 1950s and the prosecution of the leaders of the Communist Party are particularly telling examples of this).

20   See, e.g., *Adler* v. *Bd. of Educ. of N.Y.*, 342 U.S. 485 (1952) (upholding a comprehensive New York statute prohibiting public employment of teachers affiliated with the Communist Party); *Am. Comm'n. Assn.* v. *Douds*, 339 U.S. 382 (1950) (upholding a provision of the National Labor Relations Act requiring union officials to sign an affidavit that they are not members of the Community Party). *Cf. Communist Party of the U.S.* v. *Subversive Activities Control Bd.*, 367 U.S. 1, 71–74 (1961) (holding that Communist Party must register as a subversive organization pursuant to comprehensive federal legislation barring passports, public employment, social security benefits and other governmental benefits to members of such organizations).

21   344 U.S. 183 (1952).

22   Ibid. at 191. The court also insisted that its prior loyalty oath cases had also imposed a knowledge and intent requirement. Ibid. (citing *Adler*, 342 U.S. 485), *Garner* v. *Bd. of Pub. Works*, 341 U.S. 716 (1951); *Gerende* v. *Bd. of Supervisors*, 341 U.S. 56 (1951)

23   See Philip P. Frickey, Getting from Joe to Gene (McCarthy): The Avoidance Canon, Legal Process Theory, and Narrowing Statutory Interpretation in the Early Warren Court, 93 *California Law Review* 397 (2005) (documenting the incremental change in the approach of the early Warren Court to the anticommunism issue and arguing that the justices used conservative legal theory and construction rules to move the divided court toward consensus).

24   *Shelton* v. *Tucker*, 364 U.S. 479 (1960). See also *Elfbrandt* v. *Russell*, 384 U.S. 11 (1966) (striking down a similar loyalty oath in Arizona).

25   *United States* v. *Robel*, 389 U.S. 258 (1967).

26   Ibid. at 260.

27   Ibid. at 265. Cole cites *Scales* v. *United States*, 367 U.S. 203 (1961), as the source for what he calls the "specific intent" test. Cole, *supra* note 13, at 217. In *Scales*, the court upheld the defendant's conviction under the membership clause of the Smith

Act but narrowly interpreted the statute to require "active membership." Ibid. at 221. Having so construed the statute, the court rejected the Fifth and First Amendment challenges to the statute, which had both been based on the absence of a knowledge and intent requirement. The court's extensive discussion of the Fifth Amendment argument makes clear that it believed that knowledge and intent were constitutionally required. Ibid. at 224–26. It also clearly believed that the "active membership construction was akin to requiring knowledge of illegal activity and intent to participant in such activity." Ibid.

28 *NAACP* v. *Claiborne Hardware Co.*, 458 U.S. 886 (1982).
29 Ibid. at 920 (citing *Shelton* v. *Tucker*, 364 U.S. 479, 488 (1960)).
30 See Cole, *supra* note 13 at 216–17.
31 *Joint Anti-Fascist Refugee Committee* v. *McGrath*, 341 U.S. 123 (1951).
32 Ibid. at 125. President Truman established the Loyalty Review Board in Exec. Order No. 9835, 12 Fed. Reg. 1935 (Mar. 21, 1947). The Board had the authority to dismiss employees of the federal government who were affiliated with designated organizations.
33 *Joint Anti-Fascist Refugee Comm.* v. *McGrath*, 341 U.S. 123, 135 (1951). (reasoning that if the act of designating a group as communist without any process had been the purpose of the order, the case would have "bristled with constitutional issues").
34 Ibid. at 138 n.11.
35 *Communist Party of the U.S.* v. *Subversive Activities Control Bd.*, 367 U.S. 1 (1961).
36 Ibid. at 15–19.
37 Ibid. at 141.
38 Ibid. at 71–73. See Frickey, *supra* note 23, at 413–24.
39 Two terms after *Communist Party*, the court held that the individual registration provisions of the Subversive Activities Control Act were unconstitutional. *Albertson* v. *United States*, 382 U.S. 71 (1965) (holding that party officers could not be required to sign the registration documents for the Communist Party itself effectively rendering registration unworkable). See also *United States* v. *Robel*, 389 U.S. 258 (1967) (the provision barring employment in a defense facility struck down); *Aptheker* v. *Subversive Activities Control Bd.*, 378 U.S. 500 (1964) (the provision barring use of passports struck down).
40 See Redish, *supra* note 3, at 63–65 (2006) (reexamining the impact of McCarthy-era prosecutions in light of new evidence showing strong links between the Communist Party of the USA (CPUSA) and the Soviet Union, and arguing that even though the evidence now supports the American government's fear of the CPUSA, its prosecution of party leaders under the Smith Act and other laws had nothing to do with the threat of espionage and constituted unjustifiable government repression of an unpopular ideology); Richard Primus, Judicial Power and Mobilizable History, 65 *Maryland Law Review* 171 (2006) (arguing that engagement with history in constitutional interpretation bolsters the legitimacy of the constitutional system).
41 *Healy* v. *James*, 408 U.S. 169 (1972).
42 Ibid. at 185–86.
43 Ibid.
44 Ibid. at 184.
45 In his first address to Congress following the September 11 attacks, President Bush declared a "War on Terror." George W. Bush, *President's Address to a Joint Session of Congress and the American People*, available at 2001 WL 1103323 (Sept. 20, 2001). The term has come to encompass all the military, political and legal actions undertaken by the United States to prevent and respond to terrorism worldwide.
46 Pub L. No. 104-132, 110 Stat. 1214 (codified as amended in scattered sections of 7, 8, 11 15, 18, 19, 21, 28, 40 and 42 U.S.C.).
47 See 8 U.S.C. § 1189(a)(1) (2000 and Supp. I 2001). See Eric Broxmeyer, Comment: The Problems of Security and Freedom: Procedural Due Process and the Designation

of Foreign Terrorist Organizations under the Anti-terrorism and Effective Death Penalty Act, 22 *Berkeley Journal of International Law* 439, 441–46 (2004).

48 The definitions of "terrorist activity," "engages in terrorist activity," and "terrorist organizations" are complex and convoluted. In general, "terrorist activity" includes such things as hijacking; threatening to kill a person in order to pressure another person or government to release detainees; assignations; and the use of biological, chemical, or nuclear weapons. 8 U.S.C. § 1182(a)(3)(B)(iii) (2000). The term "engages in terrorist activity" includes inciting terrorist activity, preparing or planning terrorist activity, raising money for terrorism, soliciting members of terrorist organizations, or committing acts that an individual knows would afford material support to terrorism. Ibid. § 1182(a)(3)(B)(iv). A "terrorist organization" is an organization designated as such by the Secretary of State. Ibid. § 1182 (a)(3)(B)(iv).

49 22 U.S.C. § 2656f(d)(2) defines "terrorism" as "premeditated, politically motivated violence perpetrated against non-combatant targets by subnational groups or clandestine agents."

50 8 U.S.C. § 1189(a)(1).

51 For example, the Secretary of the Treasury can freeze assets of designated organizations held by American financial institutions and members of the organization cannot enter the United States. Ibid. § 1189(a)(2)(C).

52 See 18 U.S.C. § 2339B (2000 and Supp. I 2001) (criminalizing material support for terrorist organizations); 8 U.S.C. § 1182 (2000 and Supp. 2002) (limiting immigration rights of individuals found to provide support for designated foreign terrorist organization).

53 50 U.S.C. § 1701 (2000). The executive orders adopted to implement the presidential powers conferred in the act are Exec. Order No. 12,947, 60 Fed. Reg. 5,079 (Jan. 23, 1995) and Exec. Order No. 13,224, 66 Fed. Reg. 49,079 (Sept. 23, 2001).

54 50 U.S.C. § 1701–1707. See Kathryn A. Ruff, Note: Scared to Donate: An Examination of the Effects of Designating Muslim Charities as Terrorist Organizations on the First Amendment Rights of Muslim Donors, 9 *New York University Journal of Legislation and Public Policy* 447, 452–59 (2006).

55 See Ruff, *supra* note 54, at 453.

56 See Douglas Jehl, Explosion at the Twin Towers: Car Bombs; A Tool of Foreign Terror, Little Known in U.S., *New York Times*, Feb. 27, 1993, at 1:24.

57 See Bomb Rocks Federal Building in Oklahoma, *Chicago Tribune*, Apr. 19, 1995, at 1.

58 Robert M. Chesney, The Sleeper Scenario: Terrorism-Support Laws and the Demands of Prevention, 42 *Harvard Journal on Legislation* 1, 12 n.66 (2005) ("At least eight bills containing material support provisions were introduced ... [after the 1993 World Trade Center bombing in the spring and summer of 1993] during the 103d Congress"). The Clinton Administration almost immediately began to seek a broader material support statute, and, with the Oklahoma City bombing, got the boost necessary to pass broader legislation. Ibid. See also Tom Stacy, The "Material Support" Offense: The Use of Strict Liability in the War Against Terror, 14 *Kansas Journal of Law and Public Policy* 461, 462–63 (2005).

59 Anti-terrorism and Effective Death Penalty Act (AEDPA), Pub L. No. 104-132, 110 Stat. 1214 (2001) (codified as amended in scattered sections of 7, 8, 11, 15, 18, 19, 21, 28, 40, and 42 U.S.C.). President Clinton, who had issued "urgent calls" for Congress to pass antiterrorism legislation, signed the AEDPA one year after the Oklahoma City bombing. See Note, Blown Away? The Bill of Rights after Oklahoma City, 109 *Harvard Law Review* 2074, 2074–76 (1996). As he signed AEDPA into law, President Clinton said that "the legislation struck a 'mighty blow' against terrorists. 'America will never tolerate terrorism. America will never abide terrorists.'" President Clinton's Statement on Signing the Anti-terrorism and Effective Death Penalty Act of 1996, 1 Pub. Papers 630 (Apr. 24, 1996).

60 Anti-terrorism and Effective Death Penalty Act, Pub L. No. 104-132, 110 Stat. 1214 (2001) (codified as amended in scattered sections of 7, 8, 11, 15, 18, 19, 21, 28, 40, and 42 U.S.C.). See also Stacy, *supra* note 58, at 462, 468–69 ("By establishing what is essentially a strict liability offense carrying a very grave punishment, the material support offense compromises the traditional rule of culpability in the criminal law").

61 See Williams in this volume (Chapter 12; discussing the material support for terrorism crime).

62 Section 411 of the USA PATRIOT Act amends the Immigration and Nationality Act to permit exclusion or detention of immigrants who are representatives of "a political, social or other group whose public endorsement of acts of terrorist activity the Secretary of State has determined undermines the United States efforts to reduce or eliminate terrorist activities." See USA PATRIOT Act of 2001, Pub. L. No. 107-56, § 411(a), 115 Stat 272 (amending 11 U.S.C. §1182(a)(3)).

63 See, e.g., Walter Pincus and Dan Eggen, 325,000 Names on Terrorism List, *Washington Post*, Feb. 15, 2006, at A1 (reporting that an FBI database contains more that 270 names of individuals associated with domestic terrorist movements such as radical environmentalists and neo-Nazi white supremacists). For analysis of the due process issues associated with government watch lists, see Daniel Steinbock, Designating the Dangerous: From Blacklists to Watchlists, 30 *Seattle University Law Review* 65 (2006), and Peter M. Shane, The Bureaucratic Due Process of Government Watchlists, 75 *George Washington Law Review* 804 (2007).

64 One such list that has come under scrutiny is the "No-Fly" list. See, e.g., Eric Lipton, U.S. Official Admits to Big Delay in Revamping No-Fly Program, *New York Times*, Feb. 21, 2007, at A17, available at 2007 WLNR 3379704. *Compare* Justin Florence, Note: Making the No Fly List Fly: A Due Process Model for Terrorist Watch Lists, 115 *Yale Law Review* 2148 (2007), *with* Yousri Omar, Note: Plane Harassment: The Transportation Safety Administration's Indifference to the Constitution in Administering the Government's Watch Lists, 12 *Washington and Lee Journal of Civil Rights and Social Justice* 259 (2006).

65 U.S. Department of Justice, *Fact Sheet: Terrorist Screening Center*, www.fbi.gov/pressrel/pressrel03/tscfactsheet091603.htm (last visited Apr. 27, 2007); Office of the Inspector General Audit Division, U.S. Department of Justice, *Review of the Terrorist Screening Center* (June 2005), available at www.usdoj.gov/oig/reports/FBI/a0527/final.pdf (detailing a number of terrorist watch lists, including the Violent Gang and Terrorist Organizations File).

66 Michael Powell, *High Profile N.Y. Suspect Goes on Trial, Washington Post*, Oct. 19, 2004, at A2, available at www.washingtonpost.com/wp-dyn/articles/A43278-2004Oct18.html; Iraqi-Born Doctor Guilty of Charity Fraud, *Syracuse Post Standard*, Feb. 11, 2005, at A26.

67 See David Johnson, Feds Up Ante on UI Grad Students; al Hussayen Now Faces Charges of Providing Material Support to Terrorism, *Lewiston Morning Tribune* (Lewiston, Idaho), Jan. 10, 2004, at 1A; Betsy Z. Russell, Al-Hussayen Acquitted in Terror Case; Verdict Seen as First Amendment Win, *Spokesman Review* (Spokane, Wash.), June 11, 2004, at A1.

68 See, e.g., *People's Mojahedin Org. of Iran* v. *Dep't of State*, 327 F.3d 1238, 1243 (D.C. Cir. 2003). The People's Mojahedin Organization is opposed to the current regime in Iran. Its members claim to be freedom fighters. The organization has admitted activities including attacking government offices and assassinating officials.

69 See, e.g., *United States* v. *Assi*, 414 F. Supp. 2d 717, 710 (E.D. Mich. 2006) (the defendant admitted to attempting to smuggle to Hizballah, a Lebanese organization, equipment including a global positioning satellite modules, night vision goggles and a thermal imaging camera).

70 See Ruff, *supra* note 54 (arguing that charitable groups designated as terrorist organizations may be expressive associations); Fisher, *supra* note 3, at 648 (suggesting that

surveillance might violate the expressive association rights of some organizations unless the government has evidence of actual terrorist activity). The plaintiffs in *Humanitarian Law Project* v. *Reno* unsuccessfully argued that the material support statute violated their rights to expressive association by limiting their ability to provide humanitarian assistance to Kurdish groups that had been designated by the U.S. government as terrorist organizations. 9 F. Supp. 2d 1176, 1184 (C.D. Cal. 1998), *aff'd*, 205 F.3d 1130 (9th Cir. 2000).

71 8 U.S.C. § 1189(a)(2) (2000).
72 Ibid. § 1189(a)(3).
73 Ibid. § 1189(a)(2).
74 Ibid. §1189(a)(2)(A). See *United States* v. *Rahmani*, 209 F. Supp. 2d 1045, 1048 (C.D. Cal. 2002), *rev'd sub nom. United States* v. *Afshari*, 412 F.3d 1071 (9th Cir. 2005) (although reversed, the district court opinion describes the type of evidence in the administrative record supporting designation); *Nat'l Council of Resistance of Iran* v. *Dep't of State*, 251 F.3d 192, 198–99 (D.C. Cir. 2001).
75 8 U.S.C. § 1189(c).
76 *Rahmani*, 209 F. Supp. 2d at 1048.
77 *Nat'l Council of Resistance of Iran* v. *Sec'y of State*, 251 F.3d 192, 209 (relying on *Mathews* v. *Eldridge*, 424 U.S. 319 (1976), which established the due process standards with which the government must comply when depriving an individual of a liberty, interests that are consistent with the earlier notice and hearing requirements of *McGrath*).
78 Ibid.
79 8 U.S.C. § 1189(c) (2000); *Nat'l Council of Resistance of Iran*, 251 F.3d at 197.
80 8 U.S.C. § 1189(c)(3).
81 *Kahane Chai* v. *Dep't of State*, 466 F.3d 125, 129 (D.C. Cir. 2006).
82 Broxmeyer, *supra* note 47, at 482–87 (discussing the application of procedural due process rules to the use of classified evidence in designation proceedings).
83 See *infra* notes 90–94 and accompanying text. See also Williams in this volume.
84 See *infra* notes 90–94.
85 See Ellen Yaroshefsky, The Slow Erosion of the Adversary System: Article III Courts, FISA, CIPA and Ethical Dilemmas, 5 *Cardozo Public Law, Policy and Ethics Journal* 203 (2006) (arguing that the gradually increasing the use of secret evidence in criminal cases threatens the ability of courts to ensure due process).
86 8 U.S.C. § 1189(a)(8) (2000) (providing that once the designation becomes effective upon publication in the *Federal Register*, it may not be challenged in a criminal trial).
87 Ibid. § 1189(a)(7).
88 *United States* v. *Rahmani*, 209 F. Supp. 2d 1045 (C.D. Cal. 2002), *rev'd sub nom. United States* v. *Afshari*, 426 F. 3d 1150 (9th Cir. 2005) (allowing the constitutionality of the designation provisions to be raised in the context of a material support prosecution). The *Afshari/Rahmani* case has a complex procedural history. The trial judge's decision was originally reversed on appeal in *United States* v. *Afshari*, 392 F. 3d 1031 (9th Cir. 2004). That opinion was withdrawn and the substituted opinion was reported at *United States* v. *Afshari*, 412 F.3d 1071 (9th Cir. 2005). The substituted opinion was withdrawn upon the grant of rehearing. The opinion on rehearing was reported at *United States* v. *Afshari*, 426 F.3d 1150 (9th Cir. 2005). A petition for rehearing en banc was denied with a stinging dissent by Judge Kozinski, joined by four additional judges. It is reported at *United States* v. *Afshari*, 446 F.3d 915 (9th Cir. 2006). The organization involved in the *Rahmani* case is the Mujahedin-e-Khalq or (MEK). The designation of this organization as a terrorist organization has been heavily litigated in the D.C. Circuit. The designation was first upheld in *People's Mojahedin Organization of Iran* v. *Department of State*, 182 F.3d 17 (D.C. Cir. 1999). In 1999, the D.C. Circuit raised serious constitutional questions regarding the designation of the MEK in *National Council of Resistance of Iran* v. *Department of*

State, 251 F.3d 192 (D.C. Cir. 2001). Although the court found numerous due process problems with the designation, it did not revoke the designation or set it aside. It again affirmed the designation in *People's Mojahedin Organization of Iran* v. *Department of State*, 327 F. 3d 1238 (D.C. Cir. 2003).

89 See *United States* v. *Marzook*, 383 F. Supp. 2d 1056, 1059 (N.D. Ill. 2005); *United States* v. *Hamoud*, 381 F.3d 316, 331 (4th Cir. 2004).

90 See 18 U.S.C. §§ 2339A(b), 2339B(h) (2000) (as amended by the Intelligence Reform and Terrorism Prevention Act of 2004, Pub. L. No. 108-458, 118 Stat 3638).

91 *United States* v. *Afshari*, 446 F.3d at 917 (Kozinski, J., dissenting from denial of rehearing *en banc*).

92 Professor David Cole characterized the ADEPA version of the statute as a "classic instance of guilt by association." He explained:

> Under ... [the criminal material support statute as adopted in AEDPA] it would be a crime for a Quaker to send a book on Gandhi's theory of nonviolence – a "physical asset" – to the leader of a terrorist organization in hopes of persuading him to forgo violence.
> (David Cole, The New McCarthyism: Repeating History in the War on Terrorism, 38 *Harvard Civil Rights–Civil Liberties Law Review* 1, 10 (2003))

93 Alan Williams, in this volume, argues that the Constitution requires that the material support statutes be amended to include an intent standard. I will not duplicate his argument here, except to point out that the inclusion of such a standard is imperative to the protection of the rights of free association.

94 See, e.g., *United States* v. *Hammoud*, 381 F.3d 316, 328–29 (4th Cir. 2004) (noting that it is a violation of "the First Amendment to punish an individual for mere membership in an organization," but concluding that the defendant's constitutional argument "fails because § 2330B does not prohibit mere association; it prohibits the conduct of providing material support to a designated FTO"). *Cf. Humanitarian Law Project* v. *Gonzales*, 380 F. Supp. 2d 1134, 1143 n.5 (C.D. Cal. 2005). The *Gonzales* court stated:

> We therefore do not agree that the First Amendment requires the government to demonstrate a specific intent to aid an organization's illegal activities before attaching liability to the donation of funds.... AEDPA does not criminalize mere association with designated terrorist organizations by prohibiting the provision of material support regardless of the donor's intent. As previously noted, Plaintiffs remain free to affiliate with and advocate on behalf of foreign terrorist organizations.
> (Ibid. (citing prior opinions in the same case, *Humanitarian Law Project* v. *Reno*, 205 F.3d 1130, 1134 (9th Cir. 1998) and *Humanitarian Law Project* v. *Reno*, 9 F. Supp. 2d 1176, 1191 (C.D. Cal. 1998)))

95 The term "material support" is defined as:

> any property, tangible or intangible, or service, including currency or monetary instruments or financial securities, financial services, lodging, training, expert advice or assistance, safehouses, false documentation or identification, communications equipment, facilities, weapons, lethal substances, explosives, personnel (1 or more individuals who may be or include oneself), and transportation, except medicine or religious materials.
> (18 U.S.C. § 2339A(b)(1) (2000))

"Training" is defined as "instruction or teaching designed to impart a specific skill, as opposed to general knowledge," ibid., § 2339A(b)(2), and "expert advice or assistance" is defined as "advice or assistance derived from scientific, technical or other specialized knowledge," ibid., § 2339A(b)(3).

96 At least one court has held that the definitions of "training" and "expert advice and assistance" are unconstitutionally vague. See *Humanitarian Law Project*, 380 F. Supp. 2d at 1140–41.

97 *Adler* v. *Bd. of Educ. of N.Y.*, 342 U.S. 485, 492 (1952) ("[I]t is clear that such persons have the right under our law to assemble, speak, think and believe as they will…. It is equally clear that they have no right to work for the state in the school system on their own terms").

98 *Am. Comm'n. Assn.* v. *Douds*, 339 U.S. 382, 396 (1950).

99 *Dennis* v. *United States*, 341 U.S. 494, 502 (1951).

10 Domestic military intelligence activities

Stephen Dycus

Introduction

If, God forbid, the American homeland is struck by another major terrorist attack, military forces will very likely be involved in the response. There can be little doubt, for example, that if pneumonic plague bacilli were to be released in Chicago and infections resulted,[1] the entire city would have to be quarantined as soon as the contagion was detected. Nor is there any doubt that troops will be used to enforce the quarantine. Only the Pentagon and National Guard units have the personnel, equipment and training to do the job.

Military forces also may be able to help prevent another attack before it occurs, or at least to reduce its impact. In response to the September 11, 2001 terrorist attacks in the United States, for instance, Air Force and Air National Guard jets were sent aloft in an unsuccessful effort to intercept and, perhaps, shoot down the civilian airliners commandeered by terrorists.[2]

Military intelligence services directly support the military's use of force at home, just as they provide information and analysis for other military activities around the world. Inside the United States, they are concerned with protection of the military forces themselves and homeland defense generally.[3]

But these same military intelligence services have recently begun to play an even broader role in domestic counterterrorism. Such a development represents a significant change in what we have long understood to be the "normal" relationship between the military and the rest of American society.

Three decades ago, the Senate Select Committee to Study Governmental Operations with Respect to Intelligence Activities (known as the Church Committee for its chairman, Senator Frank Church of Idaho) published 14 reports describing the origins and operations of U.S. intelligence agencies, including those managed by the Pentagon.[4] The Church Committee chronicled extensive abuses of authority by those agencies at home and abroad during the 1960s and early 1970s. It found, inter alia, that both military and nonmilitary intelligence services conducted domestic surveillance of thousands of individuals and organizations, compiled records, and disrupted political activities in violation of the Constitution and of various laws and executive rules. But military intelligence services came in for special criticism, in part because they had broken with a tradition of avoiding military intrusion into civilian affairs.[5]

Several practical questions raised by the Church Committee in 1976 need to be asked again today. Will an expanded domestic role for military intelligence actually make America more secure? Will a more aggressive use of military intelligence at home make a uniquely valuable contribution to the counterterrorism efforts of the FBI, local law enforcement and other civilian agencies? Or will it be merely redundant, wasteful and perhaps even counterproductive?

Another key question is, how will these more expansive military intelligence activities affect Americans' privacy and related liberties? If sacrifices are required, will any resulting increased security make those sacrifices worthwhile? If the balance doesn't clearly favor security, should the military intelligence services perhaps be barred from actions that do not directly support the use of military force? If they are not barred, are there clear legal limits on their activities inside the United States? Should there be? And how can we ensure that any such limits will be observed?

These questions are presented in the midst of an unprecedented effort to organize and harmonize the United States' homeland security activities.[6] In the atmosphere of fear pervading American life since the terrorist attacks of September 11, 2001, the President has launched broad new intelligence initiatives at home – some with congressional approval, some secret, and some plainly illegal. Some of these precisely replicate actions of the Nixon administration during the Vietnam War that were criticized by the Church Committee.[7]

Whether the threat to national security, and particularly to the American homeland, is greater today than it was three decades ago is, of course, impossible to gauge. But the threat to civil liberties from expanded domestic use of military intelligence is surely greater now than it was then, given advances in technology. The purpose of this chapter is to describe briefly the expanding role of military intelligence in homeland security, to indicate relevant laws and regulations, to point out some possible threats to civil liberties, and to determine, finally, whether America has learned anything in this regard from the lessons of the Church Committee.

The military in American society: a cautious embrace

Since the earliest days of the Republic, Americans have worried about the risks associated with maintaining a standing army and, more generally, with giving the military a prominent role in civilian life.[8] These concerns were summed up in a 1985 judicial decision:

> Civilian rule is basic to our system of government.... [M]ilitary enforcement of the civil law leaves the protection of vital Fourth and Fifth Amendment rights in the hands of persons who are not trained to uphold these rights. It may also chill the exercise of fundamental rights, such as the rights to speak freely and to vote, and create the atmosphere of fear and hostility which exists in territories occupied by enemy forces.

The interest of limiting military involvement in civilian affairs has a long tradition beginning with the Declaration of Independence and continued in the Constitution, certain Acts of Congress, and decisions of the Supreme Court. The Declaration of Independence states among the grounds for severing ties with Great Britain that the King "has kept among us, in times of peace, Standing Armies without Consent of our Legislature ... [and] has affected to render the Military independent of and superior to the Civil power." These concerns were later raised at the Constitutional Convention. Luther Martin of Maryland said, "[W]hen a government wishes to deprive its citizens of freedom, and reduce them to slavery, it generally makes use of a standing army."[9]

In a 1972 case, the Supreme Court referred to the "traditional and strong resistance of Americans to any military intrusion into civilian affairs."[10] Four years later, in 1976, the Church Committee pointed out that "[t]he authors of the American Constitution sought to establish and preserve a clear separation of the military from the civilian realms."[11]

Domestic use of military intelligence from the founding to the Vietnam War

The Church Committee made clear that, despite all these misgivings, military forces, and in particular military intelligence personnel, have been actively involved in homeland security from the very beginning.[12] George Washington, in his capacity as general, was America's first spymaster. He made extensive use of espionage, counterintelligence, surveillance and cryptography during the Revolutionary War.[13] These efforts led, for example, to the unmasking of General Benedict Arnold as in league with the British.[14] Military intelligence also provided critical support for military successes during the War of 1812, the Mexican War and the Civil War.[15]

But between these, the only wars fought on American soil, and afterward, military intelligence gathering continued at home – not only for homeland defense and homeland security, but also for law enforcement and political purposes. During the Hayes administration, for example, Army Signal Corps weather observers collected information on labor agitators.[16] In World War I, the military conducted extensive domestic surveillance, ostensibly in search of German spies and saboteurs, although ordinary citizens who objected to wartime policies or to the war itself were also targeted.[17] Later, the focus shifted to communists, socialists and pacifists, while the military gradually began to share its domestic surveillance responsibilities with the FBI.[18]

After the Second World War, the National Security Act of 1947[19] spelled out, among other things, a structure for overall civilian control of the intelligence community. In its current form, the 1947 Act names a Director of National Intelligence (DNI) to be head of the intelligence community and "establish objectives, priorities, and guidance for the intelligence community."[20] The Act also provides that the Secretary of Defense exercises "civilian control" of the military[21] and, in consultation with the DNI, manages the operations of military intelligence components.[22] These military components, which comprise by far the largest part of the intelligence community,[23] include the National Security Agency (NSA), National Geospatial-Intelligence Agency (formerly the National Imagery and Mapping Agency), the National Reconnaissance Office, the Defense Intelligence Agency (DIA) and the intelligence elements of the three military service branches.[24]

During the 1950s and 1960s, federal troops and federalized National Guard forces, accompanied by military intelligence personnel, were deployed to help integrate southern schools[25] and to help deal with civil disorders in Detroit in 1967 and in other cities following the assassination of Dr. Martin Luther King, Jr.[26] The Church Committee investigation revealed that, throughout this period, military intelligence units also collected data on individuals and groups around the country who were suspected of involvement in "subversive" activities.[27]

Again, the Church Committee uncovered operations in which the Pentagon compiled personal information on an estimated 100,000 politically active Americans in an effort to quell civil rights and anti-Vietnam War demonstrations and to discredit protestors.[28] The Army used 1,500 plainclothes agents to watch demonstrators, to infiltrate organizations and to spread disinformation.[29] According to one report, the Army had at least one observer at every demonstration of more than 20 people.[30] It also received data about potential threats from the FBI and local law enforcement agencies.[31] And it shared extensive information with the same agencies, notwithstanding the strictures of the Posse Comitatus Act,[32] which generally prohibits the use of military forces to enforce the law. The Pentagon justified these activities as preparations for a domestic deployment of troops to help control violence associated with political protests.[33]

The Army's activities were summed up by Senator Sam Ervin:

> Allegedly for the purpose of predicting and preventing civil disturbances which might develop beyond the control of state and local officials, Army agents were sent throughout the country to keep surveillance over the way the civilian population expressed their sentiments about government policies. In churches, on campuses, in classrooms, in public meetings, they took notes, tape recorded, and photographed people who dissented in thought, word, or deed. This included clergymen, editors, public officials, and anyone who sympathized with the dissenters.
>
> With very few, if any, directives to guide their activities, they monitored the membership and policies of peaceful organizations who were concerned with the war in Southeast Asia, the draft, racial and labor problems, and community welfare. Out of this surveillance the Army created blacklists of organizations and personalities which were circulated to many federal, state, and local agencies, who were all requested to supplement the data provided....
>
> The Army did not just collect and share this information. Analysts were assigned the task of evaluating and labeling these people on the basis of

reports on their attitudes, remarks, and activities. They were then coded for entry into computers or microfilm data banks.[34]

The Department of Defense (DOD) now describes what happened in the 1960s and 1970s as

> a classic example of what we would today call "mission creep." What had begun as a simple requirement to provide basic intelligence to commanders charged with assisting in the maintenance and restoration of order, had become a monumentally intrusive effort. This resulted in the monitoring of activities of innocent persons involved in the constitutionally protected expression of their views on civil rights or anti-war activities. The information collected on the persons targeted by Defense intelligence personnel was entered into a national data bank and made available to civilian law enforcement authorities. This produced a chilling effect on political expression by those who were legally working for political change in domestic and foreign policies.[35]

These activities were not widely known until an Army intelligence officer spelled them out in a dramatic 1970 magazine article.[36] The article provoked several congressional investigations,[37] as well as modest reforms outlined below.

It also precipitated an American Civil Liberties Union (ACLU) class-action suit to stop domestic intelligence collection by the military. The plaintiffs, political activists, claimed that their First Amendment rights of free expression and association were "chilled" by Army surveillance and record collection. They feared that the improper use of information gathered about their political activities could jeopardize their jobs and reputations. They also worried that others might simply decide not to speak out, to meet with politically active persons, or even to subscribe to political publications. When the case reached the Supreme Court in 1972, the court ruled that the plaintiffs lacked standing to sue, because "[a]llegations of a subjective 'chill' are not an adequate substitute for a claim of specific present objective harm or a threat of specific future harm."[38]

As a practical matter, of course, if an activist lost her job or was denied a security clearance, she might never learn the reason why. Personal information in military intelligence files was almost impossible to obtain, certainly in advance of 1974 amendments to the Freedom of Information Act[39] or the passage of the Privacy Act the same year,[40] unless it was used in a criminal prosecution.

In 1976, the Church Committee called the Army program "the worst intrusion that military intelligence has ever made into the civilian community."[41] It proposed a "precisely drawn legislative charter" that would "limit military investigations to activities in the civilian community which are necessary and pertinent to the military mission, and which cannot feasibly be accomplished by civilian agencies."[42] More than three decades later, however, no such charter has been adopted.

Congressional and executive responses to the "worst intrusion"

Legislative limits on domestic military intelligence collection

In 1974, Congress addressed domestic intelligence excesses, both military and civilian, by passing the Privacy Act.[43] In 1978, it enacted the Foreign Intelligence Surveillance Act (FISA),[44] which now describes the "exclusive means" for electronic surveillance or the interception of domestic wire, oral, and electronic communications by any government agency without a Title III warrant.[45] The efficacy of these statutes in discouraging the improper collection and use of information about individuals and organizations is, however, far from clear.[46]

The Privacy Act generally forbids the maintenance by any federal agency of a record "describing how any individual exercises rights guaranteed by the First Amendment unless expressly authorized by statute or ... unless pertinent to and within the scope of an authorized law enforcement activity."[47] "Individual" for this purpose means a U.S. citizen or an alien lawfully admitted for permanent residence.[48] Similar provisions in FISA bar electronic surveillance or physical searches of a U.S. person "solely upon the basis of activities protected by the First Amendment."[49] But definitional problems may make these limitations illusory.[50]

The Privacy Act also bars the maintenance of personal information by an agency unless it is "relevant and necessary to accomplish a purpose of the agency required to be accomplished by statute or by executive order of the President."[51] Military intelligence agencies are charged by Executive Order No. 12,333 with collection of information concerning foreign intelligence and counterintelligence,[52] and impliedly authorized by FISA to do the same. Information about international terrorism presumably qualifies as foreign intelligence.

FISA requires agencies to follow procedures to "minimize the acquisition and retention, and prohibit the dissemination" of nonpublic information about U.S. persons, except that evidence of a crime may be disseminated for law enforcement purposes. The minimization procedures are classified, however, so it is not possible to say precisely what kinds of personal data may be collected, retained, or shared pursuant to a FISA order.

Another Privacy Act provision relevant here bars the transfer of personal information from one agency to another without the consent of the subject, except, inter alia, for a "routine use" by the transferee agency that is "compatible with the purpose for which it was collected."[53] Thus, military intelligence services may not *receive* data from other agencies if the military services are not entitled to *collect* such data directly. For example, with certain exceptions noted below, the DOD should not receive from another agency law enforcement information not related to the DOD's homeland defense mission, since the DOD could not "routinely" collect such information. But the Church Committee in 1976 thought the Privacy Act did not bar the military from "providing intelligence assistance to other agencies."[54] The Committee described the application of the Privacy Act to military intelligence activities generally as "unclear," concluding that the Act is "sufficiently ambiguous and contains enough exceptions to raise doubts as to its effectiveness as a future restraint on military investigative activity against private individuals and organizations."[55]

Individuals about whom information is collected generally have a right under the Privacy Act to inspect agency files and correct any errors about them in those files,[56] and to review any record of disclosures,[57] unless, inter alia, the information is properly classified.[58] Yet it may be exceedingly difficult to determine whether such information is in fact properly classified or, for that matter, whether it even exists.[59]

The Privacy Act does require that intelligence agents collecting personal data from human sources identify themselves to potential informants, state the authority for the collection, and describe the uses to which the data will be put.[60] Provisions of the unenacted Intelligence Authorization Acts for fiscal years 2005 and 2006 would have allowed military intelligence personnel to work undercover in the United States.[61]

The E-Government Act of 2002 requires federal agencies to prepare "privacy impact assessments" before they develop or procure new information technology or initiate any new collections of personally identifiable information.[62] The assessments must address what information is to be collected, how it will be collected, its intended use, with whom the information will be shared, and what notice, if any, will be provided to individuals described in the information.[63] Hope that this law might bring a measure of transparency to the compilation of personalized computer data must be tempered by the fact that impact assessments need only be made public "if practicable,"[64] and that even this requirement may be "modified or waived for security reasons, or to protect classified, sensitive, or private information contained in an assessment."[65] The terms "practicable," "security," and "sensitive" are not defined.

If the collection, use, or transfer of some personal information cannot be revealed because disclosure of either the process or the information itself would jeopardize national security, compliance with the law is nevertheless subject to nonpublic oversight procedures. A 1991 amendment to the National Security Act of 1947 requires the President to keep the congressional intelligence committees "fully and currently informed" about intelligence activities, including those of the Defense Department.[66] The two congressional committees provide the only systematic oversight outside of the executive branch. Inspectors General and other officials at the DOD and its various intelligence components perform internal oversight.[67]

Will these legislative initiatives reliably curb the kinds of domestic military intelligence abuses witnessed during the Vietnam War era? Maybe. Will they prevent unnecessary abridgements of civil liberties by military intelligence using computer technology that members of the Church Committee could not even have imagined 30 years ago? Probably not. Nor, it appears, will executive measures do so.

Executive measures to guide domestic military intelligence collection

Amid growing efforts by Congress to curb executive excesses and to play a more active role in intelligence, the Reagan administration in 1981 issued Executive Order No. 12,333.[68] In 2007, it is still the basic executive charter for U.S. intelligence activities. It includes a broad directive to collect intelligence "needed by" the Secretary of Defense "for the performance of [his] duties and responsibilities."[69] The Secretary of Defense is specifically authorized to collect national foreign intelligence and to conduct counterintelligence at home in cooperation with the FBI.[70] On the one hand, the order bars the collection of foreign intelligence "for the purpose of acquiring information concerning the domestic activities of United States persons."[71] On the other hand, it permits the collection, retention and dissemination of "[i]nformation needed to protect the safety of any persons or organizations."[72] Concerning collection techniques, military intelligence services may conduct electronic surveillance but generally not physical searches of U.S. persons inside the United States.[73] Thus, Executive Order No. 12,333 is an uncertain guide for military intelligence activities that purports to authorize much but forbid little. Still, it expressly disclaims any authority for acts that would violate the Constitution or statutes,[74] including, presumably, the Posse Comitatus Act, described in the next subsection.

Within the executive branch, oversight of the entire intelligence community is conducted by the Intelligence Oversight Board, a part of the Executive Office of the President.[75] The Pentagon also has an Assistant to the Secretary of Defense for Intelligence Oversight, whose job it is to monitor intelligence activities worldwide and investigate questions of their legality or propriety.[76]

Before September 11, 2001, lead agency responsibility for anticipating and responding to terrorist attacks at home was given to the FBI and the Federal Emergency Management Agency (FEMA).[77] The DOD (including, presumably, its intelligence components) was slated for a supporting role in threat assessment and in operational and tactical responses.[78]

This alignment continued after the September 11, 2001 terrorist attacks in the United States. The 2002 *National Strategy for Homeland Security*, for example, indicated that military support to civil authorities could take the form of "providing technical support and assistance to law enforcement; assisting in the restoration of law and order; loaning specialized equipment; and assisting in consequence management."[79] *Homeland Security Presidential Directive/HSPD-5*,[80] issued in 2003, named the Secretary of Homeland Security as the "principal Federal official for domestic incident management," and assigned "lead responsibility for criminal investigations of terrorist acts" to the Attorney General. The following year, the *National Response Plan* generally called for use of the armed forces only when they could be uniquely helpful in responding to a serious emergency: "DOD provides [Defense Support of Civil Authorities] in response to requests for assistance during domestic incidents to include terrorist attacks, major disasters, and other emergencies.... DSCA normally is provided when local, State, and Federal resources are overwhelmed."[81]

Yet some have argued that in a great crisis, the President ought to be prepared to deploy military forces at home in a lead role.[82] And there is evidence, described later in the chapter, that the DOD, including its intelligence components, is preparing to assume a leading role.

Do these executive measures provide sufficient clarity and adequate flexibility to allow a military response to a terrorist threat or attack at home? Almost surely they do. Do they strike a proper balance between security and liberty? It is impossible to answer without knowing how they are used. Do they provide sufficient transparency and accountability to ensure compliance with them? Probably not, especially in light of likely claims that relevant information is too sensitive to reveal.

The Posse Comitatus Act as a background principle

The 1878 Posse Comitatus Act expressly forbids the use of military forces to "execute the laws," except when expressly authorized by the Constitution or a statute.[83] It has long been thought to limit most military involvement in civilian law enforcement.[84] The Church Committee concluded that the Act "would probably prevent the military from conducting criminal investigations of civilians, but ... would not bear upon other types of investigations."[85] According to the Committee, the purpose of the Act was "to prevent federal marshals from commandeering military troops to help enforce the law, and not to prohibit investigations of civilians by the military."[86]

Military intelligence investigations not related to law enforcement are not, in principle, addressed by the Posse Comitatus Act. More narrowly, the Stafford Act gives the President authority to use the armed services, presumably including their intelligence components, in an emergency to perform work "essential for the preservation of life and property."[87] Another statute allows military forces to assist the Department of Justice in collecting intelligence or in searches and seizures when it is "necessary for the immediate protection of human life."[88]

But even if the primary purpose of an investigation is law enforcement, Congress has enacted exceptions to the Posse Comitatus Act that appear to remove any significant constraints that the Act might impose. One such exception allows the Secretary of Defense to provide law enforcement officials with "any information collected during the normal course of military training or operations that may be relevant to a violation of any Federal or State law," and to take the needs of such officials into account "to the maximum extent practicable" in the planning and execution of military training or operations.[89] The Secretary may also furnish equipment to law enforcement agencies, along with personnel to operate it, for cases involving foreign or domestic counterterrorism or violation of "[a]ny law, foreign or domestic, prohibiting terrorist activities."[90] The most important exception is the Insurrection Act, which gives the President wide latitude to use troops for almost any purpose, including law enforcement, in responding to an actual or threatened terrorist attack.[91] These statutory exceptions, designed to furnish maximum flexibility to the executive branch in a crisis, are most striking for their failure to include any meaningful limits – temporal, geographical, or situational – or any means for challenging their invocation.

The Pentagon's own regulations

What does the Pentagon believe to be the scope and limits of its domestic intelligence authority? The official answer is spread across several DOD directives, some of them written long before the threat of international terrorism became a top priority for the defense community.[92]

One directive orders that all DOD intelligence activities

> be carried out pursuant to the authorities and restrictions of the U.S. Constitution, applicable law [Executive Order No. 12,333],... and other relevant DOD policies.... Special emphasis shall be given to the protection of the constitutional rights and privacy of U.S. persons.[93]

Another, DOD Directive 5240.1-R, implements Executive Order No. 12,333, described above. It sets out 15 procedures for domestic surveillance of U.S. persons by military intelligence components, including the DIA, NSA and other DOD "organizations ... when used for foreign intelligence or counterintelligence activities."[94] It is described in the Army Judge Advocates' *Operational Law Handbook* as "the *sole authority* for DOD intelligence components to collect, retain, and disseminate intelligence concerning U.S. persons."[95] One of these procedures provides that covert collection is permitted only if "significant" foreign intelligence is sought, the head of the military agency approves, the information is not reasonably obtainable through overt means, and collection is coordinated with the FBI.[96] In addition, the information collected must not concern the "domestic activities" of any U.S. person,[97] here defined as activities that "do not involve a significant connection with a foreign power, organization, or person."[98] Other procedures contain very broad authorization for retention and dissemination of data.[99] Electronic surveillance, as well as "concealed monitoring," must follow Executive Order No. 12,333,[100] while physical searches are authorized only against current military personnel.[101] Human intelligence collection may be carried out only against prospective, current or former military personnel or contractors.[102] Undisclosed collection from a domestic organization is barred,[103] while cooperation with law enforcement officials is permitted in the investigation of international terrorist activities.[104]

A different directive, not applicable to intelligence components, covers acquisition of information about threats to DOD personnel, activities and installations; personnel security; and civil disturbances. DOD Directive 5200.27 bars acquisition of information about "a person or organization solely because of lawful advocacy of measures in opposition to Government policy," and it prohibits various intrusive measures without the express approval of the Secretary of Defense.[105]

These procedures appear to limit the collection of data on U.S. persons in some instances even more than other relevant authorities. Still, they make no provision for oversight by anyone other than the Department of Defense's own Inspector General and General Counsel.[106] And as DOD's homeland security role expands, it has become more difficult to distinguish between foreign intelligence or counterintelligence activities and force protection, raising questions about which rules to apply in a given situation.[107]

An expanding domestic role for military intelligence

The terrorist attacks of September 11, 2001 in the United States have led to the development of new strategies for protecting the U.S. homeland. Military forces, including their intelligence components, are heavily involved in some of them.

In 2005, the Pentagon published *Strategy for Homeland Defense and Civil Support*,[108] declaring that the DOD expected to "reorient its intelligence capabilities" to enable it to, inter alia, "[c]ollect homeland defense threat information from relevant private and public sector sources, consistent with [U.S.] constitutional authorities and privacy law," and to "[d]evelop automated tools to improve data fusion, analysis, and management, to track systematically large amounts of data, and to detect, fuse, and analyze aberrant patterns of activity, consistent with [U.S.] privacy protections."[109] The last objective is an apparent reference to a data mining system such as the Pentagon's Defense Advanced Research Projects Agency's (DARPA) Total Information Awareness program.[110] The document pledges that the DOD will work to "diminish existing cultural, technological, and bureaucratic obstacles to information sharing" among federal agencies, with state, local, and tribal governments, with private entities, and with "key foreign partners."[111] Other developments since the September 11, 2001 terrorist attacks in the United States that point to a growing military involvement in domestic intelligence gathering are described below.

NORTHCOM: reorganizing for homeland security

The Pentagon announced in early 2002 that it was creating a new Northern Command (NORTHCOM), based in Colorado.[112] The announced mission of the new command is to protect the U.S. homeland from foreign adversaries and assist civilian authorities in recovering from another terrorist attack at home.

NORTHCOM has its own extensive domestic intelligence operation. It collects and "fuse[s] intelligence and law enforcement information," then disseminates it to "a wide spectrum of users that consist of folks from first responders all the way up the national command authority."[113] To this end, personnel from the FBI, CIA, NSA, DIA and other intelligence agencies maintain offices at NORTHCOM and receive daily briefings on potential terrorist threats.[114]

Concerning direct intelligence collection, a former NORTHCOM commander declared, "We are not going to be out there spying on people," but added, "[W]e get information from people who do."[115] He presumably was referring to "people" in a Pentagon organization called Counterintelligence Field Activity (CIFA).[116] CIFA's stated mission is "to develop and manage DOD counterintelligence (CI) programs and functions" that protect the DOD.[117] But CIFA is also described as "a law enforcement activity within the Department of Defense."[118] CIFA is charged with maintaining "a domestic law enforcement database that includes information related to potential terrorist threats directed against the Department of Defense."[119] CIFA has been directed to develop a data mining capability that may resemble the much-maligned Total Information Awareness program, described later in the chapter.[120] In 2005, the White House reportedly considered a proposal to expand CIFA's mission to include investigation of crimes within the United States, such as treason, espionage, and foreign or terrorist sabotage, as well as clandestine operations against potential threats at home.[121]

One CIFA activity, Threat and Local Observation Notice (TALON), is officially described as "much like ... a 'neighborhood watch' program in which concerned citizens or DOD personnel report suspicious activities."[122] TALON has engaged in surveillance and data collection regarding domestic political activities, for example, compiling records on the Quakers and others who protested the Iraq War.[123] It has also monitored demonstrations against military recruitment on university campuses aimed at the DOD's "don't ask, don't tell" policy of excluding homosexuals from military ranks.[124] In early 2006, the DOD reportedly deleted 1,131 files improperly stored in the TALON database, out of some 13,000 entries, of which 2,821 involved American citizens.[125] But it is not known what became of information shared with other agencies before it was deleted from the TALON database. A 2007 report by the DOD's Inspector General maintained that the TALON database complied with U.S. law, although it violated a DOD directive.[126] Pentagon officials subsequently announced that the database would be shut down, not because of public criticism but because its "analytical value had declined," although the information would be retained "in accordance with intelligence oversight requirements."[127]

The Pentagon's relation to other domestic counterterrorism activities

The Homeland Security Act of 2002 created a new program, the Directorate for Information Analysis and Infrastructure Protection (IAIP),[128] that is "singularly focused on the protection of the American homeland against terrorist attack."[129] Its mission is to "access, receive, and analyze law enforcement information, intelligence information, and other information from agencies of the Federal Government, State and local government agencies ... and private sector entities," to integrate that information, and then to disseminate it to the same agencies and entities.[130] The Act authorizes the Secretary of Homeland Security to enter into cooperative agreements with heads of other agencies, such as the DIA, to detail personnel to the IAIP Directorate to perform "analytic functions and related duties."[131] In this role, military personnel both furnish and receive a variety of information, some of which may have no bearing on the Directorate's homeland defense mission, protection of its forces, or even support of civil authorities in homeland security.

While the Homeland Security Act expresses the "sense of Congress" that nothing in it "should be construed to alter the applicability" of the Posse Comitatus Act,[132] there is no other reference in the 2002 legislation to any limits on the military's domestic collection and use of personal information.

Intelligence components of the Defense Department also help staff the National Counterterrorism Center (NCTC), created in 2004, along with representatives of various other federal agencies.[133] The NCTC integrates and analyzes all intelligence held by the U.S. government pertaining to terrorism and counterterrorism, and it serves as a central repository for all such information, including a list of known or suspected terrorists.[134] As at IAIP, military personnel at NCTC furnish and receive a variety of intelligence. Again, it is not known whether any effort is made to restrict that intelligence to matters within the proper scope of the DOD's responsibilities.

Total Information Awareness and its progeny

In 2002, DARPA announced a new program called Total Information Awareness (TIA).[135] Developed in collaboration with the Army's Intelligence and Security Command, TIA was officially described as

> a research and development program that will integrate advanced collaborative and decision support tools; language translation; and data search, pattern recognition, and privacy protection technologies into an experimental prototype network focused on combating terrorism through better analysis and decision making.[136]

In practical terms, it was supposed to enable intelligence officials to "data-mine an indefinitely expandable universe of databases" in order to "analyze, detect, classify, and identify foreign terrorists."[137] Collecting data from government as well as public and private sources, TIA programs would automatically recognize patterns of behavior, like the purchase of bomb-making materials, or improbable medical activity, such as treatment for anthrax symptoms, that might suggest terrorist activity. They would also use biometric recognition technologies to identify individuals by, for example, their facial features or walking gait. And they would do all this on a continuing, real-time basis, in order to provide prompt warnings of potential terrorist threats.[138]

The Defense Department's association with a program to compile extensive electronic records on the American public – telephone calls, social interactions, bank transactions, medical data, credit card purchases and more – struck some as particularly threatening. Others expressed concern that the contemplated use of the technology for domestic law enforcement seemed inconsistent with the Posse Comitatus Act.[139]

In an effort to allay public fears, DARPA renamed the program Terrorism Information Awareness.[140] But without clear limits on targeting or on sharing of information (DARPA said the program would rely on existing laws and developing technology to protect privacy and civil liberties), Congress barred its deployment in early 2003, at least against U.S. persons inside the United States, pending a report to Congress on how it balanced security against privacy.[141] Then, in the fiscal year 2004 DOD Appropriations Act, Congress eliminated funding for the majority of TIA's program components.[142]

In December 2003, a number of DOD commands and intelligence services were nonetheless continuing to develop and test TIA technologies.[143] And the following year, the Defense Department was reported as the most frequent user of data mining efforts "aimed at analyzing intelligence and detecting terrorist activities."[144]

A new DOD intelligence secretariat

The 2003 DOD Authorization Act created a new Undersecretary of Defense for Intelligence.[145] He or she is responsible for coordination and management of all the Pentagon's intelligence services, as well as support for homeland defense.[146] Some believed that the DOD sought this new position to prevent the loss of control over these agencies to an intelligence czar who would operate all intelligence services not strictly military.[147] The effect, if any, on domestic military intelligence activities is unclear.

Congressional testimony by the first Undersecretary, Stephen A. Cambone, described a "horizontal integration" strategy that includes

> a planned "system-of-systems" that integrates surveillance capabilities across the various human and technical disciplines and national, theater, tactical, and commercial programs. This provides the mechanism to share information across the enterprise – increasing the likelihood that events can be correlated and fused to increase the accuracy, timeliness, and value of intelligence.[148]

Whether the "horizontal integration" and "system-of-systems" has increased domestic collection and exchange of data by military intelligence services cannot be determined from public records.

Conclusion

More than three decades have passed since the Church Committee published its dramatic reports about intelligence community violations of the Constitution, statutes and executive rules. These violations occurred in the midst of the Vietnam War and in response to a broader perceived threat of world communism. The Committee was especially critical of abuses by military intelligence services operating inside the United States. It decried the departure from an

American tradition (albeit not one observed uniformly) of avoiding military entanglement in civilian life.

Today the nation finds itself beset by a different grave threat – international terrorism – and once again locked in a protracted war. Now, as then, elements of the intelligence community have responded by violating the Constitution, laws, and regulations at home and abroad. And once again the military has apparently broken the law and intruded into domestic affairs by collecting information about the political activities of private individuals and organizations.

Without the kind of thoroughgoing investigation carried out by the Church Committee 30 years ago, it is impossible to know precisely how far military intelligence services may have strayed recently from their traditional homeland defense mission. It is clear, however, that the laws and regulations provoked by the Church Committee reports may not prevent a repeat of the earlier abuses.

Maybe, given the threat we currently face, an adjustment is needed in our thinking about the appropriate domestic role of military intelligence. If so, it should follow a determination that strengthening and refining the civilian intelligence agencies will not accomplish the same purpose. We should be satisfied, for example, that the Department of Homeland Security's IAIP or the NCTC could not furnish all the data needed to protect domestic nonmilitary targets from another terrorist attack. And any such adjustment should be the product of a robust public debate, probably culminating in legislation.

If we accept such an adjustment, we should also adopt reliable controls and measures to provide accountability. We might, for example, want to require the approval of a neutral magistrate, say one specially trained in security matters, for military investigations where a Title III warrant or FISA order would not be required. We might want to strictly limit the dissemination of military intelligence information based on particular defined needs, or to limit the acquisition of data by military intelligence components to matters bearing directly on homeland defense, force protection, or military support of civil authorities. And we might require a frequent periodic review of such data in military intelligence agency files in order to expunge whatever is not accurate or currently relevant to the agency's mission.

Even if no important changes are adopted, we urgently need to clarify our current understandings about how military intelligence activities at home should affect the balance between security and liberty. A recent Congressional Research Service report argues that the "main stumbling block" to better coordination and response between the FBI and the military is the "numerous and often confusing statutory and regulatory authorities that govern the use of the military in a domestic situation."[149] Clarifying these authorities, it says, could allow a more effective use of military forces, while ensuring respect for civil liberties and law enforcement concerns.[150] The same could be said for almost every law, directive, executive order, and regulation touching the work of military intelligence. If these various authorities are not clearly articulated and harmonized, the United States will be more vulnerable than it need be to another terrorist attack. Failure in this respect will also invite well-meaning compromises to some of the most treasured American values.

Notes

1 This scenario was posited in an exercise called TOPOFF 2, sponsored by the Departments of State and Homeland Security in May 2003. See Department of Homeland Security, *Top Officials (TOPOFF) Exercise Series: TOPOFF 2 – After Action Summary Report* (Dec. 13, 2003).

2 The sequence of events is spelled out in a report from the National Commission on Terrorist Attacks on the United States (9/11 Commission), *Staff Report No. 17: Improvising a Homeland Defense* (June 17, 2004), http://govinfo.library.unt.edu/911/staff_statements/staff_statement_17.pdf. See also Eric Schmitt and Eric Lichtblau, In 149 Minutes, Transformation to Terror Age, *New York Times*, June 18, 2004, at A1.

3 See Department of Defense, Joint Chiefs of Staff, *Homeland Defense*, Jt. Pub. 3-27, at I-11, VII-2 (July 12, 2007).

4 This chapter refers to the following reports: See S. Rep. No. 94-755 (1976) (6 Books), including *Foreign and Military Intelligence* [hereinafter Church Book I], *Intelligence Activities and The Rights of Americans* [hereinafter Church Book II], *Supplementary Detailed Staff Reports on Intelligence Activities and the Rights of Americans* [hereinafter Church Book III], and *Supplementary Reports on Intelligence Activities* [hereinafter Church Book VI]. The reports are available at www.aarclibrary.org/publib/ church/reports/contents.htm.

5 See generally Church Book III, *supra* note 4, at 787–834.

6 The Department of Defense (DOD) distinguishes between "homeland security," a national effort to prevent or reduce U.S. vulnerability to terrorist attacks, or to assist in the recovery from such an attack, and "homeland defense," the military protection of U.S. territory, population and infrastructure against external threats and aggression. DOD plays a supporting role in the former, a primary role in the latter. See Steve Bowman, *Homeland Security: The Department of Defense's Role*, Congressional Research Service RL31615 1–2 (May 14, 2003).

7 See Seamon in this volume.

8 See Church Book III, *supra* note 4 at 787–88.

9 *Bissonette* v. *Haig*, 776 F.2d 1384, 1387 (1985), *aff'd*, 800 F.2d 812 (8th Cir. 1985) (*en banc*), *aff'd*, 485 U.S. 264 (1988).

10 *Laird* v. *Tatum*, 408 U.S. 1, 15 (1972).

11 Church Book III, *supra* note 4, at 787.

12 The fascinating history is spelled out in considerable detail in Church Book VI, *supra* note 4; Church Book I, *supra* note 4, at 323.

13 See Joan M. Jensen, *Army Intelligence in America, 1775–1980*, at 7–11 (1991).

14 See ibid. at 7–9.

15 See Church Book VI, *supra* note 4, at 25–50; Church Book I, *supra* note 4, at 323.

16 See Christopher H. Pyle, *Military Surveillance of Civilian Politics, 1961–1971*, at 18 (1986).

17 See Church Book III, *supra* note 4, at 380–82; Church Book VI, *supra* note 4, at 76–94.

18 See Church Book VI, *supra* note 4, at 94–97; Jensen, *supra* note 13, at 201–15.

19 National Security Act, Pub. L. No. 80-253, 61 Stat. 495 (1947) (codified as amended in scattered sections of titles 10 and 50 of the U.S. Code).

20 50 U.S.C. §§ 403(b)(1), 403-1(f)(1)(A)(i) (Supp. IV 2004).

21 Ibid. § 401 (2000).

22 Ibid. § 403–5(b) (2000 and Supp. IV 2004).

23 See United States Intelligence Community, *Members of the Intelligence Community (IC)* (n.d.), www.intelligence.gov/1-members.shtml; James E. Meason, Military Intelligence and the American Citizen, 12 *Harvard Journal of Law and Public Policy* 541, 544 (1989); Church Book I, *supra* note 4, at 17, 319, 462.

24 The operations of these defense intelligence services are spelled out in Meason, *supra* note 23, at 547–54. See also 50 U.S.C. § 403–5(b) (2000 and Supp. IV 2004).

25 See Jensen, *supra* note 13, at 237–39.

26 Meason, *supra* note 23, at 542 n.4.

27 See Church Book II, *supra* note 4, at 77, 84–85; Church Book III, *supra* note 4, at 785–825; Christopher H. Pyle, CONUS Intelligence: The Army Watches Civilian Politics, 1 *Washington Monthly* 4 (1970). See also Jensen, *supra* note 13, at 237–47; Meason, *supra* note 23, at 542–43.

28 See Church Book III, *supra* note 4, at 789, 795–818, 822–25; Meason, *supra* note 23, at 543.

29 See *Military Surveillance: Hearings before the Subcomm. on Constitutional Rights, S. Comm. on the Judiciary*, 93d Cong. 2 (1974).

30 Pyle, *supra* note 16, at 186–87.

31 Meason, *supra* note 23, at 543.

32 18 U.S.C. § 1385 (2000). See Church Book III, *supra* note 4, at 791. The operation of the Posse Comitatus Act is described briefly in the text at pp. 170–71.

33 See Church Book III, *supra* note 4, at 793–94; Meason, *supra* note 23, at 542–43.

34 Sam J. Ervin Jr., The First Amendment: A Living Thought in the Computer Age, 4 *Columbia Human Rights Law Review* 13, 37–38 (1972).

35 Kate Martin, Domestic Intelligence and Civil Liberties, *SAIS Review*, Winter–Spring 2004, at 7, 9 (quoting Office of the Assistant to the Secretary of Defense (Intelligence Oversight), *Mission and History* (n.d.), available at www.dod.mil/atsdio/mission.html).

36 Pyle, *supra* note 27.

37 See generally *Federal Data Banks, Computers, and the Bill of Rights: Hearings before the Subcomm. on Constitutional Rights, S. Comm. on the Judiciary*, 92d Cong. (1971); Staff of the Subcomm. on Constitutional Rights, S. Comm. on the Judiciary, 92d Cong., *Army Surveillance of Civilians: A Documentary Analysis* (Comm. Print 1972); 93d Cong., *Report of the Subcomm. on Constitutional Rights, S. Comm. on the Judiciary, Military Surveillance of Civilian Politics* (Comm. Print 1973); *Military Surveillance: Hearings before the Subcomm. on Constitutional Rights, S. Comm. on the Judiciary*, 93d Cong. (1974).

38 *Laird* v. *Tatum*, 408 U.S. 1, 13 (1972).

39 Freedom of Information Act and Amendments of 1974, Pub. L. No. 93-502, 88 Stat. 1561.

40 Privacy Act of 1974, Pub. L. No. 93-579, 88 Stat. 1896 (codified as amended at 5 U.S.C. § 552a (2000 and Supp. IV 2004)).

41 Church Book III, *supra* note 4, at 792.

42 Church Book II, *supra* note 4, at 310–11.

43 5 U.S.C. § 552a (2000 and Supp. IV 2004). The workings of the Act are spelled out in U.S. Department of Justice, Office of Information and Privacy, *Overview of the Privacy Act of 1974*, May 2004, www.usdoj.gov/oip/04_7_1.html; *Litigation under the Federal Open Government Laws 2004*, at 353–401 (Harry A. Hammit, David L. Sobel and Tiffany A. Stedman eds., 22nd edition 2004).

44 50 U.S.C. §§ 1801–1862 (2000 and Supp. IV 2004).

45 18 U.S.C. § 2511(2)(f) (2000 and Supp. IV 2004). "Title III" refers to the Omnibus Crime Control and Safe Streets Act, 18 U.S.C. §§ 2510–2520 (2000 and Supp. IV 2004), which sets out the procedure for judicial authorization of electronic surveillance for the investigation, prevention, and prosecution of serious crimes.

46 See William C. Banks, And the Wall Came Tumbling Down: Secret Surveillance After the Terror, 57 *University of Miami Law Review* 1147 (2002); Steven W. Becker, Maintaining Secret Government Dossiers on the First Amendment Activities of American Citizens: The Law Enforcement Activity Exception to the Privacy Act, 50 *DePaul Law Review* 675 (2000); Technology and Privacy Advisory Committee, *Safeguarding*

Privacy in the Fight against Terrorism (TAPAC Report) 25–26 (Mar. 2004). Regarding application of the Privacy Act to military intelligence activities in the United States, see Paul M. Peterson, Civilian Demonstrations near the Military Installation: Restraints on Military Surveillance and Other Intelligence Activities, 140 *Military Law Review* 113, 130–44 (1993). See also Seamon in this volume.

47 5 U.S.C. § 552a(e)(7) (2000). The history of this provision and controversy surrounding it are described in Becker, *supra* note 46.

48 5 U.S.C. § 552a(a)(2).

49 50 U.S.C. §§ 1805(a)(3)(A), 1824(a)(3)(A).

50 See Church Book III, *supra* note 4, at 833; Becker, *supra* note 46.

51 5 U.S.C. § 552a(e)(1).

52 See the text at p. 169.

53 5 U.S.C. § 552a(b)(3), (a)(7).

54 Church Book III, *supra* note 4, at 834.

55 Ibid. at 834; *see also* ibid. at 788.

56 5 U.S.C. § 552a(d).

57 Ibid. § 552a(c)(3).

58 Ibid. § 552a(k)(1).

59 Those difficulties are outlined in *Litigation under the Federal Open Government Laws 2004, supra* note 43.

60 5 U.S.C. § 552a(e)(3).

61 S. 2386, 108th Cong. § 502 (2004); S. 1803, 109th Cong. § 431 (2005).

62 Pub. L. No. 107-347, § 208(b)(1), 116 Stat. 2899, 2921 (2002).

63 Ibid. § 208(b)(2)(B)(ii).

64 Ibid. § 208(b)(1)(B)(iii).

65 Ibid. § 208(b)(1)(C).

66 50 U.S.C. § 413(a)(1) (2000).

67 See 5 U.S.C. app. §§ 1–8, 8H, 11 (2000 and Supp. IV 2004).

68 *United States Intelligence Activities*, Exec. Order No. 12,333, 46 Fed. Reg. 59,941 (Dec. 4, 1981).

69 Ibid. § 1.4(a).

70 Ibid. § 1.11(a), (d).

71 Ibid. § 2.3(b).

72 Ibid. § 2.3(d).

73 Ibid. § 2.4. Physical searches may, however, be conducted of military personnel or defense contractors. Ibid. § 2.4(b), (c).

74 Ibid. § 2.8.

75 See *President's Foreign Intelligence Advisory Board*, Exec. Order No. 12,863, 58 Fed. Reg. 48,441 (Sept. 13, 1993); *Increasing the Number of Members on the Intelligence Oversight Board*, Exec. Order No. 13,301, 68 Fed. Reg. 26,981 (May 14, 2003).

76 See DOD Dir. 5148.11, *Assistant to the Secretary of Defense for Intelligence Oversight* ¶ 4, May 21, 2004, available at www.fas.org/irp/doddir/dod/5148_11.pdf; George B. Lotz II, Assistant to the Secretary of Defense (Intelligence Oversight), Remarks to the Technology and Privacy Advisory Committee (July 22, 2003), available at www.lotzadvisory.com/Technology-Privacy-Advisory-Jul03.pdf.

77 See *United States Government Interagency Domestic Terrorism Concept of Operations Plan (CONPLAN)* (Jan. 2001), available at www.fbi.gov/publications/conplan/conplan.pdf.

78 Ibid. at 4. See also Jeffrey D. Brake, *Terrorism and the Military's Role in Domestic Crisis Management: Background and Issues for Congress*, Congressional Research Service RL30938 (Jan. 27, 2003).

79 Office of Homeland Security, *National Strategy for Homeland Security* 44 (July 2002).

80 *Homeland Security Presidential Directive/HSPD-5: Management of Domestic Incidents* (Feb. 28, 2003), available at www.fas.org/irp/offdocs/nspd/hspd-5.html.
81 See U.S. Dept. of Homeland Security, *National Response Plan* 41 (Dec. 2004), available at www.dhs.gov/xlibrary/assets/NRP_FullText.pdf.
82 See, e.g., National Commission on Terrorism (Bremer Commission), *Countering the Changing Threat of International Terrorism* 28 (2000) ("[I]n extraordinary circumstances, when a catastrophe is beyond the capabilities of local, state, and other federal officials ... the President may want to designate DOD as lead federal agency"); Ashton B. Carter, John M. Deutch and Philip D. Zelikow, *Catastrophic Terrorism: Elements of a National Policy* (1998), available at www.ksg.harvard.edu/visions/publication/terrorism.htm (DOD primacy inevitable). *But see* Advisory Panel to Assess Domestic Response Capabilities to Terrorism Involving Weapons of Mass Destruction (Gilmore Commission), *Toward a National Strategy for Combating Terrorism* 28 (2000), available at www.rand.org/nsrd/terrpanel/terror2.pdf (the President should "always designate a Federal civilian agency other than the Department of Defense (DOD) as the Lead Federal Agency"). See also Jane Gilliland Dalton, The United States National Security Strategy: Yesterday, Today, and Tomorrow, 52 *Naval Law Review* 60, 87 (2005).
83 18 U.S.C. § 1385 (2000).
84 The Act and its application are described in Linda J. Demaine and Brian Rosen, Process Dangers of Military Involvement in Civil Law Enforcement: Rectifying the Posse Comitatus Act, 9 *New York University Journal of Legislation and Public Policy* 167 (2005–06); Sean J. Kelly, Reexamining the Posse Comitatus Act: Toward a Right to Civil Law Enforcement, 21 *Yale Law and Policy Review* 383 (2003); Matthew Carlton Hammond, Note, The Posse Comitatus Act: A Principle in Need of Renewal, 75 *Washington University Law Quarterly* 953 (1997); Charles Doyle, *The Posse Comitatus Act & Related Matters: The Use of the Military to Execute Civilian Law*, Congressional Research Service 95–964 S (June 1, 2000).
85 Church Book III, *supra* note 4, at 833.
86 Ibid. at 788.
87 42 U.S.C. § 5170b(c) (2000).
88 10 U.S.C. § 382 (2000).
89 10 U.S.C. § 371 (2000).
90 Ibid. §§ 372, 374. A related statute bars military personnel from participation in a "search, seizure, arrest, or similar activity unless ... otherwise authorized by law." Ibid. § 375. It has, however, been held not to prevent the Naval Intelligence Service from sharing with civilian police information collected in its surveillance of criminal drug activity. *Hayes* v. *Hawes*, 921 F.2d 100 (7th Cir. 1990).
91 The Insurrection Act is a collection of five statutes, 10 U.S.C. §§ 331–335 (2000), as amended by Pub. L. No. 109-364, § 1076, 120 Stat. 2083, 2404 (2006). In 1971, the Defense Department asserted that these statutes authorized the domestic collection of information in preparation for possible deployment of troops to deal with civil disturbances. See Church Book III, *supra* note 4, at 793–94.
92 DOD Dir. 3025.15, *Military Assistance to Civil Authorities*, Feb. 27, 1997, available at www.dtic.mil/whs/directives/corres/html/302515.htm; DOD Dir. 5240.01, *DOD Intelligence Activities*, Aug. 27, 2007, available at www.dtic.mil/whs/directives/corres/pdf/524001p.pdf; DOD Dir. 5240.1-R, *Procedures Governing the Activities of DOD Intelligence Components That Affect United States Persons*, Dec. 1982, available at www.defenselink.mil/atsdio/documents/5240.html; DOD Dir. 5200.27, *Acquisition of Information Concerning Persons and Organizations Not Affiliated with the Department of Defense*, Jan. 7, 1980, available at www.dtic.mil/whs/directives/ corres/html/520027.htm.
93 DOD Dir. 5240.01, *supra* note 92, at ¶ 4.1.
94 DOD Dir. 5240.1-R, *supra* note 92, at app. A, ¶ 8.

95 *Operational Law Handbook* 262 (2004) (Joseph E. Berger, Derek Grimes and Eric T. Jensen, eds., 2003), available at www.fas.org/irp/doddir/army/law2004.pdf (emphasis in original). These procedures are elaborated in Army Reg. 381-10, *U.S. Army Intelligence Activities*, May 3, 2007, available at www.fas.org/irp/doddir/army/ar381-10.pdf.

96 DOD Dir. 5240.1-R, *supra* note 92, at Proc. 2, ¶ E.

97 Ibid. at Proc. 2, ¶ E.1.

98 Ibid. at Proc. 2, ¶ B.3.

99 Ibid. at Procs. 3, 4

100 Ibid. at Procs. 5, 6.

101 Ibid. at Proc 7.

102 Ibid. at Proc. 9, ¶ C.1.

103 Ibid. at Proc. 10, ¶ C.1.b.

104 Ibid. at Proc. 12, ¶ B.1.a.

105 DOD Dir. 5200.27, *supra* note 92, ¶¶ 5.2–5.7.

106 Procedure 15 of DOD Dir. 5240.1-R, *supra* note 92, directs Inspectors General and General Counsels of the various intelligence components to seek out and investigate "questionable activities," but it offers no protection for whistleblowers.

107 See Department of Defense, *Civil Support*, Jt. Pub. 3–28, at IV-12 to -15 (Sept. 14, 2007).

108 Department of Defense, *Strategy for Homeland Defense and Civil Support* (June 2005), available at www.defenselink.mil/news/Jun2005/d20050630homeland.pdf.

109 Ibid. at 21.

110 See text at pp. 174–75.

111 *Strategy for Homeland Defense*, *supra* note 108, at 23.

112 See U.S. Northern Command, *Who We Are – Mission* (n.d.), www.northcom.mil/About/index.html; Steve Bowman and James Crowhurst, *Homeland Security: Evolving Roles and Missions for United States Northern Command*, Congressional Research Service RS21322 (Nov. 16, 2006).

113 *Homeland Defense: Old Force Structures for New Missions: Hearing before the Subcomm. on National Security, Emerging Threats, and International Relations of the H. Comm. on Government Reform*, 108th Cong. (2003) (statement of Edward Anderson III, Deputy Commander, U.S. Northern Command, Northern Aerospace Defense Command), available at 2003 WL 2008258 (F.D.C.H.).

114 See Bowman and Crowhurst, *supra* note 112, at 4; Kaye Spector, Military Commander Aims to Stay Steps Ahead of Potential Terrorism, *Plain Dealer* (Cleveland, Ohio), Apr. 6, 2004.

115 Interview by Dan Sagalyn with Ralph Eberhart, Gen. U.S. Air Force, on *The News Hour* (PBS television broadcast Sept. 27, 2002).

116 CIFA was established by DOD Dir. 5105.67, *Department of Defense Counterintelligence Field Activity*, Feb. 19, 2002, available at www.dtic.mil/whs/directives/corres/pdf/510567p.pdf. See Walter Pincus, Pentagon Expanding Its Domestic Surveillance Activity, *Washington Post*, Nov. 27, 2005, at A6 ("Northcom's intelligence centers in Colorado and Texas fuse reports from CIFA, the FBI and other U.S. agencies, and are staffed by 290 intelligence analysts.").

117 DOD Dir. 5105.67, *supra* note 116, at ¶ 3.

118 Ibid. ¶ 6.2.17.

119 DOD Dir. 2000.12, *DOD Antiterrorism (AT) Program*, Encl. 6, ¶ E6.1.2, Aug. 18, 2003, available at www.dtic.mil/whs/directives/corres/pdf/200012p.pdf.

120 Ibid. ¶ E6.1.5.

121 See generally Pincus, *supra* note 116.

122 Letter to Duncan Hunter, Representative from California, from Robert W. Rogalski, Deputy Undersecretary of Def. (Counterintelligence and Security) (Jan. 27, 2006).

182   S. Dycus

123 See, e.g., Robert Block and Jay Solomon, Pentagon Steps Up Intelligence Efforts inside U.S. Borders, *Wall Street Journal*, Apr. 27, 2006, at 1.
124 See, e.g., Servicemembers Legal Defense Network, *Pentagon Releases Documents Acknowledging Surveillance of Gay Groups* (Apr. 11, 2006), www.sldn.org/templates/press/record.html?record=2859; see also Robert Block and Gary Fields, Is Military Creeping into Domestic Spying and Enforcement?, *Wall Street Journal*, Mar. 9, 2004, at B1 (describing CIFA agents' effort to get a videotape of a law school conference attended by "three Middle Eastern men" who made "suspicious remarks").
125 See Walter Pincus, Protestors Found in Database; ACLU Is Questioning Enemies in Defense Dept. System, *Washington Post*, Jan. 17, 2007, at A8.
126 Department of Defense Office of Inspector Gen., *The Threat and Local Observation Notice (TALON) Report Program* (June 27, 2007), available at www.fas.org/irp/agency/dod/talon.pdf.
127 See *Pentagon to Shut Controversial Database*, AP, Aug. 21, 2007.
128 Pub. L. No. 107-296, § 201, 116 Stat. 2135, 2145–47 (2002).
129 Letter from Thomas J. Ridge, Secretary, Department of Homeland Security, to Senators Susan M. Collins and Carl Levin (Apr. 13, 2004), available at http://levin.senate.gov/newsroom/supporting/2004/041304TTICresponse.pdf.
130 Pub. L. No. 107-296, § 201(d), 116 Stat. 2145–48. Some details of IAIP's operations are set forth in *Homeland Security Information Analysis and Infrastructure Protection Budget: Hearing before the Subcomms. on Intelligence and Counterterrorism of the H. Select Comm. on Homeland Security*, 108th Cong. (2004) (testimony of Frank Libutti, Undersecretary of Homeland Security for Information Analysis and Infrastructure Protection). For a critique of the Directorate, see Democratic Members of the House Select Committee on Homeland Security, *America at Risk: Closing the Security Gap* 1–11 (Feb. 2004).
131 Pub. L. No. 107-296, § 201(f), 116 Stat. 2148.
132 Ibid., § 886, 116 Stat. 2248.
133 See *National Counterterrorism Center*, Executive Order No. 13,354, 69 Fed. Reg. 53,589 (Aug. 27, 2004); Intelligence Reform and Terrorism Prevention Act of 2004 (IRTPA), Pub. L. No. 108-458, § 1021, 118 Stat. 3638, 3672.
134 See National Counterterrorism Center, *About the National Counterterrorism Center* (Mar. 28, 2007), www.nctc.gov/about_us/about_nctc.html.
135 The program is described in Jeffrey W. Seifert, *Data Mining and Homeland Security: An Overview*, Congressional Research Service RL31798 5–8 (Jan. 18, 2007); *Report to Congress Regarding the Terrorism Information Awareness Program (in Response to Consolidated Appropriations Resolution, 2003, Pub. L. No. 108-7, Div. M, § 111(b))* (May 20, 2003), available at www.epic.org/privacy/profiling/tia/may03_report.pdf; Gina Marie Stevens, *Privacy: Total Information Awareness Programs and Related Information Access, Collection, and Protection* Laws, Congressional Research Service RL31730 1 (Mar. 21, 2003); and Def. Advanced Research Projects Agency, *Overview of the Information Awareness Office* (Aug. 2, 2002), available at www.fas.org/irp/agency/dod/poindexter.html.
136 *Report to Congress regarding the Terrorism Information Awareness Program*, *supra* note 135, Executive Summary at 1.
137 Stevens, *supra* note 135, at 1. Confusion about the goals of TIA is described in *TAPAC Report*, *supra* note 46, at 15–20.
138 Stevens, *supra* note 135, at 16.
139 See, e.g., Letter from Chuck Hagel, Senator from Nebraska, to Joseph E. Schmitz, Inspector Gen., Department of Defense (Dec. 2, 2002), *reproduced in* Department of Defense, Office of the Inspector Gen., *Information Technology Management: Terrorism Information Awareness Program* (Dec. 12, 2003).
140 See *Information Technology Management*, *supra* note 139, at 1.
141 Pub. L. No. 108-7, Div. M, § 111(b), 117 Stat. 534–36 (2003).

142 Pub. L. No. 108-87, § 8131, 117 Stat. 1054, 1102 (2003). A useful critique may be found in *Information Technology Management, supra* note 139.
143 See *Information Technology Management, supra* note 139, at 2; *see also U.S. Still Mining Terror Data*, AP, Feb. 23, 2004.
144 General Accounting Office, *Data Mining: Federal Efforts Cover a Wide Range of Uses*, GAO-04-548 3 (May 2004).
145 Pub. L. No. 107-314, § 901, 116 Stat. 2458, 2465 (2002) (codified at 10 U.S.C. § 137 (Supp. IV 2004)).
146 See Paul Wolfowitz, Deputy Secretary of Defense, *Implementation Guidance on Restructuring Defense Intelligence – and Related Matters* (May 8, 2003), available at www.intelligence.gov/0-usdi_memo.shtml. This change was recommended by the Church Committee in 1976. See Church Book I, *supra* note 4, at 462.
147 See, *e.g.*, Linda Robinson, *In the Intelligence Wars, A Pre-emptive Strike by the Pentagon Surprises Many in Congress*, U.S. News and World Rep., Aug. 12, 2002, at 18; see also Chris Strohm, *Defense Officials Oppose Overhaul of Intelligence Community* (Apr. 7, 2004), www.govexec.com/dailyfed/0404/040704c1.htm.
148 *Intelligence, Surveillance & Reconnaissance: Hearing before the Strategic Forces Subcomm. of the S. Armed Services Comm.*, 108th Cong. (2004) (statement of Stephen A. Cambone, Undersecretary of Defense for Intelligence).
149 Brake, *supra* note 78, at 20.
150 Ibid.

11 National security letters and intelligence oversight

Michael J. Greenlee

Introduction

For nearly 30 years, national security letters (NSLs) have served intelligence agencies as a powerful tool for collecting information. Although the initial NSL statute created a weak and often ineffective means of requesting information from financial institutions, NSL powers and authorities have developed over the years to become a vital component in the conduct of successful counterintelligence and terrorism investigations – described by some FBI personnel as "our bread and butter."[1] The information gathered through NSL requests often provides essential evidence that is required to obtain more invasive tools for intelligence gathering such as wiretaps, pen register/trap and trace devices, and search warrants. Given the potential for abuse in using these tools to gather highly personal information, Congress has sought to balance the investigative needs of intelligence agencies with the legitimate privacy and civil liberty interests of the individuals against whom these powers are used.

National security letters are a type of administrative subpoena principally used by the Federal Bureau of Investigation (FBI) in foreign intelligence, counterintelligence and terrorism investigations.[2] Although originally used to collect customer transactional records from financial institutions,[3] NSL powers and authorities were later expanded to include transactional records from electronic communication providers[4] and consumer credit agencies.[5] Transactional information provides evidence of financial or communication transactions without necessarily revealing the substance of those transactions. For example, telephone and e-mail transactional information could include historical information on telephone calls made and received from a specified number; billing records; subscriber information including name, address, and length of service; and e-mail addresses associated with an account. What is not included in transactional information is the content of these communications.

An important and controversial aspect of NSL powers is the ability of the issuing agency to enforce a nondisclosure provision, or "gag order," against NSL recipients. A gag order prevents recipients from disclosing to anyone that they have received a national security letter request or from revealing any details connected to the investigation. The original nondisclosure provisions served essentially as a permanent restriction on speech, since no mechanism existed for removing the gag order once it was in place.

Although thousands of NSLs were issued under the original authorization statutes,[6] the constitutionality of permanently gagging NSL recipients was never challenged until after passage of the USA PATRIOT Act in 2001.[7] In 2004 and 2005, two cases challenged NSL provisions on constitutional grounds, including First and Fourth Amendment challenges to gag orders.[8] Passage of the USA PATRIOT Improvement and Reauthorization Act (PIRA)[9] in 2006 met some of these challenges by amending the existing NSL statutes and providing some much-needed procedural protections.[10]

In amending the NSL nondisclosure provisions, PIRA created a judicial review process allowing NSL recipients to request that gag orders be modified or lifted. However, this process requires the reviewing court to defer to the expertise of the executive branch when designated officials certify the need for continued enforcement of the gag order.[11] This certification is considered "conclusive" when the designated official asserts that disclosure of the investigation, or any of its details, may endanger national security. Such deference is based on the "mosaic theory," which holds that the executive branch is best qualified to ascertain the importance of discrete bits of information as part of "the whole picture" in matters of national security.[12] Mosaic theory arguments have proven highly successful for the executive branch when denying Freedom of Information Act (FOIA) requests.[13]

The history of NSL powers can serve as an illuminating example of the post-Church Committee development of intelligence investigations. Many of the Church Committee findings and recommendations concerning the need for expanded oversight to prevent the executive branch from violating or ignoring the law, excessively using intrusive investigation techniques, and conducting overbroad investigations with inadequate controls on the retention and dissemination of the information gathered are all reflected in the development of NSL powers and authorities from their creation in 1978 through passage of the PIRA in 2006. At each stage of this development, Congress attempted to balance civil liberty interests with the investigative needs of intelligence agencies. Although Congress generally succeeded in striking an appropriate balance between these interests, the PIRA amendments effectively strip the courts of their power to provide any meaningful review when considering the modification or removal of nondisclosure orders. The level of deference that Congress apparently expects the courts to grant to the executive in matters of national security represents a low point in modern intelligence oversight, especially at time when the ever-expanding surveillance power of the executive requires even more vigilance from the courts and Congress.

The deployment of the mosaic theory to justify such deference can be seen as yet another example of the Bush administration's advocacy of the "unitary executive" and its desire to insulate executive actions from congressional and judicial review.[14] Such a move by the executive branch would unravel hard-won privacy and civil liberty protections that have proven so necessary in the conduct of intelligence investigations and leave those persons against whom NSL powers are used with no effective recourse when those powers are abused. The Church Committee concluded that if Americans confronted their mistakes and resolved not to repeat them, they would remain a people worthy of the best of their past. In the case of national security letter powers and authorities, and what amounts to an unchecked restriction of free speech, it would appear that the current administration is rushing to prove itself unworthy of such distinction.

National security letters prior to the USA PATRIOT Act

The structure of the contemporary U.S. intelligence community would not have been possible if it were not for the investigations conducted by the Senate Select Committee to Study Governmental Operations with Respect to Intelligence – also known as the Church Committee.[15] For 17 months in 1975 and 1976, the Church Committee's comprehensive investigation of the intelligence community revealed a horror show of government abuse in which intelligence agencies had acted virtually without oversight or restraint and with utter disregard for the law over a 30-year period.[16] Among the many documented instances of abuse, the Church Committee revealed numerous cases where intelligence agencies had conducted investigations of U.S. citizens who were not engaged in, or even suspected of, any criminal activity. Information gathered during these investigations was quite often illegally obtained and broadly disseminated between intelligence and law enforcement agencies. In some cases, this information was used to disrupt, discredit, or destroy the lives and reputations of certain individuals deemed to be subversive or national security risks – most notably, the intensive effort of the FBI to neutralize and discredit Dr. Martin Luther King, Jr., as an effective civil rights leader.

Despite the broad opposition to the Committee's investigation from the government, the media and the public, the Committee's findings and recommendations led to the implementation of a series of safeguards to restrict the collection and sharing of information about Americans by the FBI and other intelligence agencies. The most significant result of these investigations was the passage of the Foreign Intelligence Surveillance Act of 1978 (FISA)[17] and the creation of the Foreign Intelligence Surveillance Court (FISC) to provide congressional and judicial oversight of foreign intelligence investigations. This Act, in addition to subsequent Attorney General Guidelines and presidential executive orders, led to a complete reformation of the conduct of intelligence investigations within the United States and served as a stable framework preventing the recurrence of past abuses. It was within this framework that national security letters were developed as one of the FBI's vital intelligence-gathering instruments.

The first mention of the administrative tools that would later be known as national security letters is in the Right to Financial Privacy Act of 1978 (RFPA).[18] Two years earlier, the Supreme Court had held in *United States* v. *Miller* that bank customers had no legitimate expectation of privacy concerning transactional information kept in bank records, and therefore, subpoenas issued by government authorities for such information created no intrusion upon customer Fourth Amendment rights.[19] Recognizing the highly personal nature of the information that such records might contain, Congress responded to *Miller* by passing the RFPA, which provided protection of individual rights beyond that afforded in the Constitution.[20] Nevertheless, Congress recognized the importance of creating a proper balance between the right to privacy and the need of law enforcement agencies to obtain financial records in their investigations.[21]

Section 1114 of the RFPA established the provisions for the release of financial information in foreign intelligence investigations.[22] Included in this forerunner to the modern NSL is a nondisclosure provision prohibiting the financial institution from disclosing to any person that a government authority has sought or obtained access to a customer's financial records.[23] In particular, Section 1114 did not mandate compliance by the financial institution[24] but only required certification that the NSL request complied with statutory requirements.[25] Section 1114 also made no mention that the gag order could be challenged, lifted, or judicially enforced.

The need for nondisclosure is briefly addressed in the House reports accompanying the original RFPA and in the 1986 amendments to the RFPA. Although the final version of the 1978 Act represented a "substantial compromise between the original version of the title and the views of various law enforcement agencies,"[26] there is nothing to suggest that the imposition of a nondisclosure provision in foreign intelligence investigations was part of this discussion. There is brief mention of the nondisclosure provision, stating that nondisclosure is needed in order to assure the absolute secrecy required in foreign intelligence investigations.[27] Likewise, the House report accompanying Public Law 99-569,[28] amending the RFPA, notes that the effective conduct of FBI counterintelligence activities requires such nondisclosure.[29]

In addition to amending the RFPA in 1986, Congress passed the Electronic Communications Privacy Act (ECPA). This Act granted the FBI access to telephone company subscriber information, toll billing records and other electronic communication transactional records, comparable to the access to transactional records the FBI was provided under the RFPA.[30] The nondisclosure provisions contained in ECPA and in the amended RFPA are nearly identical.[31]

The 1986 amendments made significant changes to the standard for issuing an NSL. Where the original RFPA required only certification from the appropriate authority and did not mandate compliance, the amended RFPA and ECPA statutes required certification that the information was "relevant to"[32] or "sought for"[33] foreign counterintelligence purposes. In addition, NSL requests were required to show specific and articulable facts giving reason to believe that the target of the investigation is a foreign power or the agent of a foreign power. The "specific and articulable facts" standard was created specifically for use in counterintelligence investigations, balancing consumer privacy interests with the needs of law enforcement officials to maintain secrecy in their investigations.[34] Both statutes also made NSL compliance mandatory.[35] However, neither statute addressed the lack of specific language permitting a recipient to request judicial review to challenge, lift or modify an NSL or its nondisclosure provision.

In 1996, Congress created the final FBI national security letter authority when it passed amendments to the Fair Credit Reporting Act (FCRA). These amendments authorized FBI access to consumer credit agency reports during counterintelligence investigations.[36] Like the previous NSL statutes, Section 601 of the FCRA Amendments was "carefully crafted" to protect consumers' rights to privacy while allowing law enforcement agencies to obtain necessary information in foreign counterintelligence investigations.[37] The expansion of NSL authority was "not taken lightly," and the House and Senate conferees concluded that the need was genuine, that the threshold for use sufficiently rigorous, and that the built-in safeguards minimized the threat to privacy.[38] To effectively use the powers it had been granted under the Right to Financial Privacy Act, the FBI considered access to credit agency records a crucial requirement to trace the financial activities of suspected spies or terrorists.[39]

The nondisclosure provision created in Section 624(d) departed from the parallel provisions found in ECPA and the RFPA by clarifying that disclosure was permitted within the contacted institution to the extent necessary to fulfill the request.[40] Interestingly, the Conference Report states that although the conferees did not take a position on whether similar disclosures would be forbidden under the RFPA (which, like the ECPA, lacked such clarification), it notes that practicalities would dictate that the provision not be interpreted to exclude such disclosure.[41] In another departure from the ECPA and RFPA provisions, the FCRA amendments authorize judicial enforcement of NSLs.[42] Once again, no provision was made for recipients to challenge or modify an NSL in court.

In creating these NSL authorities, Congress sought to balance legitimate privacy interests with the investigative needs of law enforcement, especially in cases of foreign counterintelligence investigations. What began as a rather ineffective tool for gathering intelligence information developed into an effective and vital instrument providing carefully crafted safeguards to minimize the threat to privacy. All of the authorization acts produced informative legislative histories, which include extensive discussion of the privacy issues that were of concern at the time. However, the constitutionality of NSL gag orders was apparently not among those concerns. Congress recognized that nondisclosure was necessary for the successful conduct of foreign counterintelligence investigations. The fact that no mechanism existed, whether administrative or judicial, for modifying or terminating a nondisclosure order apparently failed to inspire any significant debate concerning the effect of permanently restricting speech.

If Congress was remiss in not providing procedural protections concerning NSL powers, it was apparently of little concern to those individuals and groups against whom nondisclosure was being enforced. Prior to passage of the USA PATRIOT Act, no court challenges to NSL gag orders were filed under any of the then existing statutes; it was not until 2004 that a judicial challenge to NSL powers and authorities was raised.[43]

Changes to NSL powers and authorities in the USA PATRIOT Act

The USA PATRIOT Act was signed into law on October 26, 2001, less than seven weeks after the al Qaeda terrorist attacks in the United States. Despite the sweeping changes it made to the investigative tools and procedures used by law enforcement agencies to investigate and prosecute terrorism, the USA PATRIOT Act encountered little opposition in either the House or Senate.[44] However, the broad expansion of intelligence and law enforcement powers under the USA PATRIOT Act generated considerable concern over the prospect of government abuse.[45]

Congress recognized the possibility of overzealous government agencies infringing civil liberties in their use of these new powers, especially in a time of national emergency. Not surprisingly, the domestic surveillance and intelligence abuses exposed by the Church Committee formed part of the Congressional debate surrounding the PATRIOT Act. Senator Patrick Leahy (Democrat from Vermont) urged the Senate to recall the Cold War abuses of investigative powers by federal agencies that had acted under the rubric of protecting national security.[46] During a time in which the executive branch had a free hand in using the FBI and the Central Intelligence Agency (CIA) to conduct domestic surveillance, with no oversight by Congress or the courts, massive files were compiled on U.S. citizens based solely on activities protected by the First Amendment. Senator Leahy and others were especially concerned that provisions of the USA PATRIOT Act – which made sweeping changes in the relationship between law enforcement and intelligence agencies, allowed the sharing of information broadly defined as "foreign intelligence," and lowered the standards for acquiring such intelligence – could serve as an invitation for government abuse and disrupt the protective framework of intelligence oversight that had emerged as a result of the Church Committee's findings.

In the end, Congress initiated a series of safeguards to ensure against unnecessary and improper use of the powers granted under the new law. Most importantly, Congress created a sunset provision that would require 16 sections of the USA PATRIOT Act to expire on December 31, 2005, unless specifically renewed by Congress.[47] These sections included some of the most troublesome provisions of the USA PATRIOT Act concerning wiretapping, the sharing of intelligence information with law enforcement agencies, and access to business records.[48] Nonetheless, many groups continued to fear that the expansion of surveillance powers under the USA PATRIOT Act would significantly weaken important civil liberty protections.[49]

Section 505 of the USA PATRIOT Act ("Miscellaneous national security authorities") broadened the FBI's NSL authority by amending three of the four existing NSL statutes and adding a fifth. These changes included eliminating the relevance standard and the need to show specific and articulable facts; expanding the scope of investigations beyond foreign counterintelligence to also include international terrorism or espionage; allowing Special Agents in Charge of FBI field offices to approve NSLs; and adding a caveat that no investigations of American citizens can be based exclusively on First Amendment-protected activities.[50] A fifth NSL authority was created by amending the FCRA to permit the FBI and other federal agencies to use NSLs to obtain consumer full credit reports.[51] Although Section 505 reduced the standard for obtaining an NSL and expanded the scope of NSL power and authority, it was not included among those provisions designated to sunset in 2005.

The many changes made by the USA PATRIOT Act to law enforcement and intelligence investigations did not extend to NSL provisions concerning nondisclosure. Also, the deficiencies of preexisting NSL authorities – such as a lack of judicial enforcement mechanisms, the absence of penalties for noncompliance, and the lack of explicit provision allowing recipients to challenge NSL requests – remained. Nonetheless, changes (or the lack of changes) to NSL powers continued to fly under the radar. It was not until the 108th Congress that amendments were first proposed to remedy some of these deficiencies.[52] These changes would later evolve into the NSL amendments found in the USA PATRIOT Improvement and Reauthorization Act of 2005.

Challenges to NSLs: *Doe* v. *Ashcroft* and *Doe* v. *Gonzales*

The first constitutional challenges to national security letters were raised during the 109th Congress. The plaintiffs in *Doe* v. *Ashcroft* (hereinafter *Doe I*) and *Doe* v. *Gonzales* (hereinafter *Library Connection*)[53] argued that NSL statutes could not withstand constitutional scrutiny unless more explicit provisions were made for judicial review and permissible disclosure by NSL recipients. Both involved only NSLs issued under 18 U.S.C. § 2709 concerning electronic communications.

Doe I raised both Fourth Amendment and First Amendment challenges. In that case, an unnamed internet service provider (ISP) received an NSL requiring the production of consumer records pursuant to § 2709. The ISP challenged the NSL, claiming that (1) the lack of an explicit judicial review mechanism under § 2709 resulted in the compulsory secret and unreviewable production of information, in violation of the Fourth Amendment; and (2) the sweeping permanent gag orders lacking any type of judicial review mechanism violated free speech protections under the First Amendment. The district court agreed with the ISP on both challenges, finding that in all but exceptional cases, § 2709 had the effect of authorizing coercive searches effectively immune from any judicial process, in violation of the Fourth Amendment,[54] and that universally applied gag orders imposing perpetual secrecy and demanding unremitting concealment placed a disproportionate burden on free speech under the First Amendment.[55]

In reviewing § 2709(c), the court found that since the nondisclosure provision operated as a content-based prior restraint on speech, it should be subject to strict scrutiny review.[56] Under strict scrutiny, a speech restriction that is either content based or acts as a prior restraint is presumptively invalid and may be upheld only if the government can demonstrate that the restriction is narrowly tailored to promote a compelling government interest. If a less restrictive alternative would be at least as effective in achieving the legitimate purpose that the statute was created to serve, then the speech restriction cannot be defined as narrowly tailored.

The district court stated that nondisclosure provisions acted as a prior restraint based on "the straightforward observation that it prohibits speech before the speech occurs."[57] The court rejected the government's argument that § 2709(c) did not act as a prior restraint because the statute did not create a licensing scheme by which the government could pick and choose among speakers to restrain. Instead, the court found that a blanket permanent prohibition on future disclosures was an even purer form of prior restraint than a licensing system, comparable to the most severe form of a licensing system in which *no* licenses are granted and the speech at issue is maximally suppressed.[58]

The court also found that the nondisclosure provision acted as a content-based restriction. The government had argued that since nondisclosure provisions acted in a content-neutral manner, they could not be considered content based. The government explained that it was not seeking to silence "less favored" or "controversial views"; rather, the prohibition on speech applied irrespective of any particular speaker's views.[59] However, the court found that even a viewpoint-neutral restriction can be content based if the restriction pertains to an entire category of speech. In the case of § 2709(c), recipients were forever barred from speaking to anyone about their knowledge and role in the events pertaining to an NSL, even at a time when disclosure of the investigation might have ceased to generate legitimate national security concerns.

On the basis of these findings, the court applied strict scrutiny in reviewing whether nondisclosure orders were narrowly tailored to promote a compelling government interest. Although accepting the government's argument that the conduct of international terrorism and counterintelligence investigations could demonstrate a compelling government interest to protect national security and that it may be necessary to impose secrecy for long periods of time, the court rejected the government's argument that a permanent application of nondisclosure orders to all persons affected, in every case, was narrowly tailored.[60]

Looking to then-pending legislation in Congress, the court found examples of less restrictive alternatives that could equally serve the government's compelling interest without imposing a categorical, perpetual ban on speech.[61] The government countered that such alternatives would be less effective because they would require the government to weigh the risk of court-ordered disclosure against the need for the information sought each time it considered issuing an NSL.[62] The court characterized the government's argument as tangential to the issue at hand – like "using the edge of the hammer to hit the nail."[63] The issue of indefinite secrecy imposed by § 2709(c) had little or nothing to do with the government's ability to gather information; rather, the question was the government's need to maintain the secrecy of discrete information and to restrict speech long after the investigation had served its purpose. The court granted that a blanket rule swearing everyone to secrecy forever certainly would be the easiest and most efficient course for the government; however, such a course would not necessarily be the most equitable and protective of fundamental rights. The court concluded that the government failed to carry its burden to show that the extraordinary scope of § 2709(c) was narrowly tailored to achieve its goals.

The court also briefly addressed the government's deployment of the *mosaic theory* in arguing for judicial deference to executive-branch national security expertise. The government argued that the court should defer to executive expertise in the case of NSL nondisclosure provisions when the government asserts that such secrecy is necessary for national security purposes. Although the court acknowledged that the judiciary should defer to executive expertise in national security matters, such deference should be conditioned on the specific facts and rationales concerning a *particular situation* involving *particular persons* at a *particular time* (emphasis in the original).[64] Furthermore, the government had cited no authority to support the open-ended proposition that it may universally apply general principles to impose perpetual secrecy on an entire category of future cases for all times and places. Essentially, the government was asking the court to assume that its use of § 2709 would always sufficiently advance asserted government interests to justify the abridgment of First Amendment expressive activity. Unwilling to accept such a dubious assumption, the court found § 2709(c) to be facially unconstitutional. In addition, the court found that since § 2709(c) could not be severed from the remainder of the statute, § 2709 in its entirety should be struck down.[65] Since all NSL nondisclosure provisions operate under the same mechanisms as found in ECPA, it seems reasonable to assume that RFPA and FCRA nondisclosure provisions would also be rendered unconstitutional.

Library Connection followed much the same reasoning as *Doe I* concerning NSL nondisclosure provisions. In *Library Connection*, a library consortium – Library Connection – offering internet access to its patrons received a § 2709 NSL requesting the subscriber and billing information for a 45-minute time period relating to a potential terrorist threat. Library Connection filed First and Fourth Amendment challenges similar to *Doe I*. However, the court only addressed the First Amendment challenge to the constitutionality of the § 2709(c) nondisclosure provision, which prevented Library Connection from revealing its identity as an NSL recipient.[66]

The district court reached the same conclusion as *Doe I* on the nondisclosure issue. After finding that § 2709 constituted a content-based prior restraint on speech, the court applied strict scrutiny to determine whether the statute was narrowly tailored to achieve the government's compelling interest. Although the court accepted the government's claim that preventing an NSL recipient from disclosing its identity could serve a compelling interest, it found nothing in the record to support that conclusion as applied in this case. Instead, the court found the government's argument that disclosure of Library Connection's identity "may" or "could" harm investigations related to national security too speculative to show a compelling interest.[67] In addition, even if the government's interest were more broadly defined as preventing an unknown subject of the government's investigation from learning of the existence of that investigation, the court found that the restraints and restrictions of § 2709(c) which served that interest lacked the narrow tailoring necessary to survive constitutional strict scrutiny.[68] The court concluded that the government failed to show a compelling interest that would be served by gagging the plaintiffs, and granted Library Connection's motion to enjoin enforcement of the nondisclosure provision.[69]

In both *Doe I* and *Library Connection*, the district courts issued a stay of enforcement pending an appeal before the Second Circuit. While the case was under consideration, the identity of the plaintiff, Library Connection, was revealed through a story in the *New York Times*, which led to a curious standoff between the government and the plaintiffs. Through an oversight by the government, the name "Library Connection" had not been redacted from part of the records that were publicly available through a court-operated website.[70] Despite the widespread publication of this information, the government insisted that the nondisclosure order be enforced, preventing Library Connection from confirming its identity as an NSL recipient. This led to a bizarre situation in which the identities of the Library Connection plaintiffs were publicly exposed, but the individual plaintiffs could not confirm to anyone, including family members, that they were involved in a national security investigation. It was only after passage of the USA PATRIOT Improvement and Reauthorization Act in March 2006 that the government ceased enforcement of the nondisclosure order against Library Connection. Finally, in June 2006, the government officially withdrew its NSL request from Library Connection, stating that it had used other means to obtain the information. By November 2006, the government was no longer seeking to obtain information from the ISP in *Doe I*, but nonetheless still sought enforcement of the nondisclosure order.[71]

The USA PATRIOT Improvement and Reauthorization Act of 2005

While *Doe I* and *Library Connection* were on appeal, a larger congressional debate was taking place concerning the reauthorization of the USA PATRIOT Act.[72] Sixteen sections of the USA PATRIOT Act were set to expire on December 31, 2005. Most of these provisions concerned surveillance and information sharing in intelligence investigations. In the debate leading up to the expiration of a raft of PATRIOT Act provisions, the federal government, civil liberty organizations and other groups argued both for and against the continuing need for the relevant measures. Some parties favored making the sunset provisions permanent or extending the sunset date, citing the dangers to national security that would emerge if law enforcement and intelligence agencies were stripped of crucial powers needed in the War on Terror; other groups favored either allowing the provisions to expire as planned or allowing their continued use only after serious revisions had been made to better protect civil liberties.[73] Although Section 505 of the USA PATRIOT Act was not included among the sunset provisions, national security letters formed a significant part of the discussion about infringements on civil liberties.[74]

The procedural protections that national security letters had lacked since their inception became a focus of the civil liberty debate. Several bills were introduced calling for explicit mechanisms for judicial review and enforcement of NSL requests, clarification of the scope of nondisclosure orders, judicial review of nondisclosure orders, more congressional oversight, and the removal of libraries and booksellers from NSL requests.[75] The intense public debate surrounding NSLs was felt in Congress, which once again sought to carefully balance the investigative needs of law enforcement and intelligence agencies with legitimate privacy interests.

After months of political wrangling, including a temporary extension of the sunset provision, Congress passed the USA PATRIOT reauthorization statutes – Public Laws 109-177 (PIRA) and 109-178 (ARAA).[76] PIRA incorporated many of the procedural protections that had been lacking in NSLs. For the first time, provisions were created for judicial enforcement and judicial review of NSL requests;[77] specific penalties were defined for noncompliance with NSL requirements;[78] clarifications were added permitting NSL recipients to contact their attorney or anyone else necessary for them to comply with NSL requests;[79] congressional oversight was expanded;[80] and a procedure was created for lifting the nondisclosure requirement.[81] These changes applied to all NSLs issued under the RFPA, ECPA, and FCRA. In addition, libraries not acting as an electronic communication service provider were excluded from NSLs issued under 18 U.S.C. § 2709.[82]

Sections 115 and 116 of PIRA established the procedure for imposing a nondisclosure order and providing judicial review to challenge enforcement of nondisclosure. To impose a nondisclosure order on an NSL recipient, the Director of the FBI or his designee must certify that nondisclosure is required to protect national security, to prevent interference with an ongoing investigation or with diplomatic relations, or to protect the life or physical safety of any person.[83] After receiving an NSL, recipients can challenge the request and the nondisclosure order in a federal district court.[84] The district court may modify or set aside the nondisclosure order if it finds no reason to believe that the original certification requires continued enforcement.[85] However, if a designated official[86] certifies that disclosure might endanger national security or interfere with diplomatic relations, then such certification is conclusive and the nondisclosure order remains in force.[87] NSL recipients are allowed to challenge nondisclosure orders once per year.[88] If a nondisclosure order is challenged one year or more after the original NSL request, then the order must either be terminated within 90 days or a designated official must recertify the need for nondisclosure.[89] Once again, it is conclusive for a designated official to certify that nondisclosure is necessary.

In amending the NSL statutes, Congress apparently had given heed to the civil liberty concerns expressed by the public, the courts and its own members by providing much-needed procedural protections, clarifications and additional oversight. These changes had an immediate effect on *Doe I* and *Library Connection*, which were on appeal before the Second Circuit when PIRA was passed. The PIRA amendments provided the explicit pre-enforcement judicial review that the respective district courts had found lacking in the original NSL provisions. In light of the congressional actions taken in 2005, which empowered NSL recipients to challenge the issuance of an NSL in court and freely communicate about an NSL request with their attorneys, the ISP in *Doe I* dropped its Fourth Amendment claims.[90] Likewise, the Fourth Amendment portion of the district court opinion was vacated.[91] The ISP's original First Amendment claims in *Doe I* were also vacated, and the case was remanded to the district court to address the constitutionality of the revised § 2709(c) and the new standards for judicial review of nondisclosure orders.[92] As was mentioned earlier, the issues in *Library Connection* became moot when the government dropped its opposition to the plaintiff's disclosure of its identity and withdrew its demand for the requested information.

The mosaic theory, judicial deference and NSL nondisclosure

Despite the procedural protections provided by PIRA, some groups believed the amendments did not go far enough to protect civil liberties.[93] The American Civil Liberties Union (ACLU), for example, accused the Bush administration of "stacking the deck" in the government's favor:

> Under the new law, if a high-level political appointee certifies that national security or diplomatic relations will be harmed, the court must consider that assertion "conclusive" unless the recipient proves that assertion was made in "bad faith" – meaning the gag order will stand. This plainly unconstitutional standard fails to comport with Americans' First Amendment rights.[94]

This statement formed the basis of the ISP's argument in the remanded case before the district court. The ISP argued that the amended nondisclosure provisions violate the First Amendment and the principle of separation of powers because they prevent courts from applying a constitutional standard of review, fail to provide constitutionally mandated procedural safeguards, and invest the FBI with unbridled discretion to prohibit speech.[95] In passing PIRA, the ISP claimed Congress overstepped the bounds of separation of powers by dictating to the courts how they must adjudicate First Amendment claims when considering nondisclosure challenges and by requiring the courts to apply a standard of review that contemplates "near-servile deference" to the executive.[96] The underlying rationale used by the government to justify such judicial deference is found in the mosaic theory.[97]

Mosaic theory claims are commonly used by federal agencies seeking to deny disclosure of information requested under the FOIA.[98] The FOIA generally provides that any person has a right, enforceable in court, to obtain access to federal agency records, except to the extent that such records (or portions of them) are protected from public disclosure by one of nine exemptions or by one of three special law enforcement record exclusions.[99] Exemption 1 of the FOIA allows agencies to prevent disclosure of all national security information concerning intelligence collection, the national defense or foreign policy that has been properly classified.[100] In conjunction with Exemption 1, Exclusion (c)(3) allows the FBI to deny the existence or nonexistence of certain records pertaining to counterintelligence, foreign intelligence or international terrorism.[101] Through the use of NSL gag orders, the executive also has the ability to prevent the disclosure of information that may threaten national security or interfere with intelligence investigations, similar to the exemptions allowed under FOIA. However, where the FOIA allows the federal government to deny access to information in the possession of the government, nondisclosure prevents NSL recipients from revealing information they already know.

In support of its decision to withhold information under the FOIA or to prevent disclosure in the case of NSLs, a federal agency will sometimes advance a mosaic claim. Such claims usually state that access to the requested materials must be denied because, when combined with other discrete bits of information, the resulting mosaic of information could reveal vital facts concerning national security. Ordinarily, judges do not have the national security expertise that would enable them to understand the sensitivity of an isolated piece of information in the context of the intelligence apparatus. Congress, the executive, and the courts all agree that the mosaic theory is basically correct: executive-branch intelligence agencies are the experts in matters relating to national security, and their judgments concerning these issues should be deferred to by the other branches of government. The real point of contention concerns the level of deference that the executive should be granted in these matters. Disagreement concerning proper deference occurs not only among the three branches of government, but within the judiciary itself. This variance of opinion within the judiciary has led to the emergence of three levels of deference.

Some courts have shown nearly complete deference, amounting almost to an *abdication* of judicial review.[102] Other courts are reluctant to evaluate and challenge mosaic claims, preferring to treat them as a distinct and privileged defense of secrecy.[103] These courts show an augmented form of deference that amounts to an effective *delegation* of mosaic theory oversight to the agencies themselves.[104] A third set of courts have opposed the application of any special treatment and evaluate mosaic claims with the *standard deference* due to the government in national security litigation.[105] Most courts have been willing to either delegate or abdicate to executive expertise in matters of national security, resulting in the phenomenal success of mosaic claims in the context of denying FOIA requests. However, courts choosing to apply standard deference when reviewing mosaic arguments have generally rejected such claims.

Between 1972 and 2001, only one court rejected outright an agency's mosaic argument involving an FOIA request.[106] Since 2001, one other court has rejected an agency mosaic argument implicating the FOIA.[107] In addition, three courts have rejected mosaic claims when considering the constitutionality of government actions restricting First Amendment rights. As was discussed earlier, *Doe I* and *Library Connection* rejected mosaic claims supporting the unconstitutional application and enforcement of nondisclosure orders. The Sixth Circuit in *Detroit Free Press* also found unconstitutional a mosaic intelligence argument concerning the closure of certain immigration removal proceedings under the "Creppy Directive."[108]

The courts in *Doe I*, *Library Connection* and *Detroit Free Press* applied standard deference in reviewing the government's mosaic claims. These courts rejected the government's mosaic theory argument for basically the same reason: In each case, the government failed to show that the restriction in question was narrowly tailored to promote a compelling government interest. *Doe I* and *Library Connection* found universally applied gag orders imposing perpetual secrecy on disclosures that "may" or "could" harm national security investigations to be too speculative and not narrowly tailored. Similarly, *Detroit Free Press* found that categorically and completely closing all special interest hearings without demonstrating, beyond speculation, the absolute necessity of such closure did not meet the requirements of strict scrutiny review.[109]

In exposing the unconstitutional manner by which the government was attempting to restrain First Amendment-protected rights, it would seem that the vital necessity for courts to engage in standard deference review of national security mosaic claims would be clear. Nevertheless, the PIRA amendments appear to leave the judiciary no choice in matters concerning nondisclosure orders. Certification by designated officials is considered "conclusive" in nondisclosure challenges when national security or diplomatic relations are threatened. Since such language seems to allow little room for courts to apply standard deference, all that remains, apparently, is for courts to either delegate or abdicate their review power to executive expertise. This has led to accusations that judicial review of nondisclosure orders is merely a rubber stamp, purely cosmetic, stunted, and a fig leaf.[110] The government denies this is the case, stating that district courts can request additional information from the government to ensure that the certification is supported by specific facts or rationales tied to the situation at issue.[111] However, this interpretation of the court's ability to review government certification is supported by neither the legislative history of PIRA nor the filings submitted in *Doe I*.

Statements in the conference report and congressional debates accompanying the PIRA amendments indicate the level of deference that was anticipated by members of Congress. The conference report accompanying H.R. 3199 states: "This provision [PIRA Section 115] recognizes that the Executive branch is both constitutionally and practically better suited to make national security and diplomatic relations judgments than the judiciary."[112] This comment is expanded upon in the *Congressional Record*:

> The standard in the conference report is the appropriate one, both constitutionally and practically, as it recognizes that sensitive national security and diplomatic relations judgments are particularly within the Executive's

expertise.... It will be an exceedingly rare case in which a judge will find, contrary to a certification by an executive branch official, that there is no reason to believe that the nondisclosure order should remain in place. It will be even rarer for a judge to find that one of the Senate-confirmed officials .. . has acted in bad faith.... I could not have supported the conference report or the explicit judicial review of nondisclosure orders if I thought that they would give judges the power to second-guess the informed ... judgments of our high-level executive branch officials. The conference report makes clear that *judges will not have such discretion.*[113]

The deference contemplated by the above statements hardly envisions a judiciary that will engage in meaningful review taking into account the "specific facts or rationales" connected to the situation at hand, as asserted by the government. The "rarity" suggested in these remarks by Senator Kyl anticipates the deference exhibited by courts that have either abdicated or delegated their responsibility to review the decisions of the executive when it raises the mosaic theory in its defense. But it is precisely in those cases in which the judiciary has requested specific facts and rationales concerning the *particular situation* involving *particular persons* at a *particular time* that the court has found the mosaic claims asserted by the government to be speculative and lacking justification for the requested restraint of First Amendment rights. However, if courts do not have the discretion to conduct meaningful review, which requires the executive to set forth particular facts for the court to evaluate, then the government will rarely be found to have failed to justify the need for nondisclosure.

For an example of the specificity to be expected from the executive when certifying the need for nondisclosure, the case *Doe* v. *Gonzales* is exemplary. The following is the text of the certification submitted by FBI Director, Robert S. Mueller, in its entirety:

I, the Director of the FBI, and an official authorized to certify as to the necessity for the non-disclosure provision, do hereby certify that disclosure that the FBI has sought or obtained access to information or records through the National Security Letter issued on or about February 10, 2004 to the plaintiff John Doe in *John Doe* v. *John Ashcroft, et al.*, No. 1:04-cv-02614 (U.S.D.C., S.D.N.Y.), including, but not limited to, the disclosure of the NSL itself or its contents, may endanger the national security of the United States.[114]

According to the text of PIRA Section 115, this certification must be accepted by a reviewing court as *conclusive* since it asserts that disclosure may endanger national security. There is no mention in the certification, the text of PIRA or in the legislative history that a reviewing court has any discretion to request more information from the government to support its need for nondisclosure. In this instance, the mere assertion that national security may be endangered is all the proof that is required of the government.

Conclusion

In March 2007, the Office of the Inspector General (OIG) issued its first review of national security letter use by the FBI.[115] Covering calendar years 2003–04 and 2005–06, the OIG reported the issuance of over 140,000 NSL requests and disclosed significant abuses by the FBI in its use of NSL powers. In the most egregious case of abuse, the OIG reported that the FBI circumvented the requirements of NSL authorities by issuing so-called exigent letters on over 700 occasions.[116] These "exigent letters" stated that the records requested were in connection with fast-paced investigations and that the subpoenas (NSLs) authorizing the request had been submitted for processing and service.[117] However, in most instances there was no documentation associating the requests with pending national security investigations; the FBI was unable to determine which letters were sent in emergency circumstances due to inadequate record keeping; and in many instances, NSLs were only processed and issued many months after the FBI had already obtained the requested information.[118] The OIG also reported that the database used by the FBI to track NSL use was inaccurate and believed the total number of NSL requests issued to be significantly higher than reported.[119]

The current rendition of NSL powers and authorities is unlike anything previously created by Congress and allows the executive to act with little restraint when gathering intelligence. The increased congressional oversight reflected in the OIG Report has shown that more scrutiny of executive intelligence-gathering activities is vital to prevent intentional or accidental violations of privacy and civil liberty interests when NSL powers are invoked. In addition, the decisions of the courts in *Doe I, Library Connection* and *Detroit Free Press* demonstrate the importance of applying meaningful judicial review to the certifications of the executive branch to prevent the unconstitutional restraint of First Amendment-protected activities. Although PIRA provides important protections related to NSL use and enforcement, to assume that continued oversight of the executive by the judiciary is unnecessary, or that the acceptance by the judiciary of unsupported assertions concerning continued nondisclosure is unproblematic, is plainly not warranted.

The tension between secrecy, privacy and liberty, which is inherent in intelligence investigations, will always demand meaningful and effective oversight of the executive branch by Congress and the courts. In the case of NSL nondisclosure orders, this will only be achieved if the executive branch is required to present hard facts to the court to support its request for continued nondisclosure. This could be accomplished by amending PIRA and applying the "specific and articulable facts" standard, specifically created by Congress for intelligence investigations in 1986, to recertifications for nondisclosure enforcement. Such a standard would defer to the expertise of the executive branch when initially imposing a nondisclosure order, but would require the presentation of specific and articulable facts if the executive seeks to extend that order after the initial investigation. Such a standard would recognize the limited ability of intelligence agencies to present such "hard" facts in the initial stages of intelligence investigations, but would require such proof after the executive branch has been given the opportunity to gather intelligence. In this way, balance could be restored by recognizing the needs of intelligence agencies to quickly initiate investigations, but also protect against the prolonged infringement of civil liberties by demanding proof that the investigation has actually "paid off" in terms of intelligence.

The Church Committee revealed in stark detail the extent to which the intelligence community will extend and abuse its powers if left unchecked. "If intelligence agencies continue to operate under a structure in which executive power is not effectively checked and examined, then we will have neither quality intelligence nor a society which is free at home and respected abroad."[120] Confronted by an administration that openly advocates for unchecked executive power and authority in the name of protecting national security, such oversight is as necessary today as it was 30 years ago.

Notes

1 U.S. Department of Justice, Office of the Inspector General, *A Review of the Federal Bureau of Investigation's Use of National Security Letters* xxii (March 2007), available at www.usdoj.gov/oig/special/index.htm [hereinafter OIG Report].
2 There are five federal statutes authorizing the use of national security letters. This chapter will not discuss NSLs issued under § 436 of the National Security Act, 50 U.S.C. § 436 (2000). Section 436 NSLs apply only to executive-branch employees who have consented to a background investigation to obtain access to classified information.
3 Financial Institutions Regulatory and Interest Rate Control Act of 1978, Pub. L. No. 95-630, § 1114, 92 Stat. 3641, 3707–08. Title XI of this Act is commonly known as the Right to Financial Privacy Act and codified in 12 U.S.C. §§ 3401–3422 (2000) [hereinafter RFPA].
4 Electronic Communications Privacy Act of 1986, Pub. L. No. 99-508, § 201, 100 Stat. 1848, 1867–68 [hereinafter ECPA].
5 Intelligence Authorization Act for Fiscal Year 1996, Pub. L. No. 104-93, § 601, 109 Stat. 961, 974–77 (1995) [hereinafter FCRA Amendments].
6 The FBI issued approximately 8,500 NSL requests in 2000, the year prior to passage of the USA PATRIOT Act. OIG Report, *supra* note 1, at xvi.
7 Uniting and Strengthening America by Providing Appropriate Tools Required to Intercept and Obstruct Terrorism Act of 2001, Pub. L. No. 107-56, 115 Stat. 272 [hereinafter USA PATRIOT Act].
8 *Doe* v. *Ashcroft*, 334 F. Supp. 2d 471 (S.D.N.Y. 2004) [hereinafter Doe I]; *Doe* v. *Gonzales*, 386 F. Supp. 2d 66 (D. Conn. 2005) [hereinafter *Library Connection*].
9 USA PATRIOT Improvement and Reauthorization Act of 2005, Pub. L. No. 109-177, 120 Stat. 192 (2006) [hereinafter PIRA]; USA PATRIOT Act Additional Reauthorizing Amendments Act of 2006, Pub. L. No. 109-178, 120 Stat. 278 [hereinafter AARA].
10 *Doe I* v. *Gonzales*, 449 F.3d 415 (2d Cir. 2006).
11 PIRA, 120 Stat. at 211–13.
12 U.S. Department of Justice, Office of Information and Privacy, *Freedom of Information Act Guide, March 2007*, at 199–201, available at www.usdoj.gov/oip/foia_guide07.htm [hereinafter FOIA Guide].
13 David Pozen, The Mosaic Theory, National Security, and the Freedom of Informa-

tion Act, 115 *Yale Law Journal* 628, 643–44 (2005) (citing only one case between 1972 and 2001 rejecting outright an agency's mosaic argument).

14 The unitary executive theory posits unchecked power in the hands of the executive branch, beyond the oversight of Congress, the judiciary, or independent agencies. See e.g., Karl Manheim and Allan Ides, The Unitary Executive, 29 *Los Angeles Lawyer*, Sept. 2006, at 24.

15 Named for its chair, Senator Frank Church (Democrat from Idaho). Over 50,000 pages of Church Committee records have been declassified for public viewing. See Assassination Archives and Research Center, Church Committee Reports, available at www.aarclibrary.org/publib/church/reports/contents.htm (last visited Oct. 12, 2007) (listing the Church Committee Reports online). These records consist of the final reports issued by the Committee and transcripts of the hearings.

16 See generally Loch K. Johnson, *A Season of Inquiry: Congress and Intelligence* (1988).

17 Foreign Intelligence Surveillance Act of 1978, Pub. L. No. 95-511, 92 Stat. 1738.

18 RFPA, 12 U.S.C. §§ 3401–3422 (2000).

19 *United States* v. *Miller*, 425 U.S. 435, 442–43 (1976).

20 H.R. Rep. No. 95-1383, at 33–34 (1978).

21 Ibid. at 33.

22 RFPA, 92 Stat. at 3707–08 (1978).

23 Ibid. at 3708.

24 The lack of compliance by financial institutions led to the amending of the RFPA in 1986. See H.R. Rep. No. 99-690(I), at 15–16 (1986).

25 RFPA, 92 Stat. at 3707.

26 H.R. Rep. No. 95-1383, at 34 (1986).

27 Ibid. at 229 (referencing the additional views of Mr. LaFalce).

28 Intelligence Authorization Act for Fiscal Year 1987, Pub. L. No. 99-569, § 404, 100 Stat. 3190, 3197 (1986) [hereinafter RFPA Amendments].

29 H.R. Rep. No. 99-690(I), at 18 (1986).

30 ECPA, 100 Stat. at 1867–68 (1986).

31 Compare ECPA, 100 Stat. at 1867, with RFPA Amendments, 100 Stat. at 3197.

32 ECPA, 100 Stat. at 1867.

33 RFPA Amendments, 100 Stat. at 3197.

34 H.R. Rep. No. 99-690(I), at 17.

35 ECPA, 100 Stat. at 1867; RFPA Amendments, 100 Stat. at 3197.

36 FCRA Amendments, 109 Stat. 961, 974 (1995).

37 H.R. Rep. No. 104-427, at 35 (1995) (Conf. Rep.).

38 Ibid. at 36.

39 Ibid.

40 FCRA Amendments, 109 Stat. at 976 (1995).

41 H.R. Rep. No. 104-427, at 39.

42 FCRA Amendments, 109 Stat. at 975.

43 *Doe I*, 334 F. Supp. 2d 471 (S.D.N.Y. 2004).

44 The House passed the USA PATRIOT Act with a vote of 357 to 66, 147 *Congressional Record* H7224 (daily edition Oct. 23, 2001); the Senate voted 98 to 1, 147 *Congressional Record* S11059 (daily edition Oct. 25, 2001).

45 See, e.g., Jim McGee, An Intelligence Giant in the Making; Anti-Terrorism Law Likely to Bring Domestic Apparatus of Unprecedented Scope, *Washington Post*, Nov. 4, 2001, at A4.

46 147 *Congressional Record* S10992–S10994 (daily edition Oct. 25, 2001).

47 See 147 *Congressional Record* S10547–S10630 (daily edition Oct. 11, 2001) (including Senate debate concerning the necessity of adding a sunset provision); 147 *Congressional Record* H7159–H7207 (daily edition Oct. 23, 2001) (including the same for the House).

48 USA PATRIOT Act, Pub. L. No. 107-56, § 224, 115 Stat. 272 (2001). Some provisions set to expire included ECPA wiretapping (Sections 201, 202), sharing of foreign intelligence information (Section 203), roving wiretaps (Section 206), FISA wiretaps (Sections 207, 218), FISA pen register orders (Section 214), FISA access to business records (Section 215), and emergency disclosures by communications providers (Section 212).

49 See generally American Civil Liberties Union, *Unpatriotic Acts: The FBI's Power to Rifle Through Your Records and Personal Belongings without Telling You* (July 2003); American Library Association, *FBI in Your Library*, www.ala.org/ala/oif/ifissues/fbiyourlibrary.htm (last visited Oct. 12, 2007).

50 USA PATRIOT Act, § 505, 115 Stat. at 365–66 (2001).

51 Ibid. § 358(g), 115 Stat. at 327 (2001).

52 See H.R. 3037, 108th Cong. § 3 (2003) (allowing judicial review to modify or quash a nondisclosure requirement and explicitly permitting disclosure to an attorney); H.R. 3179, 108th Cong. §§ 2–3 (2003) (providing punishments for violating nondisclosure orders and judicial enforcement of NSLs); S. 2555, 108th Cong. § 2 (2004) (providing judicial enforcement of administrative subpoenas, judicial review of nondisclosure orders, and limited disclosure).

53 *Doe I*, 334 F. Supp. 2d 471 (S.D.N.Y. 2004); *Library Connection*, 386 F. Supp. 2d 66 (D. Conn. 2005).

54 *Doe I*, 334 F. Supp. 2d at 506.

55 Ibid. at 524.

56 Ibid. at 511.

57 Ibid.

58 Ibid. at 512.

59 Ibid.

60 Ibid. at 516.

61 The court specifically considered H.R. 3037, 108th Cong. (2003) and S. 2555, 108th Cong. (2004).

62 *Doe I*, 334 F. Supp. 2d 471, 521 (S.D.N.Y. 2004).

63 Ibid.

64 Ibid. at 524.

65 Ibid. at 525–26.

66 *Library Connection*, 386 F. Supp. 2d 66, 69 (D. Conn. 2005).

67 Ibid. at 77.

68 Ibid. at 82.

69 Ibid.

70 Alison Leigh Cowan, Librarians Must Stay Silent in Patriot Act Suit, Court Says, *New York Times*, Sept. 21, 2005, at B2. See Alison Leigh Cowan, A Court Fight to Keep a Secret That's Long Been Revealed, *New York Times*, Nov. 18, 2005, at B1; Alison Leigh Cowan, Four Librarians Finally Break Silence in Records Case, *New York Times*, May 31, 2006, at B3; Alison Leigh Cowan, U.S. Ends a Yearlong Effort to Obtain Library Records amid Secrecy in Connecticut, *New York Times*, June 27, 2006, at B6.

71 Declaration of Jeffrey Oestericher, *Doe I* v. *Gonzales*, No. 04 Civ. 2614 (S.D.N.Y. Nov. 8, 2006), available at www.aclu.org/pdfs/safefree/decl_oester20061108.pdf.

72 See, e.g., *USA PATRIOT Act: A Review for the Purpose of Reauthorization: Hearing Before the H. Comm. on the Judiciary*, 109th Cong. (2005); *Reauthorization of the USA PATRIOT Act: Hearing before the H. Comm. on the Judiciary*, 109th Cong. (2005). For congressional debate concerning the reauthorization, especially NSLs and nondisclosure, see 151 *Congressional Record* H11515–H11544 (daily edition Dec. 14, 2005), 151 *Congressional Record* S13546–S13561 (daily edition Dec. 14, 2005), 151 *Congressional Record* S13608–S13627 (daily edition Dec. 15, 2005), and 152 *Congressional Record* S1598–S1632 (daily edition Mar. 2, 2006).

73 See, e.g., James J. Roth, Getting Terror's Number: National Security Letters Help the FBI Discover Conspirators before It's Too Late, *Legal Times*, Jan. 30, 2006; Jim VandeHei, Bush Assails Democrats over Patriot Act: Opponents Are Blocking Law's Full Renewal for Political Reasons, *Washington Post*, Jan. 2, 2006, at A2.

74 See, e.g., *Material Witness Provisions of the Criminal Code, and the Implementation of the USA PATRIOT Act: Section 505 That Addresses National Security Letters, and Section 804 That Addresses Jurisdiction over Crimes Committed at U.S. Facilities Abroad: Hearing before the Subcomm. on Crime, Terrorism, and Homeland Security of the H. Comm. on the Judiciary*, 109th Cong. 9–38 (2005); Barton Gellman, The FBI's Secret Scrutiny: In Hunt for Terrorists, Bureau Examines Records of Ordinary Americans, *Washington Post*, Nov. 6, 2005, at A1.

75 See H.R. 1526, 109th Cong. § 7 (2005) (discussing the sunset for section 505, excluding libraries from NSLs); H.R. 2715, 109th Cong. (2005) (providing the procedural protection for NSLs); S. 317, 109th Cong. (2005) (exempting libraries and booksellers from NSLs); S. 737, 109th Cong. § 5 (2005) (providing procedural protection for NSLs).

76 PIRA, Pub. L. No. 109-177, 120 Stat. 192 (2006); AARA, Pub. L. No. 109-178, 120 Stat. 278 (2006).

77 PIRA, § 115, 120 Stat. at 211–13 (2006).

78 Ibid. §§ 115, 117, 120 Stat. at 211–13, 217.

79 Ibid. § 116, 120 Stat. at 213–17.

80 Ibid. §§ 118–119, 120 Stat. at 217–21. The first audit of NSL use required under PIRA Section 119 was released in March 2007. OIG Report, *supra* note 1.

81 PIRA, § 115, 120 Stat. at 211–13.

82 AARA, § 5, 120 Stat. at 281.

83 PIRA, § 116, 120 Stat. at 213–17.

84 Ibid. § 115, 120 Stat. at 211.

85 Ibid., 120 Stat. at 211–12.

86 Designated officials include the Attorney General, Deputy Attorneys General, Assistant Attorneys General, Director of the FBI, or the head or deputy head of a department or agency in the case of an FCRA NSL. Ibid., 120 Stat. at 212.

87 The court may still modify or lift a nondisclosure order if it determines such certification is made in bad faith. Ibid.

88 Ibid.

89 In addition to the persons listed *supra* note 86, other designated officials for recertified NSLs include designees of the Director of the FBI not lower than Deputy Assistant Director at Bureau headquarters or a Special Agent in Charge of a Bureau field office. Ibid.

90 *Doe I v. Gonzales*, 449 F.3d 415, 449 (2d Cir. 2006).

91 Ibid.

92 Ibid.

93 See, e.g., 152 *Congressional Record* S1598–S1632 (daily ed. Mar. 2, 2006) (statements by Senators Kerry, Rockefeller, and Bingaman concerning PIRA amendments and civil liberties); American Civil Liberties Union, *ACLU Says Cosmetic Changes to Patriot Act Hollow, Measures Approved by the House Fail to Protect American Liberty and Privacy* (Mar. 7, 2006), www.aclu.org/safefree/general/24417prs 20060307.html; American Library Association, *ALA President Michael Gorman Responds to Senate PATRIOT Act Vote* (Mar. 1, 2006), www.ala.org/ala/pressreleases2006/march2006/PATRIOTReauthsenate.htm.

94 American Civil Liberties Union, *Reform the Patriot Act*, http://action.aclu.org/reformthepatriotact/whereitstands.html (last visited May 9, 2007).

95 Reply in Support of Plaintiff's Motion for Partial Summary Judgment, *Doe I v. Gonzales*, 04 Civ. 2614 (S.D.N.Y. Dec. 15, 2006), *available at* www.aclu.org/safefree/nationalsecurityletters/29206lgl20061215.html.

96 Ibid. at 1.
97 For cases establishing the need for judicial deference in the context of mosaic theory arguments, see *United States* v. *Marchetti*, 466 F.2d 1309 (4th Cir. 1972), *Halkin* v. *Helms*, 598 F.2d 1 (D.C. Cir. 1978), *Halperin* v. *CIA*, 629 F.2d 144 (D.C. Cir. 1980), *Cent. Intelligence Agency* v. *Sims*, 471 U.S. 159 (1985), *N.J. Media Group, Inc.* v. *Ashcroft*, 308 F.3d 198 (3d Cir. 2002), and *Ctr. for Nat'l Sec. Studies* v. *U.S. Dep't of Justice*, 331 F.3d 918 (D.C. Cir. 2003).
98 5 U.S.C. § 552 (2000).
99 FOIA Guide, *supra* note 12, at 5.
100 Ibid. at 195.
101 Ibid. at 859.
102 Pozen, *supra* note 13, at 652 (stating that the Third Circuit has countenanced an abdication of mosaic theory review).
103 Ibid. (referring to the approach adopted by D.C. Circuit).
104 Ibid.
105 Ibid. at 637 (defining "standard deference" as the court "according substantial weight" to the executive's national security judgments, but "without relinquishing its independent responsibility" to ensure that the executive's decision is lawful).
106 Ibid. at 644 (discussing *Muniz* v. *Meese*, 115 F.R.D. 63 (D.D.C. 1987)).
107 *Gerstein* v. *U.S. Dep't of Justice*, 34 Med. L. Rptr. 1111 (N.D. Cal. Sept. 30, 2005).
108 *Detroit Free Press* v. *Ashcroft*, 303 F.3d 681 (6th Cir. 2002). But see *N.J. Media Group, Inc.* v. *Ashcroft*, 308 F.3d 198 (3d Cir. 2002) (also reviewing the "Creppy Directive" but deferring to the expertise of the government to determine whether closure of special interest cases is warranted).
109 *Detroit Free Press*, 303 F.3d at 710.
110 Reply in Support of Plaintiff's Motion for Partial Summary Judgment, *Doe I* v. *Gonzales*, No. 04 Civ. 2614, at 3–4 (S.D.N.Y. Dec. 15, 2006), available at www.aclu.org/pdfs/safefree/nsl_reply_brief_redacted.pdf.
111 Reply Memorandum of Law in Opposition to Plaintiff's Motion for Partial Summary Judgment, *Doe I* v. *Gonzales*, No. 04 Civ. 2614, at 8 (S.D.N.Y. Feb. 26, 2007) (citing as authority PIRA Section 115, 18 U.S.C. § 3511(b), (e)), available at www.aclu.org/pdfs/safefree/nsl_govt_opp_reply_redacted.pdf.
112 H.R. Rep. No. 109-333, at 96 (2005) (Conf. Rep.).
113 152 *Congressional Record* S1616–S1617 (daily edition Mar. 2, 2006) (statement by Senator Jon Kyl (Republican from Arizona)) (emphasis added).
114 Declaration of Jeffrey Oestericher, *Doe I* v. *Gonzales*, No. 04 Civ. 2614, at Exhibit 1 (S.D.N.Y. Nov. 7, 2006), available at www.aclu.org/pdfs/safefree/decl_oester 20061108.pdf.
115 See generally OIG Report, *supra* note 1. Compare with 8,500 NSL requests issued in 2000.
116 Ibid. at xxxiv.
117 Ibid.
118 Ibid.
119 Ibid. at xlvii.
120 S. Rep. No. 94-755 (1976) (6 Books), including *Intelligence Activities and the Rights of Americans*, at x.

12 "Material support" prosecutions for website activities

Alan F. Williams

Introduction

Although more than 30 years have passed since Senator Frank Church of Idaho led congressional investigations that triggered a national debate concerning the balance between national security and civil liberties, America's ongoing struggle against international terrorism has kindled a new debate echoing similar themes.[1] Emerging in the wake of the shock, chaos and horror of the September 11, 2001 terrorist attacks in the United States, the Bush administration's tactics in its self-described "War on Terror" have fueled this debate while drawing severe criticism from civil libertarians. The most controversial of these tactics have included the use of military tribunals at Guantanamo Bay, aggressive interrogation techniques that have been characterized as torture, and the use of the National Security Agency to conduct domestic surveillance.

In addition, as part of an effort to preempt terrorist activity, federal prosecutors have broadly and "creatively" interpreted the scope of two "material support to terrorism" statutes in order to interdict suspected terrorists and their supporters before they have a chance to actually carry out acts of violence.[2] These creative interpretations have allowed prosecutors to arrest and detain suspects whom they suspect are not only sympathetic to the cause of the terrorists, but actively aiding their cause indirectly. Critics of this approach have quickly emerged to voice their concerns that in adopting this approach, the government has significantly expanded criminal liability and is treading on individual rights protected by the U.S. Constitution, particularly the First Amendment.

A recent case from Church's home state not only exemplified this creative prosecution strategy but also became an example for many of the government's continuing encroachment on constitutional rights after the September 11, 2001 terrorist attacks in the United States. The case involved the internet activities of Sami Al-Hussayen, an Islamic graduate student at the University of Idaho. Al-Hussayen was prosecuted under the material support to terrorism statutes, 18 U.S.C. § 2339A and 18 U.S.C. § 2339B, for designing, creating and maintaining internet websites that federal prosecutors viewed as supportive of terrorism. Although the material support statutes have been used since the September 11, 2001 terrorist attacks in the United States to cover a wide range of activities, the

Al-Hussayen case was the first time that the government attempted to use the material support statutes to prosecute conduct that consisted almost exclusively of operating and maintaining internet websites. The case attracted national attention and triggered a heated debate focused mainly on one key question: Were Al-Hussayen's internet activities constitutionally protected "free speech" or did they cross the line into criminal and material support to terrorism?

In this chapter, I will use the factual background of the Al-Hussayen case as a point of departure from which to argue that the government may criminally prosecute certain internet activities that tend to support terrorists, but that the material support statutes used in the Al-Hussayen case are ill-suited for such prosecutions. Further, I will argue that new federal criminal legislation is needed to address the extensive and alarming use of the internet by terrorist organizations. To help remedy the threat posed by these developments, I will outline a new statute to help address the difficult task of balancing security with liberty on the internet.

Background to *United States* v. *Al-Hussayen*

In early 2003, special agents of the Federal Bureau of Investigation (FBI) and local law enforcement officials launched a significant counterterrorism operation in the unlikeliest of places, the bucolic college town of Moscow, Idaho. Located in the rolling hills of northern Idaho's pastoral Palouse region, Moscow and its 22,000 citizens were caught completely off guard by the FBI-led raid that began in the early hours of February 26, 2003. That morning, agents dramatically arrested 33-year-old Al-Hussayen at his on-campus residence, a scene captured by a local television news crew and broadcast throughout the region later that day.[3] Al-Hussayen, a citizen of Saudi Arabia, had been living in Moscow since 1999 and was pursuing a Ph.D. in Computer Science. Since his arrival, he had become a beloved member of the University of Idaho. The community recognized him for his friendly and unassuming nature and for his public calls for reconciliation between Muslims and Christians in the wake of September 11.[4] Thus, his arrest on suspicion of terrorist-related activities sent shock waves through an incredulous, close-knit university community.

The arrest of Al-Hussayen came after a comprehensive year-long investigation by the FBI that began shortly after the events of September 11, 2001. During the investigation, FBI agents sought and received court orders that allowed them to tap Al-Hussayen's phones and to monitor his personal e-mail accounts.[5] The FBI also conducted physical surveillance of Al-Hussayen's activities on the University of Idaho campus.[6] During the investigation, FBI agents discovered evidence of Al-Hussayen's internet activities that seemed to connect him with terrorism through websites belonging to organizations that described themselves as Islamic charities.[7] The FBI had long been suspicious of Islamic charities because there was a well-documented pattern of them serving as a legitimate face or "front" for international terrorist organizations.[8] When the FBI discovered evidence of Al-Hussayen's extensive involvement in the financial management and leadership of a major Islamic charity along with evidence that he created and maintained websites containing exhortations to violence and efforts to recruit new members and fund terrorist activity, the Department of Justice began to consider a criminal prosecution.

In particular, the FBI investigation revealed that Al-Hussayen was the registered webmaster[9] for websites belonging to the Islamic Assembly of North America (IANA), the Al-Haramain Islamic Foundation (AHIF), and Dar Al-Asr.[10] The IANA and AHIF purported to be charities dedicated to spreading the cause of Islam, and Dar Al-Asr was an information technology company based in Saudi Arabia.[11]

Al-Hussayen's most extensive involvement appeared to be with the IANA, an organization known to advocate Wahhabism – a conservative and radical sect in modern Islam closely associated with modern international terrorism.[12] The Saudi Embassy labeled IANA members as Muslim extremists, and the FBI had reason to believe that the IANA was actively involved in fundraising for fundamentalist Muslim terrorist organizations.[13] The FBI concluded that Al-Hussayen played a major role in the IANA organization, not only by serving as an officer in IANA but also through his substantial personal efforts in creating, operating and maintaining websites that appeared to be designed and intended to recruit mujahideen and to raise funds for violent jihad.[14] The FBI discovered that Al-Hussayen designed and maintained an IANA website, www.al-multaqa.com, that published articles extolling the virtues of mujahideen, describing and encouraging jihad, and praising *shaheed* – the act of dying as a martyr – as the ultimate honor for a Muslim.[15]

According to the FBI, Al-Hussayen also created and maintained websites for the AHIF – another self-described Islamic charity with its world headquarters in Saudi Arabia and offices in the United States (Ashland, Oregon), Chechnya, Bosnia, Somalia, Indonesia, Pakistan and Kenya.[16] According to the indictment, AHIF used the websites designed and managed by Al-Hussayen as one of the ways it carried out its mission of disseminating fundamentalist pro-jihadist Islamic materials.[17] At the time of Al-Hussayen's arrest, the U.S. State Department had designated numerous branches of Al-Haramain as "Specially Designated Global Terrorists" pursuant to the International Emergency Economic Powers Act.[18]

In addition to his extensive involvement with these purported charities, Al-Hussayen was also identified as the registrant, editor and manager of an Al-Asr website that published fatwas by radical sheikhs Safar Al-Hawali and Salman Al-Ouda justifying and encouraging violent jihad, including suicide attacks.[19] Al-Hawali and Al-Ouda had been identified after the first World Trade Center bombing in 1993 as spiritual advisers to Usama bin Ladin, the putative leader of al Qaeda.[20] According to the FBI, Al-Hussayen provided internet-related services for these two Saudi clerics by publishing the fatwas justifying violent jihad.

Furthermore, the FBI determined that Al-Hussayen had set up a web-based system whereby contributions could be made to HAMAS, a Palestinian terrorist organization best known outside the Palestinian territories for its suicide bombings. According to the indictment, the website Al-Hussayen helped to create and maintain, www.islamway.com, included links to a variety of articles, speeches and lectures promoting violent jihad in Israel.[21] One page within the site allegedly included a section entitled "What is your role?" This question was answered on the same page as follows:

> Participate with money, and this is [via] The Palestinian Information Center (the official mouthpiece of the Islamic Resistance Movement, HAMAS) which opens the door of donations for all Muslims to assist their brothers in their honorable jihad against the dictatorial Zionist Jewish enemy.[22]

This webpage also provided a link to www.palestine-info.org for donations to HAMAS.[23] Another website developed and maintained by Al-Hussayen, www.almultaqa.com, included hyperlinks to the same page for donations to HAMAS.[24]

According to the FBI, Al-Hussayen also maintained and moderated an internet e-mail group that the government alleged had the purpose of facilitating the recruitment of mujahideen for violent jihad.[25] This site contained a posting that the government alleged Al-Hussayen made to all members of the group urging them to donate money to support those who were participating in violent jihad.[26] Another posting attributed to Al-Hussayen included materials entitled "Virtues of Jihad" and glorified those who die while performing violent jihad.[27] According to the indictment, Al-Hussayen also stated in his postings that the "problem today is that Muslims have given up on violent jihad and are not practicing it enough."[28] In addition to his personal postings, the indictment also alleged that in his role as webmaster, he had control of the content of the websites – that is, he had the power to review all postings and to delete the ones that were inappropriate, irresponsible or criminal.[29] Among the postings of the group, one included detailed instructions on how to travel to and train at a particular terrorist training camp outside the United States; another included an "urgent appeal" to Muslims serving in the U.S. military requesting information about potential terrorist targets including American military bases, logistical support (including drinking water) for bases, storage facilities for weaponry and ammunition, and routes followed by oil tankers.[30]

On the basis of all this information, in the second superseding indictment the government charged Al-Hussayen with two counts of violating 18 U.S.C. § 2339A and one count of violating 18 U.S.C. § 2339B.[31] The first § 2339A count alleged that Al-Hussayen had conspired to provide and conceal material support or resources to terrorists, and the second count under § 2339A charged him with *actually* providing material support or resources to terrorists.[32] He was also charged with a sole count under § 2339B for conspiracy to provide material support to HAMAS, a U.S. State Department-designated foreign terrorist organization (FTO).

The "material support" statutes

The material support to terrorism charges were predicated on Al-Hussayen's alleged design and maintenance of internet websites for charitable organizations that the government believed were encouraging jihad, recruiting terrorists and funneling money to international terrorist groups. Although frequently referred to as USA PATRIOT Act innovations, § 2339A and § 2339B in their original forms predate the USA PATRIOT Act by more than half a decade.[33] The first material support to terrorism statute, 18 U.S.C. § 2339A, was enacted as part of the Violent Crime Control and Law Enforcement Act of 1994.[34] As amended by the Antiterrorism and Effective Death Penalty Act of 1996[35] (AEDPA) and in force at the time of the Al-Hussayen prosecution, 18 U.S.C. § 2339A provided as follows:

> Section 2339A: Providing material support to terrorists
> (a) Offense: Whoever provides material support or resources or conceals or disguises the nature, location, source, or ownership of material support or resources, knowing or intending that they are to be used in preparation for, or in carrying out, a violation of [certain sections of the U.S. code prohibiting terrorist activities], or in preparation for, or in carrying out, the concealment of an escape from the commission of any such violation, or attempts or conspires to do such an act, shall be fined under this title, imprisoned not more than 15 years, or both, and, if the death of any person results, shall be imprisoned for any term of years or for life. A violation of this section may be prosecuted in any Federal judicial district in which the underlying offense was committed, or in any other Federal judicial district as provided by law.
> (b) Definition: In this section, the term "material support or resources" means currency or monetary instruments or financial securities, financial services, lodging, training, expert advice or assistance, safehouses, false documentation or identification, communications equipment, facilities, weapons, lethal substances, explosives, personnel, transportation, and other physical assets, except medicine or religious materials.[36]

The original version of § 2339A passed by Congress did not include the "expert advice and assistance" language; it was added in 2001 to § 2339A, and by reference to § 2339B by the USA PATRIOT Act.[37] Indeed, the inclusion of this language was critical in the Al-Hussayen case, as is discussed later in the chapter, because the prosecution expansively interpreted "expert advice and assistance" to encompass Al-Hussayen's internet activities.

In addition to being charged with a violation of § 2339A, Al-Hussayen was also charged with a violation of § 2339B. The "second" material support statute, § 2339B, provides:

Section 2339B: Providing material support or resources to designated foreign terrorist organizations
(a) Prohibited activities
(1) Unlawful conduct: Whoever, within the United States or subject to the jurisdiction of the United States, knowingly provides material support or resources to a foreign terrorist organization, or attempts or conspires to do so, shall be fined under this title or imprisoned not more than 15 years, or both, and, if the death of any person results, shall be imprisoned for any term of years or for life....
(4) [T]he term "material support or resources" has the same meaning given that term in section 2339A (including the definitions of "training" and "expert advice or assistance" in that section).[38]

Congress enacted 18 U.S.C. § 2339B in 1996 as part of the same AEDPA legislation that amended § 2339A, and § 2339B was designed to cover what was perceived as a "gap" in the law left open by § 2339A.[39] The passage of § 2339B was motivated by government concerns that terrorist groups were diverting funds donated for humanitarian purposes to support acts of violence in their campaigns of terror.[40] Even though § 2339B adopted the definition of material support to terrorism contained within § 2339A, it was written so that donors could no longer provide funds to terrorist organizations under the pretext that the funds were intended for humanitarian purposes. Congress believed that § 2339A continued to leave open this source of terrorist funding and had determined to close it.[41] Under the newly created § 2339B, all donations to designated FTOs would be prohibited, even if the donors intended their money go only to the nonviolent or humanitarian wings of the designated FTOs.[42]

Before the trial began, Al-Hussayen filed motions arguing that prosecution under these material support statutes for his internet activities would violate his rights to freedom of association and freedom of speech guaranteed by the First Amendment. However, the court ruled that the First Amendment did not foreclose prosecution for these activities.[43] The trial finally began in Boise in April 2004, more than a year after Al-Hussayen was taken into custody. After a trial lasting six weeks, the jury returned a mixed verdict. Al-Hussayen was found not guilty of all three material support counts, and not guilty on one of the false statement counts and two of the jury fraud counts, but the jury was unable to reach a decision on three additional false statement charges and five visa fraud counts.[44] The trial judge declared a mistrial as to these eight counts, leaving open the possibility of a retrial on those counts.[45]

Following the verdict, negotiations between the U.S. Attorney's Office and Al-Hussayen's attorneys resulted in an agreement under which Al-Hussayen waived his right to object to deportation in his immigration case in exchange for the government's agreement to dismiss the eight counts on which the jury had hung.[46] Al-Hussayen agreed to go back to Saudi Arabia rather than face a retrial on the remaining visa and false statement charges, and returned to Saudi Arabia in July 2004.[47] His departure brought some measure of closure to the case, but left many questions unresolved.

Should Al-Hussayen-type activities be protected by the First Amendment?

Although the trial court ruled that Al-Hussayen's internet activities were not protected by the First Amendment, the rationale for this decision was never set forth on the record, nor has the ruling been subject to appellate review since Al-Hussayen was acquitted.[48] Notwithstanding the absence of appellate review, there is substantial legal support for the court's conclusion that the First Amendment does not protect these types of internet activities.

Al-Hussayen's alleged misconduct may be roughly divided into three main categories: encouragement and advocacy of terrorist violence, recruiting of new members for terrorist organizations, and fundraising for terrorist organizations. Since each of the activities is expressive in nature, their criminal proscription potentially triggers the protection of the First Amendment.

In beginning the First Amendment analysis, we must first determine whether these activities actually qualify as speech. In *Texas* v. *Johnson*, the Supreme Court held that in determining whether something is speech one must consider "whether an intent to convey a particularized message was present and whether there was a great likelihood that the message would be understood by those who view it."[49] The only plausible explanation for Al-Hussayen allowing or personally posting this type of information on websites he controlled was that he intended to have persons understand the information and the nature of its content. Because the information on the websites was written in simple and unpretentious language, there seems to be a great likelihood that it would be understood by those who read it. We may therefore tentatively conclude that Al-Hussayen's internet activities were speech and potentially protected under the First Amendment. Our next task is to determine whether these activities fall into one of the categories of protected speech divined from the First Amendment by the Supreme Court.

In general, cases from the Supreme Court have consistently recognized the principle that the First Amendment is not an absolute protection for all forms of speech. In its First Amendment jurisprudence, the Supreme Court has repeatedly refused to extend full First Amendment protection to many forms of expression that might qualify as speech under *Texas* v. *Johnson*. These forms of expression have included such categories as obscene material,[50] fighting words,[51] hate speech,[52] and libel and slander.[53] In these and other categories, such as commercial speech,[54] the court has repeatedly recognized significant limits to the First Amendment's protections. The Supreme Court in *Chaplinsky* v. *New Hampshire* summarized this approach as follows:

> There are certain well-defined and narrowly limited classes of speech, the prevention and punishment of which have never been thought to raise any

Constitutional problem. These include the lewd and obscene, the profane, the libelous, and the insulting or "fighting" words – those which by their very utterance inflict injury or tend to incite an immediate breach of the peace. It has been well observed that such utterances are no essential part of any exposition of ideas, and are of such slight social value as a step to truth that any benefit that may be derived from them is clearly outweighed by the social interest in order and morality.[55]

Al-Hussayen's alleged conduct seems to fit best within yet another category of cases where the court has dealt with speech that arguably poses some type of threat to public safety or national security. In a series of cases beginning in 1919 with *Schenck* v. *United States*,[56] the court has repeatedly recognized significant governmental authority to regulate speech that falls into this category. In *Schenck*, a case arising from World War I, the court reviewed the conviction of a defendant for conspiracy to cause insubordination in the armed forces and to obstruct recruiting in violation of the Espionage Act of 1917.[57] The defendant passed out leaflets which the government considered as encouraging conduct that hampered the war effort. Justice Oliver Wendell Holmes, Jr., writing for a unanimous court, held that the First Amendment did not protect speech that encouraged insubordination and obstructed recruiting during World War I.[58] The court upheld the conviction, and in the opinion's most famous passage, Justice Holmes set forth the famous "clear and present danger" standard:

> The question in every case is whether the words used are used in such circum-
> stances and are of such a nature as to create a clear and present danger that they
> will bring about the substantive evils that Congress has a right to prevent."[59]

Holmes further emphasized the significance of the national and international political context when he stated that

> [w]hen a nation is at war many things that might be said in time of peace are
> such a hindrance to its effort that their utterance will not be endured so long
> as men fight, and that no Court could regard them as protected by any con-
> stitutional right.[60]

However, later that year when the court in *Abrams* v. *United States*[61] upheld a conviction under the Espionage Act as amended in 1918, Holmes found himself writing a dissenting opinion. Although Holmes dissented, it was not because he had renounced the principles set forth in *Schenck*, but rather on the ground that he felt the evidence insufficient to convict in this particular case.[62] In his influential dissent, he seemed to attempt to both refine and reaffirm his "clear and present danger" test when he said:

> I do not doubt for a moment that by the same reasoning that would justify
> punishment for persuasion to murder, the United States may constitutionally

punish speech that produces or is intended to produce a clear and imminent danger that will bring about forthwith certain substantive evils that the United States may constitutionally seek to prevent. The power is greater in time of war than in time of peace because war opens dangers that do not exist at other times.[63]

His articulation of an imminent danger requirement as part of the clear and present danger test was largely ignored for the next 50 years as the court drifted toward a very deferential standard that essentially remained in place until the Supreme Court decided *United States* v. *Brandenburg*.[64] Of particular pertinence to the Al-Hussayen case is that Holmes' opinions in *Schenck*, *Abrams*, and others during this period consistently advance the proposition that when the country is on a war footing, legislation that may punish or restrict speech should be given greater deference because of the unique dangers to national security that such speech may pose.

A series of cases dotted the First Amendment landscape as the court continued to grapple with the challenge of balancing rights to speech and association with measures aimed at protecting the United States from the perceived threat posed by international communism.

The most important of these cases were decided during the McCarthy era when the court was called upon to review convictions under the Smith Act.[65] The Smith Act made it a crime

> to knowingly or willfully advocate, abet, advise or teach the duty, necessity, desirability or propriety of overthrowing the Government of the United States or of any State by force or violence, or for anyone to organize any association which teaches, advises or encourages such an overthrow, or for anyone to become a member of or to affiliate with any such association.[66]

In 1951, the court decided *United States* v. *Dennis*, a case in which the court reviewed the convictions of several defendants under the Smith Act.[67] The court upheld the convictions, holding that the Smith Act did not inherently violate the First Amendment and emphasizing the distinction between the *mere teaching* of communist philosophies and *active advocacy* of those ideas.[68] The court ruled that while the First Amendment protected abstract teaching of communist philosophies, active advocacy, which constituted a "clear and present danger" threatening national security, was subject to criminalization by the government.[69] Writing for the majority, Chief Justice Fred Vinson stated:

> Obviously the words [clear and present danger] cannot mean that before the Government can act, it must wait until the putsch is about to be executed, the plans have been laid and the signal is awaited.... The damage which such attempts create both physically and politically to a nation makes it impossible to measure validity in terms of the probability of success or the immediacy of a successful attempt.[70]

This language in the decision indicated that the court had concluded that when the risk of harm to the government is so enormous, the likelihood of success and the imminence of the threat are not particularly determinative factors when deciding whether the government may regulate the speech at issue.

Six years later, the court decided *Yates* v. *United States*,[71] another case challenging a conviction under the Smith Act. In *Yates*, the court reversed the Smith Act convictions of 14 individuals who had been prosecuted for being members of the Communist Party. The court held that "passive" membership in the Communist Party was insufficient to sustain convictions. Writing for the majority, Justice John Marshall Harlan II declared:

> The indoctrination of a group in preparation for future violent action, as well as exhortation to immediate action ... is not constitutionally protected when the group is of sufficient size and cohesiveness, is sufficiently oriented towards action, and other circumstances are such as to reasonably justify the apprehension that action will occur.[72]

The language in *Yates* reinforced the *Dennis* court's rationale that an essential distinction must be made between those who actually urge others to do something illegal and those who merely urge others to *believe* in something. Curiously, *Yates* also seemed to resuscitate the "imminence" and "likelihood of success" factors that *Dennis* had seemingly extinguished. On the whole, these line cases, although varying in rationale and somewhat schizophrenic, seemed to consistently give the government significant deference when dealing with the use of speech that it considers a threat to national security or public safety.

In 1969, however, in a terse *per curiam* opinion in *United States* v. *Brandenburg*, the Supreme Court seemed to take a more restrictive view of the government's ability to criminalize such advocacy, despite purporting to follow the court's reasoning in *Dennis*. *Brandenburg* involved the State of Ohio's prosecution of a rural Ohio Ku Klux Klan (KKK) leader under an Ohio criminal syndicalism statute for his participation in a KKK rally.[73] During the rally, the KKK members burned a cross and the defendant made a speech referring to "revengeance" against "niggers" and "Jews," and announced plans for a march on Washington, D.C., St. Augustine, Florida, and Mississippi.[74] Even though the defendant never directly threatened or encouraged the participants in the rally to take any action, he was convicted of advocating violence under the Ohio statute for his participation in the rally and for the speech he made. The Ohio statute proscribed "advocat[ing] ... the duty, necessity, or propriety of crime, sabotage, violence, or unlawful methods of terrorism as a means of accomplishing industrial or political reform" and "voluntarily assembl[ing] with any society, group or assemblage of persons formed to teach or advocate the doctrines of criminal syndicalism."[75] In reversing Brandenburg's conviction, the court discussed its jurisprudence in this area:

> [Past decisions] had fashioned the principle that the constitutional guarantees of free speech and free press do not permit a State to forbid or proscribe

advocacy of the use of force or of law violation except where such advocacy is directed to inciting or producing imminent lawless action and is likely to incite or produce such action.[76]

This statement from the opinion seems at odds with the position taken in *Dennis* in that it emphasizes the "imminence" and "likelihood of success" factors alluded to in *Yates*. Because of the reemergence of these factors, many have interpreted *Brandenburg* and its progeny as imposing a major obstacle to the government's prosecution of those who, like Al-Hussayen, "merely" advocate lawless or dangerous behavior. Indeed, the language arguably requires that the advocacy have a *likelihood* of producing *imminent* lawless behavior. Under a restrictive interpretation, the inciting statement and the accompanying act would have to be in very close proximity.[77] However, this is not the only possible interpretation of the much-conflicted precedent in this area.

To fully understand the scope of the law, we must look beyond the text of *Brandenburg* and *Dennis* to establish a workable constitutional framework. In *Scales* v. *United States*, the court held that while the advocacy and teaching of forcible overthrow of government as an abstract principle is immune from prosecution, for those who have guilty knowledge and specific intent or aim to overthrow the government, mere "active" membership may be prosecuted.[78] In reaching its decision, the court established the requirement that for the government to punish such association, it must prove that the individual actively affiliated with the group, knew of its illegal objectives, and had the *specific intent* of furthering those goals.[79]

An important recent case reaffirmed the viability of *Scales* in addressing First Amendment issues. In *Rice* v. *Paladin Enterprises*, the Fourth Circuit read *Brandenburg* very narrowly and relied in part upon the specific intent requirement of *Scales* in coming to the conclusion that while *Brandenburg* protects mere *abstract* advocacy, it is not an absolute bar to liability in all circumstances.[80] In holding that the First Amendment did not bar a suit against the publisher of a "hit man" instruction book, the court held that since *Brandenburg* protects only abstract advocacy, it could offer no protection to the publisher of the hit man book because it was a detailed instructional manual on how to commit murder for hire and avoid discovery and prosecution. Basing potential liability on a complicity theory with evidence that the book was actually used by a hit man to murder a mother, her child and the child's caregiver, the court held that the publisher was not protected – even under the *Brandenburg* standard. The court concluded that there was no First Amendment protection if (1) the defendant has a specific intent of assisting and encouraging the commission of criminal conduct, and (2) the alleged assistance and encouragement takes a form other than abstract advocacy.[81] Citing *Brandenburg* as authority, the court stated, "The cloak of the First Amendment envelops critical, but abstract discussions of existing laws, but lends no protection to speech which urges the listeners to commit violations of current law."[82] In denying certiorari, the Supreme Court passed up an opportunity to state definitively whether the Fourth Circuit's interpretation was correct. Thus, questions remain as to precisely how to apply *Brandenburg* and the limits of its holding. Since neither *Brandenburg* nor its progeny establish how imminence and likelihood are to be assessed, one possible interpretation suggested by *Dennis* is that the greater the potential harm, the less in the way of imminence and likelihood will be required.

With this doctrinal framework in mind, we may now begin to consider how it relates to the creation, development and maintenance of internet websites like the ones in the Al-Hussaysen case. In developing our framework, we must not forget to consider Justice Holmes's repeated observation that in the context of a wartime environment the government is entitled to greater deference. This is a particularly important factor when considering that Al-Hussayen's internet activity was occurring in the immediate aftermath of the September 11 attacks by terrorist elements and that Al-Hussayen's internet sites appear to have been intended to encourage further violence and to strengthen international terrorist organizations with financial support.

Thus, if we synthesize these cases, we may conceive a standard that takes into consideration the Supreme Court's jurisprudence and lower court interpretation discussed above. Internet communications *specifically intended* to enable terrorist groups or cause acts of terrorist violence that are concrete and detailed in nature may be criminally prosecuted, provided that the government has a substantial interest in regulating the communication and that the regulation is narrowly tailored to encompass no more internet activity than is necessary. The government's interest is to be measured by the magnitude of the potential threat against which it seeks to protect its citizens. In light of the failure of the court to overrule *Dennis*, a case that applied this formula, this interpretation is consistent with both *Dennis* and *Brandenburg*. Since this rule depends on the magnitude and context of the government interest, we now turn to the question as to whether the government would have a substantial interest in regulating internet communications like Al-Hussayen's.

Is there a substantial government interest?

The United States is currently engaged in a conflict with a number of terrorist groups that has many of the characteristics of war. Particularly when one considers that the United States has been engaged in protracted ground campaigns in Afghanistan and Iraq since 2001 and 2003 respectively, one can hardly debate that the country is at war. The terrorist groups with which the United States is at war have established kidnapping, torture and killing of Americans as a primary goal in order to achieve their political objectives.[83] While they been have successful in killing Americans on many different occasions throughout the world, these actions would not in and of themselves justify the regulation of speech.

However, the sheer magnitude of the threat that the United States faces in its conflict with terrorist groups may be best judged to some extent by the nature of the attacks on September 11, 2001. On that date, the United States suffered serious and potentially crippling attacks on its financial, political and military centers. The World Trade Center towers and the Pentagon are penultimate symbols of United States' financial and military might. The attacks were interpreted as an attempt to destroy the ability of the United States to govern and protect itself, something analogous to an attempt to overthrow the U.S. government. The Supreme Court has stated:

> Overthrow of the Government by force and violence is certainly a substantial enough interest for the Government to limit speech. Indeed, this is the ultimate value of any society, for if society cannot protect its very structure from armed internal attack, it must follow that no subordinate value can be protected.[84]

As evidence indicates that the same terrorist entities are in search of nuclear technology, the magnitude of the threat is even more serious.[85] To borrow the language of *United States* v. *Yates*, in repeated violent attacks many terrorist groups, such as al Qaeda, have repeatedly shown themselves to be "successfully oriented towards action" of "sufficient size and cohesiveness ... as to allow the apprehension that action will occur."[86] Using Holmes's oft-repeated principle that during wartime the government is entitled to greater deference in restricting certain types of speech, it is reasonable to conclude that the current state of war is sufficient to warrant some degree of deference to the government in the regulation of speech that is directed toward inciting more attacks and funding and supporting the organizations responsible for carrying them out.

The internet is a critical resource for the continued development of terrorist groups. Terrorism experts have reached a consensus that the internet is a particularly effective and important tool of contemporary terrorists.[87] Terrorists make use of the internet for its commonly accepted purposes, including communications, propaganda, marketing, fundraising and recruiting.[88] Research has also shown that terrorist groups routinely use the internet to plan and coordinate attacks on American citizens and allies throughout the world,[89] and their propaganda uses of the internet for the broadcast of videos depicting acts of violence are well known. However, the last two uses are particularly important to any sustained terrorist efforts; if fundraising and recruiting were significantly diminished, it would have a fatal effect on the viability of these organizations.[90] Ironically, radical Islamic groups who criticize and attack Western modernity, technology and media are among those who are making the most effective use of the West's most advanced modern medium – the internet.[91] Gabriel Weimann states in his comprehensive study of terrorists' use of the internet:

> Terrorists use the Internet for its commonly accepted benefits: communication, propaganda, marketing, and fund-raising. Other uses of the internet by terrorists include data mining, networking, and sharing information.[92] And yet, despite this growing terrorist presence, when policymakers discuss the combination of terrorism and the internet, they focus on the overrated threat posed by cyberterrorism or cyberwarfare (i.e., attacks on computer

networks, including those on the Internet) and largely ignore the numerous uses that terrorists make of the Internet every day.[93]

Because the internet is such a critical tool for modern terrorist organizations, it follows that the government has a substantial interest in regulating advocacy on this medium specifically intended to encourage violent attacks on the United States and its citizens – particularly messages specifically intended to assist in the recruitment of a new crop of terrorists, and efforts specifically intended to raise funds for terrorist organizations. All these activities are crucial links in per-petuating and sustaining terrorist activity against the United States.

In *Reno* v. *American Civil Liberties Union*, the Supreme Court found the internet to have full First Amendment protection given to media such as the print press, thus refusing to concede that the internet should be subject to the greater regulation allowed over broadcast media.[94] In its decision declaring the Communications Decency Act of 1997 facially overbroad, the *Reno* court went to some pains to catalog the unique strengths of the internet: a vast virtual library of information, the ability of those with limited means to "publish," a decentralized structure, the lack of significant control or supervision, and ease of access.[95] Ironically, the advent of these unique capabilities and the coincident expansion of international terrorist groups and acts of terrorism pose an unprece-dented threat to United States and international security. The structure of modern terrorist organizations is in many ways compatible with the structure of the internet.[96] Through a decentralized and loosely structured network of cells, modern terrorist groups are able to take full advantage of the internet's strengths. The internet can allow groups located throughout the world to plan and coordinate their actions in cyberspace without having to congregate in a single physical location, thus providing Hydra-like survivability and regenera-tion capability for the rest of the organization if one part were to be destroyed.

A prime example of the importance and power of the internet for terrorist groups may be seen in the case of al Qaeda. Even though much of al-Qaeda's organization and training facilities were lost after the U.S. invasion of Afghanistan in 2001, the organization has reemerged in a "virtual Afghanistan" in cyberspace through the power of the internet.[97] Through the internet, members and trainees can now log onto a computer and have access to a multimedia "virtual training camp" complete with instructions on bomb making, suicide bombing, kidnapping and murder.[98] Al Qaeda is also effectively using the inter-net to incite, recruit and fundraise the same activities that the government alleged Al-Hussayen was conducting with his internet websites.[99]

The scale, scope and rapidity of terrorist attacks demonstrate the magnitude of the potential threat in the current world situation, and those tasked with protecting the populace need to intervene earlier in the process to ensure public safety. This earlier intervention includes efforts to starve terrorist organizations of the continu-ous source of money and personnel that are the lifeblood of their operations.

Other mature democracies, such as the United Kingdom, France, Germany and Australia, have recognized the potential harm of these types of activities by passing laws aimed at preventing the encouragement and incitement of terrorism.[100] For example, the United Kingdom's Terrorism Act of 2006 created the offense of the "direct or indirect encouragement or inducement of terrorism."[101] The Act prohibits

> [the publishing of] a statement that is likely to be understood by some or all of the members of the public to whom it is published as a direct or indirect encouragement or other inducement to them to the commission, preparation or instigation of acts of terrorism or Convention offences.[102]

Indirect encouragement statements include every statement that (1) glorifies the commission or preparation (whether in the past, in the future or generally) of such acts or offenses; and (2) is a statement where members of the public could reasonably be expected to infer that what is being glorified is being glorified as conduct that should be emulated.[103]

The threat posed by use of the internet by terrorists or their indirect supporters creates substantial national security dangers that outweigh any potentially offsetting social value associated with this type of expression. In particular, the rise of a decentralized network of violent international terrorist organizations coupled with the technical advances in internet technology poses a tremendous neoteric threat to U.S. national security.

Why the current material support statutes are inadequate

Given the substantial government interest at stake, the government needs properly tailored and constitutionally sound means of addressing the unique threat posed by terrorist use of the internet. In retrospect, it appears that the prosecution of Al-Hussayen under the material support to terrorism statutes was an ill-advised attempt to expand the reach of the material statutes beyond the ambit of activity they were designed to proscribe. While I believe that the government was correct in viewing Al-Hussayen's activities as potentially criminal, these statutes were the wrong tools for initiating a prosecution.

There are three main reasons why the material support statutes are inadequate for prosecuting these types of internet activities: First, these statutes are not specifically directed at internet activity; second, the statues are too vague and do not provide sufficient notice; and finally, they do not collectively provide a specific intent element sufficient to pass constitutional muster within the framework established by Supreme Court precedent.

While it is true that the charges of material support based on Al-Hussayen's internet activities survived motions to dismiss at trial, the prosecution was unable to overcome significant questions about the theoretical underpinnings of their case, ultimately failing in its efforts to convince a jury that Al-Hussayen's internet websites constituted material support to terrorism.

Although U.S. jury secrecy requirements shield the jurors' reasons for acquitting Al-Hussayen, we may reasonably infer that the jury was ultimately unconvinced that Al-Hussayen's internet activities, even if as alleged by the prosecution, amounted to material support to terrorism. In an interview after the Al-Hussayen case, a member of the jury summarized the problems for the prosecution when he stated, "There was a lack of hard evidence. There was no clearcut evidence that said he was a terrorist, so it was all on inference."[104]

Although the jury members apparently were looking for "hard evidence" of Al-Hussayen's support for terrorism – providing weapons to terrorists, hiding terrorists, or even driving them to a target – they were instead provided with vast amounts of evidence showing that Al-Hussayen had built internet websites aimed at recruiting, funding and encouraging jihadists in their worldwide campaigns of violence. The evidence of internet activity apparently was not the "hard evidence" they expected for a terror prosecution.

Given the rapid advance of internet technologies and substantial uncertainty not only in the general public but even within the courts concerning the extent of First Amendment protections, a prosecution for internet activity under the broadly worded material support statutes was risky to the government from the outset – especially when one considers that neither of the material support statutes mentions the words "internet," "websites," or even "computer."

The internet's stunning and disconcerting rise to dominance has left hidebound legal definitions struggling to keep up. Because of its unique and pervasive influence, the public needs specific notice as to the limitations of this powerful medium. In *Grayned* v. *City of Rockford*, the Supreme Court has clearly explained the significance of this proposition:

> It is a basic principle of due process that an enactment is void for vagueness if its prohibitions are not clearly defined. Vague laws offend several important values.... A vague law impermissibly delegates basic policy matters to policemen, judges, and juries for resolution on an ad hoc and subjective basis, with the attendant dangers of arbitrary and discriminatory application. ... [W]here a vague statute "abut(s) upon sensitive areas of basic First Amendment freedoms," it "operates to inhibit the exercise of (those) freedoms." Uncertain meanings inevitably lead citizens to "'steer far wider of the unlawful zone' ... than if the boundaries of the forbidden areas were clearly marked."[105]

The material support statutes are broadly written with language aimed at the provision of funding and services, categories quite distinct from building websites to support a cause.

The plain language of the statutes does not give adequate notice that internet website creation and maintenance might expose one to criminal liability. We know this because of the confusion and often diametrically opposed holdings that have emerged from federal courts attempting to interpret these statutes. For example, in *United States* v. *Sattar* the district court found § 2339B unconstitutionally vague because the statute had been used to criminalize mere use of phones and other means of communication.[106] The *Sattar* court also found that it was not clear from the statute what behavior constituted an impermissible provision of personnel to an FTO.[107] (After this decision, the U.S. Attorney recharged the case under § 2339A, and the court upheld the prosecution on the ground that 18 U.S.C. § 2339A's specific intent requirement allowed the indictment to proceed and was not impermissibly vague.[108])

Similarly, the Ninth Circuit affirmed the lower court's conclusion the terms "personnel" and "training" in 18 U.S.C. § 2339A(b)(1) were impermissibly vague.[109] In contrast, in *United States* v. *Lindh* the court held that the term "personnel" in the definition of material support is not unconstitutionally vague,[110] and in *United States* v. *Goba* the court held that the term "training" was not unnecessarily vague.[111] The results of these cases lead one to believe that if federal courts, with highly competent and learned judges, are unable to consistently agree on what the statutes mean, it is unlikely "ordinary people can understand what conduct is prohibited."[112]

The Supreme Court has also expressed that the constitutionality of a statute may depend on whether it incorporates adequate *mens rea* elements.[113] The material support statute, 18 U.S.C. § 2339B, establishes essentially a strict liability regime whose inadequately crafted *mens rea* elements have also been litigated in federal court.[114] Read literally, § 2339B could impose criminal liability on someone who knowingly provided support to a terrorist organization even if he did not know that the organization he supported had been designated as such by the Department of State. For example, if a taxi driver picked up a customer and was aware that the person to whom she was giving a ride was a member of HAMAS, she could be found guilty even if she did not know of HAMAS's status as a designated FTO. This is because the statute is silent as to defendants' *mens rea* with respect to HAMAS's designation as a foreign terrorist organization. In *Humanitarian Law Project* v. *Department of Justice*, the Ninth Circuit addressed the question as to whether § 2339B requires proof that the defendant knew that the organization was a designated FTO.[115] In order to avoid declaring the entire statute unconstitutional, the court construed § 2339B to require proof that a person charged with violating the statute had knowledge of the organization's designation or knowledge of its unlawful activities.[116]

It is significant to note that § 2339A, in contrast with § 2339B, contains a "specific intent" *mens rea* requirement established by "knowing or intending that they are to be used in preparation for, or in carrying out, a violation of..." in subparagraph (a). As shown above, at least one court has relied upon this specific intent aspect of the statute to hold the statute constitutional in a federal prosecution.[117]

Moreover, because of widespread notions that "anything goes" on the internet, it is plausible that one might erroneously believe that building a website would never rise to the level of "material support" to terrorism. Without clearer distinctions about what constitutes material support with respect to internet activities, future cases will proceed uncertainly, with little sense of predictability for the defendant or the government. Establishing a more specific, concrete set of elements defining an offense targeting this activity would likely result in more selectivity, efficiency and fairness in future prosecutions.

One could argue that prosecutors could simply charge under § 2339A and avoid using § 2339B. However, this does not satisfy the need for internet-specific legislation, a need resulting from the internet's vast importance in American life. In addition, the problem is compounded by the fact that the statutes are conjoined like Siamese twins by § 2339B's incorporation of the definition of "material support and resources" by reference from § 2339A(b)(1). In order to fairly criminalize this type of internet activity, we must remove these types of internet prosecutions from the material support statutes and approach the problem with specifically tailored legislation. The public would be much better served by starting afresh.

The proposed legislation and how it fixes the problems

I propose the enactment of the following statute as a means of addressing the problems we have identified in pursing these types of activities under the material support statutes:

Section 2339E: Use of Internet Websites with Specific Intent to Facilitate Terrorism
Offense: Any person who:
(a) Establishes and maintains internet websites or posts detailed information on such websites with the specific intent to recruit persons to join terrorist organizations (as designated under Section 219 of the Immigration and Naturalization Act), or with the specific intent to recruit persons to engage in acts of violence against the United States or citizens of the United States, or
(b) Establishes and maintains internet websites or posts detailed information on such websites with the specific intent to encourage violent attacks against the United States government or its citizens, to include, but not limited to, violations of those criminal code sections set forth in 18 U.S.C. § 2339A(a), or
(c) Establishes, maintains or posts detailed information on internet websites with the specific intent to assist, encourage or facilitate funding to designated terrorist organizations in violation of 18 U.S.C. § 2339B, or
(d) Attempts or conspires to do such acts as defined by paragraphs (a) through (c) shall be fined under this title, imprisoned not more than twenty years, or both, and, if the death of any person directly results from such acts, shall be imprisoned for any term of years or for life. Violations of this section may be prosecuted in any Federal judicial district through which any computer network providing access to such internet website passes, or in any other Federal judicial district as provided by law. To violate subparagraphs (a) and (c), a person must have knowledge that the organization is a designated terrorist organization,

that the organization has engaged or engages in terrorist activity (as defined in Section 212(a)(3)(B) of the Immigration and Nationality Act), or that the organization has engaged or engages in terrorism (as defined in Section 140(d)(2) of the Foreign Relations Authorization Act, Fiscal Years 1988 and 1989).

(e) Limitations: Criticism of United States officials or United States policy, or the advocacy of peaceful change, is specifically excluded from the proscriptions of this statute.

This proposed legislation offers several advantages. First, it is specifically addressed toward the use of the internet, a unique and pervasive feature of modern life that warrants particularized legislation. The proposed statute also provides greater precision than the material support statutes concerning the specific conduct that is prohibited, establishes specific intent requirements to ensure that it will pass constitutional muster, and contains a provision designed to ameliorate any chilling effect on speech that it might otherwise have. By incorporating these protections, the statute serves to eliminate doubt about the point at which internet website design and maintenance may cross the line and become criminal conduct. This important aspect is achieved by requiring the government to establish that the defendant had the specific intent to encourage, request, aid, abet or facilitate the violent acts, as well as proof that the defendant actually knew that the organization was a terrorist organization, or that the organization has engaged in, or intended to engage in, acts of terrorism, for a conviction under subparagraph (a). Further, the information must be more than abstract objection to U.S. policy or purely theoretical discussion; it must be detailed and concrete. This ensures that the statute does not sweep within its scope those who are unwittingly relaying information that might otherwise qualify as criminal under the statute. Making these *mens rea* requirements manifest will place future prosecutions in harmony with an Anglo-American jurisprudence that places great importance on the idea that proving criminal intent is a condition precedent to conviction and punishment in the criminal justice system.

Finally, one must always be concerned about the "chilling effect" that restriction on speech may create. The proposed statute explicitly states that mere criticism of officials of the United States or United States policy, or advocacy of peaceful change, is not prohibited by the statute. Making this explicit in the statute will reassure members of the public that they will not be prosecuted for purely political speech, which is absolutely protected by the First Amendment.

Conclusion

The legislation I advocate is not designed to chill free speech, lessen peaceful dissent or erode precious liberties. The proposed legislation is reasonable in light of the Supreme Court's jurisprudence and the recognition that during a time of war there should be deference extended to legislative attempts to narrowly circumscribe speech that creates substantial risks for the public. The speech of individuals and groups directly and concretely advancing the cause of those whose goal is violence and destruction should not be protected by the First Amendment. In *Speech, Crime, and the Uses of Language*, Kent Greenawalt makes the astute observation that "a sensible interpretation of the First Amendment requires evaluation of the value of liberty of speech and the dangers of particular kinds of communications."[118] Failing to recognize and prohibit the clear threat posed by unimpeded terrorist use of the internet is not a sensible interpretation of the First Amendment. If faced with this issue today, the *Chaplinsky* court perhaps would decide that websites and internet activities seeking to recruit, fund, and encourage violence are "no essential part of the exposition of ideas, and are of such slight social value as [to be] ... clearly outweighed by the social interest in morality and order."[119]

Justice Robert Jackson perhaps said it best in his famous dissent in *Terminello* v. *City of Chicago*:

> The choice is not between order and liberty. It is between liberty with order and anarchy without either. There is danger that, if the Court does not temper its doctrinaire logic with a little practical wisdom, it will convert the constitutional Bill of Rights into a suicide pact.[120]

Notes

1 For an excellent overview of the background and conduct of the Church Committee hearings, see Loch K. Johnson, *A Season of Inquiry: Congress and Intelligence* (1998).
2 Robert M. Chesney, The Sleeper Scenario: Terrorism-Support Laws and the Demands of Prevention, 42 *Harvard Journal on Legislation* 1, 35–36 (2005).
3 Maureen O'Hagan, A Terrorism Case That Went Awry, *Seattle Times*, Nov. 22, 2004, at A1.
4 Ibid.
5 Ibid. As part of this investigation, the FBI read approximately 20,000 of Al-Hussayen's e-mail messages and monitored approximately 9,000 of his personal phone calls.
6 FBI Application and Affidavit for Search Warrant (Mar. 10, 2003), *United States* v. *Al-Hussayen*, No. CR03-C-EJL (D. Idaho Mar. 4, 2004).
7 Second Superseding Indictment at 4, *United States* v. *Al-Hussayen*, No. CR03-C-EJL (D. Idaho Mar. 4, 2004). The indictment alleged that Al-Hussayen maintained at least six U.S. bank accounts, in Indiana, Texas, Idaho and Michigan.
8 *The Terrorist Financing Operations Section: Hearing before the H. Comm. on Fin. Serv. Subcomm. on Oversight and Investigations*, 108th Cong. (2003) (statement of John S. Pistole, Assistant Director, Counterterrorism Division, FBI), available at www.fbi.gov/congress/congress03/pistole092403.htm.
9 See *American Heritage Dictionary of the English Language* (4th edition 2004) (defining webmaster as "a person whose occupation is designing, developing, marketing, or maintaining websites").
10 Second Superseding Indictment, *Al-Hussayen*, *supra* note 7, at 3.
11 Ibid. at 5.
12 See Susan Schmidt, Spreading Saudi Fundamentalism in U.S., *Washington Post*, Oct. 2, 2003, at A1.
13 Schmidt, *supra* note 12, at A1.

14 Second Superseding Indictment, *supra* note 7, at 3. *Mujahidid* is an Arabic word meaning "one who struggles" or "holy warrior" and refers to one who engages in "violent jihad." "Violent jihad" is "the taking of action against persons or governments who are deemed to be enemies of fundamental Islam." Ibid. at 2.

15 Ibid. at 6.

16 Ibid. at 3.

17 Ibid.

18 Second Superseding Indictment, *supra* note 7, at 3. The indictment states that branches of Al-Haramain were so designated pursuant to the International Emergency Economic Powers Act, 50 U.S.C. § 1701 (2000), as implemented by Exec. Order No. 13224, 66 Fed. Reg. 49079 (Sept. 23, 2001). Al-Haramain Islamic Foundation was a charity front, based in Saudi Arabia, for the international terrorist organization al Qaeda.

19 See *American Heritage Dictionary of the English Language* (4th edition 2004) (defining a fatwa as a legal opinion issued by an Islamic scholar).

20 See William McCants, *Militant Ideology Atlas, Research Compendium* 344 (2006), available at http://ctc.usma.edu/atlas/Atlas-ResearchCompendium.pdf (describing Al-Hawali). McCants describes Al-Hawali as

> [The] current secretary general of the Supreme Council of Global Jihad ... one of the 26 Saudi scholars who issued an open letter in late 2004 calling on Iraqis to fight the US. [He is] closely associated with Salman al-'Awda [Ouda] and is considered by some to be a significant mentor to Usama bin Ladin. [He is] named as a "theologian of terror" in the 10.2004 petition to the UN signed by 2,500 Muslim intellectuals calling for a treaty to ban the religious incitement to violence.

(Ibid.)

21 Second Superseding Indictment, *supra* note 7, at 8.

22 Ibid. at 8–9.

23 Ibid.

24 Ibid.

25 Ibid. at 9.

26 Ibid. at 8–9.

27 Ibid. at 9.

28 Ibid. at 9–10.

29 Ibid. at 5.

30 Ibid. at 10.

31 In the first indictment, Al-Hussayen was charged only with the false statement and visa fraud charges. This indictment was superseded by the first superseding indictment that added charges of violations of 18 U.S.C. § 2339A. The second (and final) superseding indictment was the one considered by the jury at trial.

32 Second Superseding Indictment, *supra* note 7, at 11–12.

33 For an excellent discussion of the evolution of U.S. laws aimed at addressing international terrorism see Chesney, *supra* note 2, at 4–12.

34 Violent Crime Control and Law Enforcement Act of 1994, Pub. L. No. 103-322, 108 Stat. 1796.

35 Antiterrorism and Effective Death Penalty Act of 1996, Pub. L. No. 104-134, 110 Stat. 1214.

36 18 U.S.C. § 2339A (2000).

37 Uniting and Strengthening America by Providing Appropriate Tools Required to Intercept and Obstruct Terrorism Act of 2001, Pub. L. No. 107-56, § 805(a), 115 Stat. 272.

38 18 U.S.C. § 2339B (2000).

39 Antiterrorism and Effective Death Penalty Act of 1996, Pub. L. No. 104-132, 110 Stat. 1214.

40 H.R. Rep. No. 104-383, at 43–45 (1995).
41 Ibid.
42 Under AEDPA, the Secretary of State may designate an organization as an FTO if the Secretary finds: (1) the organization is an FTO, (2) the organization engages in terrorist activity, and (3) the terrorist activity of the organization threatens the security of U.S. nationals or the national security of the United States. Prior to designation as an FTO, the Secretary must notify certain members of Congress and publish the designation in the Federal Register. See 8 U.S.C. § 1189(a)(2)(A) (2000). The designation is effective upon publication. See ibid.
43 District Court Order (Apr. 12, 2004), *United States* v. *Al-Hussayen*, No. CR03-C-EJL (D. Idaho Mar. 4, 2004). Although Judge Lodge denied the motion on the basis of First Amendment grounds, his reasons for doing so were never placed in the record.
44 Verdict (June 10, 2004), *United States* v. *Al-Hussayen*, No. CR03-C-EJL (D. Idaho Mar. 4, 2004).
45 Judge Edward J. Lodge Trial Minutes (June 10, 2004), *United States* v. *Al-Hussayen*, No. CR03-C-EJL (D. Idaho Mar. 4, 2004).
46 Betsy Z. Russell, Sami Al-Hussayen on His Way Home Free After Months in Idaho Jails, *Spokesman Review* (Spokane, Wash.), July 22, 2004, at 1B.
47 Ibid.
48 Although Al-Hussayen also made arguments at trial that the prosecution implicated his First Amendment rights to freedom of association, owing to space constraints I address here only the freedom of speech aspects of the prosecution.
49 *Texas* v. *Johnson*, 491 U.S. 397, 404 (1989) (citing *Spence* v. *Washington*, 418 U.S. 405, 410–11 (1974)).
50 *Roth* v. *United States*, 354 U.S. 476 (1957).
51 *Chaplinsky* v. *New Hampshire*, 315 U.S. 568 (1942).
52 *Virginia* v. *Black*, 538 U.S. 343 (2003).
53 *N.Y. Times* v. *Sullivan*, 376 U.S. 254 (1964).
54 *Cent. Hudson Gas and Elec. Corp.* v. *Pub. Serv. Comm'n*, 447 U.S. 557 (1980).
55 *Chaplinsky*, 315 U.S. at 571–72.
56 *Schenck* v. *United States*, 249 U.S. 47 (1919).
57 Espionage Act of 1917, ch. 30, tit. I, §3, 40 Stat. 219 (codified as amended in scattered sections of 18 U.S.C.). This law prohibited any person from willfully making or conveying false reports or false statements with intent to interfere with "military success" or "to promote the success of its enemies" as well as "obstructing the recruiting or enlistment service of the United States."
58 *Schenck*, 249 U.S. at 249.
59 Ibid.
60 Ibid.
61 *Abrams* v. *United States*, 250 U.S. 616 (1919).
62 Ibid. at 626 (Holmes, J., dissenting).
63 Ibid. at 627–28.
64 *Brandenburg* v. *Ohio*, 395 U.S. 444 (1969).
65 18 U.S.C. § 2385 (1940).
66 Ibid.
67 *United States* v. *Dennis*, 341 U.S. 494 (1951).
68 Ibid. at 515–16.
69 Ibid. at 517.
70 Ibid. at 509.
71 *Yates* v. *United States*, 354 U.S. 298 (1957).
72 Ibid. at 321.
73 Ohio Rev. Code Ann. § 2923.13 (1919).
74 *Brandenburg* v. *Ohio*, 395 U.S. 444, 446 (1969).
75 Ohio Rev. Code Ann. § 2923.13 (1919).

76 *Brandenburg*, 395 U.S. at 447.
77 Much of the broad First Amendment protection that many interpret *Brandenburg* to mandate depends on the meaning of the word "imminent." Despite the nearly 40 years since *Brandenburg*, the meaning of "imminent" remains problematic. The most obvious meaning of an imminent event is one that is "likely to occur immediately." *See American Heritage Dictionary of the English Language* (4th edition 2004). Some have argued that a more expansive interpretation of "imminent" is possible and would urge that the necessities of increasingly aggressive extremist groups compel such an interpretation. *See* Robert S. Tannenbaum, Comment, Preaching Terror: Free Speech or Wartime Incitement, 55 *American University Law Review* 785 (2006). This is a strained interpretation of *Brandenburg* which I refuse to accept.
78 *Scales* v. *United States*, 367 U.S. 203, 229–30 (1961).
79 Ibid.
80 *Rice* v. *Padalin Enters., Inc.*, 128 F.3d 233 (4th Cir. 1997); see also *United States* v. *Sattar*, 272 F. Supp. 2d 348, 359 (S.D.N.Y. 2003).
81 *Rice*, 128 F.3d at 242–43.
82 Ibid. at 246.
83 See Fed'n of Am. Scientists, *Intelligence Resource Program: Al-Qa'ida* (Oct. 12, 2005), www.fas.org/irp/world/para/ladin.htm. According to the Federation of American Scientists, al Qaeda's current goal is to establish a pan-Islamic caliphate throughout the world by working with allied Islamic extremist groups to overthrow regimes it deems "non-Islamic" and expelling Westerners and non-Muslims from Muslim countries – particularly Saudi Arabia. Al Qaeda issued statements saying it was the duty of all Muslims to kill U.S. citizens – civilian or military – and their allies everywhere.
84 *Dennis* v. *United States*, 341 U.S. 494, 509 (1951).
85 Bob Woodward, Robert G. Kaiser, and David B. Ottway, U.S. Fears Bin Laden Made Nuclear Strides: Concern over "Dirty Bomb" Affects Security, *Washington Post*, Dec. 4, 2001, at A1.
86 *Yates* v. *United States*, 354 U.S. 298, 321 (1957).
87 Gabriel Weimann, *Terror on the Internet* 109 (2006).
88 Ibid. at 50.
89 Ibid. at 129–30.
90 Ibid. at 117–19, 134–35.
91 Ibid. at 51.
92 Ibid. at 50.
93 Ibid.
94 *Reno* v. *Am. Civil Liberties Union*, 521 U.S. 844, 870 (1997).
95 Ibid. at 849–53.
96 Weimann, *supra* note 87, at 25.
97 Internet Jihad: A World Wide Web of Terror, *The Economist*, July 12, 2007, available at www.economist.com/world/displaystory.cfm?story_id=9472498; see also Weimann, *supra* note 87, at 117.
98 Weimann, *supra* note 87, at 117.
99 Ibid. at 118–20, 138–40.
100 See George H. Pike, Global Reach of Anti-Terrorism Laws, 23 *Information Today*, Jan. 2006, at 17, 17.
101 Terrorism Act of 2006, c. 11 (U.K.).
102 Ibid. at c. 11, pt. 1, § 1.
103 The Act also prohibits the "dissemination of terrorist publications." See ibid. at ch. 11, pt. 1, § 2.
104 Bob Fick, Saudi Grad Student Cleared of Terror Charges in Idaho, *Boston Globe*, June 11, 2004, available at www.boston.com/news/nation/articles/2004/06/11/saudi_grad_student_cleared_of_terror_charges_in_idaho/.

105 *Grayned* v. *City of Rockford*, 408 U.S. 104, 108–09 (1972) (citations omitted).

106 *United States* v. *Sattar*, 272 F. Supp. 2d. 348 (S.D.N.Y. 2003).

107 Ibid. at 383.

108 *United States* v. *Sattar*, 314 F. Supp. 2d 279, 321 (S.D.N.Y. 2004)

109 *Humanitarian Law Project* v. *Reno*, 205 F. Supp. 3d. 1130 (9th Cir. 2000), *aff'g Humanitarian Law Project* v. *Reno*, 9 F. Supp. 2d 1176 (C.D. Cal. 1998).

110 *United States* v. *Lindh*, 212 F. Supp. 2d 541, 574 (E.D. Va. 2002).

111 *United States* v. *Goba*, 220 F. Supp. 2d 182 (W.D.N.Y. 2002) (holding that the federal statute criminalizing provision of material support to foreign terrorist organizations was not unconstitutionally vague when applied to defendants accused of training at a known terrorist organization's camp).

112 *Grayned* v. *City of Rockford*, 408 U.S. 104, 108–09 (1972).

113 *Colautti* v. *Franklin*, 439 U.S. 379, 395 (1979).

114 For a good discussion of § 2339B strict liability regime, see Tom Stacy, The Material Support Offense: The Use of Strict Liability in the War Against Terror, 14 *Kansas Journal of Law and Public Policy* 461 (2004–05).

115 *Humanitarian Law Project* v. *U.S. Dep't of Justice*, 352 F.3d 382, 385 (9th Cir. 2003).

116 Ibid. at 402.

117 See *United States* v. *Sattar*, 314 F. Supp. 2d 279, 321 (S.D.N.Y. 2004).

118 Kent Greenawalt, *Speech, Crime, and the Uses of Language* 339 (1989).

119 *Chaplinsky* v. *New Hampshire*, 315 U.S. 568, 571–72 (1942).

120 *Terminello* v. *City of Chicago*, 337 U.S. 1, 36 (1949) (Jackson, J., dissenting).

13 Comparative law and Germany's militant democracy

Russell A. Miller

Introduction

The terrorists who perpetrated the September 11, 2001 attacks in the United States clearly benefited in their plot from the individual liberties secured by the United States Constitution. They freely associated with one another.[1] Their mission seems to have been emboldened, if not inspired, by the religious convictions they freely exercised.[2] Most importantly, they operated in a sphere of privacy free of the government's intrusive scrutiny; and they could have been certain to avoid such scrutiny as long as the discrete acts leading up to the attacks did not raise the suspicion necessary to permit a criminal investigation or attract permissible intelligence monitoring.[3] Not surprisingly, the terrorist attacks have given rise to a vigorous debate over the balance that must be struck in a constitutional democracy between security and liberty.[4] Liberty may be getting the worst of the bargain, as the other chapters in this book make clear.

From the clamor of voices urging the recalibration of that balance for the United States in the era of global terrorism,[5] a common refrain has been to propose the examination of other countries' national security regimes.[6] Bruce Ackerman, after recognizing that "terrorism is a challenge facing all liberal democracies,"[7] suggested:

> [The United States] has much to learn from the experience of other countries. Most of them haven't had the protection of two great oceans, or the luxury of looking upon grave threats as rare events. By the luck of the geographic draw, they have been forced to live with extreme danger for centuries. As a consequence, their constitutions often contain elaborate political safeguards ... providing ideas for the work before us.[8]

For good reason, Germany has attracted some of this comparative attention.[9] Like the United States, Germany is a well-established and well-respected constitutional democracy. Of greater relevance in this context are the constitutional peculiarities that have resulted from Germany's three historical encounters with violent authoritarian and antidemocratic movements. The first of these confrontations, of course, is the legacy of National Socialism, against which

Germany's post-World War II constitutional order is fundamentally defined.[10] The second is the reaction of Germany's maturing democracy to the leftist terrorism of the 1970s and 1980s. The third is Germany's still-unfolding confrontation with radical Islamic terrorism. Fitting Ackerman's description, almost throughout the whole course of its 60-year existence the Federal Republic has been engaged with balancing security and liberty in response to actual authoritarian and terrorist threats in a manner and to a degree that the United States, at least prior to 2001, had been privileged to avoid.

The most sensational and unique contribution Germany's national security constitution[11] has made to the common constitutional struggle to balance security and liberty is the theory of "militant democracy." It is unfortunate that the radically peaceful, thoroughly internationalist, and uncompromisingly democratic Federal Republic must be associated with a constitutional construct that sounds so unflatteringly aggressive, so *Prussian*. But this is how *"wehrhafte Demokratie"* long has been translated; although I might have preferred "proactive democracy" or "self-sustaining democracy."

And now, András Sajó, the best-known contemporary theorist of militant democracy, has written to advocate the implementation of militant democracy in the present struggle against terrorism. "The counter-terror state, following the logic of militant democracy," he explained, "intends to protect certain fundamental rights and values by denying those rights to some people who are believed to abuse the system."[12] This claim has been endorsed by Jürgen Habermas, among the world's leading public intellectuals and a committed democrat. "How tolerantly may a democracy treat the enemies of democracy?" Habermas has asked. "If the democratic state does not wish to give itself up, then it must resort to intolerance toward the enemy of the constitution," particularly including "today's terrorists."[13] Since the September 11, 2001 terrorist attacks, U.S. policymakers have demonstrated themselves, through an array of measures, eager to express such intolerance. Without explicitly invoking the phrase, the United States has noticeably "militarized" its democracy in the years since 2001 and might do more if voices like Sajó's gain momentum.

How should a comparatist analyze the claims that America can borrow and transplant Germany's militant democracy as a weapon in the struggle against global terrorism? On one hand, comparative claims like Ackerman's and Sajó's represent the traditional, *functional* answer to that question. *Contextualists*, on the other hand, are doubtful of the prospects of borrowing a normative construct like militant democracy for use by another country. They argue that a focus on the context in which specific problems and their national legal solutions arise reveals the difficulty, if not the impossibility, of transplanting norms. In order that comparative law remain relevant in the face of these contending approaches and the new demands being placed upon it by the new terrorist paradigm, I propose a discursive comparative methodology that rejects the focus on the viability and propriety of borrowing a norm that is at the heart of the functionalist and contextualist approaches and instead recognizes comparative law's potential as a powerful instrument for social critique.

Germany's militant democracy provides a timely case study for a survey of these approaches to comparative law, including the discursive comparative method I propose. In the following section, I introduce Germany's militant democracy. Thereafter, the chapter's final section will describe the three comparative methods under consideration, including my proposal for a discursive comparative approach, and demonstrate the application of the approaches through a case study of Germany's militant democracy.

Militant democracy

The theory of militant democracy introduced

The fire that terrorists set to the German Reichstag (Parliament) building during the night of February 27 and 28, 1933 was so symbolically potent as to offer Hitler a "pretext for intensifying the repressive measures [the Nazis] had already initiated against all forces opposed to the regime."[14] We are all too familiar with the horrors unleashed by the Nazi tyranny, which was, in part, presented as the necessary response to the threat terrorism posed to German democracy. Still, it bears repeating, especially today: The seeds of World War II and the Holocaust were planted in the fertile dictatorial soil cleared away by Hitler's emergency decree issued on February 28, 1933, the day after the Reichstag fire. The decree suspended "key basic rights and all constitutional guarantees."[15]

But democracy itself, enshrined and preserved in many of the rights that Hitler hastily abolished after the Reichstag fire, was just as much an accomplice to Hitler's rise to power as it was his victim. Certainly with no small amount of thuggery,[16] but also through effective electioneering,[17] by as early as 1930 the Nazis could claim that they drew their support from all sectors of German society.[18] In the snap parliamentary elections held in early March 1933, shortly after the Reichstag fire – the last credibly free elections of the German Weimar Republic – Hitler and the Nazis fairly became the German parliament's largest party. Joseph Goebbels ridiculed the system, declaring: "This will always remain one of the best jokes of democracy, that it gave its deadly enemies the means by which it was destroyed."[19]

In view of this history, the framers of Germany's new postwar constitution were preoccupied with the terrorism inflicted on the German state by Hitler's democratically imposed fascism and not by the terrorists of Dutch communist Marinus van der Lubbe's ilk, who was accused of the Reichstag arson. Having witnessed firsthand the havoc fascism had set loose and the historic trauma it had inflicted on German democracy, the framers, in a series of constitutional provisions, saw fit that the enemies of democracy would never again be able to exploit the freedoms secured by democracy only to subvert it. *"Keine Freiheit für die Feinde der Freiheit!"* the sentiment ran.[20] The resulting finely wrought system of undemocratic provisions – meant to preserve and protect democracy – has been described as "militant democracy."

For inspiration in fashioning their new militant democracy, the Federal Republic's founding fathers and mothers turned to the political theory of Karl Loewenstein. Reacting very specifically to the death-grip of European fascism in the interwar years, Loewenstein, a German émigré to America, coined the phrase "militant democracy" in a pair of articles he published in 1937. Loewenstein argued:

> A virtual state of siege confronts European democracies. State of siege means, even under democratic constitutions, concentration of powers in the hands of the government and suspension of fundamental rights. If democracy believes in the superiority of its absolute values over the opportunistic platitudes of fascism, it must live up to the demands of the hour, and every possible effort must be made to rescue it, even at the risk and cost of violating fundamental principles.[21]

Fascism, he agonized, had already forced democracy to succumb in Italy, Germany, Turkey and Spain.[22] He saw Austria, Bulgaria, Greece, Portugal, Hungary, Romania, Yugoslavia, Latvia and Lithuania tipping precariously towards authoritarianism.[23] In each case, he decried the "democratic fundamentalism"[24] and "exaggerated formalism of the rule of law"[25] that had prevented democracy from forbidding to "the enemies of its very existence the use of democratic instrumentalities."[26] Democracy's tolerance and freedom, Loewenstein lamented, had been the "Trojan horse by which the enemy [entered] the city."[27]

For the contemporary proponents of militant democracy, Loewenstein's characterization of the fascist threat arrayed against constitutional democracies in the 1930s resonates strongly today. First, he argued that fascism was a political technique and not a substantive ideology. Fascism, he explained, "simply wants to rule."[28] Second, he noted fascism's dependence on emotionalism as opposed to an epistemology dependent on rationality.[29] Third, he remarked fascism's unique dependence on the technology of mass communication.[30] Finally, he argued that fascism sought, in particular, to exploit democracy:

> Democracy and democratic tolerance have been used for their own destruction. Under cover of fundamental rights and the rule of law, the anti-democratic machine could be built up and set in motion legally. Calculating adroitly that democracy could not, without self-abnegation, deny to any body of public opinion the full use of the free institutions of speech, press, assembly, and parliamentary participation, fascist exponents systematically discredit the democratic order and make it unworkable by paralyzing its functions until chaos reigns.[31]

Writing more recently and with an eye toward the terrorist threat confronting liberal democracies today, Sajó described the democratic dilemma in very similar terms:

Majority rule creates the opportunity for the deformation of democracy and the imposition of a concept of the good life that does not allow for alternative forms and autonomous definition of the good life. Within the framework of the democratic process, using the mechanisms of democracy (free speech, assembly, elections), a regime may be established that dissolves democracy.[32]

To meet the fascist threat, Loewenstein proposed giving modern liberal democracies the power to defend themselves against challenges to their political existence.[33] "If democracy is convinced that it has not yet fulfilled its destination," Loewenstein argued, "it must fight on its own plane a technique which serves only the purpose of power. Democracy must become militant."[34] Thus, democratic societies must give force to the principle that those who use freedom "aggressively against the free and democratic order" surrender any right to the enjoyment of liberty.[35] Loewenstein hurled down disdain on those who would refrain from curbing liberty out of a fundamentalist respect for the core democratic principle that holds that "citizens must rule themselves, and in modern parlance, they must possess the rights necessary to permit self-rule without undue impediments or constraints."[36] The principal obstacle to democracy's defense, Loewenstein said, was "democratic fundamentalism itself."[37] Max Lerner accused democracies of exhibiting "a creeping paralysis of will."[38] This fundamentalism, this lack of will, so the criticism went, refused to acknowledge the differences in motive, method and mechanism that distinguish the illiberal elements of militant democracy and the illiberal, authoritarian essence of fascism:

> Of course, there is a fundamental difference between the fighting spirit of the dictators on the one hand, who aim at imposing a total system of values and a strait-jacket social organization upon their citizens, and a militant democracy on the other, which becomes militant only in the defence of the agreed right procedure of social change and those basic virtues and values – such as brotherly love, mutual help, decency, social justice, freedom, respect for the person, etc. – which are the basis of the peaceful functioning of a social order.[39]

A democracy "assured enough of its tolerance,"[40] however, could marshal positive legislative measures of containment and repression, which might be discomfortingly undemocratic in their nature but would be used for the defense of democracy. Most of the undemocratic measures Loewenstein prescribed for combating the "suicidal lethargy" of democracy were specifically tailored to the distinct nature of the interwar fascist threat and its domestic political manifestation.[41] Three of his recommendations, however, seem to be more amenable to adaptation and use in the "War on Terror." The first is what Loewenstein described as the thorny problem of "curbing the freedom of public opinion, speech, and press in order to check the unlawful use thereof by revolutionary and subversive propaganda."[42] The measures in the "War on Terror" having negative impacts on speech and press freedom are expertly critiqued elsewhere in this book.[43]

I will not seek to add to the impressive body of literature comparing the distinct German and American constitutional traditions of free speech. Apart from the fact of its thorough treatment elsewhere, I have chosen not to concentrate on this aspect of militant democracy because, as those surveys reveal, neither country recognizes an absolute constitutional protection of these freedoms. The distinct limits each country recognizes in its ordinary constitutional jurisprudence, though very often cognizant of and sensitive to security concerns, operate independently of the unique threat to democracy posed by fascism and terrorism. They are equally applicable to a Nazi, an al Qaeda terrorist and the less ideologically charged prankster who shouts "fire" in a crowded theater.[44] But as limits on freedoms that might otherwise have aided the destruction of democracy, this ordinary jurisprudence nonetheless has a "militant" quality.

This gives rise to Otto Pfersmann's disillusionment with the special attention bestowed on militant democracy. "Militant democracy," he explained, "is on a scale of degree with other forms of democracy, in other words, that democracies are always more or less militant."[45] Certainly, the commonplace rejection of constitutional absolutism locates the United States and Germany at a point along the scale that is more militant than what Pfersmann called an "open democracy," namely, the pure setting in which the only constitutive features are the traditional democratic expectation that "addressees participate in the production of the general norms by majoritarian decisions, directly or through the election of representatives in charge of enacting such general rules."[46]

Germany's more unique contribution is its constitutional establishment of a "whole set of strong obstacles to anti-democratic action";[47] direct, higher-order limits on freedom that are different as a matter of degree and quality than more common constitutional limits on free speech, even as those limits might be expanded during times of stress or suspended altogether during times of crisis.[48]

The strong, higher-order forms of militant democracy that interest me, and which are now drawing attention in the "War on Terror," are demonstrated by two of Loewenstein's more exceptional recommendations. First, he proposed that democracies "proscribe subversive movements altogether."[49] In Germany, this has taken the form of a constitutional provision that permits the banning of antidemocratic political parties.[50] This calls to mind the "guilt by association" provisions of the USA PATRIOT Act, which was enacted in the wake of the September 11, 2001 terrorist attacks in the United States "to deter and punish terrorist acts in the United States and around the world, to enhance law enforcement investigatory tools, and for other purposes."[51] The USA PATRIOT Act's "guilt by association" provisions build on the web of related provisions enacted in 1996 as part of the Antiterrorism and Effective Death Penalty Act.[52] These laws attract comparison with Loewenstein's proposal that antidemocratic groups be banned outright because they strike at suspected terrorist groups[53] and their constituents by (1) directly sanctioning the group by freezing assets and prohibiting members' entry into the United States, (2) making aliens deportable for wholly innocent associational activity with the organization, and (3) criminalizing the provision of material support to the groups.[54] Cole and Dempsey summarized the increasing reliance on this brand of militant democracy in these terms:

> Building on the 1996 Antiterrorism Act, the PATRIOT Act expands guilt by association,... which has been making a strong comeback in recent years under the guise of cutting off funding for terrorism. Under immigration law that existed before September 11, aliens were deportable for engaging in or supporting terrorist *activity*. The PATRIOT Act makes aliens deportable for wholly innocent associational activity with a "terrorist organization," irrespective of any nexus between the alien's associational conduct and any act of violence, much less terrorism.[55]

Second, Loewenstein proposed that democracies "select and train political police for the discovery, repression, supervision, and control of anti-democratic and anti-constitutional activities and movements."[56] In Germany, this proposal has manifested itself in the form of domestic intelligence agencies, operated by federal and state governments, known as the Offices for the Protection of the Constitution.[57] Such domestic intelligence gathering calls to mind the Bush administration's warrantless domestic surveillance regime that was conducted by the National Security Agency in the aftermath of the September 11, 2001 terrorist attacks in the United States.[58] The parallel between the NSA warrantless domestic surveillance regime and Loewenstein's proposed domestic intelligence operations is captured by Katherine Wong's description of the former:

> In 2002, the President signed an order secretly authorizing the NSA to eavesdrop on individuals within the United States without [Foreign Intelligence Surveillance Court] approval. Surveillance activity under the order has encompassed the communications of potentially thousands of Americans, signaling a shift from intense, long-term monitoring of a few individuals to data mining.[59]

John Cary Sims emphasized the domestic implications of the NSA warrantless surveillance regime when he claimed that it represented a radical departure from preexisting surveillance policy. "The warrantless surveillance program," Sims noted, "appears to significantly expand the interception of international electronic communications involving United States persons by taking 'unintentionally' intercepted communications to, from, or about an individual, and using them as a basis for targeting future communications involving that person."[60] Perhaps Richard Seamon, in his contribution to this book, best captured the menacing domestic ramifications of the NSA warrantless surveillance regime and its parallels with Loewenstein's proposal. In the simplest terms, Seamon concluded, "In 2001, the President began spying on Americans again."[61]

Germany's militant democracy outlined

Germany's militant democracy takes up these strong, higher-order militantly democratic mechanisms. Most prominently, the *Grundgesetz* (Basic Law or Constitution) provides for the outright exclusion of some groups. Article 9(2), for example, prohibits "associations whose aims or activities contravene the criminal laws, or that are directed against the constitutional order or the concept of international understanding."[62] A similar provision permits a ban on political parties. Article 21(2) says, "Parties that by reason of their aims or the behavior of the adherents, seek to undermine or abolish the free democratic basic order or to endanger the existence of the Federal Republic of Germany shall be unconstitutional."[63]

In addition to these constitutional provisions, the somewhat Orwellian-sounding Federal and State Offices for the Protection of the Constitution can be credited as examples of Germany's adoption of Loewenstein's militant democracy. According to the federal enabling law, these federal and state agencies are "tasked with the collection and analysis of information, especially of such information, intelligence and documents relating to" threats to the "free democratic basic order."[64]

David Currie concluded that Germany's militant democracy represents the most "startling aspects of the Basic Law to an observer from the other side of the Atlantic."[65] His estimation has held up in the limited comparative law literature that has taken notice of Germany's militant democracy. Norman Dorsen and his coauthors, again focusing on the free speech facets of militant democracy, noted that "[m]any European countries prohibit the public display of emblems or symbols or the wearing of clothes connected with extreme-right ideologies or racial hatred; the U.S. does not."[66] Elsewhere, the tone struck in the North American literature is often dismayed or disapproving.[67]

Surveying comparative methods

Considering the socio-legal differences that inform the general discomfort expressed by Americans with respect to Germany's militant democracy, how should a comparatist analyze the claims that America might nonetheless borrow and transplant Germany's militant democracy as a weapon in the struggle against terrorism? Two established approaches present themselves. I suggest a third.

Functionalism

For some time, comparative law has been in thrall to a methodology of the kind illustrated by Sajó's proposal that liberal democracies might benefit from borrowing Germany's militant democracy as a functional solution to the problem that liberal democracies provide the means of their own destruction.[68] The functionalist tradition "considers legal problems and their solutions in isolation" and "treats comparative law as a technique of problem solving. The subject of comparative analysis is the legal problem, excised from its context."[69] As Konrad Zweigert and Hein Kötz, the architects of the functional method, explained:

> The reception of foreign legal institutions is not a matter of nationality, but of usefulness and need. No one bothers to fetch a thing from afar when he has one as good or better at home, but only a fool would refuse quinine just because it didn't grow in his back garden.[70]

The problem-solving emphasis of the functional method led to an understanding of comparative law that was "distinguished by a universalizing method and epistemology ... [aimed at] arriving at practical solutions ... that was the vehicle to legal truth."[71] The result was that comparative law presented issues "generically," "detached" from specifics, and abstracted from their relevant contexts in an effort to construct the ideal law.[72]

Ruti Teitel associated Sajó with the reemergence of the functional method, now applied to constitutional law as comparative law's last frontier.[73] Sajó's book *Comparative Constitutionalism*, Teitel argued, "endeavors to abstract the constitutional problem from its contextual factors in the hope of identifying the best practices. The relevant issues are represented as timeless and universal."[74] Sajó's commitment to the functional method is exemplified by his assertion that "[e]lements of militant democracy ... might be relevant in the analysis of the state's reactions to terror."[75] Sajó also goes to great lengths to establish a convergence between interwar fascism and the contemporary terrorist threat.[76] Thus, Teitel focused her critique of Sajó's "neofunctionalism," in particular, on the treatment of militant democracy in his book *Comparative Constitutionalism*:

> Consider the [book's] treatment of political parties in U.S. and European constitutional law. Although in the United States, except with respect to the First Amendment, political parties do not have special status under the Constitution, in Europe party politics are subject to greater scrutiny and have more constitutional significance. Understanding the basis for these differences requires a consideration of the differences between the natures of presidential and parliamentary democracies. In the casebook's discussion of Germany's close constitutional review of political parties, known as "militant democracy," the editors assert that "the protection of democracy against its enemies is a matter that states confront at all times," suggesting that vigilance is essential to constitutionalism. Yet militant democracy is a distinct postwar response that is associated with a particular political and constitutional history and that assumes a normative take on constitutional democracy. The editors' inquiry does not address the relevance of values to constitutional protection of democracy or the extent to which "militant democracy" raises critical tradeoffs best understood in light of the unique features of a particular legal and political culture.[77]

Contextualism

A comparative law methodology has arisen that turns away from functionalism's utility-enhancing presumption that legal systems and problems are essentially similar.[78] As Teitel's critique of Sajó's book hints, this turn in comparative law methodology is interested in a more nuanced consideration of the socio-legal context of the foreign norms under examination. Teitel explained the contextual critique in these terms: "[T]he functionalist project is of limited value because the functionalist comparative constitutional analysis tends to elide political, economic, and social realities in its quest to identify legal regimes that can be transplanted across national lines."[79] Mary Ann Glendon and her coauthors urged that "[l]egal norms cannot be fully understood without some knowledge of their sources; their political, social, and economic purposes; the milieu in which they operate; the role of the legal profession; the operation of the court system."[80] Vivian Grosswald Curran has given us a succinct description of this contextual method, what she termed "cultural immersion": "[A] valid examination of another legal culture requires immersion into the political, historical, economic and linguistic contexts that molded the legal system, and in which the legal system operates."[81] Angus McDonald argued that the contextual method is all the more appropriate as regards a comparative discussion of a constitutional law construct like militant democracy. "As a constitutionalist and a comparatist," McDonald explained,

> I believe I have two good reasons for being a contextualist. Even if other legal fields might make a convincing argument for a "black letter" conceptual purity, constitutional questions at their very heart address the point where law meets government meets democratic demands meets economics meets social response.[82]

Tietel ascribed a similar vision to Vicki Jackson and Mark Tushnet, coauthors of a comparative constitutional law casebook that competes with Sajó's:[83]

> The relevant inquiry [for Jackson and Tushnet] is historical and political. From the perspective of a hermenutics associated with political, historical, and cultural contingency, [the contextual method] better accounts for constitutionalism's changing and particular dimensions.... While [Sajó and his coauthors] seek to abstract, [the contextual method practiced by Jackson and Tushnet] endeavors to situate various constitutional problems in their animating political circumstances.[84]

This contextualization of problems and norms greatly complicates, if it does not confound, attempts at borrowing a legal regime, like Germany's militant democracy, for use in another setting, like America's struggle with terrorism. In fact, a contextual comparative analysis identifies a number of variables that argue against the viability of transplanting Germany's militant democracy.

First, as Teitel notes, a mechanism of militant democracy like Germany's party-ban is not easily converted for use in the United States where political parties play a distinctly different role and have a distinctly different constitutional standing. In a passage already quoted, Tietel explains:

> [I]n the United States, except with respect to the First Amendment, political parties do not have special status under the Constitution, in Europe party politics are subject to greater scrutiny and have more constitutional significance. Understanding the basis for these differences requires a consideration of the differences between the natures of presidential and parliamentary democracies.[85]

Second, it is questionable whether Sajó is correct in suggesting that fascism and terrorism are comparable. Invoking Loewenstein's characterization of fascism, Sajó argued, "The only genuine goal of such politics and movements is to seize and retain power at all costs. This description applies to al Qaeda. It can succeed in this goal only if it operates within the democratic institutional infrastructure."[86] Fundamentalist Islamic terrorism shares, Sajó has argued, the emotionalism of the fascist movement, which militant democracy was originally intended to combat: "[T]he intimidation and fear resulting from terror also generate a kind of politics of emotion, or other forms of irrationality."[87] Ultimately, Sajó understands the goals of Islamist terrorism to consist of the less refined aims of public intimidation and disruption of governmental function, as well as the more sophisticated objective of the creation of radically Islamist states.[88] Fascism, according to Sajó, had a range of similar goals. But Loewenstein's theory was preoccupied with the internal political threat fascism posed to democracies. The aim of fascism, in Loewenstein's view, was to replace constitutional government with emotional government; rationality and the rule of law with unchallengeable commands. Militant democracy was uniquely tailored to respond to fascism's essence: "[T]o arouse, to guide, and to use emotionalism in its crudest and most refined forms ... the movement and emotion are identical."[89] Sajó is certain that fascism and terrorism are comparable enough to justify the application of militant democracy against terrorism. Acknowledging that the comparison is complicated by international Islamist terrorism's suicidal element, Sajó nonetheless argues that terrorism shares fascism's emotionalism and the practice of operating within democratic infrastructure or availing itself of democratic freedom.[90]

Not everyone agrees that terrorism presents the same kind of unique political threat that made fascism susceptible to militant democracy. Kent Roach, for example, concluded that "[a]nti-terrorism laws could be constructed and defended without reference to the problematic idea of militant democracy.... Terrorism, as violence directed at civilians, could be punished as ordinary crime. Murder is murder."[91] And contrary to the governing ambitions of fascism, terrorism, by its nature, cannot seek to achieve government power because it is inherently always oriented against established authority.

Third, the translation of militant democracy's illiberal political structures into the contemporary intellectual and ideological milieu neglects militant democracy's relationship to the intellectual and ideological milieu prevalent in the interwar, Great Depression era. The spirit of the age was deeply skeptical of the liberal tradition in ways that are wholly unimaginable today. Max Lerner captured the mood when he declared, "The central tragedy of our age, in short, lies not alone in fascism; it lies even more in the liberalism which has thus far proved feckless to cope with social collapse and the fascism that follows it."[92] Karl Mannheim was equally dispossessed of liberalism: "If I had to summarize the situation in a single sentence I would say: 'We are living in an age of transition from laissez-faire to a planned society.'"[93] At least Lerner and Mannheim expressed skepticism of liberalism in its economic *and* political manifestations. Our increasing political militancy, however, curiously parallels an entrenched, unabashed liberal-economic triumphalism. In this respect, it seems that economic freedom might be diverging from political freedom. This gap would have interested Lerner, who already in 1943 recognized that the social and economic failings of liberalism had contributed to its political failings.[94] In any case, it is clear that invocations of Loewenstein's militant democracy today occur against the backdrop of a radically different liberal epistemology.

Fourth, an examination of Germany's militant democracy in its context reveals its bankruptcy as a mechanism for ensuring political stability in Germany, undermining claims that importing it for top-down use in the "War on Terror" would enhance American security. Germany's militant democracy has been very rarely and only symbolically implemented across the nearly 60 years of the life of Federal Republic, including a disastrous recent attempt at putting militant democracy into practice.

Very early in the life of the Federal Republic, the Federal Constitutional Court imposed bans on the Socialist Reich Party (SRP) and the German Communist Party (KPD). Although often portrayed as a dramatic example of the implementation of Germany's militant democracy, these cases must be viewed as chiefly symbolic. The bans were not essential to promoting deeper stability in Germany because neither the SRP nor the KPD represented a significant political movement that threatened to seize the democratic machinery through democratic means. For example, in the May 6, 1951 state elections in Lower Saxony, the SRP's supposed stronghold, the party drew only 11 percent and four direct mandates, "below what many observers had feared."[95] Donald P. Kommers remarked on a similar state of affairs with respect to the KPD. Chancellor Konrad Adenauer's government initiated a party-ban action against the KPD in 1951, the same year it sought a declaration of unconstitutionality against the SRP. But, it took the court four additional years to decide the *Communist Party* case. Kommers explained:

The delay reflected the growing feeling among some of the justices [on the Federal Constitutional Court] that the Adenauer Government's action against the KPD was premature and that it would be more prudent to allow the party to bury itself in an open political contest than to have it banned by judicial decree. The KPD's electoral strength dipped to 2.3 percent of the national vote in 1953, and by 1956 its popular support had almost vanished. On August 17, 1956, convinced that the government would not withdraw the case, the Court handed down an opinion declaring the Communist Party unconstitutional.[96]

More suggestive of the symbolic rather than actual impact of the court's bans was the significant concern that the western occupying authorities had shown for these parties. For example, the record is clear that the Allies wanted the SRP banished, whether by legal or political means, and that they were determined to see the work done if the Adenauer government proved inadequate to the task. Norbert Frei reported that the Americans informed Adenauer that "'we will intervene' if it 'should prove necessary'" to stamp out the reemergence of Nazism in Germany.[97] Ultimately, Frei concluded that "much speaks for the assumption that the Allies were the main reason for the West German government trying to stamp out right-wing radicalism by banning."[98] And Kommers placed the KPD ban in the broader context of the Cold War, again suggestive of the United States' immense external interest and influence over matters. "[I]n the face of rising Soviet–American tensions," Kommers explained, "tensions exacerbated by the division and rearming of both Germanies [*sic*] – the *Communist Party* case was important *symbolically* in the bitterly Cold War between East and West Germany."[99]

If a deeper examination of the context in which Germany first sought to implement its militant democracy suggests that those efforts were primarily symbolic, claims of the efficacy of Germany's militant democracy are further undermined by militant democracy's long dormancy after the SRP and KPD cases. The court has not banned a party since. Perhaps most tellingly, Kommers noted,

> [the authorities did not seek a ban of the] reorganized Communist Party, now called the German Communist Party (DKP). The new party could have been suppressed as a successor organization of the banned KPD, but security officials failed to move against the party, and it continued to operate openly. As one commentator noted: "The toleration of the DKP and the [right-wing National Democratic Party (NPD)] probably reflects a sense that it would be improper to move to ban parties that act lawfully within the liberal democratic system, even when they clearly aim to have that system replaced by an illiberal, anti-democratic one."[100]

The relative quiet of the last decades regarding militant democracy was broken in 2002 when the court threw out the most recent attempt at implementing a party-ban. It is my view that the failure of the National Democratic Party (NPD) party-ban application has finally discredited militant democracy as a viable device for promoting stability and security in a mature democracy, a fact which, in turn, should undermine claims that Germany's militant democracy is appropriate for transplantation in the American struggle against terrorism.

Beginning in the 1960s, the rise of the extreme right-wing NPD, with its neo-Nazi politics, stirred concern in Germany. The NPD, however, was not declared unconstitutional, and the government did not petition the court to declare it unconstitutional until the emergence of a startling rise of neo-Nazi and anti-Semitic incidents in Germany a quarter-century later, many occurring in the new, economically depressed states of the former East Germany. The center-left government of SPD Chancellor Gerhard Schröder seized on those events as the justification for seeking a ban of the NPD. In October 2001, the Federal Constitutional Court found the party-ban applications to be admissible.[101] But in January 2002, just days before the planned hearings in the case, the court suspended the proceedings.[102] Through *ex parte* communications, the court learned that much of the evidence it considered in the admissibility phase of the case, and upon which it would be expected to rely in its substantive ruling on the ban, had come from highly placed state agents and informants working within the NPD.[103] These *V-Männer* worked primarily for the Federal and State Offices for the Protection of the Constitution, the secret political police forces that Loewenstein had urged and which Germany had adopted as part of its militant democracy. These domestic, political spies are

> already part of a criminal or extremist organization [who are] paid to provide information on a regular basis over a long period of time. These persons are not occasional informers but are continuously guided, directed and supervised by the [state] agency receiving the information.[104]

The potential these state agents pose for manipulated evidence and state influence on the activities and policies of the party is obvious. In fact, the NPD had planned to argue in its defense that the evidence offered against it was the product of so-called *V-Männer*. At a hearing on the scope of the phenomenon in the case, it was revealed that 15 percent of the NPD's Executive Council consisted of agents who "were supervised and paid by Federal or State Offices for the Protection of the Constitution."[105]

In a March 2003 ruling dismissing the party-ban case against the NPD, the court focused on the procedural implications of the deep infiltration of the party by state agents and not on the substantive question of the NPD's compatibility with the free democratic basic order. The outcome hinged on the application of the rule requiring a two-thirds majority for decisions in party-ban proceedings that negatively impact the party.[106] Thus, a minority of three justices prevailed in having the case dismissed, even though a majority of the court would have allowed the proceedings to go forward. The prevailing three-justice minority concluded that the role of the state agents violated the high standard of procedural fairness required of such a radical measure of militant democracy. The decision suggests an increasingly strict jurisprudence that should make party-bans even more difficult to obtain.[107] Some herald this as a sign of political and democratic maturity. Germany, so the argument goes, need not resort to illiberal measures in order to preserve its liberal character.

It is possible to argue that Germany never relied on militant democracy to promote democratic stability. Certainly, the foregoing contextual examination of Germany's militant democracy greatly undercuts claims that it might be of some use in the American "War on Terror."

A discursive comparative method

The contextual method is susceptible to the well-known limits of critical, post-modern perspectives, including charges of dead-end relativism.[108] On this account, law's contextual particularity, especially constitutional law's contextual imbed-dedness, raises questions about "whether transcultural comparativism is even pos-sible."[109] If the contextualists are right and context thwarts the borrowing that functionalism sought to promote, comparative law runs the risk of being reduced to little more than socio-legal tourism. Besides this relativism, the contextual method "does not appropriately account for areas of [legal] affinity and consensus ... [evident in] recent globalizing political changes that have invigorated" transna-tionalism – a phenomenon demonstrated most ominously by global terrorism.[110]

To overcome these critiques of the contextual method, I propose yet another turn for comparative law, one that is discursive. I begin with the recognition that both the functional and the contextual approaches are preoccupied with the pro-priety of norm borrowing and transplantation as a top-down process: The func-tional approach simplifies variables to embrace the norm in question; the contextual approach complicates variables to reject the norm. Departing from this borrowing paradigm, however, I acknowledge that the contextual approach reveals a wealth of sociological information which, even if excluding the possi-bility of borrowing the norm in question, might be of value in critically examin-ing the comparatist's system. It is this body of information on which I propose opening discourse between two systems: the sociology, history, economics and politics the comparatist discovers in the foreign context might come to inform the comparatist's understanding of the sociology, history, economics and poli-tics of her or his own socio-legal culture. Drawing more explicitly on the horti-cultural imagery of norm transplantation, the functional and contextual methods focus on the norm as a plant that might (functional) or might not (contextual) be plucked and transplanted into a new setting. I propose, on the contrary, a focus on the social milieu in which the norm is found – the dirt out of which it grows. Something revealed in that examination might enlighten, as a social critique, the understanding of one's own social milieu. Comparative law, thus, might inform the growing of our own norm as a bottom-up process.

As applied to Germany's militant democracy, the contextual approach notes the social and political realities in which Germany's militant democracy is embedded as limitations on its viability as a transplant in the "War on Terror." Among these limiting variables, the most compelling might be that militant democracy made no real contribution to Germany's postwar stability and security. My examination of Germany's militant democracy, however, revealed one interesting factor that might inform a critique of American policy in the "War on Terror." Nearly every account of postwar Germany attributes Germany's political stability and security to the country's rapid and robust economic development.[111] Frank Tipton, for example, recognized Germany's postwar "economic miracle" as one of the "fundamental facts" essential to understanding Germany's first postwar generation.[112] The economic recovery (substantial in both East and West Germany[113]) was fundamental to peace, stability and security because of the widespread devastation confronting the Germans. The Germans had been decimated. By the official end of the war,

> Allied bombing had laid waste to Germany's great cities, and the total German war dead would climb to 4.5 million. Of those, 500,000 were civilians incinerated in the cities, 2 million soldiers who died on battlefields, and another 2 million refugees forced from German-occupied Hungary, Poland, and Czechoslovakia between 1944 and 1946 in what has been called "the greatest migratory movement of modern times."[114]

There was no housing.[115] There was no transportation.[116] There was no food.[117] Tipton flatly summed up the postwar period in these terms: "Germany could not feed itself."[118] For the ordinary German, "the most pressing problem was survival itself."[119] And these problems were exacerbated by the westward migration. In the end, "West Germany absorbed an influx of over 10 million persons.... There was, of course, no housing, nor were there social services to accommodate this mass of people."[120]

On these facts, it is clear why economic development, and not the largely symbolic gestures of militant democracy, came to be widely regarded by the Germans and the Allies alike as the best tool for stabilizing West Germany's democracy. Tony Judt explained that "[t]he prospects for political stability and social reform in post-World War Two Europe all depended, in the first place, on the recovery of the continent's economy."[121] Exactly mirroring the twin concerns putatively addressed by the German Constitutional Court's seminal partyban cases, "the Allied authorities feared that nostalgia for the better days of Nazism, together with a reaction against denazification programmes, food shortages and endemic minor crime, could yet turn to neo-Nazi or even Soviet advantage."[122] The answer to these concerns, however, depended less on militarizing German democracy, as exemplified by the bans on the SRP and KPD, and more on substantial and swift economic recovery. West Germany's first Chancellor, Konrad Adenauer, understood that

> economic upswing – [was] the recipe for freeing the Germans from their transfigured memories of material glory and national greatness. In view of the fact that more than half the SRP's followers gave improvement of the economic and social situation as their main aspiration, the chancellor's approach was certainly not false.[123]

According to Norbert Frei, the Germans understood, perhaps better than the Allied occupiers, that, to borrow a phrase, "it was the economy, stupid." The West German government would have allowed neo-Nazi and communist tendencies to be snuffed out by economic growth alone, without resort to mechanisms of militant democracy.[124]

Something dramatic had to be done to "deliver the economic goods, 'both figuratively and literally.'"[125] Political stability was not achieved through the mostly symbolic measures of militant democracy. Instead, it was achieved as a consequence of economic recovery fueled, in no small part, by the Marshall Plan. Marshall's European Recovery Program "put food in people's mouths and this was what mattered most."[126] Tony Judt explained, "The Marshall Plan was an economic program but the crisis it averted was political."[127] The Western Allies, particularly the British and the Americans, understood that "[i]f the Germans in the Western zone of occupation remained beaten down and impoverished, and were offered no prospect of improvement, they would sooner or later turn back to Nazism – or else to Communism."[128] Although it was certainly not the sole factor, the German postwar "economic miracle" was nonetheless significantly aided by the Marshall Plan.[129]

In any case, the economic upswing that saw the end of the postwar hardships of homelessness, unemployment and near-starvation replaced with full employment and exemplary social security was the most significant driver for West Germany's enduring resistance to antidemocratic movements.

Even if the comparative consideration of militant democracy led (the contextualist) to the conclusion that militant democracy would be a poor fit for the American struggle with terrorism, the contextual comparative effort nonetheless revealed the fact that economic development played a critical role in securing postwar Germany against the enemies of democracy. This discovery, if placed into discourse with American antiterror policy, would certainly pose an important and unique critique of American policy. Indeed, might this social, political and economic fact about the German experience with authoritarian threats to democracy support the widely held thesis that poverty is a significant (if not determinative) driver of terrorism? That question, made uniquely possible by the comparative examination of Germany's militant democracy, has as its focus a critical examination of American policy. It is a critical perspective that is particularly worth noting in light of the fact that, as noted earlier, the United States is busy militarizing its democracy while pursuing a weaker commitment to global economic development and justice. This discursive method makes no claim whatsoever about the transplantability of militant democracy, but it credits the comparative effort with significant resonance.

Conclusion

Terrorism, it seems, has been good for comparative law. But existing approaches to comparative law are plagued by claims of abstraction and relativism. Thus, reference to the policies of other countries may not serve to improve the

American response to terrorism. The discursive approach to comparative law I suggest here demonstrates a novel use to which comparative law might be put. Without concentrating on borrowing norms, the comparatist nonetheless has much to offer by way of social, legal, political, historical and economic critique. The promise of these insights, made possible by exposure to a foreign socio-legal milieu, is a better-informed and more self-conscious approach to American policy. This might be a most important improvement in the American approach to the "War on Terror."

Notes

1 "[F]reedom of speech and of press is accorded aliens residing in this country." *Bridges* v. *Wixon*, 326 U.S. 135, 148 (1945). *See Kwong Hai Chew* v. *Colding*, 344 U.S. 590, 596 n.5 (1953); *United States* v. *Verdugo-Urquidez*, 494 U.S. 259, 271 (1990). The Supreme Court has recognized that freedom of association is part of the liberty protected by the First Amendment, even absent an explicit textual mention of the right. *NAACP* v. *Alabama ex rel. Patterson*, 357 U.S. 449, 460 (1958).
2 *Kwong Hai Chew*, 344 U.S. at 596 n.5.
3 Foreigners within the United States are protected by the Fourth Amendment. *Almeida-Sanchez* v. *United States*, 412 U.S. 266, 273 (1973).
4 "Democracy is not an end unto itself: it is a means for the achievement and preservation of a proper balance between liberty, law and order." Yoram Dinstein, The Dilemmas of Democracy, 26 *Israel Yearbook on Human Rights* 1, 5 (1996).
5 David Cole and James Dempsey admit that "[i]n the wake of [the September 11, 2001 terrorist] attacks, calls for new security measures are undoubtedly warranted, particularly in light of the ongoing threats that the country faces as it fights a war against terrorism...." David Cole and James X. Dempsey, *Terrorism and the Constitution* 148 (2002).
6 See, e.g., Arunabha Bhoumik, Democratic Responses to Terrorism: A Comparative Study of the United States, Israel, and India, 33 *Denver Journal of International Law and Policy* 285 (2005); Jonathan Grebinar, Responding to Terrorism: How Must a Democracy Do It? A Comparison of Israeli and American Law, 31 *Fordham Urban Law Journal* 261 (2003); Amos N. Guiora, Where Are Terrorists to Be Tried: A Comparative Analysis of Rights Granted to Suspected Terrorists, 56 *Catholic University Law Review* 805 (2007); Amos N. Guiora, Transnational Comparative Analysis of Balancing Competing Interests in Counter-terrorism, 20 *Temple International and Comparative Law Journal* 363 (2006); John Ip, Comparative Perspectives on the Detention of Terrorist Suspects, 16 *Transnational Law and Contemporary Problems* 773 (2007); Ralph Ruebner, Democracy, Judicial Review and the Rule of Law in the Age of Terrorism: The Experience of Israel – A Comparative Perspective, 31 *Georgia Journal International and Comparative Law* 493 (2003); Michel Rosenfeld, Judicial Balancing in Times of Stress: Comparing the American, British, and Israeli Approaches to the War on Terror, 27 *Cardozo Law Review* 2079 (2006); Jeremie J. Wattellier, Comparative Legal Responses to Terrorism: Lessons from Europe, 27 *Hastings International and Comparative Law Review* 397 (2004).
7 Bruce Ackerman, *Before the Next Attack* 3 (2007).
8 Ibid.
9 See, e.g., Francesca Bignami, European versus American Liberty: A Comparative Privacy Analysis of Antiterrorism Data Mining, 48 *Boston College Law Review* 609 (2007); Shawn Boyne, The Future of Liberal Democracies in a Time of Terror: A

Comparison of the Impact on Civil Liberties in the Federal Republic of Germany and the United States, 11 *Tulsa Journal of Comparative and International Law* 111 (2003).

10 Norbert Frei described it as "the postwar democracy's foundational anti-Nazi consensus." Norbert Frei, *Adenauer's Germany and the Nazi Past* xii (Joel Golb, trans., 2002).

11 I borrow this phrase from Harold Hongju Koh, *The National Security Constitution* (1990).

12 András Sajó, From Militant Democracy to the Preventive State?, 27 *Cardozo Law Review* 2255, 2269 (2006).

13 Jürgen Habermas, Religious Tolerance – The Pacemaker for Cultural Rights, 79 *Philosophy* 5, 8 (2004).

14 German Bundestag, *Questions on German History: Paths to Parliamentary Democracy* (1998).

15 Ibid.

16 Gregory H. Fox and Georg Nolte, Intolerant Democracies, 36 *Harvard International Law Journal* 1, 11 (1995). Fox and Nolte state:

> Not surprisingly, Hitler abused his power over the few key ministries held by his party by arresting and intimidating opponents before calling for new elections. Despite rampant intimidation of other parties and their candidates by the now unchecked Nazi storm troopers, the elections of March 1933 still did not yield an absolute majority for the Nazis.

(Ibid.)

17 Steven Ozment, *A Mighty Fortress: A New History of the German People* 269 (2004). Ozment comments:

> Using airplanes (the campaign was called "Hitler over Germany") and film commercials for the first time in a German political campaign, [Hitler] took 30 percent of the vote [in the 1932 presidential election] to Hindenburg's 49 percent, rising to 37–53 percent in the runoff in May.

(Ibid.)

18 Ibid. at 260 ("Over the years the [Nazi] party would win more white-collar than blue-collar voters, while demonstrating a substantial appeal across the social spectrum").

19 *Nationalsozialistische Diktatur, 1933–1945: Eine Bilanz* 16 (K.D. Bracher *et al.* eds., 1983) (quoting Joseph Goebbels, translation from Sajó, *supra* note 12, at 2262 n.20).

20 "No freedom for the enemies of freedom!"

21 Karl Loewenstein, Militant Democracy and Fundamental Rights, I, 31 *American Political Science Review* 417, 432 (1937).

22 Ibid. at 417.

23 Ibid.

24 Ibid. at 424.

25 Ibid.

26 Ibid.

27 Ibid.

28 Ibid. at 423.

29 Ibid. at 418.

30 Ibid. at 423.

31 Ibid. at 423–24.

32 Sajó, *supra* note 12, at 2262.

33 Stephen Holmes, Book Reviews, 4 *International Journal of Constitutional Law* 586 (2006) (reviewing *Militant Democracy* (Andras Sajó ed., 2004)).

34 Loewenstein, *supra* note 21, at 423.

35 Jochen A. Frowein, How to Save Democracy from Itself, 26 *Israel Yearbook on Human Rights* 201 (1996).

36 Michael Rosenfeld, A Pluralist Theory of Political Rights in Times of Stress, in *Political Rights under Stress in 21st Century Europe* 12, 15 (Wojciech Sadurski, ed., 2006).

37 Loewenstein, *supra* note 21, at 431.

38 Max Lerner, *It Is Later than You Think – The Need for a Militant Democracy* 103 (New Brunswick, NJ: Transaction Publishers, 1989) (1943).

39 Karl Mannheim, *Diagnosis of Our Time* 7 (1943).

40 Lerner, *supra* note 38, at 103.

41 Karl Loewenstein, Militant Democracy and Fundamental Rights, II, 31 *American Political Science Review* 638, 644–56 (1937).

42 Ibid. at 652.

43 See Brandt (Chapter 9), Williams (Chapter 12), and Greenlee (Chapter 11) in this volume.

44 See *Schenck* v. *United States*, 249 U.S. 47 (1919), overruled by *Brandenburg* v. *Ohio*, 395 U.S. 444 (1969).

45 Otto Pfersmann, Shaping Militant Democracy: Legal Limits to Democratic Stability, in *Militant Democracy* 47, 53 (András Sajó ed., 2004). Pfersmann argued that *every* constitutional limit or departure from spontaneous, open democracy represents a kind of militant democracy. But for the minimal practice of majority decision making, all constitutional democracies "are therefore more or less militant, according to the intensity of the first- and higher-order obstacles." Ibid. at 56.

46 Ibid.

47 Ibid. at 57.

48 Rosenfeld, *supra* note 36, at 13. Rosenfeld states:

> Should political rights in times of stress fall somewhere between political rights in times of crisis and those in ordinary times? Should political rights in times of stress be the same as those prevalent in ordinary times, but be protected to a lesser extent than the latter? Should there be any special political rights for times of stress?
>
> (Ibid.)

49 Loewenstein, *supra* note 41, at 645.

50 Grundgesetz [GG] [Constitution] art. 21(2) (F.R.G.).

51 Uniting and Strengthening America by Providing Appropriate Tools Required to Intercept and Obstruct Terrorism Act of 2001 (USA PATRIOT Act), Pub. L. No. 107-56, 115 Stat. 272 (codified as amended in scattered section of 8, 15, 18, 22, 31, 42, 49, and 50 U.S.C.) (quoting the preamble).

52 Antiterrorism and Effective Death Penalty Act of 1996 (AEDPA), Pub. L. No. 104-32, 110 Stat. 1214 (codified as amended in scattered sections of 7, 8, 11, 15, 18, 19, 21, 28, 40, and 42 U.S.C.).

53 A category that also is now extremely broadly defined and left to the discretion of a number of executive branch officials. See Cole and Dempsey, *supra* note 5, at 153.

54 See the chapters by Brandt and Williams in this volume; see also Cole and Dempsey, *supra* note 5, at 118, 153–54.

55 Cole and Dempsey, *supra* note 5, at 118, 153–54.

56 Loewenstein, *supra* note 41, at 655.

57 Bundesverfassungsschutzgesetz [BVerfSchG] [Act Regulating the Cooperation between the Federation and the Federal States in Matters relating to the Protection of the Constitution and on the Federal Office for the Protection of the Constitution], Dec. 20, 1990, BGBl. I at 1818, § 2 Nos. 1 and 2 (F.R.G.). See Bundesamt für Verfassungsschutz [Federal Office for the Protection of the Constitution], www.verfassungsschutz.de/en/index_en.html (last visited Nov. 9, 2007).

58 See Seamon (Chapter 8) in this volume. See also James Risen and Eric Lichtblau, Bush Lets U.S. Spy on Callers Without Courts, *New York Times*, Dec. 16, 2005, at A1.

59 Katherine Wong, Recent Developments – The NSA Terrorist Surveillance Program, 43 *Harvard Journal on Legislation* 517, 518 (2006).

60 John Cary Sims, What NSA is Doing … and Why It's Illegal, 33 *Hastings Constitutional Law Quarterly* 101, 121 (2006).

61 See Seamon in this volume.

62 Grundgesetz [GG] [Constitution] art. 9(2) (F.R.G.).

63 Grundgesetz [GG] [Constitution] art. 21(2) (F.R.G.).

64 Bundesverfassungsschutzgesetz [Act Regulating the Federal and State Protection of the Constitution], Dec. 20, 1990, BGBl I. at 1818, § 3(1) (F.R.G.).

65 David P. Currie, *The Constitution of the Federal Republic of Germany* 213 (1994).

66 Norman Dorsen *et al.*, *Comparative Constitutionalism* 1284 (2003).

67 See, e.g., G. Brinkmann, Militant Democracy and Radicals in the West German Civil Service, 46 *Modern Law Review* 584, 592 (1983); Fox and Nolte, *supra* note 16, at 69–70; Judith Wise, Dissent and the Militant Democracy: The German Constitution and the Banning of the Free German Workers Party, 5 *University of Chicago Law School Roundtable* 301, 303 (1998); Ronald J. Krotoszynski, A Comparative Perspective on the First Amendment: Free Speech, Militant Democracy, and the Primacy of Dignity as a Preferred Constitutional Value in Germany, 78 *Tulane Law Review* 1549, 1564 (2004).

68 See Vivian Grosswald Curran, Cultural Immersion, Difference and Categories in U.S. Comparative Law, 46 *American Journal of Comparative Law* 43, 46–54 (1998). See also Ralf Michaels, The Functional Method of Comparative Law, in *The Oxford Handbook of Comparative Law* 339 (Mathias Reimann and Reinhard Zimmermann eds., 2006); Michele Graziadei, Comparative Law as the Study of Transplants and Receptions, in *The Oxford Handbook of Comparative Law*, *supra*, at 441.

69 Ruti Teitel, Comparative Constitutional Law in a Global Age, 117 *Harvard Law Review* 2570, 2573–74 (2004).

70 Konrad Zweigert and Hein Kötz, *Introduction to Comparative Law* 34 (Tony Weir trans., Oxford University Press, 3d edition 1998) (1977).

71 Teitel, *supra* note 69, at 2575.

72 Ibid. at 2577.

73 Ibid. at 2573–76 (The casebook *Comparative Constitutionalism*, which Sajó coauthored, "posits a return to [functionalism]").

> [The book] represents a sustained endeavor to revive this approach – this time with respect to constitutional law. Historically, functionalism assumed that legal problems could simply be excised from their political context, a notion easy to sustain in private law. By contrast, the crux of neofunctionalism is the plausibility of the method's application to constitutional law – an area beyond its traditional purview.
>
> (Ibid.)

74 Ibid. at 2579.

75 Sajó, *supra* note 12, at 2255.

76 Ibid. at 2261–65.

77 Teitel, *supra* note 69, at 2579–80.

78 According to the functionalist method, one always conducts the inquiry with an eye to convergence. Ibid. at 2576 (quoting Mary Ann Glendon *et al.*, *Comparative Legal Traditions* 1 (1994)).

79 Ibid. at 2581.

80 Mary Ann Glendon *et al.*, *Comparative Legal Traditions* 12 (1994).

81 Curran, *supra* note 68, at 46–54.

82 Angus McDonald, Hundred Headless Europe: Comparison, Constitution and Culture, in *Comparative Law in the 21st Century* 193, 195–96 (Andrew Harding and Esin Örücü, eds., 2002).

83 Vicki C. Jackson and Mark Tushnet, *Comparative Constitutional Law: Cases and Materials* (1999).

84 Teitel, *supra* note 69, at 2581–82.

85 Ibid. at 2579–80.

86 Sajó, *supra* note 12, at 2263.

87 Ibid. at 2264.

88 Ibid.

89 Loewenstein, *supra* note 21, at 423.

90 Sajó, *supra* note 12, at 263–65.

91 Kent Roach, Anti-terrorism and Militant Democracy: Some Western and Eastern Responses, in *Militant Democracy* 171, 171 (András Sajó ed., 2004).

92 Lerner, *supra* note 38, at 3.

93 Mannheim, *supra* note 39, at 1.

94 Lerner, *supra* note 38.

95 Norbert Frei, *Adenauer's Germany and the Nazi Past* 259 (Joel Golb trans., 2002).

96 Donald P. Kommers, *The Constitutional Jurisprudence of the Federal Republic of Germany* 222–23 (2nd edition 1997); Donald P. Kommers, *Judicial Politics in West Germany* 190–91 (1976).

97 Kommers, *The Constitutional Jurisprudence*, *supra* note 96, at 222–23.

98 Ibid. at 263.

99 Ibid. at 222–23 (emphasis added).

100 Ibid. at 224 (quoting Dan Gordon, Limits on Extreme Political Parties: A Comparison of Israeli Jurisprudence with that of the U.S. and the Federal Republic of Germany, 10 *Hastings International and Comparative Law Review* 376 (1987)).

101 Felix Hanschmann, Federal Constitutional Court to Review NPD Party Ban Motion, 2 *German Law Journal* (Nov. 1, 2001), at www.germanlawjournal.com/article.php?id=104.

102 Bundesverfassungsgericht [BVerfG] [Federal Constitutional Court], 2 BvB 1/01 from Jan. 22, 2002, www.bundesverfassungsgericht.de/entscheidungen/bs20020122_2bvb000101.html.

103 Alexander Hanebeck, FCC Suspends Hearing in NPD Party Ban Case, 3 *German Law Journal* (Feb. 1, 2002), at www.germanlawjournal.com/article.php?=129.

104 Ibid. at ¶ 3.

105 Felix Hanschmann, Another Test in Proceduralizing Democracy: The Oral Proceedings in the NPD Party Ban Case Before the Federal Constitutional Court, 3 *German Law Journal* ¶ 3 (Nov. 1, 2002), at www.germanlawjournal.com/article.php?id=204.

106 Bundesverfassungsgerichtsgesetz [BVerfGG] [Federal Constitutional Court Act], Aug. 11, 1993, BGBl. I at 1473, art. 15.3 (F.R.G.).

107 See Felix Müller, Report – Bundesverfassungsgericht (Federal Constitutional Court) – 2003, in *Annual of German and European Law – 2004*, at 333 (Russell A. Miller and Peer C. Zumbansen eds., 2006).

108 See Stanley Fish, Condemnation without Absolutes, *New York Times*, Oct. 15, 2001, at A19 (confronting these critiques, especially as they related to the confrontation with terrorism).

109 Teitel, *supra* note 69, at 2581.

110 Ibid. at 2583–84.

111 Another variable that contributed to Germany's postwar stability and security, which also might be instructive for the American "War on Terror," was the economic and, eventually, political integration of Europe.

112 Frank B. Tipton, *A History of Modern Germany since 1815*, at 496 (2003).

113 Tipton notes:

> The German economies did more than merely recover, however; both East and West Germany grew very rapidly during the 1950s and 1960s. West German output rose more than 6 per cent per year in real terms from 1950 to 1970. East German growth is more contentious. The East German government's own statistics showed output rising even more rapidly, at more than 7 per cent per year. Western estimates were more modest, but were still over 4 per cent per year. Substantial increases in total and per capita output appeared to have been achieved despite the heavy loss of population before the closure of the border in 1961 and despite the burden of reparations and occupation costs imposed by the Soviet Union.
>
> (Ibid. at 514–15)

114 Ozment, *supra* note 17, at 289.

115 Tony Judt, *PostWar* 82 (2005).

116 Ibid.

117 Ibid. at 86. Judt explained that in the critical year of 1947, "the fundamental problem of food supply was not yet overcome.... In French opinion polls taken in the course of 1946 'food,' 'bread,' 'meat' consistently outpaced everything else as the public's number one preoccupation." Ibid.

118 Tipton, *supra* note 112, at 502.

119 Jürgen Weber, *Germany 1945–1990: A Parallel History* 3 (2004).

120 Tipton, *supra* note 112, at 508.

121 Judt, *supra* note 115, at 82.

122 Ibid. at 88.

123 Norbert Frei, *Adenauer's Germany and the Nazi Past* 263 (Joel Golb trans., 2005).

124 Ibid.

125 Tipton, *supra* note 112, at 515 (quoting Charles S. Maier, The Two Postwar Eras and the Conditions for Stability in Twentieth-Century Western Europe, 86 *American Historical Review* 327, 334 (1981)).

126 Judt, *supra* note 115, at 96.

127 Ibid. at 97.

128 Ibid. at 122.

129 Weber writes:

> The Marshall Plan developed into an aid programme with long-term benefits for West Germany, which may be summarized as follows: 1. It supplied the momentum for the creation of a West German state with an economic and social structure based on American precepts. 2. It accelerated the already increasing industrial production and thereby contributed significantly to economic recovery. 3. It provided the Germans with a psychological orientation towards the Western democracies.
>
> (Weber, *supra* note 119, at 22–23)

Index

CPSIA information can be obtained at www.ICGtesting.com
Printed in the USA
BVOW11s0503190515

400857BV00006B/14/P